Designing the Requirements

Designing the Requirements

Building Applications that the User Wants and Needs

Chris Britton

✦✦Addison-Wesley

New York • Boston • Indianapolis • San Francisco
Toronto • Montreal • London • Munich • Paris • Madrid
Capetown • Sydney • Tokyo • Singapore • Mexico City

Library of Congress Cataloging-in-Publication Data
Britton, Chris, author.
  Designing the requirements : building applications that the user wants and needs / Chris Britton.
      pages   cm
  Includes bibliographical references and index.
  ISBN 978-0-13-402121-8 (pbk. : alk. paper)—ISBN 0-13-402121-5
  1. Computer software—Specifications. 2. Application software—Development. I. Title.
  QA76.76.S73B75 2016
  005.302'18—dc23
                                                                        2015028696

ISBN-13: 978-0-13-402121-8
ISBN-10: 0-13-402121-5

Text printed in the United States on recycled paper at RR Donnelley in Crawfordsville, Indiana.
First printing, October 2015

This book is dedicated to my mother, who died early in 2015 at the age of 98. When she was young, horse-drawn carts were common, she lived in a house without a telephone, and TV hadn't been invented. The Internet wasn't even a dream.

Contents

Preface xiii

Acknowledgments xxi

About the Author xxiii

Chapter 1: Introduction to Context-Driven Design 1

    Designing Requirements 2

    What Is Design? 9

        Ad Hoc Design 12

        Planned Design 14

        Engineered Design 14

        Summary of Design Approaches 18

    Making IT Application Development More of
      an Engineering Discipline 19

    Taking IT Architecture into Account 20

    Concluding Remarks 21

Chapter 2: A Hierarchy of Designs 23

    Justifying the Hierarchy of Designs 23

    Context Design 28

        Tasks 28

        User Groups 30

        Data Tables 30

        Messages between Tasks 31

        Task Dependencies 31

        Putting It All Together 32

        Analysis of the Context Design 34

    Integration Design 35

    Technical Design 41

    User Interface Design 44

Database Design 46

Implementation 47

Is It Really Engineering? 48

Concluding Remarks 51

Chapter 3: Reusing Existing Methods and Practices **53**

Agile 54

Individuals and Interactions over Processes and Tools 55

Working Software over Comprehensive Documentation 56

Customer Collaboration over Contract Negotiations 58

Responding to Change over Following a Plan 59

Conclusion 60

Upside-Down Design 60

Use Cases 62

Atomicity 63

Confusion of Design Layers 64

Use Cases Are Confusing 66

Large Use Case Documents Are Hard to Understand 67

Use Cases Do Not Assist Engineered Design 67

Conclusion 68

The Problem with Estimating Cost 68

Why Is BDUF Big? 72

Iterations 74

Quality 75

Testing and Inspection 76

Using Existing Practices in Context-Driven Design 78

Learning Organizations 80

Concluding Remarks 80

Chapter 4: The Problem of Large Applications **83**

The Dimensions of Size 84

Problems with Large Projects 88

Requirements Problems 88

Lack of End User Support 91

Technical Design Problems 93

Procurement and Outsourcing 96

Can Large Projects Be Avoided? 100

Concluding Remarks 103

Chapter 5: The Relationship with the Business **105**

Understanding Business Processes 106

When It's Not a Process 112

    Business Services 112

    Resource Management 113

    Reviewing and Monitoring 115

The Need for a Wider View 115

Applying the Business Strategy to Application Development 118

    Speed of Development 119

    Cost versus Performance and Availability 119

    Experimental Business Programs 120

    How Long Before the Benefits 120

    The Need for Security 120

    Designing for the Existing Culture 120

    Design for a Culture to Which the Organization Aspires 121

    Allow for Changing Plans 122

    Support a Learning Organization 122

    Non-Business Applications 122

Analysis 123

    Is the Process Well Formed? 123

    Dependency Analysis 123

    Objectives Analysis 127

Concluding Remarks 128

Chapter 6: The Relationship with the Users **129**

Adding the Detail 129

    Task Details 131

    Task Fragments 135

    Common Purpose Groups 135

    Data Tables 136

    Messages 137

    Nonfunctional Requirements 138

    Who Uses the Context Design? 140

Who Are the Users? 141

    Business Process Operations 142

    Monitoring by Management 143

    Data Used by Other Applications 147

    Data Analysis 148

Application Administration 149
Analyzing the Context Design 151
Process Layer 151
Task Details 153
Data Table Details 154
User Group Details 155
Message Details 155
Reviewing the Context Design 156
Concluding Remarks 158

Chapter 7: The Relationship to Other IT Projects **159**
Integration Design 161
Applications 161
Services 162
Databases 165
Services Interface Design 170
Service Interface Definition 172
Designing Reusable Services 176
Existing Applications 178
Knowing What Is There 178
Replacing Existing Applications 180
Fashioning Services from Existing Applications 184
Looking Back at the Design Process 186
Concluding Remarks 188

Chapter 8: User Interface Design and Ease of Use **189**
Logical User Interfaces 191
From Tasks to Clicks 194
Ease of Use 199
Function 200
Information 201
Navigation 202
Text 202
Help 203
Intuitive and Likable Applications 203
Ease-of-Use Design 205
Monitoring Ease of Use 208
Transaction and Task Integrity 208

The User Interface Design and the Other Detailed Designs 212
Concluding Remarks 212

Chapter 9: Database Design **215**

Database Design 215
Database Design Theory 223
Programmers versus the Database Designer 233
Database Access Services 236
NoSQL 238
Concluding Remarks 242

Chapter 10: Technical Design—Principles **243**

Principles of High Performance on a Single Machine 244
    Cache 245
    Multithreading and Multiprocessing 248
Principles of High Performance on Many Servers 252
    Front-End Parallelism 252
    Back-End Parallelism 256
Principles of High Resiliency 260
The Need for Testing and Benchmarking 263
The Technical Design Process 265
Concluding Remarks 268

Chapter 11: Technical Design—Structure **271**

Program Structure 272
What Is a Framework? 276
The Variety of Programming Languages 281
Choosing a Programming Language and Framework 286
    Choose a Language that Fits Your Organization's Skill Set .. 287
    Choose a Language that Is Appropriate for
      Your Application's Performance Goals 287
    Choose a Language that Can Meet Your
      Integration Requirements 287
    Choose a Language that Supports Group
      Working If Needed 287
    Choose Version Control Software and Project Management
      Software as Well as a Language 288
    Choose a Language that Chimes with Your Development
      Methodology 289

Extending the Framework 290

Implementing Common Functionality 293

Concluding Remarks 295

Chapter 12: Security Design **297**

IT Application Security Principles 299

Authentication 300

Access Control 302

User Administration 303

Security Protection 304

Security Monitoring 306

The Security Elements of Each Design 307

Context Design 307

Integration Design 311

User Interface Design 312

Database Design 312

Technical Design 314

Security Programming 316

Concluding Remarks 319

Chapter 13: The Future of Application Development **323**

How Context-Driven Design Changes Application Development . . . 323

Context-Driven Design Opportunities 325

New Tools 326

Context and Integration Design 328

User Interface and Database Design 328

Technical Design 329

The Application Development Challenges 332

Flexibility 332

Operations 334

Correctness 335

Quality 336

Professionalism 337

Concluding Remarks 339

Appendix A: Context Design Checklist **341**

Description 341

Elaboration 344

Analysis 344

References **349**

Index **353**

Preface

This book is the fruit of about 15 years of thinking about IT application development. It started when I was working on IT architecture in the late 1990s. At that time I wrote a book called *IT Architecture and Middleware: Strategies for Building Large, Scalable Systems* (a second edition coauthored with Peter Bye in 2004 is still available). This was about the technology for building integrated applications and about how to make the applications scalable, highly available, and secure. Other people were thinking along similar lines at the time, and the kinds of solutions Peter and I were proposing came to be called Service Oriented Architectures (SOAs) because the basic idea was to have reusable services with which you can rapidly assemble new applications using integration technology. In spite of the advantages of SOA, which we thought were obvious, very little happened. IT managers liked the SOA story but didn't get around to implementing anything. Something was missing, and almost from the beginning I had the suspicion that the missing something was application development. In other words, we didn't have a good answer to the question, "How do you develop an SOA application?" Or perhaps the question is better expressed as, "I have a bunch of requirements; what do I have to do to ensure that I end up with an SOA solution rather than a stand-alone application?" Over the next few years I did less and less thinking about architecture and more and more thinking about application development.

I first did application programming in the late 1970s. Since that time I have mostly worked in the system and environmental software arena, fixing and designing. I spent a lot of time mending data management software and occasionally would be thrown a compiler bug or an operating system bug to fix. I have done a fair bit of designing and programming system software. Later on I worked on database design and repository design (I could give a long discourse on version control—strangely, very few people wanted to hear it). By the year 2000, I was experienced in many aspects of computer technology, but I hadn't done a lot of straightforward application design and programming, so I couldn't in all honesty go to the application developers and tell them they were doing it all wrong.

At that time, application development gurus showed little interest in architecture. Instead they were at war among themselves. In one corner was the "big design up front" (BDUF) crowd who promoted designs based on Unified Modeling Language (UML) modeling. The designs were structured, well documented, and full of quality control procedures. In the other corner was the "agile" crowd who believed in delivering software first and then, through a series of short iterations, amending it to suit the stakeholders. At the core of their disagreement was the relationship with the stakeholders. In BDUF it was contractual and there was a formal step to gather requirements. In agile they believed it was best to split the functionality into small chunks, to elicit detailed requirements just before implementing a chunk, and to show the stakeholders the working software shortly after it was finished. Thus by continual feedback they hoped to navigate to the implementation by making small, but frequent, adjustments to the steering. Whenever I have tried to explain agile to people outside of IT, they have clearly thought it verges on the irresponsible. But the agile community's criticism of BDUF has resonance. Stakeholders do have trouble understanding the proposed application until they actually see it running. A contract doesn't magically make an IT application loved.

Neither side, however, could give any insight into why SOAs weren't being developed. It was as if the problem didn't exist.

So why should application development be resistant to SOA? One reason is that IT projects have a poor reputation for delivering on time and on budget and delivering what the stakeholder wants. This leads to pressure on IT developers, and one reaction to this pressure is to insist on strong project boundaries. They want to control everything within the boundaries and to be able to ignore everything outside them. Thus what tends to happen is that the outcome of one application development project is one stand-alone application. If you have one big project, you develop one big application, while if you have many small projects, you end up with many small applications. Furthermore, it is well established that large IT projects are particularly prone to failure, and thus there is a drive to have many small projects rather than one big one; hence many small applications rather than one big one. IT architects, on the other hand, are trying to persuade application developers to build services rather than stand-alone applications and to build the wherewithal for the services to cooperate. They don't stand a chance. I didn't realize how inward-looking projects could be until I started seriously looking again at application development in the early 2000s and was appalled to discover that there was even a simmering tension between programmers and database designers. Programmers were so focused on their immediate project aims that they had no interest in the notion that data was to be shared and managed across the organization.

Thus came the first change I wanted to make to application development—I wanted to find a way to open it up to the architecture so that all the applications would work to take the overall architecture forward rather than to undermine it.

If projects are inward looking, one reason has to be that the requirements are inward looking; in other words, they focus on a particular problem rather than the needs of the organization as a whole. When I was working on architecture, I did a great deal of work investigating how IT applications support the business. In particular, I looked at how IT supports business processes and at how to achieve data consistency across multiple databases. In each case, integration of the IT applications was enormously important. So why wasn't this being reflected in the requirements; why weren't business managers telling IT application developers to create integrated applications? I already knew the answer to that one. I have worked in management and I have worked with sales people, marketing people, and finance people, and I know something about what makes them tick. Furthermore, I had seen sales processes and other business processes come and go. In short, I had seen the frustration from the other side. I know that managers are often clever and sometimes devious. I know that managers don't always agree; not only do they not always agree with their peers, but they also do not always agree with their bosses. Into this cauldron walk the innocent IT guys who happily tell everyone that they are going to build an application that's going to change everyone's life so please can you tell them what you want it to do. Perhaps the IT guy should act differently and perhaps business management should act differently, but I think the fundamental problem is deeper than this.

An IT application is not like a photocopier or an iPad; it is not a stand-alone thing that can assist businesses but whose use is optional. Rather, IT applications are integral to the business activities; these days you cannot do business without them. Thus, before implementing the application you had better be sure that it is designed to support the right business activity; it would be good to get the details right and to ensure that the organization knows what it is getting and is truly behind it. There is an acceptance in IT circles that the application requirements change; there is even a term for it: *requirements churn*. It is frequently suggested that this has to do with the fast-changing business environment. Yes, the business environment does change, but I say that by far the most common reason for requirements churn is the fact that people are designing the business activity itself on the fly. The solution is to persuade both the IT application designer and the business management that simply gathering requirements won't do. Whether they like it or not, they are engaged in a design exercise to make a better business solution supported by IT. I think giving requirements gathering the aura of a design rather than the aura of writing a shopping list will have a transformative effect on how both business management and IT application designers approach the task of creating the requirements.

This was the second change I wanted to make to application development— I wanted to change the relationship with business management by making requirements gathering itself a design project.

One of the problems that always nagged me when I was working on IT architecture was that the diagrams we drew for visualizing IT applications were so unsatisfactory. There were—and are—two problems. The first is that to describe a system you needed to look at it from multiple angles and create multiple views. You can take, for instance,

- **A business organizational view**—splitting the business according to the organization chart
- **A business process view**—processes often cross business functional boundaries
- **A data view**—showing what data there is and where it is
- **A programmer's view**—how the business rules are converted to code
- **A hardware configuration view**—how all the boxes fit together

There are many other ways proposed for having multiple views [1]. (The references are listed at the back of the book.) The problem with all these view models is that seeing the dependencies among the different views is very hard, especially in large organizations with complex IT systems. And large organizations do have truly mind-boggling complexity in their IT systems. A thousand applications or more and a hundred databases or more are not uncommon. (I have long suspected that complexity of software is proportional to the number of programmers tasked with writing the software rather than to the complexity of the problem they are trying to solve, but that is another story.)

The second problem with architectural diagrams is that many of the views aren't strictly hierarchical. This might seem an odd thing to be worried about, but let me explain. For any view what you want to see is the information at a high level—the 10,000-foot view if you will—and you want to be able to zoom in to see the detail—the 100-foot view. There are two ways this can be done, which I will call the "map" and the "engineering drawing." As you zoom in with a map, new things pop into view. At the high level you see the major roads, but at the low level you see the minor roads. This has problems; for instance, you are never entirely sure you can find the best way to get from A to B because there may be a shortcut on a road that you can't see on the map. With an engineering drawing, on the other hand, the object is described as being made up of components, and the drawing shows how the components fit together. Furthermore, any component itself might be made up of subcomponents, and there might be another engineering drawing explaining how such a component is assembled from subcomponents. As you go down the hierarchy, new objects don't pop into view; instead, existing objects break apart. This makes a difference. For example, you can look at the engineering drawing of a car and ask the question, "How much does it weigh, and where is the center of gravity?" By knowing the weight and position of each component you can calculate the answer because you don't have to worry about additional stuff popping into view. Unfortunately, IT architectural views are like maps. For instance, a high-level network diagram will show all the major servers and major network connections. As you zoom in, it will start to show the small servers, the routers, and the PCs. Similarly, a high-level view of the data will show the major data tables. The many hundreds of other data tables won't be shown until you zoom in to see the greater detail.

Why should this matter? It has long been observed by practically everybody that IT applications are less reliable than engineered vehicles and buildings. At one stage in my career, job titles like software engineer were common but then went out of fashion. Maybe I'm being cruel, but I have the impression that the programming profession has given up on the dream of being an engineering discipline. I have an explanation of why programming isn't engineering and it is simply this: we don't have anything equivalent to engineering drawings. Why this is an explanation should be clear by the end of the first chapter. So, I started to wonder whether there was a high-level engineering view of IT applications. Naturally—since I am writing this book—I think I have succeeded, albeit in a rather different form from that of classic engineering diagrams.

This was the third change I wanted to make—I wanted to make application design more like an engineering discipline.

When I started thinking about application development and had some ideas I wanted to tell to the outside world, I found I had few listeners. I didn't have the case studies and the prestige, and I have never had the instinctive marketing *nous* for telling my story that some people seem to possess. I wrote papers and gave presentations, but while everyone listened politely, there was no reaction. But since it was at the height of the BDUF-versus-agile wars I suppose I shouldn't have been surprised. It was like walking into a crowded room where everyone is shouting at each other and the only thing they want to hear is whose side you are on.

That was ten years ago. The arguments between BDUF and agile have degenerated into an uneasy truce, and application development is still as unloved by the business world as it has ever been. In the meantime, I have returned to being a programmer. I have spent most of my time trying to develop tools to draw the diagrams you see in this book, and I have spent some time doing application programming. Though my ideas in essence haven't changed much, I think I am now in a position to make the arguments much richer. In my earlier attempt to tell the story it was in disjointed short papers. I am now in the position to pull it all together and to lay out a comprehensive picture of how to do application development top to bottom.

I am conscious that some of my readers will have strong opinions, and some of them will also believe that they have solved all the problems of application development and don't need a lecture from me. Much of this book is an analysis of the problems, so even if you don't believe in my solutions, I urge you to think about the problems. I hope this book encourages you to do so.

There are many books, papers, and Web sites on application design. They are full of good advice. They have numerous checklists. They tell you about iteration and how to split your project into phases. They give you wise pointers on how to deal with stakeholders and how to present to management. They lay down principles to guide your work, and some of them tell you when to have meetings, who should be there, how to structure the meetings, and what to discuss. What is there for me to add to all this? Let me put it this way: if application development were a religion—and sometimes it seems as if the practitioners think it is—these other books would tell you how to be a priest and how to run a religious service. This book is about what you should believe in.

In a nutshell, what I believe in is that application design should

- Be built on the recognition that you don't gather your IT application requirements, you design them

- Be more like an engineering discipline, in particular, by analyzing the designs and looking for flaws before implementation

- Act with other applications to create a coherent IT architecture

The Structure of the Book

This book is split roughly into three parts; four chapters of scene setting, seven chapters on the detail of design, and two chapters tidying up at the end.

The first scene-setting chapter, Chapter 1, "Introduction to Context-Driven Design," discusses why the three points I listed in the previous section are important and also discusses the nature of design itself. I think this is widely misunderstood, in particular what is meant by engineered design.

An important aspect of engineered design is a hierarchy of designs that go step by step from requirements to implementation. This is discussed in Chapter 2, "A Hierarchy of Designs." The designs identified are described in more detail in Chapters 5 to 11.

Chapter 3, "Reusing Existing Methods and Practices," has two tasks. One is to position my design approach relative to existing design approaches, and the second is to point out where I am building on existing design and project management practices.

However, existing design practices are particularly bad at handling the development of large applications; why this is so and possible remedies are discussed in Chapter 4, "The Problem of Large Applications."

The next chapters go into more detail about design. Chapter 5, "The Relationship with the Business," and Chapter 6, "The Relationship with the Users," are about designing the requirements, in other words, designing the business solution of which the IT application is but a part.

Chapter 7, "The Relationship to Other IT Projects," is about ensuring that your application works well with other applications and databases. It is also about IT application services and splitting up large development efforts into a number of more easily digestible, smaller projects.

One of my big concerns with application development is ease of use. I believe strongly that ease of use must be designed up front. This is the topic of Chapter 8, "User Interface Design and Ease of Use."

Chapter 9, "Database Design," is about, as it says on the can, database design. This book is not a detailed book about database design, so this chapter is written for people who are not database designers to help them understand the concerns of the people who are.

Chapter 10, "Technical Design—Principles," and Chapter 11, "Technical Design—Structure," are about technical design. Again, I cannot teach you all there is to know about technical design, or anywhere close to it. The idea is to help nontechnical designers communicate with technical designers. The chapter on technical design principles is largely about the difficulties of making an application very scalable and very resilient and how these difficulties can be overcome, at least in principle. The chapter on technical design structure is about how building a software framework for an application makes life for the programmers easier and helps the project run smoothly.

At the end of the book are a couple of other chapters. Chapter 12, "Security Design," focuses on security. Security should be designed into the application at all levels, so I could have incorporated security design into all the other design discussions. The reason I have not done so, but have instead gathered all the security design discussion into one chapter, is that I think the treatment of security would be too fragmented otherwise. In a chapter of its own I can give the topic the whole sweep from top to bottom, from security strategy to programming implementation.

Finally, Chapter 13, "The Future of Application Development," is where I summarize the points and discuss where application development might go in the future.

At the end of the book, there is also an appendix that gives a checklist of some analysis techniques for context design which I anticipate is the most unfamiliar topic in the book. There is also a list of references.

Who Should Read This Book

This book is targeted at designers and project managers. I hope programmers will be interested as well, as I hope it will expand their horizons.

I have tried to make this book nontechnical. I do mention IT technologies and methods but mostly as examples rather than as part of the main argument. Just because I mention some product or technology does not mean I expect you to know about it; it's just a guide for people who do know about the product. I find that when I read a book like this one, I cannot stop myself from reading it through the lens of my past experiences. Sometimes I mention technologies and existing design approaches to clarify more accurately what I am trying to say. In any case, if I mention something you don't know about, it shouldn't matter.

In a large, demanding application there is unlikely to be a single IT application designer; there will be a team, some of whom will need specialist skills, for instance, in technical design, database design, and security design. Part of my aim is to give the different members of the design team the information they need to understand each other. If there is one aim for the book it is this: to help the design team work together to create a design that the organization truly wants.

Acknowledgments

Many people have helped me with this book, sometimes without realizing it. In particular I wish to thank Peter and Alison Bye, Andy McIntyre, Graham Berrisford, Kevin Bodie, Robert Bogetti, Celso Gonzalez, and David Janzen. Also, I would like to thank the publisher's team—Chris Guzikowski, Michelle Housley, Chris and Susan Zahn, Mary Kesel Wilson, and Barbara Wood—for taking a risk on this book and guiding me through the publishing process. And, of course, my wife, Judy, for putting up with me working on this book rather than working in the garden or mending the hole in the front windowsill.

About the Author

Chris Britton has worked in many areas of the IT business. He started in IT in the 1970s programming COBOL and Algol and joined Burroughs (which after the merger with Sperry became Unisys) in 1976, quickly becoming a database specialist for large mainframe systems. For a while in the 1980s he worked in the United States developing SIM, a semantic database product. Back in the UK and working in the Burroughs' European headquarters, he worked in a variety of roles, often simultaneously, in systems support, marketing support, IT architecture, and management. During the 1990s he increasingly worked on IT architecture and wrote the book *IT Architecture and Middleware: Strategies for Building Large, Scalable Systems*, now in its second edition (Addison-Wesley, 2004). In 2001 he left Unisys and worked in his own company doing consultancy and developing software applications. Outside of IT, his main interest is classical singing. He sang in the choir when a student at Trinity College, Cambridge, and has sung in operas and choirs, large and small, ever since.

Chapter 1

Introduction to Context-Driven Design

This book is about how to design IT applications. I have written the book because I want to persuade people to design differently. In particular, I want to change application design by

- Basing it on the recognition that you don't gather your IT application requirements, you design them

- Making it more like an engineering discipline, in particular, by analyzing designs and looking for flaws before implementation

- Ensuring that the application works with other applications that exist or are in development to create a coherent IT architecture

This book is about how you think about application design and how you analyze designs. It says little about how to structure your development team, how you manage the team, and how frequently you give your end users a new version of the application. If you follow the precepts in this book, you can structure and manage your project in many different ways, and there is no right way that suits every organization and every kind of project.

I start by examining the first of these points: designing requirements. This is followed by a section called "What Is Design?" This is preparation for a discussion on the second point above which is in a section entitled "Making IT Application Development More of an Engineering Discipline." The third point is addressed in "Taking IT Architecture into Account."

Designing Requirements

Designing requirements—surely that must be wrong, isn't it? For design in general, perhaps, but for design of IT applications, no, it is not. The reason is simple. IT applications in business don't exist in a vacuum; they are there to support the business. Thus the design of the IT application should reflect the design of the business solution, just as the design of a house's foundations reflects the design of the whole house.

Several chapters of this book are about replacing a passive exercise of gathering requirements for an IT application with an active exercise of designing a business solution supported by an IT application. Let me explain why this is important.

Implementing business change is hard. There are some business changes that executive management can force on the business by moving around money and resources; that is the easy way to make change happen. The difficult way is making existing operations more error free, less costly, and more flexible, in other words, changing what employees are doing and consequently moving them out of their comfort zone. Add an IT application into the mix and it becomes harder still. If the IT application is late, it can delay the introduction of the new way of working. If the IT application is clumsy, unreliable, or slow, it can engender resentment against the whole program of change. If the IT application's functionality is not what people expected, they will start to question the basis of the program for change.

One of the root causes of these dangers is that when an IT application is involved, the desire for business change must be converted into precisely defined demands for people to do their work differently. But even with the same goal in mind, different people will have different ideas on the best way to achieve a goal. When you add competing departments, a changing business environment, and differing practices and traditions in different geographies, differing visions and conflicts are almost inevitable. With other approaches to business change, like training, you can skate over these differences, sweep them under the carpet as we say, but with a new IT application you can't. IT applications demand precision; that is the nature of computing and programming. Let us look at a very simple example. You will no doubt have come across a Web site that will accept your input only if you put data in fields marked by an asterisk. Someone somewhere has made the decision that the data is so important (and so unlikely to be faked) that it is worth their while to force potential customers to fill in these fields in spite of the annoyance it causes. Does everyone in the organization agree with the decision on how much data is required? I doubt it. IT applications are full of decisions like this. Some can be easily changed late in the day, like this example of required fields. But some are more structural to the application, and some are structural to how the business is done and cannot easily be changed.

Let us look at a more complex example. I live and work in England, and here in the last few years the banks have been handed down large fines for mis-selling, for abusing the ignorance and naïveté of their customers to sell them inappropriate financial products such as overly expensive or unnecessary Payment Protection Insurance (PPI) that insures against not being able to repay a loan. Our example is an imaginary bank that wants to prevent these practices. First, they have to understand what went wrong; after all, no one instructed people to sell inappropriate products. Mis-selling happened because the bank put pressure on sales through targets and bonuses to sell, sell, sell. The pressure was not only direct but also indirect through the refurbishment of bank branches to make them selling spaces and training that told sales to attach a PPI sale with every loan. Looking forward, the bank still wants to sell, but it wants to do it more subtly, and with more understanding of the customer's wants and needs. The bank is not going to succeed in making its employees work differently by just telling them to be nicer. Sure, it can put some retraining in place, but all the good words are likely to be forgotten the next time bonus plans are announced or the bank starts a drive for greater efficiency. So how can the bank make the message stick? Eventually the bank decides to make the employees ask key questions during an interview to validate the sale and to record the answers. The questions are designed to ensure that the customer needs the product. It's not long before someone suggests that the answers to the questions be put into a new database so that if there is a later problem, there is traceability of who said what to whom. Not much longer after that it is realized that the answers to these questions provide valuable marketing information. Shortly after, somebody else (perhaps a golf buddy of the CEO who happens to work for a big consultancy firm) will say that it is really simple to write an application that captures the answers to a bunch of questions and puts them in a database, and it should be done in the twinkling of an eye at practically no cost. However, think about it a bit longer and there are many questions, such as these:

- To what financial products does this apply—all of them?
- If the sales people try to sell to the same customer twice, do they annoy the customer by asking the same set of questions the second time?
- How much time should be spent asking questions rather than selling, and what is the cost to the bank?
- Does the application take input from existing data in the bank? If so, what data and where is it?
- How and who should be allowed to change the questions?
- If the questions are changed, how does this affect the analysis of the data (e.g., analysis that spans the time before and after the change)?

- For some products, such as a mortgage for a house, sales have been asking lots of questions for a long time, so is this a new system, or is it an extension of an existing system; and if it is a new system, how do we prevent the same questions from being asked all over again?

- If the bank hears of a customer's change of circumstance (such as a new job, moving, a divorce), does the bank go back and reassess the products sold to that customer?

And so on. It's easy to see how asking many questions could degenerate into laborious bureaucracy to the annoyance of customers and sales staff alike.

In addition to these questions around the process of selling, there are many questions about the IT aspects of the development, such as these:

- To what degree will the new application be integrated with existing applications or databases?

- How should the application be integrated with existing security systems?

- How can we ensure that sales people aren't given carte blanche to access anyone's personal financial details?

- Are there any existing tools for analyzing the data?

And so on.

Today in IT application development the approaches to gathering requirements fall into two camps. In one, a team asks the stakeholders questions, singly or in groups, written or verbally, perhaps by having brainstorming sessions or other techniques for developing business ideas. The team then writes a document that specifies the requirements. When the requirements document is reviewed and signed off, it is passed to an IT development department for implementation. In the other school of thought, a short list of pithy statements of the requirements is written, and then the programmers start development. The software is developed in small increments, and detailed requirements are taken on board by talking to the business representative just before the development of each increment. There is also continual feedback on the product as it is produced, expanding the list of pithy statements.

Whichever way the requirements are gleaned, both approaches rely on a set of assumptions that, if not true, can lead the project to go dangerously awry.

The first assumption is that business managers will give clear answers to all questions posed to them. Look back at the list of questions in our bank example. Many managers simply won't have thought about these questions when the IT requirements are being set. Even worse, some of them will pretend to answer the questions by giving vague, waffly answers, probably with an upbeat, sales-y tone that attempts to push all difficult questions under the carpet. When you have worked gathering requirements for even a short period, you realize that it requires a fanatical attention to detail. Many business managers simply aren't details people, and they find being pressed on detailed questions uncomfortable.

There are some people who insist that all requirements are measureable, partly to counteract management waffle. For instance, instead of saying, "The application must be easy enough to be used by the general public," they say things like "Users must complete the task within five minutes and abort the task less than 5% of the time." Setting metrics is hard. Is a 5% abort rate a good measure of ease of use? Should it be 1% or 10%? And, of course, people abort for reasons other than ease of use, so it is not clear what the metric means. The other problem with such metrics is that they increase costs. Someone has to write extra code in the application to capture the raw information. Someone else has to analyze the data, and if the application fails the test, the project has to be delayed while the problem is fixed—if it can be fixed. And if the abort rate is 6%, what is the business going to do—cancel the application? Sometimes a better approach is to set a requirement to gather the metrics and set the targets as an aspiration, not a showstopper. But there is no point doing even this unless someone is prepared to look at the metrics and do something about them. Business managers will rarely give you target metrics, especially for something as nebulous as ease of use. When they do, they are likely to get it wrong by asking for something that is either far too easy or far too hard. This is where professionalism comes in; the person gathering the requirements should know what is reasonable and help guide the interviewee.

The second assumption is that all stakeholders give consistent answers. This simply isn't true. Managers disagree with managers. Managers disagree with workers. Headquarters disagrees with the branch or department managers. In our example, different managers are likely to say that different people will set the questions. Perhaps the head of the sales force demands that sales managers can override the questions, changing them for their local offices. The head of marketing might completely disagree.

The third assumption is that all the important stakeholders will be found. Not only do requirements gatherers often leave out important stakeholders, especially, for instance, stakeholders who are based abroad, but sometimes they are instructed to leave out important stakeholders. In our example bank, the central management might anticipate pushback from the branches about having to spend time asking questions the customers don't want to answer so hope to present them with a fait accompli rather than address the issue up front.

There are cultural differences here. I once heard of a Japanese business manager who characterized the Western approach to business with a gunslinger analogy as

"Fast draw, slow bullet." In other words, Western businesses get a product to market fast, but the details and the backup aren't there to make it a success. Furthermore, someone is given the role of hero or fall guy, and the rest of the corporation stands back and watches from the sidelines rather than falling in line and giving support. This is a real danger for IT application development as only one person or a few people are providing answers when a wide range of views is necessary. (On the other hand, the problem with many non-Western cultures is that no one tells the manager that he—it is usually a "he"—is wrong.)

The temptation for the person or team gathering the requirements is to answer the requirements questions themselves. It is easy to do this unconsciously, to over-interpret what you are being told or to listen to what is being said with your mind already made up. It is common that if you are sure of the direction in which the project should be going, you only hear statements that confirm your view. Psychologists call this "confirmation bias."

This leads to the fourth assumption: that business executives and managers will read and understand the requirements specification and give intelligent and well-considered feedback. For projects where feedback is given after looking at an early version of the finished product, confirmation bias works the other way around; managers assume the application will support what they want it to do even if they don't see it in front of them—they assume it is in another part of the application or that they have misinterpreted how the applications works.

Any business project must be assessed by comparing the cost and time to deliver against the benefits. The fifth assumption is that the requirements team is in a position to give a good estimate of the application development and runtime costs and that senior managers have a sufficient understanding of the functionality proposed that they can make good trade-off decisions.

The final assumption I discuss has to do with the IT department. In many proposed applications these days—and the bank example we have been discussing is typical—there is a question about the degree of integration with other IT applications. Sometimes more integration means more up-front cost, though often with gains later on because some features are built that future development can use. In our bank example, the integration could range from using a common single sign-on for security to integrating the data with existing customer tables in the database. In the latter case, the designer may have to decide which of several customer tables to integrate with. For instance, there may be customer tables in the accounts database, the mortgage database, and the insurance database. (In real life, I expect most banks have many more than three customer tables.) The assumption, therefore, is that the degree of integration and the pros and cons of different options will be sufficiently visible to business managers that they can make a considered decision.

On a small project with a small number of stakeholders who work well together and where there is little or no integration with other IT applications, these assumptions may well be true. But as projects increase in size and integration becomes more important, these assumptions are far less likely to be true. The consequence is mainly that the IT application does not meet the business need. It commonly happens that someone notices that the project won't do what he or she thought it would do, and hence the requirements change mid-project, leading to delays and cost overruns. (As I said in the preface, it is commonly said that rapid business change is the reason for requirements changing, but I think that by far the most common reason is a realization by the stakeholders that the project is going in a direction they never wanted.) Sometimes the requirements gatherers themselves realize these assumptions are wrong and react by making the requirements overblown because they are trying to include all possible business practices.

This book is about a different way to engage with the stakeholders to build requirements. It is based on a simple observation, which is that the requirements for an IT application are the output from a design process. Put another way, you cannot just "gather" requirements for an IT application like picking apples from a tree. You have to design the business solution to the business problem where part of the solution is an IT application.

Our example illustrates this point. The top-level requirement is that the bank wants to sell within legal bounds because if it does not, the sale will damage the reputation of the bank and the bank may incur a fine. That single statement is the nub of the requirements, although you might need to fancy it up a bit with cost criteria and so forth. It is typical that the essence of a real high-level requirement in business is a single simple statement such as this one. Stating what a business wants to do is rarely complex; it's figuring out how to do it that is. In our example, the response to this requirement is to design a business solution that consists of adapting a number of existing sales processes and adding some additional management processes (to monitor the answers) and marketing processes (to set the questions and analyze data gathered). In support of the business solution and integral to it, a new IT application is designed.

You may be thinking that *design* is too pompous a word for fixing a business problem. I suspect that this is partly because many business managers like a more free-flowing approach—trying something out and adapting it as they go along. Let me make it clear that a free-flowing exploratory approach is a perfectly acceptable way of doing design in general—this is discussed in more detail in the section called "Ad Hoc Design"—but it does not sit well with IT applications, at least with large applications. IT applications are rigid, brittle things, and while in this book I discuss how to make them more flexible and more responsive to change, this is much easier to do when you have a good understanding of which parts are likely to change. Put another way, you can make IT applications bendy but only in part. I once heard a certain well-known application software product described as being "as flexible as concrete"; it can be molded into any shape you like when wet, but when it sets, that's it. A lot of IT applications are like that.

Let us see how turning "gathering requirements" into "designing a business solution" makes our assumptions come true. The key stage in any design is what I call the "design hypothesis"—it is the basic idea for the solution. In our example the design hypothesis is that during a sale, questions are asked and the answers are recorded. The most time-consuming part of the design process is elaborating the design, by which I mean working out what it means in practice and tidying up all the details. The big difference between a design approach and a "requirements gathering" approach is that in a design approach you spend little time asking people to fill in a blank sheet of paper and a lot of time presenting them with a possible solution and listening to their feedback. People find it much easier to criticize than to create. If asked for their needs, they will have difficulty listing them all; but presented with one or two possible solutions, they will quickly identify additional needs, errors, issues, and problems. Furthermore, differences of opinion among the stakeholders become apparent quickly when they are all reviewing the same design. The design provides a framework from which you can try to find a compromise. Here are our assumptions:

- **Assumption one: clarity.** You are not relying on the clarity of the people giving you requirements; you are relying on your own clarity to present to them an accurate picture of the solution.

- **Assumption two: no disagreements.** It is easier for people to raise alternative approaches when they can frame them as criticisms of a possible solution because it allows stakeholders to express disagreement without directly criticizing their peers. If disagreements are in the open, they can be more easily resolved.

- **Assumption three: no unknown or ignored stakeholders.** With the emphasis on feedback and openness it is easier to include people simply by sending them the electronic copy of the design presentation.

- **Assumption four: feedback is clear.** It is easier for the stakeholders to describe precisely how the solution is wrong than to describe what the solution should look like.

- **Assumption five: cost estimates and trade-offs are included in the design process.** Actually, I don't think you can give a cost estimate from a business design alone; you have to go one step further and design the technical solution before making an accurate cost estimate. This is discussed in more detail in Chapter 3, "Reusing Existing Methods and Practices." The good news is that taking this further step is not time-consuming in relation to the total time of the project. It is sufficiently short that it is reasonable to design alternative business solutions and alternative technical designs (for instance, with different availability goals) so that the organization can make an informed decision that suits its time frame and the size of its wallet.

- **Assumption six: business managers understand integration options sufficiently that they can provide guidance in this area.** As we shall see, integration options are presented as part of the design, not in techno-speak but in terms of access to data and passing messages.

The output from designing requirements is what I call a *context design* because it provides the context for the IT design. As you can see from my previous comments, it is vitally important that the context design give a clear picture to business managers of what the proposed IT application does.

I call the whole design approach *context-driven design*.

But before I discuss the other two points I raised at the beginning of this chapter (being more like engineering and working for rather than against the architecture), I need to discuss design in general.

What Is Design?

Design is so familiar that few people give it any thought, but the more you think about design in general, the more peculiar the design of IT applications is shown to be. This peculiarity provokes a question: Is application design really so different, or do we go about it in such an odd way that we are obscuring some fundamental truths?

To begin with, let us define design. A design is a conceptualization of the thing or system you wish to build. The word *design* is both a noun and a verb, but the definition in the previous sentence is for the noun. So we supplement it by saying that the verb *design* means to create a design (the noun).

This definition is broad, deliberately so. Even if you haven't drawn a nice diagram of the imagined final product or written a textual description of the thing or system, even if the conceptualization consists only of a thought in your head, it is still a design.

Of course, people do design in many different ways, but when you take design down to its essential structure, there is a deep similarity among all kinds of design. I think most designers understand this intuitively, though I have to admit I have never seen it articulated like this (though I once saw it articulated somewhat like this but in a manner that was so opaque I'm not absolutely sure).

The structure of design is as follows. Design is a three- or four-step process:

1. **Understanding**. Understand what you are trying to achieve—people's ambitions for the development—and the problems that you will need to overcome. The outcome is the list of requirements.

2. **Hypothesis**. This is the creative bit; this is where hunches and informed guesswork come in. Have some ideas and choose one (or maybe more) to carry forward.

3. **Elaboration**. Flesh out the design by making sure you have covered all the requirements and have fixed all identified weaknesses.

4. **Analysis**. Perform checks, tests, and/or calculations on the design. Try to kill the hypothesis.

It is the fourth step that is optional—or at least it is often not done.

An example is designing a bridge. The requirement is simply to create a way X vehicles per hour can cross a river at point Y, give or take half a mile each way, at no more than Z cost. A tunnel is ruled out on cost grounds. The design hypothesis would be whether to build a suspension bridge, a box girder bridge, a Japanese traditional wooden-style bridge, a typical stone arched bridge, or one of the many other types of bridges. The elaboration would determine what it looks like, where the columns are placed, what it is made of—the details, in other words. The analysis would be the calculations to see whether it could carry the load and won't fall down if the river is flowing fast and other checks.

While I have described these as steps, in practice the process is rarely so clear-cut. In particular, analysis may be spread throughout the elaboration step, although it is important to redo the analysis when you think the design is finished. Even choosing a design hypothesis may be immediately followed by a quick analysis check to establish that the idea is sound. Part of elaboration is driven by looking for weaknesses in the design and finding ways to fix them. Analysis checks are one tool for looking for weaknesses.

In IT, a popular notion is the idea of *patterns*. Patterns are rather like prepared design hypotheses. The idea is an old one. In the recent past it was associated with the architect Christopher Alexander, but in the eighteenth century there were many pattern books published to help less well-trained builders create classical-style houses. Patterns are good, but there is a point where designers must be more creative and think afresh to find a solution.

In design there is feedback, meaning that you might have to loop back to an earlier step. During the elaboration step, you might find that the design hypothesis doesn't work and you have to go back to try another approach, in other words, select another hypothesis. Also—and this is important—you may find that during the elaboration step you have to add to or change your requirements because you uncover gaps or inconsistencies. When the hypothesis changes, the requirements focus changes. For instance, if you are designing a bridge and you decide to change the design hypothesis from a suspension bridge to a bridge that lifts or moves the roadway (like Tower Bridge in London or the swiveling bridge at Wuhan), a whole new set of requirements come into play, like how often it raises or swivels. Thus in design even the requirements aren't fixed. This is illustrated in Figure 1.1.

The analysis step may, of course, reveal an error. Sometimes you can fix the error by tinkering with a detail, in other words, by redoing part of the elaboration step. Sometimes you have to go all the way back to step 2—that is, look for another hypothesis.

One of the requirements is likely to be cost. During the elaboration or analysis steps you may realize the cost is too great and the whole design must be reconsidered.

The word *hypothesis* points at the similarities between design and advancing a scientific theory. This is deliberate. The notion of a hypothesis and trying to disprove it is associated with Karl Popper and is now more or less accepted as how we do science. Before Popper advanced his hypothesis about hypothesizing, it was thought that scientific progress took place by accumulating facts until a scientific law emerged. This model of accumulation and emergence is similar to how most people think of design, and I think this is how most people think of application development; we gather requirements and the design emerges. It is as wrong for application design today as it was wrong for science in the past, for two main reasons. First, we are not dealing in certainties; we are dealing with guesswork, intuition, and gut

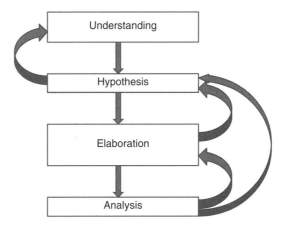

Figure 1.1 *Design Feedback*

feeling—there is no one answer. The elaboration and analysis steps are about keeping the guesswork, intuition, and gut feelings in check, putting them on a sound basis. The second reason is that, as previously noted, the hypothesis and the elaboration may change the requirements. There is a kind of conversation between the requirements and the solution that needs to take place.

Because of the feedback between the steps, design does not work well in a fixed time frame. All we can hope for is that the duration of doing the design is much less than the duration of the implementation. This is a problem for IT design because programming is itself a design exercise. The aim of much of this book is to look for ways of making important decisions early (but not too early) so that the programming is relatively routine.

I believe the best designers go through these four steps instinctively. They have two behaviors that poor designers don't have. First, they avoid many of the problems of looping back by keeping in their heads a picture of the design that is way ahead of what they are actually doing. Put another way, they loop back but in their heads. Second, they take their time on major decisions like choosing the hypothesis; they don't leap to conclusions, and they are happy to listen to suggestions and explore alternatives. At various points in this book I urge you to think like a designer; what I mean by this is that I would like you to think deeply about the hypothesis and what it means for the elaboration step and about the dialogue between design and requirements. You should also be looking for ways to analyze the design.

Design is done in many different ways. I group these broadly into ad hoc design, planned design, and engineered design. These are discussed in the following sections.

Ad Hoc Design

In ad hoc design you start with a simple sketch or just an idea and start building. As you go along, you are likely to find that the design is incomplete or has problems, so you tweak it. Sometimes you have to make changes to the design that are so fundamental that you have to undo some of the completed work.

Ad hoc design is extremely common in IT, and I have used it myself a lot. It works well when you are building something that is routine—you have done something similar before and more or less know what to expect. More precisely, it normally works fine if the project has these characteristics:

- The project is small. The design is in one person's head and therefore the designer is able to set very well-defined jobs for anyone else on the team. Alternatively, the designer can subcontract part of the design to another member of the project, but again only if the scope and the requirements for the subdesign can be set precisely.

- The project is self-contained, by which I mean that other development projects happening at the same time aren't dependent on it. In general, if a project depends on another IT project, it must define precisely the nature of the dependency. For instance, it must specify exactly what data it receives and what data it sends or what data it shares in a database. This is hard to do in an ad hoc design project because by the nature of the process the designer is likely to change his or her mind, which may infuriate the designers of the dependent project.

- The relationship between the designer and the stakeholders is very close because the stakeholders have to trust the designer to deliver what they want with very little evidence. This problem can be alleviated by frequently showing the stakeholders the partially completed build, which is fine if the stakeholders have the time and energy continually to review the work in progress.

There is another scenario where ad hoc design works, and that is when you start on a project and don't know where you are going to end up. Essentially it becomes design by trying things out. An example I use in this book is an application I built for drawing diagrams from data. I used ad hoc design partly because the stakeholder was me, and partly because when I started I didn't have a clear idea of what the final product would look like.

Ad hoc design works best if you are mentally prepared at the beginning to throw away work you have already done. This happens because as you go along the design road, you sometimes reach a roadblock or you realize there is a better solution to the problem. I reckon that in my diagram-drawing application I threw away about 20% of already-tested code I had written. Artistic work can also be seen as a kind of design, and it is often achieved using ad hoc design. A characteristic of great artists is their willingness to destroy work that isn't good enough. I would go as far as to say that you can design a solution to a complex and challenging problem with ad hoc design but only if you are prepared to throw away large parts of the unfinished product. Put simply, you code something, realize you can do better, and code it again.

It is commonly observed that the second or third release of a software product is much better than the first release. Clearly the interrelationships among parts of the system are much better understood if a version of the system already exists, and thus it is easier for different designers to be working on different parts of the system in harmony. And it's partly a marketing thing; it is better to have something working to gain entry to the market, so the first version might be a bit sloppy. (That said, I have never known good programmers to write sloppy code even if they are under time pressure because it is usually counterproductive.) But I suggest a major reason is that when writing the second or third release, people are much more willing to throw away code belonging to the old release, which they wouldn't have done while programming the first release.

One way to create a large product using ad hoc design is to have many small releases. A complex design builds up gradually, and as it emerges it is understood by all members of the implementation team. As a tangential point, observe that something very odd is happening here. Why is it we can understand a large, complex piece of software in our heads, but it seems we can't express the design on paper in such a way that people can understand it? Much of this book is about my attempt to do this.

Planned Design

In planned design you draw a diagram of the product you are designing or describe it in words. Most of the fine historical buildings you see today were designed using planned design; an architect drew a diagram of the building's floor plan and exterior walls and specified what materials and/or techniques to use. I expect most of the wonderful Gothic cathedrals in Europe were designed using planned design; it is hard to imagine how the builders could have done it any other way, especially when you consider someone carving a block of stone to fit exactly into one position in the window tracery. But Gothic cathedral builders used rules of thumb to decide how thick to build the columns, and they relied on craftspeople to know how to build what was in the drawing.

A great benefit of planned design is that, assuming you are using competent craftspeople, you don't have to supervise them as much as in ad hoc design. They can look at the drawing and build from that.

When you have something complicated to build, design hierarchies come into play. Suppose I am designing a medieval cathedral. At the top level of design is the basic shape. This defines where the pillars and the walls go but not the internal structure of the pillars or roof. This detailed design is left to others, or more likely to craftspeople who will build it according to the same designs they have used for centuries. Someone else might design the stone tracery, the stained-glass windows, and the layout of the altar and choir stalls.

Planned design tends to be conservative because it relies on a body of knowledge and skills in the craftsperson's head, whereas moving away from the familiar requires developing a new body of knowledge and skills.

IT has used planned design a great deal, especially in large projects. I think it is fair to say that planned design has a mixed record of success in application design.

Engineered Design

Engineered design is very much like planned design in that the design is represented by drawings or text; the difference is that in engineered design the design is tested. In other words, engineered design is the only kind of design that includes the formal analysis step previously described in the four-step process. I am not saying that in planned design or ad hoc design there is no analysis, because I suspect good designers often do some analysis in their heads even if it is something as simple as running through different scenarios of how the product will be used. I even suspect that Gothic cathedral designers in the Middle Ages thought long and hard about how the cathedral would be used, perhaps even working out how the space could give added flexibility to processions and services. Unfortunately the cathedral builders did not understand forces and load-bearing calculations, and quite a number of cathedral towers fell down shortly after they were built. The difference in engineered design is that formal analysis is done and there is a body of knowledge about what analysis is appropriate. A modern civil engineer will calculate the loads and will have confidence that, so long as the build is done correctly, the building will be structurally sound. There are other forms of analysis besides calculation. You can analyze a building design to check how long it will take people to escape if there is a fire by using computer modeling. You can analyze a car design for wind resistance by putting it in a wind tunnel.

For engineered design of anything beyond the very simple, there will be a hierarchy of designs. For instance, if you are designing a new passenger jet plane, the top-level design describes the shape of the plane in terms of how all the components fit together. Each component has its own design, and a complex component like an engine is also broken down into numerous subcomponents, each with its own design. The hierarchical nature of the design is illustrated rather abstractly in Figure 1.2.

Each small box is a component, and each big box enclosing the small boxes is a design. Thus the top-level design shows how the aircraft is an assembly of body,

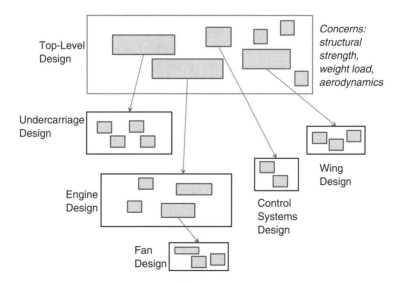

Figure 1.2 *Hierarchical Design of an Aircraft*

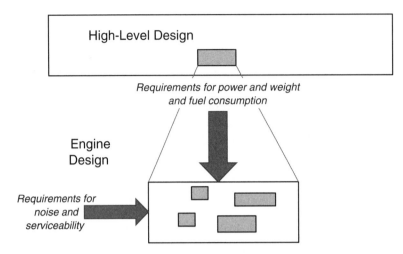

Figure 1.3 *Requirements on a Component*

wings, engines, undercarriage, and so forth, and the engine design shows how the engine parts fit together.

The requirements for the component design come both from the higher-level designs and from the outside. For instance, an aircraft engine's requirements come from the higher-level design—power needed, weight limits, size limits—and from the outside—noise limits and serviceability requirements. This is illustrated in Figure 1.3.

In engineered design each component design is tested.

There are two important points about engineering calculations. The first is that the calculations depend on the components satisfying their requirements. For instance, an aircraft designer will do a calculation to check whether the plane will fly. This calculation relies on assumptions about how much the engines weigh and how much power they deliver. Any factor of a component used in the analysis must be underpinned by a requirement on the component design. If the engines cannot deliver the power for the prescribed weight, the higher-level design must be redone. In other words, there is a feedback loop from component design to the higher-level design. This is illustrated in Figure 1.4.

The second important point about engineering calculations is that they do not prove that something will always succeed. All they do is show that the product won't fail under a set of predefined circumstances. Reverting to the building example, structural engineers can calculate loads to be sure that a building won't collapse when people walk in and furniture is added. But to be sure the building won't fall down in a high wind you have to do another set of calculations. Likewise for earthquakes, floods, and so on. In other words, calculations prove only that problems you

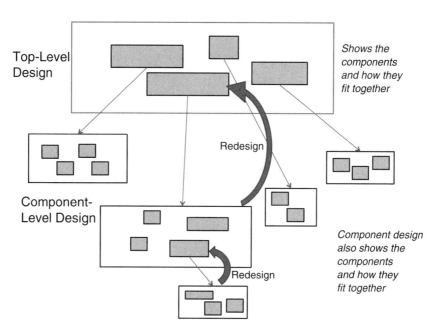

Figure 1.4 *Redesign Feedback Loop*

have identified are prevented. It does not prove that problems you haven't identified are prevented. I make this point because in IT there is this nirvana that people hanker for, which is that a program is *provably correct*. Engineers don't prove that a design is correct; instead, they prove that it does not suffer from a predefined set of problems. It is time we stop trying to be mathematicians and concentrate on being engineers instead.

The point that failure has to be anticipated before it can be fixed is illustrated by the famous example of the Tacoma Narrows Bridge collapse in 1940 [2]. What happened was that a medium-strength wind caused resonance, and the swaying built on itself. The consequence was that a small up-and-down movement became a large up-and-down movement, and the bridge eventually writhed about until it broke. These days engineers understand resonance and do calculations to ensure that a structure does not suffer from it. Sometimes they get it wrong, as with the Millennium Bridge in London. This had resonance, not from wind but from people walking over it. The bridge was closed shortly after opening while the problem was fixed.

There is always a danger that some problem is found that cannot be surmounted without a redesign. And there is always a danger that a redesign of a component will cascade, leading to a further redesign of the whole product. Both dangers are likely to be more serious in planned design than in engineered design because in engineered design the analysis is likely to catch problems early.

Summary of Design Approaches

There were a number of concepts in the last few sections, and I think it is worth a recap.

- Design is essentially a four-step process: understanding, hypothesis, elaboration, and analysis.

- Complex designs can be split into a hierarchy of components being separately designed.

- Broadly speaking, there are three kinds of design:

  - **Ad hoc design.** There is no formal design, which means the design resides in the designer's head. It works well for small, well-understood products but can also be used for exploratory design if the designer is willing to rework large parts of the product that were previously thought to be finished.

  - **Planned design.** There is a formal design that allows the build to proceed without continual guidance from the designer. It can be used for any scale of project (even large—think of the pyramids!). There is no formal analysis; therefore, the performance of the product is reliant on the designer's intuition.

  - **Engineered design.** This is like planned design, but formal analysis is applied to the design. Building products that are complex, that have many internal dependencies, or whose performance is hard to predict demands engineered design.

To support the arguments in the next two sections, I have drawn in Figure 1.5 a diagram representing engineered design.

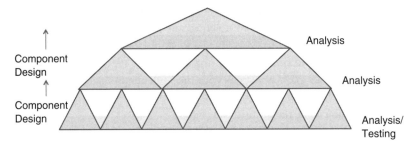

Figure 1.5 *Engineered Design*

So can we make application development an engineering discipline, and if we can, do we want to?

Making IT Application Development More of an Engineering Discipline

Engineered design in IT is almost nonexistent. There are two main reasons. The first is that an IT application is a component of a business solution; from the design perspective it is not a complete system. The second is that analysis of the design—in contrast to testing and inspection of the code—is hardly ever done. Using the diagram style of Figure 1.5, typical IT design is illustrated in Figure 1.6.

Does this matter? Imagine you were designing a new kind of aircraft and the only testing you could do was to fly the plane. The dangers are obvious. The design might not have the weight distributed properly, leading to dangerous flying behavior. The structure might not be strong enough, leading to it falling apart. You would probably anticipate these problems and compensate by making the structure far stronger than it needed to be, resulting in excess weight and poor flying ability. Similar arguments apply to IT application design, especially for large applications because design flaws are always harder to spot in a larger, more complex design.

I hope to convince you that it is possible to make IT application development an engineering discipline—to change Figure 1.6 into Figure 1.5. It needs a complete hierarchy of designs, and each design needs analysis techniques.

The hierarchy of designs I have developed is described in the next chapter. It is rather different from a classic engineering hierarchy of designs, but I hope to convince you that it still supports engineered design principles.

The analysis techniques tend not to be engineering-style calculations but checking for completeness and consistency and looking at how data is used. They are described in detailed in Chapters 5 through 12.

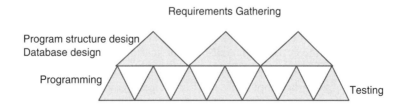

Figure 1.6 *Typical IT Application Design*

Taking IT Architecture into Account

At the beginning of this chapter I wrote that I have three objectives; so what about the third of these—support for IT architecture?

Unfortunately I have to explain some terminology here. I have used the words *IT architecture* as a catchall term for different kinds of architecture in the IT development space such as enterprise architecture, information architecture, and technical architecture. What I mean by *taking IT architecture into account* is having a concern for the whole of the enterprise's IT resource rather than the single application. It is about looking for synergy, looking for data consistency across the organization, and creating an IT application portfolio that can be easily extended to support new functionality. It is about taking care of the integration across applications as well as the applications themselves.

Note that if IT application development becomes an engineering discipline, it would not, per se, be more likely that the applications will support the IT architecture. The same is true in civil engineering—just because a civil engineer has helped to design a building it is no more likely that the building will be in keeping with its environment.

There are several areas of design where architectural concerns are particularly important. One is the *technology design*. For most projects, there are a huge number of technology products you could use, so you have to select which technology to work with. You want to use technology in which your organization has expertise, and technology that is easy to integrate with your existing applications. The technical design must also help you decide how to structure the application and how to integrate with the organization's systems management and security services. There are opportunities for reusing ideas, technology, and sometimes programmed code across many applications.

Another area is *database design*. The issue here is consistency of data across the organization, for instance, by having one copy of data for each customer or, if you have multiple copies, ensuring that they have the same information. The new application should be built to use data that already exists, or at least it should work with other applications to keep the data consistent.

However, the linchpin for ensuring that wider concerns are taken into account is deciding, early in the design, what existing applications and services to keep and what applications and services to replace, and identifying and implementing services that can be reused by other applications. This I call *integration design*, and I put it high up in the design hierarchy because the decisions just cited are central to deciding the scope of the development.

Concluding Remarks

This chapter is about why I think application design methods need to change. It is structured around the three areas where I think change is most necessary:

- Basing IT application design on the recognition that you don't gather your requirements, you design them

- Making application design more like an engineering discipline, in particular, by analyzing designs and looking for flaws before implementation

- Ensuring that the application works with other applications that exist or are in development to create a coherent IT architecture

In the course of expanding on these points, I also discussed the nature of design and the three kinds of design: ad hoc design, planned design, and engineered design. I noted how design consists of four steps, albeit often interwoven and with loopbacks: understanding requirements, design hypothesis, elaboration, and analysis. It is the inclusion of the analysis step that characterizes engineered design. This notion of analyzing design is a thread that runs throughout this book. I also described the notion of design as a hierarchy, how a large-scale design is broken up into smaller component designs. How to do this for IT application design is not obvious and it is the topic of the next chapter.

Chapter 2

A Hierarchy of Designs

As I pointed out in Chapter 1, "Introduction to Context-Driven Design," engineered design depends on having a hierarchy of designs. In this chapter I examine whether we can construct an engineering-quality hierarchy of designs for IT software development and whether it is worth our while to do so.

This chapter has three parts. In the first section, "Justifying the Hierarchy of Designs," I examine the design hierarchy from the bottom up with the aim of justifying the hierarchy of designs. In the following sections—"Context Design," "Integration Design," "Technical Design," "User Interface Design," "Database Design," and "Implementation"—I look at the hierarchy of designs from the top down to give a feel for the flow of information through the design. Having presented all parts of the hierarchy, I return to the question posed at the start of the chapter in a section called "Is It Really Engineering?" The chapter ends with "Concluding Remarks."

Justifying the Hierarchy of Designs

I start by examining *implementation design*—in other words, programming.

Programming is a design exercise. I have discovered that not all people agree with that statement, but it is my experience of programming. You start with a design hypothesis—often called a program pattern. You elaborate it by writing code, and you analyze it by compiling, inspection reviews, and testing. But, as illustrated in Figure 1.6 in the previous chapter, the program—at least in a business application—is not the whole of the design.

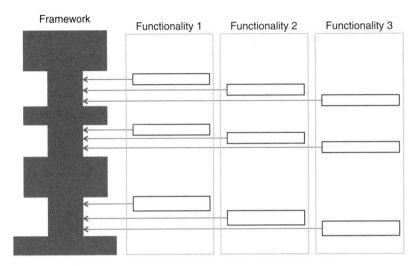

Figure 2.1 *Frameworks*

Most programs these days are built on frameworks. The concept of a framework is illustrated in Figure 2.1.

The idea of frameworks is that there is some skeletal code into which code segments are placed. The code segments deliver the user functionality; the skeletal code makes it all hang together and provides common system facilities such as security, message passing, and systems management.

For instance, there are many frameworks that support the MVC (Model-View-Controller) pattern. The basic idea is that the input comes to a controller, which uses the model to access the data and uses the view to display the data on the screen. Thus to implement some functionality, you write code for models, views, and controllers, and these are then slotted into the framework.

Frameworks are often supplied by software vendors. Most major application development software vendors have their own framework—often more than one—and there is a host of open-source frameworks. But often application developers need to extend vendors' offerings to meet their requirements. This is particularly true for multitier applications because most vendors' frameworks don't extend beyond the bounds of a single machine.

With framework development, you can subdivide the work programmers must do into three areas: framework development, functional code development, and common utilities development. Common utilities are functions like programmatically sending e-mails, turning a list of data into a PDF file, and reporting an error. This is illustrated in Figure 2.2.

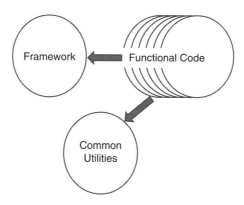

Figure 2.2 *Different Areas of Programming*

With this in mind, imagine you are a programmer who needs to program some new functionality. What do you need before you can begin? You need to know

- **The user interface design**—the layout of the user interface, the inputs, what needs to be done to process each input, and the output display
- **The database design**—the structure of the database or non-database files
- **The integration design**—the messages (if any) that are sent to or received from other applications
- **The technical design**—the choice of which framework and software to use and the design of additional common code to make the framework, administration, and operations work best

The user interface design, the database design, and the technical design form the next level up in the design hierarchy. The integration design is described later in this section.

If we have three designs, we need three designers: the user interface designer, the database designer, and the technical designer. Let me make it clear that these are roles, not people. In a small application one person may do all three jobs as well as programming. However, if one person is doing, say, the user interface design and the implementation, he or she should not interleave it. You should not do the user interface design in small increments just before each increment is coded—just-in-time user interface design if you will. Let me clarify. The look and feel of the user interface design (the font size, position of the buttons, choice of colors, etc.) can be changed with little impact on the code and therefore can be left until late in the project. But the flow from screen to screen, the data displayed on each screen, and the function of each button need to be designed as a whole. This way the design can be analyzed for completeness and examined carefully for ease of use. Similar arguments apply to database design and technical design.

Ah, I hear you protest, when you are programing, you can find flaws in the design. Yes, sometimes this is true, and as I pointed out in the previous chapter, this is the nature of design; there is always the possibility of feedback from detailed design to the higher-level designs. In the military there is a saying, "No plan survives first contact with the enemy." But that does not mean they don't believe in planning. On the contrary; the better the plan, the easier it is to make changes to the plan. It is the same with designs; you are in a much better position to understand the ramifications of change when you have completed the top-level designs; you are much more likely to find the best way to mend any flaws you find.

So what do the user interface, database, and technical designers need in order to do their jobs? They need to know

- **What the organization needs the application to do.** As I describe in detail later, I split the application functionality into tasks—one person at one time doing something. Thus the designers need to know what tasks to implement and what each one of them does.
- **Which data tables the tasks use.** Often the description of a task does not make sense without talking about the data.
- **About the users.** The designers need to group the users according to what they do and hence according to what data they can see and update.

These three pieces of information I put into one design because the information is tightly woven together. I call this the *context design*.

But in a complex integrated system, the context design might cover more than one application and service, while a user interface design is associated with only one application or service. Moreover, the database design may be for a database that serves several applications or services. Thus there may not be a simple one-to-one relationship between the context, user interface, and database designs. To show how the applications, services, and databases implement the context design, we need an *integration design* showing how the parts exchange messages and share common resources.

Finally, for the technical design we need to know some metrics like how many tasks are done per hour or per second, and the application availability target.

Diagrammatically the designs are illustrated in Figure 2.3, which I call, with a striking lack of originality, the *six-box model* of design.

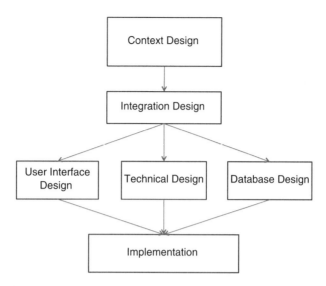

Figure 2.3 *The Six-Box Model*

Is it a problem to have so many designs? It is not, for three reasons. First, the output from the database design is the database schema, and the main output from the technical design is framework code; in other words, both are part of the final deliverable. Second, the user interface design is lightweight, by which I mean it is far above the level of code—one line of design translates into many lines of code. Third, information is reused from design to design. Parts of the specification in the context design are unchanged by the integration design and reused in the user interface design. This is different from classical engineering design; integration design to user interface design and integration design to database design are transformations rather than divisions into components.

In the following sections I will describe this model from the top down—context design to implementation. The emphasis is on the design output rather than how you develop and analyze the designs, which is a topic for later chapters.

While I am concentrating on business application development, I think the six-box model also holds for other kinds of IT applications, although some applications may have a negligible database component and others may have a negligible integration component. There are some applications where it is ridiculous overkill—for instance, designing and implementing a word processor application. But for some non-business applications, while I would expect the context design to change substantially, I would still expect it to be there. For instance, the design of the software for the real-time control of a rocket should have a context design that defines what the controls are and how they behave, as well as the rules for changing the controls.

The user interface design would in this case be not for humans but for electronic measurement devices. I would expect, too, a significant difference in the implementation of real-time applications because often the program needs to do some action within a precise timing window. However, there would still be six boxes. Even the database design might still be there because there is a need to keep persistent data in order to have a record of the recent past states, and the integration design might be there because the processing is spread over several processing units. Similarly, in games programming a six-box model may apply, but I would expect the context design to outline the story of the game and the integration design to be relevant only for multiuser games.

In the following sections I return to the mundane world of business computing.

Context Design

The context design needs to explain the business requirements of the IT development. The elements of the context design are tasks, user groups, data tables, and messages between tasks, and this chapter includes a subsection on each. They are followed by subsections called "Task Dependencies," "Putting It All Together," and "Analysis of the Context Design."

Tasks

As previously noted, I split the business into *tasks*. So what is a task?

If you could view an organization by wandering around the offices and every time people sent or received a message from an IT application a halo of red glowed from their heads, what you would see is that the halos come in short bursts. These are the tasks. Most tasks are short—a few minutes or less—and most people spend more time between tasks than doing them. Even in a job like a bank teller when there is a queue of people waiting to be served, the bank teller will spend a short period of time using the IT application and the rest counting money, waiting for customers to fill in or sign forms, and waiting for someone to leave and the next person to arrive. Examples of tasks are

- Checking a guest into a hotel
- Withdrawing money from an ATM
- Recording a delivery
- Assigning a car to a police incident
- Raising an order

Let me add some precision to the definition of task. First, let me be clear that using the word *task* to have a precise meaning in a business modeling context is not common. I have stolen the word *task* in the hope that it isn't as loaded as all the other words I could use here like *activity, use case, transaction,* and *action.* When business process analysts want to express the same idea as tasks, they sometimes use the expression "One person, one place, one time." I've always found the *one place* somewhat odd (one person at one time is usually in one place, right?) and think that perhaps it would be better expressed as *one device* so we can capture the idea of one person doing one thing on a PC and another on a mobile, both at the same time. Or to be accurate, since some interfaces like Web browsers allow you to be connected to many applications at the same time, perhaps we should say *one device/tab.* So we have "One person, one time, one device/tab." It hasn't got much zing to it, has it? Which is why I call them *tasks.*

But for a formal definition we need to discuss *atomicity.* To model a business operation you need a unit of work at the bottom rung. That unit of work must be atomic, meaning that all of it must be done or none of it is done. Atomic does not mean one outcome. There can be many outcomes, but they must be definable—we must be able to list them all and define exactly what each outcome is. The outcomes may include updates to the database. Thus, a better definition of a task is

An atomic unit of work done by one person at one time

By saying that tasks are atomic, we mean that if a task fails before it has reached one of the outcomes, it must be undone as if it had never happened. Having several outcomes to a task is usually the consequence of the user making decisions, but for every task the context designer must also consider the following two possible events:

- The IT application fails (e.g., the server is subject to a power cut).
- The user stops doing the task (goes to lunch, must rush home, etc.) and leaves the task unfinished.

The context designer may decide in these two cases to save the updates in the database instead of undoing all the work. If so, we must define two tasks—a *start and maybe finish X* task and a *complete X* task—because *complete X* may take place a long time after the *start X* task.

You will probably recognize the task's concept of atomicity as similar to the database transaction's concept of atomicity. The database notion of transactions has, as you probably know, not only atomicity but also consistency, isolation, and durability—the ACID properties—which makes one wonder whether the *C*, *I*, and *D* in ACID also apply to tasks. They do in weakened form, and this is discussed in Chapter 8, "User Interface Design and Ease of Use." So are tasks simply transactions? Unfortunately not, because tasks often require several messages to be passed to and fro from user to IT application; thus tasks usually cannot be implemented directly by database transactions. Nonetheless they rely entirely on the database transaction functionality; a task that updates a database is implemented by one or more database transactions.

A simple way of thinking about all this is that the business moves forward in task steps.

I can see many of my readers thinking, "What's wrong with using use cases?" It is true that a use case may be a description of a task, but the trouble is that use cases are also used for many other things. This is discussed in more detail in the next chapter.

Other readers may be asking, "Aren't tasks business process activities (i.e., the boxes in business process diagrams)?" An activity can be broken down into several tasks. An activity to dig a hole in the road may have one task at the beginning when the team leader indicates that the crew should start the dig, and another task at the end indicating that the activity is finished. This is discussed in Chapter 5, "The Relationship with the Business."

In the old days, when people were searching for a new technical word, they found one in Latin or ancient Greek. I sometimes wonder if we in IT should do the same.

User Groups

Another piece of information user interface designers need is user groups. User groups are categories of users, such as sales people, warehouse managers, security staff, and so on. But note that one person may belong to several user groups; for instance, one person might be a sales person (for submitting orders), a sales manager (for accessing sales reports), an employee (for submitting expenses), and a manager (for doing personnel reviews). Different groups of users of an application will have different access rights to the application; they will see more or less data than other user groups, and they will do different tasks, albeit possibly with some overlap. The user interface designer will need to make decisions about whether to give different user groups different screens or to give them the same screen but tailor the screen differently according to which user groups the user belongs to.

I have used the words *user groups* rather than *roles* or *user roles* because I think using the word *roles* will make some people leap to conclusions about implementation. I have also avoided the word *actor* because users aren't actors.

Data Tables

The main purpose of a business-style application is usually to store data for later retrieval. Without having a notion of what the data is, describing an application is impossible. In a bank we talk about *crediting an account*. What is an account? It is data. In a business we talk about *order processing*. What is an order? It is data.

Typically the nouns used in a description of an IT business application refer to data. Thus a business-level description of an application is largely about what tasks do to data. This is why we need some understanding of data in the context design. But we don't want to clutter the context design with all the detail you find in a database schema. In fact, when we start thinking about the context design, we may not even have identified how many databases we want.

In the context design I use the term *data table* to indicate a group of *data objects*, where a data object holds data for something like an account, a product, or a customer. The structure of the data object is not defined; we know we have some data, we give it a name, and we figure out which task created, read, updated, or deleted the data, and that is mostly it. We define a data attribute for data objects in a table only when we need that attribute in order to define rules in the task. When we come to define the database schema, we will not only give the data tables some attributes but may also find that the data tables in the context design split into several database tables.

Messages between Tasks

Tasks might send messages to each other rather than just share data.

I find that specifying message passing in a context design is rare. It is common for an implementation to call a service—some application code—over a network. But this is an implementation detail not needed in a functional description (which the context design is).

Also, when tasks need to pass data to each other, it is often a better design to put the data into a data table. When using messages to send data, there is one provider task of the data and one consumer task. Often we find that we need to have more than one consumer of data; hence it makes sense to put the data in a data table. Using tables also allows the consumer to read the data in a different order from the order in which the data was provided.

In practice, most examples of sending or receiving messages are about passing data to other applications outside the scope of the context design. But an example where messages are useful within an application is to send an alert to a task that tells its user that something important has happened.

Note that because a task might be entirely driven by processing input messages, it may have no users. This is also true for batch tasks—tasks that run at certain times of day, night, week, month, or year. An example of a batch task is a task that pays interest on bank accounts.

Task Dependencies

Tasks are great for specifying what needs to be done, but they do not operate in a vacuum. To really get a grip on the tasks for the purpose of analyzing the context design for completeness and consistency, you must understand how tasks depend on other tasks.

One way tasks depend on each other is that the tasks implement activities in a business process. A process is about how activities cooperate to do things; in other words, processes have outcomes. The point of analyzing processes is to understand how the outcome is achieved. For instance, to pay expenses, someone submits an expense claim—that is one activity; someone signs off on it—another activity; and there is an automatic activity run, say, once a month to pay the expenses. Thus in this example there are three activities in a simple sequence and the output is a payment. If a manager decides that some expenses should be paid by another group, the manager transfers the expenses to another manager to sign off, and the process is no longer three simple activities in a sequence, especially if the receiving manager disputes the claim. It is common for there to be a simple sequence of activities when everything goes right and a complex network of activities with loops back to previous activities to handle problems. From the task-level view, a process is often helped along by tasks sharing data and tasks sending messages to other tasks.

Processes are not the only dependencies between tasks. If you are allocating resources—for instance, assigning trucks to do deliveries—you may have a number of tasks that have to do with assigning, releasing, buying, and servicing the trucks which make the trucks available or unavailable. Several tasks are bound together by the fact that they manage the same resources.

In both of these examples—processes and resource allocation—the dependencies between tasks are usually converted into dependencies of tasks on data tables. For instance, a data object representing an order should tell you where in the order processing that particular order is. To find out whether a truck is available you would look at the status in the data object representing the truck. This triggers an analysis question: "How can we be sure that the information in the database accurately describes the state of the resource in the outside world?" To answer this question, we have to think of the people, places, and times in an organization where there is an interaction with the resource and what happens when someone finds that the resource is not in the state in which the database said it should be.

Some data does not manage a process or a resource; it is information in its own right, and here again it may be shared across many tasks. For instance, data about products is used by ordering, manufacturing, storage, sales, marketing, and billing.

Putting It All Together

There can be hundreds of different kinds of tasks performed in a medium-size business, so it may make sense to group them. I call these groups *common purpose groups*. Naturally you try to group in such a way that there are few dependencies between the tasks in one common purpose group and tasks in another, but there are likely to be some. This is discussed in Chapter 6, "The Relationship with the Users."

The business functionality is described by

- The tasks
- The user groups
- The data tables
- Messages between tasks
- The dependencies between the tasks

The first three of these elements is drawn diagrammatically in Figure 2.4.

The top line shows user groups. (Remember that one person can belong to more than one user group.)

The middle line shows the tasks. The description of the tasks is supplemented by text. This is described in Chapter 6. I haven't drawn any message sending, but if there was any it would be just an arrow between tasks.

The bottom line shows data tables, not databases.

Other dependencies—for instance, the fact that several of the tasks are part of a business process—would be drawn in separate diagrams as needed. All dependencies should be documented somewhere because the information is needed to understand the ramifications of change and for context design analysis. I like to have each dependency illustrated in at least one diagram because I use the diagrams for review.

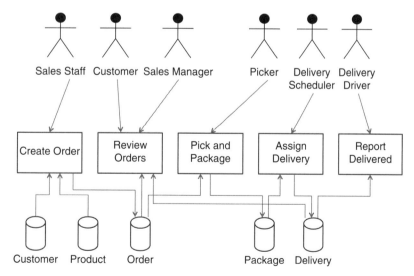

Figure 2.4 *Task View Diagram*

Alternatively you can document dependencies in a table with a list of tasks on the column and row axes by putting a check mark in the intersection box if they have a dependency or, better, one or more letters that indicate the nature of the dependency. You can do the same with tasks against data tables and tasks against user groups. Tables are good for looking things up, but they aren't very user friendly in reviews; diagrams make the reviews more engaging.

Note that most of these other dependencies between tasks while identified in, say, process diagrams end up as dependencies of tasks on data or messages sent between tasks, and thus for implementers they are a nice-to-know, not a need-to-know.

You may be thinking that identifying the tasks is easy; in fact, you may think that the business managers should already have done this. It is true that sometimes the tasks are obvious and sometimes so trivial that there is little point in drawing a diagram to represent them. In other cases they are most certainly not trivial. For instance, the diagram in Figure 2.4 looks rather straightforward and easy, but even such a simple diagram should provoke questions. For instance:

- Are picking and packing one task or two?

- What happens if the picker has run out of product? There needs to be a task to report back to the customer.

- What happens if the delivery fails?

As we noted earlier, processes become complicated when something goes wrong.

Analysis of the Context Design

With a context design, you can ask questions such as these:

- Does every data table have tasks that create the data, other tasks that use the data, and tasks that delete the data?

- If the data is tracking an entity in the real world (e.g., data about a customer), is it accurate? What happens when the real world changes (e.g., customers change their names or addresses)? If the data is inaccurate, does it matter?

- Does every task have the information it needs to do its job?

- Do the tasks and data support the business processes well? For instance, in order processing there should be a rule that the customer is invoiced for what is delivered, not what was ordered. The analysis question is whether this rule is obeyed.

- What is the impact of an IT failure on a business process?

- Are users being given too much work to do collecting data?

- Are there security (or even legal) implications of people seeing the data?

These questions hint that a context design can be analyzed, which in turn means that it can be used to support engineered design. It's not analysis that relies on calculations; it is more about tracing data flows and studying dependencies. Even a small amount of simple analysis can help you avoid costly mistakes.

I expect you know of organizations that have never done any analysis of anything equivalent to a context design and seem to be doing just fine. So why is analysis important? Actually, in my experience, almost no companies have done a comprehensive analysis equivalent to developing a context model. What they have are small islands of consistency, forced upon them the hard way by the needs of some business functionality, among a sea of vagueness. The consistent areas are glued together by manual procedures and guesswork. This is why

- You have to give the same organization the same data time and time again.

- Two airline passengers have the same seat number.

- Organizations sell you products that have been discontinued.

- A utility company bills my daughter for the next-door address and continues to do so long after being told of the error.

Recall that a weakness in planned design versus engineered design is a tendency to overengineer because you don't dare risk failure. Exactly the same happens with IT applications. Because the application can't rely on the accuracy of the information in the database, it rechecks the data or forces the user to re-input it. Also, because the application doesn't know who needs the data, it sends the data to everyone. In most cases, people aren't killed and we can live with the inefficiency, but it would be kind of nice not to.

Integration Design

The main purposes of integration design are

- To partition the tasks into applications and services

- To decide how to allocate data tables to databases

- To define integration requirements in terms of messages sent between applications

Integration design defines the scope of the more detailed designs. User interface design is done independently for each application or service (the user of a service being another program). Database design is done independently for each database. Technical design could be done for each application or service individually, but in most organizations it makes sense that a number of applications and services share a common technical design.

Partitioning tasks into applications and services is illustrated in Figure 2.5.

However, as diagrams go it isn't very useful, because in a real-life application the number of tasks is much greater and diagrams such as these are hard to draw. So I draw a diagram like Figure 2.6 and make a list of the tasks implemented by each application. The boxes are applications or services. Arrows indicate request/response calls unless they have some annotation like "SP" on the lines between the databases. SP stands for "select and project," meaning that not all the data objects are transferred (but only selected ones) and of those that are, not all their attributes are included in the data stream. (Taking some but not all of the attributes from a data object is known as projection; *select* and *project* are database jargon words.) At the bottom of the diagram is a message with a "D" in it. *D* stands for "deferrable,"

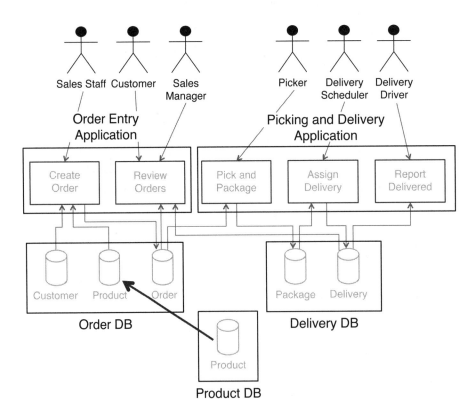

Figure 2.5 *Application View Diagram*

meaning that this is a send and forget message. Its purpose in Figure 2.6 is to record in the Order database that the order has been packed and is awaiting delivery.

Applications can be of three sorts:

- **Online applications.** They have end users driving them. When I call something an *application* I mean an online application. In the diagram, Order Entry Application and Warehouse Front End are applications.

- **Batch applications.** They are triggered by some time event. An example is a banking application to calculate account interest payments. I mark a batch application on a diagram by drawing a simplified clock face in the box's top left corner.

- **Service applications.** These are applications called by other applications. When I call something a *service* I mean a service application. In the diagram, Picking Services is a service. (Note: Take care not to confuse a service application with a business service, for instance, a library service. A business service may be provided by staff who use an online application. A service application never has any direct users.)

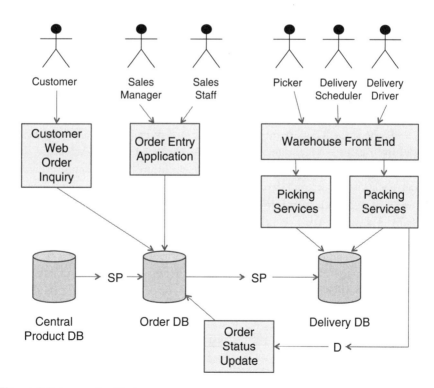

Figure 2.6 *Integration Design*

So what precisely is an application? The notion that an application equals a program is long gone. We implement applications in components and possibly put the components into tiers or replicate them across many servers. Components are units of installation, but since components can be very small, you often want one project or subproject to look after a group of components that work together. I call these *applications*. Here is a definition:

> An application is a collection of compute code files and settings that you release and put into production all at the same time.

There is a big implication here, which is that if application A sends messages to application B, you had better be ready for the likelihood that application A and application B won't be installed into production at exactly the same time. For instance, a new order entry application may need to be able to send orders to an old order fulfillment application as well as to a new order fulfillment application. This *unit of release* property is important even for application development because it implies that the applications can be developed with at least some degree of independence.

A similar argument applies to databases: if you move to a new version of a database, you don't want to be forced to move all the applications to a new release at the same time. Sometimes you are forced to release both the application and the database simultaneously—for instance, if you rename a column—but in general this should be avoided if possible.

The diagram in Figure 2.6 is meant to be illustrative. It is not meant to be the best solution to the business problem. The best solution will depend on circumstances. Historically, some organizations developed giant applications that covered many tasks, and others developed many small applications. When SOA—Service-Oriented Architecture—came along, some organizations developed giant services and three-tier applications consisting of a presentation application (for communicating with the user), a business logic service, and a data service. Some of these SOA projects didn't go well, and many people these days are trying to distance themselves from the term SOA. The latest trend is *microservices* [3]. Microservices differ from traditional SOA services primarily by splitting the functional requirements so they can be implemented by many small services rather than a few enormous ones. The justification—and it is a good one—is that small projects have a better success rate than large ones.

Beware that both SOA and microservices have been defined in many different and contradictory ways. Some people have defined SOA to be services that are implemented by Web services technology like SOAP. The Wikipedia entry [4] says microservices aren't the same as SOA because they implement only a single application rather than being integrated across applications. If that is really the case, microservices are doomed because the reason why integration is important is to support business functionality and not because the developers think it's so much fun. Martin Fowler [3] says microservices are about giving the service developers responsibility for a piece of functionality, which (since there must still be some application handling the user interface) I think means merging the business logic layers with the data-handling layers. This is an excellent idea because most "business logic" is about handling the data (and it is an idea I advocated way back in the 1990s). Eric Knorr [5] says that SOA was management led (boo, hiss) while microservices are developer led (hooray). And then there is the technology—microservices use recent technology, which is more lightweight than the old-fashioned technology used in SOA. The argument about which technology to use is about whether you want the middleware vendor to provide additional functionality like system monitoring and reformatting the data, which can easily be implemented in application code.

Microservices have many good features, but I am frustrated by these hyped-up "savior" technologies/architectures/processes in the IT industry, so while it is unfair to single out microservices, it is the first time in this book I have discussed something that is part good idea, part fad. We in the IT industry have one bandwagon after another; people rush to join, the talent is diluted, people apply rote learning rather than thought, the concept is tarnished, and the idea is thrown on the rubbish heap, often to be resurrected in a slightly different guise by the next bunch of people who want to be proclaimed as the saviors of the IT world. Sir Isaac Newton wrote, "If I have seen further, it is by standing on the shoulders of giants" [6]. If Sir Isaac had worked in the IT industry, he surely would have hacked the giant's legs off.

One reason for faddishness is that the noble gurus in the IT industry do not untangle business needs—in the case of SOA, the need for data accuracy and efficiency—from an IT concept—in the case of SOA, calling a service by a program, usually over a network—or from a specific technology (such as Web services) that implements the concept.

Obscured in all this hype are some simple questions that we struggle to answer. In the case of services, the simple questions have been the same for 30 years at least. They are:

1. Should we use services at all?

2. How big should the services be?

Let's look at each in turn.

There are several reasons for implemention using services, such as

- **To reuse logic and data.** For instance, many banking applications take money out of accounts (and some even put money back in), and it is good to write the code once to manage account credits and debits.

- **For performance reasons.** You may want multiple servers and backup servers for greater performance and greater resiliency.

- **For security.** For instance, you probably don't want your customer-facing Web site to be directly connected to your Order database as I have drawn in Figure 2.6, because you want the network traffic to go through extra layers of firewalls and you want to restrict the kinds of messages that can be sent to the server.

- **To split a large project into several smaller projects.**

There are many applications to which none of these points applies, so the only reason for these applications to use services is to anticipate reuse at a later date. Since writing both a service and a front-end application requires more work than simply writing one application, this is not a great reason.

So how big should services and applications be? There are a number of points. First, look after the user. This means that a user-facing application should support all of the work from one user group (recall that each person belongs to more than one user group), and if two user groups are closely linked (e.g., sales staff and sales managers), it may make sense to have one application handle both. Of course, the underlying processing can be largely handled by services. The second point is to look after data accuracy, by which I mean ensure that you have one authoritative copy of each piece of information. Data can be duplicated, but it is not good for the business to have two conflicting views of one fact. That does not mean one enormous database. You can in theory have one database for each context design data table, though that first requires much more managing and second is inefficient since many transactions update more than one data table. So it would be good for data tables to be grouped so that a single task updates only one of them. However, some data tables are pervasive (like customer tables, order tables, and product tables), so you may choose to put the same data tables in more than one database. This is illustrated in Figure 2.6 where product and order data is duplicated. However, if you are duplicating a data table, you need to duplicate only the information that is needed, which is good for performance and security. Thus only information about actively sold products need be stored in the Order Processing database, and only information pertaining to the delivery of submitted orders need be sent from the Order database to the Delivery database. The third point is that you should split your applications and services so they can be developed with small, responsible teams and have a minimum of dependencies between them (which is hard to know unless you have a context design). Points one, two, and three may push the design in opposite directions. These kinds of compromises and having the creativity to find an effective solution are what design is about.

You can analyze the integration design first by checking that every task is implemented somewhere and has access to all the data it needs. If data is being transferred, you can do a rough calculation to find out how much data is being passed from application to application. If data is copied from one database to another, there is a question of what happens if the data copy is delayed for whatever reason.

The other big reason why integration design is necessary is to integrate with existing applications or with applications developed by a third party. In reality you are unlikely to be implementing everything from scratch, and some of the applications may already exist. It might be that the cost-effective solution is to live with the inadequacies of the existing or third-party applications. Or it might be that the move from current application to future application is staged, which may mean a partial replacement of the old application.

It is possible to reconstruct a context design from existing applications, in which case I call the result a *context model*. If your design calls for changes to an existing application, it is desirable to build a context model of the existing applications. You can then compare the context design with the context model and figure out what the differences are. This is especially useful if there are complex interdependencies between a new application and an existing one.

A context model of existing applications is also a good check on a new design in the same or overlapping area, because it helps you check whether you have covered all of the functionality needed. It also helps you write the business case for the new development.

Technical Design

The next level down from integration design is split into three areas: technical design, user interface design, and database design. In this section I discuss technical design.

Technical design has two broad aims:

1. Design a solution that can meet the nonfunctional requirements.

2. Design a solution that makes the functional programmer's job as easy as possible.

Nonfunctional requirements are requirements that are not about direct support for business work. They cover points like

- The desired throughput and response time
- The availability target

- The disaster recovery requirement

- The security design—you need to know where the security vulnerabilities are, how to fix them, and how and where security monitoring and administration will be done

- Ease of use for systems operations and administration

- Efficient handling of new releases of hardware and software

- The cost target

When people think of nonfunctional requirements, they normally think of only the first two of these—the performance and availability targets. It is true that those two have the most impact on the design, but the rest should not be ignored.

As I write (in 2015), there is a lot of noise about DevOps [7]. The main thrust of DevOps is to make the time between the finish of programming and the release into production much faster, partly by breaking down the barriers between development and operations (e.g., by using the same tools to manage versions) and partly by reducing or eliminating the process steps needed to release software. As microservices followers sneer at SOA, DevOps followers sneer at ITSM (IT Service Management). There is no question that the procedures for installing new versions of software in many IT departments are dysfunctional. But there is also no question that procedures are needed. If you want to see just how bad it can get, I refer you to the great NatWest Bank fiasco in 2012 [8], which was caused by a software upgrade snafu. Processes everywhere in business evolve, and unfortunately they have a tendency to evolve toward greater complexity, greater cost, and slower speed. Also, the people working in the process become comfortable with it and resist change. It's good that DevOps has been used as a club to make people rethink their practices, but unless you have the discipline in place to improve the processes continually, they will again start their slow evolution toward stultification.

But one reason why large, complex applications have long-winded and tortuous change control procedures is that they evolved piecemeal. The technical design is the point where you at least attempt to start with a fresh approach. It needs to address issues such as

- The tools to use by both development and operations for version control

- The operational procedures such as for error reporting, switching to backup, and so on

- The need (or not) for putting additional monitoring code in the application to assist with detecting failures and monitoring performance

Version control and installation procedures cannot be developed without considering the systems test environment. The technical design should also consider how testing should be done.

Many of these operational and systems test issues also play to the second goal of technical design: helping the programmers. But more generally, as illustrated in Figure 2.1, the most important way technical design helps the programmers is by designing and implementing an effective framework. This starts with the selection of the hardware and software technology, but it is more than that. The technical design should lay down guidelines for how the functional code is implemented. It should provide some common services like security authentication and identifying the user's user group. It should show the programmers how to use the middleware if there is some. If the application is being relied on to detect a network time-out when calling a service, the technical design should show how this is done.

For some IT applications the technical design will be trivial. For others, like multitiered business applications, with backup servers for disaster recovery and dark room operations, the technical design will be complex. You will find that one technical design might cover many applications and services, especially if you are using an external or internal cloud.

There is possible feedback from the technical design to the context design, especially because, having done the technical design, you may realize that you can't afford the project. Instead of canceling the project, you may decide to scale back your ambitions, and that too may mean changing the context design. This feedback is so critical that you should take your time and get the designs right.

I strongly believe that the only way of finding out if the technology design is capable is to build it. Whatever the framework, you want to ensure that the framework is up to the job as soon as possible and before too much application functionality has been committed to the design. The way to check whether it is fit for purpose is to test it by putting it under load.

I suggest the sequence for developing code for a complex, highly demanding application that is illustrated in Figure 2.7.

At the start are experimental prototypes. Their purpose is to explore new technology or new ideas. If the technology is well understood, this stage can be skipped. The next stage is to build the framework and the test environment. The framework is then populated by some stub components and tested under load. Other tests like switching to backup and for operational ease of use are useful at this point. When people are happy with the solution, the stub components are removed and, as they become available, the real components put in.

There is little wasted effort in this scheme because the benchmark machine becomes the systems test machine. The driver used to flood the benchmark machine with input messages becomes the systems test driver.

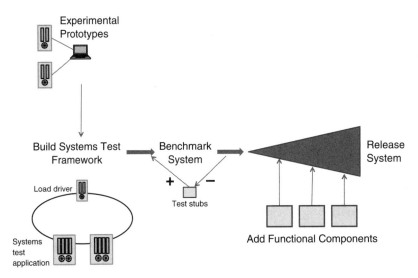

Figure 2.7 *Technical Design Implementations*

Naturally, for a simple application this is overkill; technical designs vary enormously in size and complexity.

User Interface Design

User interface design is about the design of the end user interface for applications and about the programmatic interface for services.

For an online application, the user interface consists of the screens the application will display. During user interface design I don't design the detailed layout of the screens or their look and feel; that can be done later and is best done with the help of a specialist graphic designer. Instead, I design what I call the logical screen design, which defines what data is displayed on the screen, what actions the user can do on each screen, and how the screen flow works—in other words, how the user goes from one screen to another. An example is Figure 2.8, which shows part of an Internet banking application. The boxes represent screens, and the lines show the flow between screens. The dotted box in the top left-hand corner is a menu bar that is included on every screen.

The diagrammatic form of showing the user interface design has the disadvantage that you end up with many diagrams, each showing a different subset of the total interface, because to show it all on one diagram would be to draw a diagram that is far too busy.

I also have a simple textual way to express screen flow that also defines more of the detail: the data displayed, the input data fields, and the effect of clicking buttons and

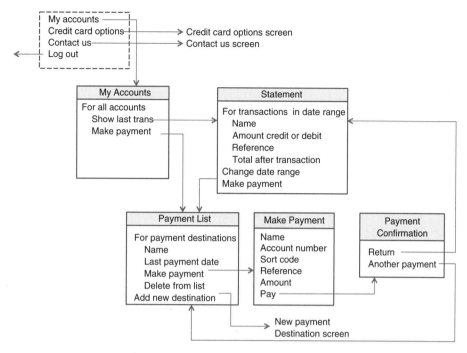

Figure 2.8 *Diagram of a Logical User Interface*

links on the database. The details of what each of these does can usually be copied from the context design. In practice, I find I start with the textual form because it can be edited easily and draw diagrams only when I need to present the information to other people. The nature of the textual forms is discussed in more detail in Chapter 8.

The main reason why the user interface design should be logical is to focus on ease of use. Ease of use is much more than the look of the screens. With a lightweight way of expressing the design, people can concentrate on non-look aspects, and the designer, because he or she hasn't committed large amounts of time to the design, will be much more willing to discuss alternatives.

You can check that the user interface design is complete by making sure that every piece of functionality in the context design has a corresponding part in the user interface design.

There are also various questions to ask to help assess the ease of use. You should also take the stakeholders through the design; you will find that it is not only an excellent check on the user interface, but it also validates the context design.

Services, of course, don't have end users; their users are other programs. The user interface design of a service is the design of the programmable interface to the service. Typical issues you have to face are whether to supply the data to the service in one big message or to supply it in many little messages. The skills and technical expertise needed are completely different from those needed for screen design and are described in more detail in Chapter 7, "The Relationship to Other IT Projects."

Database Design

The database has to be designed independently from the user interface design for three reasons:

- More than one application may use each database, and their differing needs must be reconciled.

- The data may be searched by management or used for marketing research. Those users may need additional data that is not needed by operational requirements. The database design will typically take on board requirements that have not gone into the context design.

- In large companies, the application developers may know that they want some data but don't know where to find it in the organization's many databases.

The database design should be done or at least heavily influenced by the organization's central database team, who should be able to provide knowledge of all the organization's data. (Knowledge of an organization's data resources is needed for business analysis.) Knowing the true nature of data in a database is not easy. One problem is simply finding your way around the organization's business and technology terms and definitions. Another problem is that the meaning of the data is colored by where the data comes from. I remember dealing with a brewery many years ago that wanted to know how many outlets they had. Three different databases produced three different answers; one included hotels and another didn't, one included sports clubs and another didn't, and so on.

These are the three main analysis checks on the database design:

- All data must be created by some application, used by some application, or used for data analysis and deleted or archived by some application.

- If data is duplicated (and in large organizations some data almost certainly is), there should be a mechanism in place to make sure the data is consistent.

- If the data represents something in the outside world (e.g., a customer), there should be mechanisms in place to ensure that it remains accurate.

These are a repeat of some of the analysis checks on the context design, but this time we are closer to the implementation and may have introduced additional data tables.

Implementation

As previously mentioned, the implementation—in other words, the programming—is itself a design exercise. The output is a working application or service.

Since programming is design and designs have loopbacks, there is always a possibility that during programming you will find errors or improvements to the higher-level designs.

The literature is full of descriptions of program design diagrams. I personally don't use any of them while programming except occasionally object diagrams so I can figure out the shape of a complex data structure.

Design diagrams and documents serve three purposes. One is to think about the design. If that is their only purpose, they can be thrown away once the design has been thought about. In fact, they should be thrown away because there is a danger that the design will change and the diagrams will be misleading. Another purpose is for communicating with others. Thus the logical user interface is for communicating the user interface design to programmers. The final purpose is for use in a later project. The context design is useful to keep because other development projects may later need to integrate with the application you are designing. Programmers communicate with the stakeholders by means of the working application, so the only use for diagrams is for thinking about difficult programming problems.

In common with many in the agile programming movement, I find that the best technical documentation for a program is the source code.

As previously noted, it is best to complete all the higher-level designs before embarking on implementation. The actual writing of a design document for a user interface design of 100 screens or writing the schema for a database of 100 tables is not a long exercise. One person can do either of these tasks in a few weeks. It is making the decisions that takes the time—the discussion, the feedback, and the reworking. And of course it is because of the feedback and so on that the implementation shouldn't start until the dust has settled. There is one exception: the technical design flows into the implementation of the systems test environment and common routines and can be started as soon as the nature of the application, its size, and its nonfunctional requirements become clear.

As the implementation is done, the systems test application grows. At any point the systems test application could be shown to stakeholders. I would personally try to do this quite often for two reasons:

1. It gives the stakeholders a warm feeling that the project is progressing.

2. If the stakeholders change their minds, I would rather they do it early.

But let's be realistic here; trying to get the attention of key stakeholders and putting a slot into their diaries can be a challenge.

You want the first release to make a good impression but to have a sufficiently small number of features that it can be delivered fast. Once the first release is done, it might be criticized by the users who are not formally stakeholders. It is a good idea to react to such feedback. It makes the stakeholders feel they are being listened to and helps the application be accepted well in the business, which ultimately is the aim.

Is It Really Engineering?

The six-box model for design is not really the same as a classic engineering component breakdown. So can it really support engineered design as I described it in Chapter 1? Well, yes and no.

In civil engineering and mechanical engineering, the high-level design and the component design are mostly drawn the same way—you define shapes and surfaces, and all the components have dimensions and weights. Furthermore, there is no limit to the number of levels of design from top to bottom; in other words, you can have components split into subcomponents, which are split into additional subcomponents any number of times. IT software development designs aren't like that. Instead, each design—context design, user interface design, database design, technical design, and implementation design—is represented in a different way, and there are only three levels of design: context, detailed, and implementation. (Strictly speaking, it is even a DAG—a directed acyclic graph—not a hierarchy, but since the implementation is much bigger in time and effort and is usually split into many components, it feels like a hierarchy, so I call it a hierarchy.)

The question is, Can the idea of a hierarchy of designs taken from civil and mechanical engineering apply to something so different?

I visualize the breakdown of context design into user interface, database, and technical designs as horizontal slices, as illustrated in Figure 2.9.

There is not much overlap between the user interface design and the database design—though they have to be designed with close cooperation—but the technical design overlaps everything. One might expect a traditional component breakdown to be possible by expanding each task into screens, logic, and databases, but not only do the tasks share data, they also sometimes share screens. What is happening with the three detail designs is that the context design is being split into three different views, each of which informs three different aspects of the implementation. In our example the user interface design devises a set of screens and screen flows that enable warehouse pickers and packers to do their tasks; the database design creates the database to provide data storage for the tasks; and the implementation design identifies the technology and defines how the technology

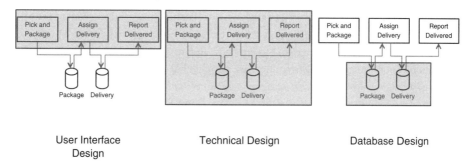

User Interface Design   Technical Design   Database Design

Figure 2.9 *Horizontal Slicing*

will be used to service the code that drives the screens and accesses the databases. So—is it engineering?

I suggest that there are three tests that together are enough to ascertain whether a hierarchical series of designs can support engineering design. The first test is whether the design is *complete*. Completeness means that what is specified in the top-level design is what you get in the implementation; in other words, you don't lose information as you go down the design hierarchy. In a normal engineered design completeness is obvious. At every point in the high-level design you see something either that you can build directly (like a piece of shaped metal) or that is a component that has its own design. In our six-box model it is not so obvious. To prove completeness we have to do a series of checks, first that every task is implemented in the user interface design and that every part of the user interface design is programmed. We must also check that all data tables in the context design are implemented in the database schema and that controls exist in the code to ensure that members of user groups can do only what they are allowed to do. The important point is that we can check for completeness.

The second test is *consistency*. We have to check that the three detailed designs are consistent with each other; put informally, we have to be sure they fit together. For instance, if an action in the user interface needs to access a data object, it must have at hand all the data to find the data object in the database. Consistency between designs is also an issue for classic engineering. For instance, when designing a car, you must ensure that the gear box is compatible with the engine.

While completeness gives you confidence that you have finished the implementation, completeness and consistency give you the confidence that any assertion made about the context design will remain true for the implementation.

I think of testing for completeness as looking downward from the top of the design hierarchy into the lower-level designs, and testing for consistency as looking across the design hierarchy. Sometimes we want to look upward from the lower levels of the design hierarchy. This is the third property of engineered design: *traceability*. Traceability is about knowing the correspondence between elements in the low-level design and elements in the higher-level designs. With traceability we can answer questions like, "If this line of code breaks, what is the impact?" Looking back at Figure 2.2, we see that code is primarily there either to support functional requirements or to support nonfunctional requirements (the framework code). That said, all code must take some responsibility for some nonfunctional requirements such as performance and quality. We can trace functional code to actions in the user interface, and we can trace the user interface actions back to the task description. The framework code is more difficult to trace. Some of it can be traced back to supporting a systems management function; other code is simply there to enable the functional code. Looking at the traceability back up to design requirements is a useful exercise when doing code reviews.

In the preface I made a comment about how engineering designs and maps can show more or less detail depending on whether you are taking a high-resolution view or a low-resolution view. When using, say, online maps, high resolution shows more detail than low resolution; hence things are visible in the high-resolution map that are not visible in the low-resolution map. Thus mapping does not have the property of completeness because new things pop into view as you look in more detail. Furthermore, an object in the high-resolution map may not be in the low-resolution map, hence there is no property of traceability.

Of course, a design can be complete, consistent, and traceable and still have errors in it.

Let's ask a simple and, on the face of it, stupid question: "What is a program error?" An error is any behavior of a program that deviates from the specification. Some specifications are probably not written down anywhere, such as the requirement that the program must not stop unexpectedly. In general, though, you cannot define an error unless you have a specification to compare it against, and in the six-box model the specification is the context design. This is where completeness and traceability become important. Completeness means you can check that all of the specification is implemented. Traceability means that all code can be linked back to a statement in the specification. One way of looking at it is that completeness is ensuring that we don't lose information as we go down the hierarchy of designs, while traceability means that we don't lose information as we go up the hierarchy of designs.

In most projects today there is no formal specification, so how do programmers in these projects know when they have errors? The answer is that they develop tests; in other words, the tests themselves have become the specification. I have two objections:

- It is hard to figure out if the tests are a true reflection of what the stakeholders want.

- It encourages the programmer to cut corners by ignoring subtleties in the requirements that are hard to spot (like dependencies between tasks).

Please don't conclude from this that I don't believe in testing. Actually, developing tests can be far more rigorous when the test developers have a user interface design and a context design to guide them. I just don't think tests are a good alternative to a context design.

In the previous chapter I said that application development should be an engineering discipline. Is there then no role for formal methods, which can be characterized as a mathematical rather than an engineering approach? Formal methods typically require reformulating the requirements in terms of mathematical set theory. For each state the system can be in, you identify the facts that must be true within that state. You then must identify all the possible transitions between the states and the rules that govern the transitions. The problem with formal methods is that they are not very user friendly; your average stakeholder who needs to review the specification is going to be baffled rather than enlightened. They have been applied well in technical areas—such as defining a specification for a cache controller chip—but haven't been used successfully as far as I know in general business applications. I have a suspicion that formal methods are due for a revival; see the articles on Amazon's use of TLA+ ([9] and [10]), which used formal methods to analyze tricky problems such as what happens when there is a failure within recovery code. But this is a long way out of sight from a typical business reviewer. It may be possible to make task descriptions more "formal," though it will be a challenge to make them formal and keep them readable (though I know some people think it is possible [11]). I will leave this as a research topic.

Concluding Remarks

I have presented an outline of design for IT applications with an emphasis on business applications. This chapter lays the groundwork for the rest of the book by explaining in outline what is done in each design and how information flows between the designs. The output from the context design step is, of course, the context design. The output from the user interface design is the logical user interface and the service interface description. The output from the database design is the database schema, and the output from the technical design is briefing for the programmers and stakeholders and a working systems test application ready to receive the code the implementation programmers write. Of these design artifacts only the context design and user interface design don't become part of the application itself.

I have also described in outline some of the analysis techniques for each design.

This schema of design—the six-box model as I call it—is different from a traditional engineering set of designs. I have laid out arguments for why we can still achieve engineering-quality design, the essential point being that the six-box model can still be complete, consistent, and support traceability. Is it worth doing? I believe so, if only for the promise of fewer late design changes and better ability to handle change when it happens.

The next chapter looks at other design approaches and contrasts them with context-driven design. It also looks at all the parts of design and implementation I haven't mentioned and where I believe there is a best practice that should be followed.

Chapter 3

Reusing Existing Methods and Practices

In the preface I mentioned that there has been a conflict between BDUF (big design up front) on the one hand and agile design on the other. Is context-driven design really a variant of BDUF design? Or is it agile with a bit of icing on the top? One purpose of this chapter is to position context-driven design in relation to other existing methods. I am not going to describe agile and BDUF methods in detail—that would require another few books—but will instead discuss the concepts that drive these methods. The other purpose is to explain what you can retain from existing methods in context-driven design, which, fortunately for you and for me, is a lot.

I am conscious that many of my readers have been successful IT application developers and are likely to have strong opinions about what works and what does not. While it would be nice to convert you to context-driven design, my secondary objective is to provoke you to think about what you are doing, and about why some practices work and other practices do not.

This chapter is organized by topic:

- Agile

- Upside-down design

- Use cases

- The problem with estimating cost

- Why is BDUF big?

- Iterations

- Quality

- Testing and Inspection

Finally, I will discuss the point of using existing practices within context-driven design and the notion of a *learning organization*.

Agile

The agile movement was triggered by some like-minded experts who met together and wrote a manifesto. You can see the result of their work at "The Manifesto for Agile Software Development" [12]. They say they value

- Individuals and interactions over processes and tools
- Working software over comprehensive documentation
- Customer collaboration over contract negotiation
- Responding to change over following a plan

Besides the values there are 12 principles:

1. Our highest priority is to satisfy the customer through early and continuous delivery of valuable software.

2. Welcome changing requirements, even late in development. Agile processes harness change for the customer's competitive advantage.

3. Deliver working software frequently, from a couple of weeks to a couple of months, with a preference to the shorter timescale.

4. Business people and developers must work together daily throughout the project.

5. Build projects around motivated individuals. Give them the environment and support they need, and trust them to get the job done.

6. The most efficient and effective method of conveying information to and within a development team is face-to-face conversation.

7. Working software is the primary measure of progress.

8. Agile processes promote sustainable development. The sponsors, developers, and users should be able to maintain a constant pace indefinitely.

9. Continuous attention to technical excellence and good design enhances agility.

10. Simplicity—the art of maximizing the amount of work not done—is essential.

11. The best architectures, requirements, and designs emerge from self-organizing teams.

12. At regular intervals, the team reflects on how to become more effective, then tunes and adjusts its behavior accordingly.

It is easy to pick holes, starting with "What the heck is a *principle,* and what does *value* mean?" For instance, I enjoy interacting with individuals more than I enjoy filling in forms. Does that mean I am in agreement with the first value? But instead of losing ourselves in semantic nitpicking, it's worth trying to get behind these statements to try to understand what the authors were really concerned about and how context-driven design responds to the same concerns.

Individuals and Interactions over Processes and Tools

Actually I think all that they are saying here is "Get rid of unnecessary bureaucracy"— and I can't imagine anyone who would disagree. But you have to ask yourself why application development has so often become overburdened with bureaucracy. I suggest it all starts with management fear.

Management has several fears:

- That something will be forgotten, for instance, a requirement will be missed

- That the designers and programmers aren't competent

- That the project will slip without them knowing

They try to overcome their fears by

- Developing checklists and processes to ensure that every item in the list has either been handled or is shown to be unnecessary

- Developing progress reporting processes

I think the agile answer to this is twofold. First, the agile developer will show results early and often. This is the idea behind principles 1, 2, and 3. The second is: Trust us. This is why principles 5, 9, and 11 are important.

My answer to overcoming the fear of omission is that the analysis of designs is, in part, about ensuring that nothing is forgotten. Moreover, when the context and user interface designs are done, the stakeholders should have a reasonable idea of what is being proposed in its entirety. This is in contrast to an agile project, which is like setting off on an adventure with no clear idea of whether you will reach the end or indeed where the end is.

I am told that the previous paragraph will make people leap out of their seats shouting, "Waterfall design—told you so!" The main issue I have with waterfall design is not that the design is done up front; it is that the design is not being done properly—the team is gathering requirements, not designing requirements. Furthermore, because they are not documenting the dependencies, they are not in a position to manage change. Traditional waterfall design also did not have iterations, and I see no problem with iterations so long as you have a concept of the whole before you start iterating. This is discussed further in the "Iterations" section later in this chapter.

Back to management fear. It is true that managers feel more confident in the implementation team when they see the delivered product. But it is much easier to assess the implemented solution when there is a context design and a user interface design to compare it against. Software development often seems to suffer from a malicious form of the 80:20 syndrome; when it seems that 80% of the application is implemented, it is in fact only 20% complete. This is partly because so much of the complexity often lies in handling the error and exception cases as we noted earlier. With context-driven design you are in a better position to understand where you truly are in a project. With agile development the stakeholders see the 20% and leap to the conclusion that the application is almost finished. Then developers and stakeholders start to understand the problem better and the list of requirements grows, sometimes faster than they are being implemented. Trust is strained when this happens.

But note that trust is still important. The organization relies on the professionalism of the project delivery team, and I don't think there is any way around this.

In conclusion, management fears are justified and the agile movement is correct in saying that bureaucracy is not the answer. But frequent software deliveries are at best only part of the answer.

Working Software over Comprehensive Documentation

Documentation has several uses:

- To tell the end user how the software works
- To communicate between teams in the development project
- To communicate with stakeholders
- To help a designer think through a problem

Is working software a substitute for any or all of these?

There are many people who never read software documentation, preferring instead to learn by trying out the software itself. This surely is because much software documentation is so bad. Much of it concentrates on telling you the obvious, treating you like a dimwitted automaton; little of it tells you what problems the software is trying to solve, how the software works, or what principles it follows (such as "All popular commands can be found by right-clicking over an item on the screen"). Even software documentation from well-established vendors often seems to take the lazy option; for instance, why are there so few diagrams? But complicated software needs explanation; no one in their right mind would try to learn a programming language by randomly pressing keyboard keys.

But again I suspect that the Agile Manifesto authors are arguing about something rather different. Their gripe is that they don't like voluminous program design documents, not end user documentation.

In the past, there have been numerous techniques for describing program logic before writing code. Examples are flow charts, hierarchical input-process-output (HIPO) diagrams, hierarchical structure charts, class diagrams, object diagrams, and state transition diagrams. I don't use them either except occasionally. There are several reasons. One reason is scale. Think of an architectural drawing of a house. You want to see a side of the house on one piece of paper that corresponds to a scale of 1:50 to 1:100. An architect's drawing of a bigger structure might use a scale of 1:1,000. All the programming diagrams tend to show one aspect of the program at a level of detail not far from the code (a 1:4 or 1:10 scale if you will), and few of them provide any opportunity for scaling up or down. The program documentation therefore tends to be very large, and it can be difficult to find your way around it. The diagrams themselves usually concentrate on one aspect of the program, like the process logic, the data structure, or timing, but they don't represent a complete design. Many of the flaws in a program design lie in the interaction of the different views. Like many programmers, I mostly don't find them useful—it is better to go straight to code.

The only times I think any detailed programming design documentation is needed are

- When the technical design team needs to explain their design to the implementers (though note that the most valuable part of such an explanation is often some example code).

- When you are designing a particularly complicated piece of programming and you want to visualize aspects of the implementation before rushing to code. The important point here is that the diagrams should be thrown away.

In my experience, which I am not sure is typical, the diagrams are out-of-date as soon as I start writing code because when I write code, I find flaws with the paper design, and I find that the best way on paper is frequently not the best way in code.

Context-driven design is not documentation free. The main documents over and above working code and a database schema are

- The context design document
- The integration design diagram
- The user interface document
- Internal presentations, such as the presentation to be given during reviews or to instruct the implementation programmers
- Project management plans

I don't believe this is excessive. It is several orders of magnitude smaller than the program source code.

Customer Collaboration over Contract Negotiations

In a sense, of course, customer collaboration is more important than contract negotiations because there have been plenty of projects that have been run without a formal contract—for instance, most projects implemented by in-house IT developers.

But when it comes to contract negotiations, you either have to do it or you don't; there is no possibility of replacement here, no either/or.

Also, there are projects that cannot have customer collaboration, at least not until near the end. This is true of almost all projects that are being developed to sell—you have to guess how your potential customers are going to react to your product. Instead of actual customer collaboration you have proxies, like a marketing manager whose job is to do the guessing for you.

But agile developers are asking for more, as principle 4 and, to some extent, principle 6 imply. They are asking for very close collaboration. The logic goes thus: agile developers don't think documented requirements specifications work; therefore they think you can't write a meaningful contract and therefore you must rely on stakeholders telling you what they need as you go along. I don't think that is true, as will be discussed later in the section on pricing.

One reason for contracts is that business management must have a cost estimate. The lack of accurate costing is one of the worst problems of IT application development and needs to be fixed.

Responding to Change over Following a Plan

The implication of this value statement is that in nonagile projects the plan somehow gets in the way of responding to change. I think this is unfair; nonagile projects may be reluctant to change the plan, and they may charge more for changing the plan, but they still change the plan.

I have already mentioned the military's love of planning in spite of the chaos of war, and that the underlying reason is that they respond to events not by throwing the plan out of the window but by changing the plan.

The chief advertised advantage of agile approaches such as Scrum [13] and Extreme Programming [14] is that they can cope with late-changing requirements, or requirements churn as some call it. Naturally, I believe that one of the big positives of context-driven design should be that there are far fewer late-changing requirements. This is not only because of the rigor of the design process; it is also because the programming implementation phase is shorter because programmers have clear instructions for what to do.

However, late-changing requirements do happen, so how does context-driven design handle them? Rather easily, actually. The first action when handling a change of requirements is that you have to figure out whether the change is cosmetic or fundamental. A requirements change will mostly require a change to the user interface, so a good starting point is often the user interface design. Here you will find out what screens to change and hence what code needs to be redone. If the change is more fundamental, you will have to go back to the context design. Whatever you do, you can change the design or designs and quickly identify the code that needs to change. But the huge advantage of managing change in context-driven design over other approaches is that you can look at the dependencies between tasks, which allows you to figure out the consequences of change in one place on the other tasks. You can say to the user, "If you change X, that affects Y and Z." Not only that, you can illustrate your point by showing the user the designs. In short, you can have an intelligent, business-led discussion about the change. What happens in agile development? Programmer A changes some code and programmers B and C have no idea that what they coded four weeks ago has a dependency with programmer A's code. This is why agile projects work best when they are small enough that at least one person has a working knowledge of what everybody else has done and is doing. In other words, that person must have a mental picture of the total design. On a project with, say, 100 programmers, that is too much to ask.

I am not alone in thinking this. Alistair Cockburn, who is one of the use case gurus and a participant in the original meeting that drew up the Agile Manifesto, thinks that there is value in supplementing an agile methodology like Scrum with use cases [15], and I see no reason to disbelieve him.

Conclusion

Let me summarize what I think about agile. Agile has two revolutionary ideas:

- Trust in the programmer
- Just-in-time design

I am strongly in favor of the former and strongly against the latter.

Upside-Down Design

While I dislike agile approaches in general, are they good in part? Are there exceptions where an agile approach works?

A possible example of an exception is an application I wrote for doing business reviews. There was a need for reports, and while some of the reports could be easily specified from the user's requirements, some could not. In particular, part of the application was the ability to record constraints—external factors that were preventing people from achieving their goals. The main stakeholder wanted some way of analyzing all the text in the constraint descriptions to identify common themes; he told me he knew a friend of a friend who was an expert in artificial intelligence and this was right up his street. While I have nothing against AI (though I had an ulterior motive, which was not throwing a lot of money away on an open-ended research project), I thought that before we looked to AI we should attempt some simple analysis such as listing the common words and common word combinations. So I wrote some code along these lines. It needed tweaking, so I tweaked it. I showed it to the stakeholder and tweaked it some more. As it turned out, the application is in limbo at the moment, but if it ever bursts back into life again, we will let the users run with it and see if it satisfies their needs. If it does not, we might revert to a more AI-like approach after all.

I call this upside-down design because the order is reversed—from programming to requirements rather than requirements to programming. You can, in my experience at least, easily identify areas where upside-down design works; essentially they are the areas where the requirements are vague and there is an element of being a research project about them. They are particularly common, again in my experience, where information is being presented in some way to the end users and they don't know what they want until they have seen it. In a larger project where some of the design is upside down but most isn't, the upside-down part must be tightly constrained—its boundaries must be strict. You must ensure that the upside-down bit doesn't leak out into the rest of the code; in other words, the programmer does not have the authority to change what he or she likes.

I have the following suggestions about writing upside-down code:

- Do the easy part first. If you do the easy part, often the difficult part is seen to be unnecessary. It is also encouraging for the stakeholders because they see progress.

- Be ready to throw away code. Refactor often and sometimes redesign. In the previous example about reports, a big question that needed several attempts to answer was the design of the screens for setting the report parameters. It sounds easy, but the basic question was how much should be canned and how much driven by setting fields like the date range.

- Have frequent (e.g., once every two weeks) reviews. You must avoid someone disappearing into a dark corner and working unmolested for months and finally producing something nobody wants.

- Try to show the stakeholders some design options.

The last suggestion is an attempt to counteract one of the problems with upside-down designs: the programmer tends to assume authority over the design and won't listen to the stakeholders.

Having said all this, does upside-down development really exist? Let us look at this example again. Essentially you must still define what you want the reports to do and what the report output looks like. Second, you must design the user interface, the database design, and the technical design before writing code. In other words, you have done the design in the normal way but you know even before starting to design that there is a good chance that the stakeholder won't like the result. Put another way, it is not upside down; it is repeat again. This can, of course, be true of any aspect of the application.

Early on in a design, it is common that there are parts of the design where we are sure that the stakeholders want precisely what we have designed and parts of the design where we think the stakeholders are uncertain about what they want. In the latter case, we anticipate that we will have to reiterate through the design from context design through user interface design to implementation. Put another way, on all parts of the context design and the user interface design we can put an "uncertainty score." An uncertainty score is a measure of the likelihood of a redesign. A high uncertainty score against an element in the context design is normally more serious than a high uncertainty score put against an element in the user interface design. For instance, in the example at the head of the section I could mark an uncertainty of 0 that users want a report to analyze the text, but then mark my initial design with an uncertainty of 7 out of 10, indicating that there is a 70% chance it will change somewhat when the users look at it. At least we know then where we stand.

Sometimes the uncertainty is not related to the stakeholders not knowing what they want, but to the user interface design not having enough detail. As I have described user interface design so far, I haven't mentioned the possibility that the output might be diagrams or maps. In these circumstances, you will need to supplement the user interface design with some drawings or other collateral. But even in these cases—cases where you expect a few iterations to get it right—it is always worth trying to scope the entire problem first and understand what is being requested. Knowing why some fancy feature is important helps greatly toward pointing the solution in the right direction.

The simple act of asking a stakeholder the uncertainty score will often make the stakeholder think more deeply about the requirement and, hence, reduce the uncertainty score. Sometimes the solution is to implement the feature as specified but put in code to monitor what the users actually do with the feature. In general, I think applications could be a lot better at analyzing themselves by recording what features are being used and what features are not being used and by providing facilities for users to give their feedback, perhaps on a screen-by-screen basis.

Another way to reduce uncertainty is to present the stakeholders with alternative designs. This provokes discussion, helps eliminate misunderstanding, and, again, helps everyone think that little bit deeper.

If the uncertainty score is high, there are various actions you can take. You can put that feature into a later release so that other important features are not delayed because of it. Another technique is to show the implemented feature before it is finished and ask the stakeholders, "Are we going in the right direction?"

In general, sometimes uncertainty is unavoidable, but the context design and the detailed designs help you manage change.

Use Cases

In the preceding sections I have focused my criticism on agile development. Today the alternative to agile development is almost always to write use cases as a means to capture the requirements. In this section I want to discuss the differences between use cases and context design.

Essentially a use case is a simple textual way of describing a scenario using a sequence of numbered steps, and as such use cases can be and have been applied at all sorts of levels of detail. There are also use case diagrams that show which actors

(actors are more or less the use case equivalent of user groups) use which use cases and which use case extends another use case. I will discuss "extends" later. Thus a use case diagram often looks a lot like my context diagrams but without showing the data tables. Furthermore, in Chapter 6, "The Relationship with the Users," I show a textual description of tasks that is a lot like a use case description. The main differences are, first, I have a section on the data access needed by the task, and second, I split the description of what to do into a narrative and a rules section in contrast to use cases, which have only a narrative. In short, there are large areas of commonality between use cases and task descriptions, and if you think about it, it would be surprising if there weren't.

I have serious problems with use cases, namely:

- There is no formal concept of atomicity.
- There is a confusion of design levels.
- They are confusing, even for the people who use them.
- A large application described in use cases is hard to understand.
- They do not support analysis well and hence do not support engineered design well.

I will discuss each of these in turn.

Atomicity

Use cases can be used to describe tasks, in other words what one person is doing at one time, but they don't have to. You can elide the description of a couple of related tasks into one use case. For instance, you will often come across applications in which you have filled in a long form (e.g., a tax form) and you have the option of saving your updates and resuming later, eventually submitting the form for further processing. A use case description may have filling in the form as one use case, but I insist that there are two kinds of tasks here:

1. A task to start and possibly finish filling in the form
2. A task to resume and possibly finish filling in the form

Of course, most of the logic of these two tasks is the same, and I would document this by having both tasks include a common task fragment rather than writing the same text in both of them. It is hard for me to say if eliding two tasks like this in a use case is the recommended approach because the literature on use cases does not, to my knowledge, discuss the concept of atomicity and therefore lacks the vocabulary to discuss this issue.

So why is it important to define two tasks and not one use case? Because you must "design the gaps." Even in this very simple example you must ensure that

- The user must be able to see that there are forms waiting to be finished.

- There is always the possibility that a form is never finished. Thus the designer must decide whether to leave the unfinished form hanging around forever or to delete it and, if so, how old a form must be before it is deleted.

And there are also questions to answer:

- Must the same person who started the form always finish it? If so, how is that enforced? If not, how does the other user see the unfinished form?

- If the application fails or the user goes away during a form-filling exercise, is the partially completed form saved by default?

- Should the user be forced to complete one form before starting another?

If you elide the tasks into one use case, you can (you don't have to, but you can) brush these questions under the carpet where they will reappear later, probably when the implementation is well under way.

Confusion of Design Layers

Another example raises a more complex issue. Suppose the actor is a delivery driver and the use case is about picking up a parcel, delivering it, and having the customer sign for it as received. Again I would define two tasks—one to assign the parcel to the delivery run and the other for the customer's signature—whereas a use case might elide them into one. Let us consider the case of the delivery driver having a crash. Clearly at the very least the parcel will have to be assigned to another delivery or, if you are less lucky, written off. But which task is going to record the crash? There may be one task recording that the truck is out of service. There may be another task to retrieve the parcel and decide what to do with it. This is all becoming rather complicated. Furthermore, there may be one business process defined that shows how parcels are delivered and another business process that is all about managing the fleet of trucks. At the time of the crash, these two processes interact. In theory you can put all of this into one use case, though I don't advise this since the use case will be very complex (but people tell me that use cases often run to many pages, so I suspect it happens in practice). But because there are two processes involved, this scenario may be documented by two use cases—along the lines of the two business processes—which interact in subtle ways. To analyze the interaction between long, complex use cases is very difficult. In fact, to do the analysis the first step must be to split the use cases into units where one person does one thing at one time. In other words, the first step in understanding a complex scenario is to identify the tasks.

In this example, the confusion of levels is about the confusion between the process level and the task level since in both these examples bits of process description have been used to join two or more tasks.

However, use cases in practice not only merge the process and task levels, they also merge the task level and the logical user interface design.

To be fair, experts on use cases clearly state that they don't specify the user interface, and I think they mean by this not only the actual physical layout of the screens but also the logical user interface. I strongly suspect this command is honored more in the breach than in the observance. The designer is being encouraged to think in terms of scenarios, which surely means imagining the user sitting in front of a workstation. Moreover, the examples (from the same experts) often tell a different story. For instance, in a couple of places I have seen logging in included in the steps. In context-driven development, logging on isn't even part of user interface design, let alone context design; it is instead part of technical design.

The reason for having a clear distinction between task design and user interface design is that it is always a good idea in design to be clear in your mind what you want to achieve as opposed to how you want to achieve it. If you skip the "what you want to achieve" step, it is easy to omit something important. If you omit the "how you want to achieve it" step, you will often overlook better designs. Specifically, if you omit the user interface design and go straight from use case to programming, you miss out on several opportunities for better design:

- Seeing the user interface design as a whole helps make the application easier to use. The user interface design can be a significant transformation of the task design as discussed in Chapter 8, "User Interface Design and Ease of Use."

- Reviewing the user interface design is a check on the context design.

- Having a user interface design speeds up programming. Not only will the programmers spend less time doing the user interface design in their heads (without all the information) and redoing it when their first attempt is wrong, but also project managers will find it easier to pick the difficult problems to be coded by the better programmers.

- There is additional information in the user interface design—the detailed data fields—that is not in the context design, which means the context design is more compact. In the use case equivalent, these fields must be documented in the use case, which makes them long and wordy.

It is important to be clear about what level you are working at and allow no leakage between the levels. Each level has its own integrity constraints and its own recovery techniques. At the database transaction level recovery is handled by the database system. At the task level it is handled in various ways to make it look like it has transaction-like atomicity.

Use Cases Are Confusing

There is a subindustry in explaining use cases. There are numerous books, numerous experts, and several different styles of use cases. I suspect that at least in the early days of use case writing, experts found that use cases were badly written and felt the need to prescribe rules and guidelines. Since use cases are in essence so simple—they are basically a numbered list of actions—it comes as a surprise that so much expertise on display is necessary.

There are areas that obviously puzzle many people. A particular case of this is the application of use cases to the strategic level—so-called strategic use cases. Here is a quote from a comment on a Web site [16]: "I don't think I quite understand the subtleties between System Scope and Strategic Scope, and I've been writing Use Cases for years!!" Personally I am hard pressed to think of anything strategic that can be defined in terms of a sequence of steps; the use case form of expression is aimed at the "how," while strategic ideas are aimed at the "what." So personally, I would discourage using use cases for defining anything strategic.

Another feature of use cases that is an area of misunderstanding is the ability to say one use case "extends" or "includes" another. They are both about capturing common logic and documenting it once. "Includes" is about use cases picking up a use case fragment, which makes sense when two or more use cases have some steps in common. "Extends" is about one use case being like another use case but different in some way. "Includes" is more restrictive because you can only include the entire fragment, while when you extend a use case you can indicate changes in several places. On the other hand, you are meant to extend only a full use case, not a fragment. You must be really careful using either "includes" or "extends" in real life. It is easy to extend a use case without considering all the consequences, perhaps because you are in a bit of a rush.

(This situation is not helped by examples in the literature. For instance, if I look up "use case" on Wikipedia—this is in January 2015 and it may have changed by now—I find a diagram where "eat food" extends "drink wine." I just find this unhelpful and bizarre.)

But the main reason why use cases are confusing has to do with the mixing up of levels of design described in the previous section.

The following statement will annoy many: I think that one of the underlying problems with use cases is that they lack a good theory. This means it is difficult to be precise about what you must or must not do, and there is little notion of correctness.

Large Use Case Documents Are Hard to Understand

Documenting a large application with use cases makes for a very dull document. Going through the exercise of developing and documenting, say, 100 to 1,000 use cases no doubt gives the authors of the use cases a good understanding of the application. But the second job of the requirements document is to explain the proposed application to the stakeholders in the hope that they will verify the design and give good feedback. Large, boring documents are not a good way to do this.

Use Cases Do Not Assist Engineered Design

The fundamental reason why use cases are poor at supporting engineered design is that they are hard to analyze.

Let us step back a moment and ask what is needed for a design to be easily analyzable:

- It must be compartmentalized into chunks that aren't too complex. This is not only about splitting a design into functional areas; it is also about why we need a hierarchy of designs. Use cases are all at one level.

- All dependencies must be documented. Having split the design into components, we must be completely sure that we have documented all the relationships between the components. Many of the dependencies between tasks are in their shared data. Use cases don't document this explicitly. You have to figure it out from reading the text.

- The notion of atomicity is fundamental. Components are black boxes, if you will, for which you know only what they do, not how they do it. In any design you have to assume that the components have a fixed and prescribed number of outcomes. You can analyze only what you can see. If a component has a hidden outcome, all the analysis in the world won't reveal it.

- It must be easy to link solution to requirement, in other words, to answer the question, "How is requirement X implemented?" At the top level you need the basic business requirements. I think it is very hard to check whether 100 to 1,000 use cases support the business requirement, even assuming that the underlying business requirement is actually written down anywhere.

• It is easier to analyze rules rather than steps or loose descriptions. You can apply mathematics to rules. Even without a mathematical analysis, it is normally straightforward to see if rules contradict each other. One problem with analyzing steps is that you are always faced with the question, "Is the order of the steps important or arbitrary?"

Put simply, use cases were designed to help gather requirements; they were not designed to support the analysis of requirements.

Conclusion

In a nutshell, use cases make business design difficult.

In the course of writing this book, people have told me that they enjoy writing use cases and use cases are good. I have a theory that the people writing use cases think they are good since having to think about scenarios is undoubtedly a good way of starting to understand what an application needs to do. But the people who have to read use cases thoroughly dislike them.

There is a further problem with the use case approach that is rather subtle: it is not a good basis for estimating project cost. This I discuss in the next section.

The Problem with Estimating Cost

One of the major problems with IT projects, especially large IT projects, is that the projects overrun their planned duration and exceed their planned cost, often by huge factors. It is probably this that exasperates business managers about IT application development more than anything else. Put bluntly, to make an important business decision you need to know how much the options cost.

Today's best practice for estimating the effort required to do a project is to use function points. The basic idea of function points is to take a unit of work, count the number of inputs and outputs to users and to external data sources (in other words, the number of database tables read and updated or the number of other files read or written), and multiply that by a factor that is an educated guess based on the complexity of the unit. There is data available [17, 18] that gives you estimates of historically how long projects have taken to implement. However, organizations should have their own records and be able to verify whether the averages seen in other projects apply to them or not.

Let us assume you are setting out on a project with some guess at the cost and time to deliver. In my experience, the project at this point looks relatively easy. As you work on the context design, you realize the business complexities of what you want to do and the estimates grow. Projects always seem to get more complex, not easier, maybe because so much of the complexity lies in handling errors and occasional events that aren't obvious until you have thought about the application in depth. I see no difficulty in estimating the number of function points from a context design rather than any other kind of design. Furthermore, if the context design has been analyzed for consistency and completeness, there is more hope that all complexities have been identified than there is with other design methods. Thus, one would expect that the effort required to implement a project is at a first approximation proportional to the size of the context design.

That said, you may be able to make an even better estimate when the user interface design and the database design are done. However, one would not expect the estimate to be different from the context design estimate by more than a few percentage points each way.

But if you look at a paper called "Software Estimating Rules of Thumb" [19], you will see a table of total lines of code in an application versus the average time taken to develop one line of code. In large projects the effort needed to code one line of code is much higher than—at least twice—that of small projects. What is going on?

One answer is that large projects tend to have more demanding technical requirements that impinge on the technical complexity of the solution. Imagine you are developing a Web application. At one end of the scale you could be implementing a cheap and cheerful Web application using a product like PHP or Ruby, and at the other end of the scale you could be implementing a multitier Java application with routines for security monitoring, detecting failures, and switching to backup. In these complex systems not only is the task implementation more difficult—and therefore longer—but there is also a big initial fixed cost to develop the environment, set up the systems test system, set up the product system, and do performance and availability testing.

Put another way, the complexities in the technical design don't add to your estimate; they multiply your estimate by some factor. In general, therefore, during design you should expect the estimates to increase until both the context design and the technical design are finished, and thereafter it should be relatively stable. The need for having both context and technical designs done before having an accurate estimate is illustrated in Figure 3.1.

Is technical complexity the only reason why the cost per function point is greater the more function points you are implementing? One possible reason might be that the functionalities are more intertwined and thus there are more relationships between the different elements of the design. This should not be true in

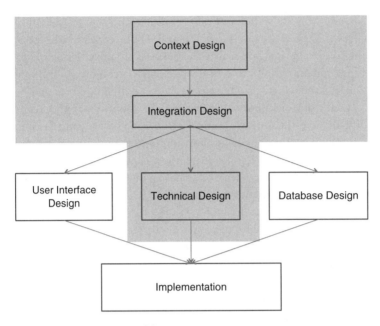

Figure 3.1 *The Minimum Required for an Accurate Price*

context-driven design because the relationships between the elements should have been understood and designed in the context design. Another possible explanation is that the number of late changes to the design is proportional to the number of months taken to implement the solution. There are some statistics to back this up (Capers Jones reckons that on average software requirements increase by 1% to 2% every month [19]). While context design does not stop business managers from changing their minds, it should at least reduce the incidence of late realization of design flaws. Taking all these considerations together, it should be possible to make the cost per function point much less dependent on the number of function points. The ideal, of course, would be no dependency at all.

It isn't only IT projects where estimates change over time. In large engineering projects, like the London Olympics and the London to Channel Tunnel railway line, the preliminary estimates were wildly wrong. For instance, the bid cost estimate for the 2012 Olympics was £2.4 billion. When the UK won the bid, the organizers did some detailed planning and design and came up with a new estimate, which was £9.28 billion. The completed project came in at £8.921 billion. The difference between these projects and a typical IT project is that the calculation of the final estimate proceeded relatively quickly after the initial go-ahead. Clearly, to make the better estimates, they needed to do some detailed design—in other words, go through the design elaboration step. Clearly, too, the outline of the design—which was detailed enough to be sold to the Olympic committee—wasn't enough. However, once they had done the detailed design, they got the pricing right. Personally I think the engineers did as much as could be asked of them. Yes, the initial estimate was way off, but they did some work and came up with an accurate estimate. If the project had been canceled at that point—which of course for the Olympics was politically unacceptable—not a lot of money would have been spent.

Thus part of the problem with pricing is managing expectations. Do not expect the estimates to be close until the context and technical designs are done. And when I say not close, I mean not close. My guess, for what it is worth, is that the Olympic experience is typical; the initial estimate can be off by a factor of four, and for some reason it is almost always four times too low. When the technical design is done, you should be able to make a good estimate (assuming you have a good record of past projects that allows you to estimate the development effort). Also remember that the total cost includes development, procurement of production hardware and software, operational costs, training, and other rollout costs across the organization. The estimate should be even more accurate when the user interface and database designs are done.

Putting this together, the ideal place in the project plan to do major reviews is illustrated in Figure 3.2. This diagram shows time moving from left to right. Thus the initial estimate review comes after completing the context design and integration

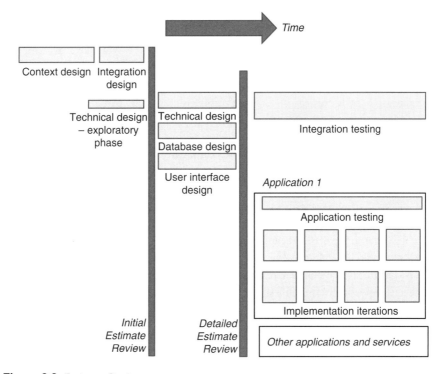

Figure 3.2 *Estimate Review*

design, and the detailed estimate review comes after the detailed designs are done. You can be flexible. Some of technical design—the coding of the systems management interface, for instance—can be done after the detailed review and overlap with the main implementation. You can move the user interface design into the application box, implying that each application has its user interface designed separately from the rest. In each of these cases, there is a very small chance that design problems will be uncovered that lead to a more substantial change. It may be that the applications are phased over time, and some applications may be more important than others. So there is flexibility; if you understand the basis on which the estimates are done, you can take calculated risks.

The implication of the estimate not being accurate until the technical design is done is that there should be a major review when the technical design is finished. The review could easily mean reworking or even canceling the project.

Why Is BDUF Big?

I expect many of my readers are thinking that I have just presented a new method of doing BDUF—big design up front. Put simply, I do agree with DUF—design up front. It is the *B*—the big—that I object to. The question is, Does having design up front encourage the design to be big? Unfortunately the answer is yes. It all has to do with psychology, especially the psychology of meetings. If you have a group of experts in a room, all of them will feel that they have to contribute something, and they won't want to challenge other people in the room. The least confrontational approach is to include everyone's suggestions in the final product. Also, people bounce ideas off each other, which is often a good thing, but it often makes people find additional features they hadn't considered before.

Incidentally, the way committees fall into complexity by its members trying to agree with each other is true not only of business applications; it is how Greece got into the eurozone. Standards committees suffer from the same problem. I have a copy of the 1992 SQL standard. It is 600 pages of impenetrable prose without any examples, and it does not cover the later additions like object-oriented extensions and spatial data. What is notable about many of the technologies that have made the most impact—like TCP/IP, the Web, and the C language—is that they were not developed by committee but were developed in an environment where there was a vested interest in keeping things simple.

The agile approach is much less likely to fall into the trap of overcomplexity, first because the designers talk to fewer people (committees are more likely than single people to produce complexity) and partly because the people giving the input are much more cognizant of the cost of implementing the features because they are slowly seeing the application being developed before their eyes.

So what can you do about it? You can

- Trim—try to cut the requirements list down
- Organize the features into phases
- Look for existing implementations (the SOA approach) and try to piggyback on those
- Try to design a simpler solution that satisfies most of the demands and can be easily extended.

One useful technique for both trimming and splitting into phased releases is to define the MVP—the minimum viable product.

When you decide to cut back on a specification—either to trim or to put features into releases—you must take into account the dependencies. If task A depends on data table B, you cannot eliminate task A without also eliminating data table B. Envisage all the tasks, data tables, and user groups drawn on a diagram and the dependencies drawn between them so it looks like a great big bird's nest. You can eliminate by trimming the outside of the nest, or if you find that an interconnected bunch is hanging off but connected to the rest by only one dependency thread, the bunch can be cut off as a unit. This is another reason why it is so important to capture all the dependencies in the context design.

The fourth option—a simpler solution—is well worth looking for. One example is as follows. Suppose you are programming a banking application and the complexity comes from having many different kinds of accounts. A possible solution is to create a table of account types like so:

```
Table Account .. attribute AccountType
Table AccountType ... attributes for fees, overdraft limit,
interest rates, etc.
```

In other words, you are parameterizing all the characteristics of the account. You can then easily create a new type of account without any additional programming. This may not be simpler for three account types, but it is a lot simpler if there are 200 account types—which is quite likely since historic account types linger on the system. Another example is when you have requests for many kinds of reports, so you code the most common ones and provide an option to download selections of data so the users can do detailed searching in a spreadsheet. A simpler solution is often a better solution, so be creative.

What you must not do is cut costs by reducing quality. In a small project this is unlikely to be cost-effective because you will have to fix the problems sometime or other. This is especially true if you take into account the business costs of using an unreliable application. On a large project reducing quality can be disastrous because many of the later work items will be dependent on the earlier delivered code working properly. If the earlier work items perform badly or are full of bugs, it will seriously hamper the later work.

Iterations

There are three sorts of iterations:

1. **Systems test iterations.** Programmers are assigned work items, and the code produced is tested locally (for instance, on the programmer's workstation) and loaded into the systems test environment. The new systems test version is then tested. One should expect a certain number of version mismatches and misunderstandings between the programmers. Having frequent systems test iterations eliminates most of these early, which improves the smooth running of the project.

2. **Design iterations.** Every now and then a new systems test iteration is shown to the stakeholders. The outcome may be design changes. Hopefully in a context-driven design project the changes will be minor. If they are not, the change request can be analyzed by going back to the context design and looking at the dependencies of the task that is being changed. In any large project it is unlikely that you will be able to show the new version to more than a small proportion of the stakeholders. You may need to show the application to several stakeholders at different times. Judgment is called for here. If you are aware of differences of opinion between stakeholders, you should aim to show the new version to both at once. You don't want to find yourself in the situation where one stakeholder says *do this* and the other says *do that*.

3. **User iterations.** These are the production releases to the end users. Sometimes an end user release must be preceded by hardware installation and/or training. Also, many users do not appreciate the application changing often; familiarity is important. Thus user iterations are not to be undertaken lightly.

These iterations may dictate the number of systems test versions currently being managed. There may be the latest version used by the programming teams, the latest stable version used by the programming teams, the latest version shown to the stakeholders, and the latest version released to production. And often there are many more. Managing many versions is time-consuming, in particular when you find yourself having to put the same bug fix into multiple versions.

There has been in the past an enormous amount of discussion about the desirability and frequency of iterations. I find that stakeholder iterations and user iterations are often driven by external events and don't happen as often as the development team would like. But I strongly believe it is best to manage iterations when you have a view of the total design. It allows for better prioritization of features, and it allows you to see better the dependencies between the changes so you can group them into feature sets more intelligently.

Quality

Quality is about consistency and improvement. The two go hand in hand since consistency provides the baseline for improvement.

In the minds of many, quality management has become associated with comprehensive and large documentation. This is a pity, and I think the fundamental reason is a lack of trust in the programmer's and designer's skills, which has led management to try to use quality programs to compensate. To understand why this is wrong, let me paint an analogy. A good chef knows how to cook a soufflé. A quality program does not teach a chef how to cook a soufflé or even supply a recipe to cook a soufflé; a quality program is about ensuring that soufflés are cooked consistently well.

There is evidence that quality programs work well in IT development. In "Evaluating Agile and Scrum with Other Software Methodologies" [17], Capers Jones shows some measurements of the effectiveness of various methodologies. One of the methodologies that does very well is TSP—Team Software Process. I have to admit I was surprised when I saw this since many of the comments on TSP that I have seen on the Web are, frankly, hostile. TSP is led by an organization that for a long time provided thought leadership in quality processes: the Software Engineering Institute based at Carnegie Mellon University.

There are three lessons that I have learned from studying TSP. The first is that quality runs from top to bottom. TSP is built on PSP—Personal Software Process. Programmers and designers are meant to monitor what they are doing, identify their weaknesses, and better themselves. TSP builds on PSP by applying similar processes to the team.

The second lesson is that quality is built on measurement. If you don't measure how fast function points are implemented, how many bugs are found, and the nature of the bugs that are found, you are unlikely to think about how the work can be done better. PSP has arguably taken this to extremes. Programmers complain that they are forced to document not only for how long they actually write code each day—down to the minute—but also what numbers and kinds of compiler errors they have. This strikes me as excessive, though it would be nice if the development tools themselves kept track of all these measures. With measurements in place you are in a good position to identify and fix your weaknesses.

In other words, quality should not be about bureaucracy; it should be about engendering a learning organization. A learning organization is not only one that sends people on courses and has regular meetings to discuss procedures; it is also one in which complaints can be raised without retribution and people have a willingness to try something different. In Chapter 2, "A Hierarchy of Designs," I fleetingly discussed DevOps, which is in part an objection to so-called quality systems in the operations department. What I have said about measurement and learning organizations applies to the operations department as well.

The third lesson I have learned from quality practices is the use of inspections. This is discussed in the next section.

Testing and Inspection

A large project will have many layers of testing. Having all of unit test, function test, regression test, component test, performance test, systems test, and acceptance test is common. Testing consumes an enormous amount of resources and time, irrespective of the number of bugs it finds. In "Software Estimating Rules of Thumb" [19], Capers Jones states his "Law of Software Development Cost Drivers," which is "Finding and fixing bugs is the most expensive activity in all of software." For your information, the next-most expensive activities in a BDUF project are producing documentation, coding, and meetings and management. In military projects producing documentation rises to first! In agile projects the second and fourth swap places.

The disappointing thing about testing is how ineffective it is. There are several reasons for this:

- Testing is usually focused on proving that the program implements the asked-for functionality. It is rarely focused on finding errors. You write a fix to a bug and write a test to prove it works, and then the same test is run over and over again, where it is found (not surprisingly) that it is working every time. In short, you are testing the parts of the program that are most likely to work.

- Tests are written by people who know how the application should work. The application is used by people who don't know how the application should work and therefore use it in unanticipated ways. This was startlingly shown back in 1989 by Miller and others who simply input rubbish commands into Unix utilities [20]; 25% to 33% of all utilities failed this test.

- Tests are laborious to build, and therefore not many of them are built.

- The tests themselves often have errors!

- There are some errors that are hard to detect by testing such as timing errors, errors that happen because of missing data in the database, and the security issues that hackers exploit.

- Most tests are done on test applications, and other errors arise through version or configuration mistakes caused when moving the application to the production system.

Organizations should put their best brains into developing a good systems test implementation. Let me rephrase that somewhat: your best programming brains are not necessarily your best testing brains. The best testers will be creative and enjoy trying to break the application.

I was once told that the difference between professional classical musicians and amateurs is that the amateurs practice until they can play a piece correctly, while the professionals practice until they don't make mistakes. There is a world of difference; the amateur is looking only at capability, whereas the professional is looking for consistency. There is a similar gap in testing. Testing to make sure the application works is the amateur level. Testing to make sure it does not fail is the professional level. To break a program I suggest you look at the following:

- Try to break it under load, especially load that looks to the application as if it is coming from many users simultaneously.

- Try to break it by causing errors and furthermore by causing errors within the error recovery process.

- Look at the seams—examine all the dependencies between parts and test them.

If the application is already released and there is some real data in the database, try to devise tests that use the real data, perhaps anonymized to protect the innocent. Many tests use the same data over and over again, and especially if the database has been changed, the existing data may be different.

But to achieve a quality program, you should not rely only on testing. You should also

- Use static analyzers to analyze the code and look for code and variables that are never executed, variables that aren't initialized before use, loops that may not terminate, and maybe performance and security issues.

- Use code inspection. I suggest two levels of code inspection, one by peer programmers in the team and the other by the systems test group. The first should help eliminate simple mistakes and misunderstandings of how the system is configured. The latter should eliminate more subtle issues like security problems.

There are good statistics showing that these are as effective as testing for identifying bugs, and they find different bugs from the bugs found in testing.

If you have good measurements of the number of bugs, you will probably notice that some parts of the code seem to attract bugs like moths to candlelight. These are the parts of the code to examine in detail and maybe rewrite.

Using Existing Practices in Context-Driven Design

In these last few sections—on iterations, quality, testing, and inspection—I have not been saying anything that has not been said at greater length and in more depth by others. Essentially they can be summed up in the statement "Use the best practice."

Taking the implementation phase first, I would do as follows:

- Split the work into assignments using the user interface design as a guide, and calculate how many function points there are in each assignment. Keep the assignments small, aiming for each to be completed in two to four weeks.

- Programmers aren't finished with their assignments until they can demonstrate working code running in the systems test configuration. After the code passes the demonstration, the systems test hounds are let loose to try to break it. Thereafter all bugs are public.

- Have a code inspection within the team before putting anything into systems test and another code inspection by an external person after the code has been put into systems test.

- Keep records of how long programmers took on their assignments and how many errors have been discovered after completion of each assignment. Metrics are of no use unless lessons are learned. Every few months the metrics should be discussed and personal and team practices improved.

This is close to best practice on methods such as Scrum [13] and Kanban [21], the main difference being that splitting the work after the user interface design is much easier than splitting it before the user interface design.

However, this applies only to the implementation; project management of the earlier phases, the context design and the detailed designs, have a distinctly different flavor. Context design can realistically be done only by self-directing, self-motivated teams. Their work is not easily split into well-defined units, and their time frame will depend a great deal on whether they can get access to the stakeholders in a timely manner and whether there is general agreement or disagreement. The same is true of the integration design, the user interface design, and the database design. This does not mean that the design projects should not be regularly reviewed. In fact, the design teams should welcome reviews as they are an easy way to meet their stakeholders.

One of the problems with interleaving requirements design and programming implementation is that it forces you to manage the whole project in the same way. It does not give the flexibility to have a dispute about an aspect of the design without disrupting the delivery.

Technical design is more difficult. If the project is a rush, the exploratory part of technical design can be started well before the context design is finished since all that is needed is an idea of the size and nature of the application. The details cannot be finalized until integration design is done, though it is likely that the technical designers will provide a great deal of input into the integration design and hence have early knowledge of its contents. Technical design is closer to designing system software; its main differences from typical commercial programming are as follows:

- The stakeholders are programmers, security experts, operations managers, network managers, and context designers. These people aren't typical business managers, and all have technical expertise.

- It is much more difficult to split the work into neat chunks that take, say, two to four weeks.

I still recommend agile-like small teams that have regular coordination meetings, even in a very large project. Each member of the team should also spend a sizable part of his or her time inspecting other team members' code.

Learning Organizations

Many of the difficulties met in IT departments would lessen if people in the IT department took active steps to improve their skills and processes; the department should become a learning organization. It should take steps such as

- Keeping project metrics

- Sharing designs and developing best practices for design

- Giving internal presentations about how well or badly the project, or an aspect thereof, has gone

- Giving programmers time (perhaps between projects) to experiment with new technologies

- Sharing war stories with other organizations

A framework for design like context-driven design helps structure such learning. You should see where your organization is weak and where it is strong and see how you can improve the former and exploit the later.

In Chapter 2 I discussed DevOps. One of the principles behind DevOps is that programmers should be skilled in operations so that they implement solutions that are easy to operate. I recently wrote an application that runs in the cloud, and since I was implementing the project myself I had to do all the installation and administration. I suppose this makes me a DevOps developer. So what do I think of programmers doing operations? Simple: I hate it; I am just not interested in all the little details of installation, administration, and monitoring, and I loathe wading through the morass of documentation. However, the fact that I don't like it doesn't make it a bad idea, and the other principles in DevOps, like unified version handling between development and operations, I completely support. Ideally, new programmers should spend six months in operations. But ideally they should also spend six months in database design and administration, six months doing context designs, six months in the security department, and six months helping out the technical designers. Moving programmers around and trying to build IT experts, not just programming experts, is an important aspect of developing an IT learning culture.

Concluding Remarks

You will notice that there is a great deal missing in my description of IT design that is documented in other methodologies, such as principles, practices, policies, meetings, task boards, and so on. This is because best practice should be reused in context-driven design. While I see the design phases as being fairly free-flowing, I see the programming as feeling much like today's agile projects.

Even if you design up front, you can still have multiphase releases, you can still split the work into small slices and deliver it incrementally, and you can still show the latest working version to stakeholders, fully expecting that sometimes they are going to change their minds. The great advantage of context-driven design is that you can quickly work out the impact of change, both on the code and on the business, and you can ensure that the change does not affect the integrity of the whole system. The ability to understand change and manage change is one of the key advantages of context-driven design over existing methods.

Another area where I think existing practice should change is in bringing forward the technical design and insisting that it not be finished until it is proved to be fully working and meets the requirements. This is to counter the temptation to say that we'll sort out the performance and availability issues at the end when all the functional code is written. Again, you might find you need to make tweaks to the technical design later on, but this is much easier when you have a solid design to start with and you have the ability to retest the new design.

The third difference I see from current practice is that there are different project styles for different designs. The context design, integration design, user interface design, and database design need self-motivated teams, while the implementation can use existing practices like Scrum, possibly adapted somewhat. Technical design is somewhere in between.

The next chapter looks at the issue of why large IT application projects are particularly prone to failure, and from then on I concentrate on the core subject of this book: how to think about design.

Chapter 4

The Problem of Large Applications

Large application design projects are famously prone to failure. The paper "The Impact of Size and Volatility on IT Project Performance" [22] reports a survey of project managers, which showed that 77% of projects requiring over 1,000 person-months to implement underperformed while 100% of projects requiring over 2,400 person-months to implement underperformed. In contrast, projects requiring under 500 person-months to implement underperformed less than 38% of the time. Under-performance here means going significantly over budget, being significantly behind schedule, or having significantly reduced scope.

The IT industry in general is appallingly deficient in good statistics. One reads so much about how such-and-such methodology/product/service/idea revolutionizes application development, but the fact is that in terms of solid numbers we haven't the faintest idea. It's just as well that in the IT industry you don't have to prove a statement's validity through something like an airworthiness certificate or a drugs trial. (To be fair, I think academia would love to do more studies, but acquiring the raw data has proved difficult.) Such studies as there are don't tell a consistent story; for example, the study I quoted in the preceding paragraph is at variance with the Standish Chaos report (the study on IT project success and failure from the Standish consultancy group that has been repeated several times since the 1990s [23]). I am not blaming anyone because there really are difficulties. Take the metrics of going over or under the budget or schedule. At the start of a project, the best you can do is estimate a range, but often management demands a single budget figure. In their paper "The Rise and Fall of the Chaos Report Figures" [24], Eveleens and Verhoef report that one organization almost always took the top end of the range for its budget figure and another organization almost always took the bottom end of the range.

The reasons for the bias had to do with office politics. In the first case the priority was to get a project started; in the second it was to be seen to perform to plan. Then take the notion about implementing all the scope. In an agile project, since there is no clear definition of the scope early on, I have no idea how this could be measured. In a BDUF project, it may be possible to measure scope after the requirements have been gathered and the use cases have been written but not before. Even so, a measurement based on use case implementation is the view of the project manager, but it does not necessarily coincide with the view of the stakeholders; you can implement all your use cases and still not satisfy the end users or business management. Thus there are two different answers to the question of satisfying scope: the project manager's view ("I did what I was asked to do") and the business manager's view ("It satisfies the business need"). All is not bleak, however; there are many examples of IT applications that were late and over budget but over the years have done their organizations proud.

But in spite of all this statistical murkiness, both the Sauer study and the Standish Chaos report are clear on one point: large projects are prone to failure. This point is corroborated by statistics on government projects that are publicly available.

In this chapter, I discuss not only why there are special reasons why large projects go wrong but also whether large projects can be avoided by simply having many small projects. Let me begin by giving you a sense of what makes an application large before I turn to the discussion of specific problems.

The Dimensions of Size

Applications are large in different ways. I think of largeness in three orthogonal dimensions.

In the first dimension, the application may support a large number of tasks. Obviously an application that supports 200 tasks, is described in 200 use cases, and has 1,000 screen formats and a database of 100 tables takes a lot of effort to implement. I think of this as the horizontal dimension—such applications are large horizontally. I suppose it comes from the idea of drawing them and ending up with lots of boxes in a horizontal line.

In the second dimension, the application may support a large number of people simultaneously. I say simultaneously because one of the joys of Web applications is that there is no restriction on the number of people who can use the application; the application has a problem only if many of the users use it at the same time. If you support a large number of people simultaneously, you obviously have to pay attention to scalability, by which I mean the application's ability to grow in line with the increasing number of users. But you must also pay attention to reliability, because if it fails, you are going to upset a lot of people all at once. In the worst case, a failure can make the national news. I think of this dimension as the vertical dimension, possibly because when you draw it you often find yourself drawing multiple tiers vertically on the page.

There is a third dimension, which is complexity. Large projects are not necessarily complex, but they often are. Whenever you start to program a different type of application from what you are used to, you are going to struggle to begin with. For instance, the first time you write a games program, or a compiler, or some artificial intelligence routines, you are going to find it difficult. It's the same if you start using different technology, such as a new programming language or a new operating system. Familiarity counts for a lot in this business. But this kind of technical complexity can be overcome with training or by hiring some outside expertise. On the other hand, some programs are inherently complex, because what they are doing is complex; they are complex algorithmically. This kind of complexity does not require a technical expert but an expert on thinking through complex problems, a problem solver. Examples of difficult problems are how best to design the layout of a chip, how to run the best investment strategy, and how to write a database recovery utility that will run on unreliable hardware. I visualize this dimension as the depth dimension going into the page.

Each of these dimensions requires a different approach. If there are many tasks to implement, the project must be strong on relationships with the business users and management because the tasks have to be the right tasks. On the other hand, the programming—so long as the application is not large in the third dimension of complexity—may be relatively straightforward. In the second dimension, you need technical expertise to build a platform that can really perform. When it comes to the application coding, the programmers may be told to write the application rather differently from the way they would if there were no performance challenges. For example, there may be special ways of handling sessions because the work is spread over many servers (an issue discussed in Chapter 10, "Technical Design—Principles"). In the third dimension, you need to find the right person or people; technical problems need someone with the right expertise, and algorithm complexity needs someone who is good at solving complex problems.

It is worth noting that only projects that are large in the first dimension of supporting a large number of tasks benefit from having large teams, and it is large teams that are prone to project failure. It is these applications that we are mostly concerned about in this chapter. But it is also worth noting that the style of management often used to manage large teams, especially if it is very rule bound and bureaucratic, can put off the quality people you need to hire to handle the other two dimensions.

While there are large applications that are large in only one of these dimensions, many large applications are large in more than one dimension; an application not only has many users, but it also supports many tasks. You can envisage the effort to write such applications as the area created by great horizontal width and great height because the high performance requirement adds complexity to every part of the application.

One place to find applications that have high volume requirements and support many tasks is in areas where IT applications have been around a long time. When applications age, they tend to become more and more complex; they accrue new reports, new interfaces, tweaks in the ways of doing things. It can be difficult to figure out which of the application's features are unimportant and can be forgotten. Some of the most ancient applications are in businesses that took to computing early, such as banking and airline ticketing. The reason they were interested in computer applications many years ago was that they had large volumes of repetitive work, and thus today they have applications that support large numbers of people and have large transaction volumes. Government applications, too, often have a similar profile of large size and having been built on old foundations. These organizations have ended up with large, high-performance systems, written over 30 or more years ago, understood by fewer and fewer people and then only in part, and with all the complexity that comes from applying many short-term fixes. Then someone comes along and says, "Rewrite the lot."

Actually, before anyone says, "Rewrite the lot," he or she probably says, "Why do I have so many programmers in my organization? Move to a package." I always encourage people to look around for packages before embarking on any development. Packages in areas where all businesses do more or less the same thing—payroll, accounting, and human resources—work well. There seem to be some industries in which packages are pervasive and also work well. But I have seen several examples of failure to implement a package. The two most common reasons are:

- The package is not sufficiently scalable.
- The package came from another country and required large changes due to different business operations, different legal systems, and different regulatory environments.

For instance, I have heard several stories about large banks taking on applications written for small-scale banks and failing to make the applications work for them. In general, packages work least well for large, high-performing applications where the complexity is of the horizontal dimension—lots of tasks. In fact, they work least well for the same kinds of applications that seem to be the most prone to development project failure.

It is rare that senior managers decide on a rewrite for technical reasons only. They want some change to business functionality. Thus the project team is encouraged not only to reimplement everything that was done before but also to rethink how parts of the business will change at the same time.

When I talk about large project failure, I imagine that most of my readers assume that I mean public-sector projects. Actually, no. The major reason why project failure is associated with the public sector is that there it cannot be hidden. Businesses sometimes find themselves in the public eye if there is a failure (e.g., a bank stops accepting credit cards for a few hours), but many companies have managed to hide the cancellation of large IT projects that have cost hundreds of millions of dollars from both the general public and the company's shareholders. Moreover, in the public sector there is increasing use of outside contractors and outsourcing. One of the biggest IT fiascos in recent times was the NHS National Programme for IT in the UK. (For my American readers, the NHS is the National Health Service, and this program is a series of interlinked projects that provide centralized IT functions like booking hospital appointments and holding health records.) The program was established in October 2002, and it was meant to cost £2.3 billion and take three years to complete. By 2013 a fraction had been delivered, the cost overrun was probably on the order of £10 billion, and it was embroiled in legal disputes. It is hard to know exactly what went wrong, because it is still shrouded in secrecy [25]. But it cannot be blamed on public-sector workers, at least below the level of senior management, because all of it was subcontracted to large IT services companies like Accenture, CSC, Fujitsu, and BT.

That said, there are some reasons why public-sector projects are particularly vulnerable to failure:

- Their applications have large numbers of users.

- Their IT applications are allowed to grow very old before investments are made in a new application. This has two consequences. First, the organization is forced into a rewrite rather than making incremental changes. Second, all users of the system realize they have one and only one chance to have the IT application do what they want, so requirements come flooding in.

- They are forced to use open-tender procurement rules that give the job to the lowest bidder. It is likely that the lowest bidders will play the flawed specification game—instead of reporting a problem with the specification, they deliberately underbid, knowing the procurer will have to change the spec, for which they can charge an outrageous price.

In this chapter I discuss the underlying problems with large projects and suggest some solutions.

Problems with Large Projects

So why do large projects fail? I will list some possible reasons and then discuss them.

1. Requirements problems.

    a. The requirements are inconsistent.

    b. The requirements as specified don't meet the needs of the organization.

    c. The requirements keep changing.

2. User acceptance problems.

    a. The new application meets resistance from end users.

    b. IT is used as crowbar to leverage organizational change.

3. Methodology problems. The project follows a methodology that is not suited to large applications.

4. Technical design problems. The nonfunctional requirements—scalability, resilience, security, and so on—are not designed properly.

5. Procurement problems.

    a. The project is outsourced or the project is not outsourced.

    b. Procurement practices destroy trust.

I discuss four of these in the following subsections. I am not going to discuss methodologies since all the other problems can be seen as methodology problems. Besides, if you don't have the rigorous notion of an engineered design, it is difficult to put your finger on the reasons why methodologies fail.

Requirements Problems

If the requirements aren't right, the project is doomed from the outset. Requirements not being right may mean that they are incomplete or inconsistent. But it may mean that the requirements don't meet the true needs of the organization; they meet the needs only of the few people who have been asked for their requirements. If the requirements are wrong to begin with, the consequence may be that the requirements keep changing during development.

These are all symptoms of not having a well-thought-through context design—in other words, the underlying cause is that requirements have been gathered, not designed. It is an obvious point, but the larger the project, the larger the context design and the more difficult it will be to spot incompleteness and inconsistencies. Naturally, I believe that taking a more rigorous approach to context design will solve most of these problems. Furthermore, the awareness of dependencies in the context design and the traceability from code to application design to context design will make the management of changing requirements much easier.

But a consistent and complete context design is not necessarily a design that meets the needs of the organization. This is true even if the context design has been reviewed extensively, because it is easy to lose touch with the overall objectives when you are spending your time designing the detail. The solution to this problem is to remember that developing a context design is a design exercise, and the first step of a design exercise is understanding the requirements. What then are the requirements of the context design itself? Recall that in Chapter 1, "Introduction to Context-Driven Design," I wrote that the main thrust of real high-level requirements can often be captured in a single statement. There may be a few more requirements, but many of these will be unsaid, and (say it softly) some of them may be unsayable. For instance, the overriding requirement may be to save money, but the hidden requirement may be the degree to which quality and service can be degraded to save money. When you are embarking on a complex context design, it is important to take time to list the real high-level requirements. If, for instance, you are imposing a new business process, why are you doing so? List the reasons why you hope the new process will be better than the old process. List the circumstances when it might be worse—the risks inherent in the new process. If you are moving to a new business model, again, what are the hopes for the new model and what are the risks? When the context design is finished, analyze it for completeness and consistency, but also analyze its effectiveness in reaching your goals and mitigating the risks.

Most context design requirements fall into one of the following three categories:

- Reduce cost.
- Reduce errors.
- Improve service.

When analyzing the context design, it is good to be able to

- Explain how you achieve any of the goals
- Define metrics to underpin the targets
- List what has to be done outside of the IT application development to achieve the goals

The list of requirements and the metrics will help drive the project, especially on the question of whether you want to cancel or redefine the project later on.

The more people who provide requirements, the more likely you are to have conflicting views. Look at a simple example. Suppose you are implementing an application that supports a parcel delivery company. What happens if the receiving person is not at home? In the UK, one of four things might happen: the parcel goes back with the driver, who tries to deliver it again the next day; the parcel goes back with the driver and the customer has to collect it from the depot; the parcel is left somewhere for the customer to find, such as beside the house behind the garbage cans; or the parcel is left with a neighbor. It is not unlikely that different managers will have different views about what choice is acceptable. If you talk to only one manager, other managers might be very upset when they eventually find out that you haven't implemented their preferred option. You could, of course, implement all the options, but this way madness lies because you, the non-expert, are trying to think of all the alternatives. Furthermore, implementing multiple options increases the complexity of the user interface and increases costs. Of course, you can meet conflicting views in an application of any size, but in a large application it is much more likely. You want to resolve the disagreements during the context design, and thus it is important that the context design not be hidden from view; you need the arguments to be out in the open. If you do not take steps to inform all relevant parties, the arguments will surface halfway through the implementation, giving rise to late requirements changes. It is also important that the person who signs off on the context design be seen by everybody to have signed off. The organization must realize that this is the direction of travel whether individuals like it or not.

Late-changing requirements are often blamed on the speed of change in business life today. I think only a tiny fraction of late-changing requirements can be put down to business change. Much more likely reasons for change are the following:

- A stakeholder was not included in the initial design phases.

- A stakeholder makes his or her views known only well after the project has started.

- A stakeholder misunderstood what was being proposed and realizes that only when shown the "finished" product.

- The management changes and there are new stakeholders who have different views.

The first of these points should be addressed by openness. The next two points should be addressed by an effective review of the context design. Only the last point should mean a redesign. But at least with a sound context design and traceability from context design to code, it should be possible to identify the parts of the design and the implementation that can be retained and the parts that should be thrown away.

The worst case happens when there are not so much conflicting views as conflicting visions. At its heart, this is probably what went wrong with the NHS National Programme for IT. The vision of a unified IT structure came from the top, but the thrust of other developments in the NHS was to introduce more internal competitiveness, such as hospitals competing for patients—and therefore funds—against other hospitals. One way for hospitals to improve their efficiency was to improve their IT, so it was contrary to this aim to then centralize many of the IT applications, and it could easily throw the hospital's IT strategy into chaos. So there was resistance. The project team was (as I previously mentioned) secretive, which I would argue was exactly what wasn't needed since the rollout had to be in many ways a marketing exercise in convincing semiautonomous organizations to do things their way.

Lack of End User Support

That a new application meets resistance from its end users is common. Often an application is meant to make the end users' lives easier, but even that sometimes has an implied threat because if it makes their lives too easy, the organization will be able to lay off some of them. That said, often the resistance is simply because the end users don't like change.

Resistance is much more likely if the context design is demonstrably wrong, even in trivial ways. If there is likely to be resistance, you cannot afford to make mistakes.

The other reason there is resistance is that the new application makes the end users' lives more difficult. This is surprisingly easy to do. A simple way to annoy end users is to make them gather a lot of extra data (the usual justification is that the data is needed for marketing reasons). Another way is for the new application to be slow. A third is to makes the end users do work that they consider worthless. A classic example is the Choose and Book application that was introduced by the UK's National Health Service. The idea was that a doctor could sit with a patient and choose online to which hospital to refer the patient. "What's not to like about this application?" you may ask. What was not to like was that it was time-consuming and often pointless as there was often only one local hospital that supplied the service needed. The result was that after its rollout in 2005 and 2006, by 2012 it was used by only half of the GPs (general practitioners—the UK local doctors).

It is important that the project study the impact of a new application on the end users. This should be an analysis test applied to the context design and the user interface design. It can be further tested by a rollout to a small number of real end users before a full rollout across the whole organization. One way to perform this analysis test on the user interface design is to playact some scenarios. Have an end user pretend to use the application and a member of the team pretend to be the application and pass paper with data on it rather than have screens. When these two people are playacting, do two things:

- Time it. Find out how much time is saved or lost. If you are not saving time, you are in trouble.

- Ask what happens when a step goes wrong.

As noted previously, rolling out a new application is in part a marketing exercise. The rollout will be a lot easier if people feel they were listened to during the design. Secrecy is a vice people succumb to in large projects. The project team often justifies it on the grounds that competitors shouldn't know what they're doing, but in truth most of it comes about because it's a habit. If you are less secretive, you will have more input, more problems will be identified, more early gains will be found, and the workforce will be more enthusiastic about the final product.

In a large project, it is logistically infeasible to talk to all the people who will use the new application. People are sent out to ask opinions and solicit input, but there is a natural reluctance to report bad news, and there is a strong tendency to ask management a lot and ask the end users a little. Projects get caught up in office politics. Senior management thinks the project is a good idea; therefore naysayers and doom mongers aren't good corporate citizens. But however strong-willed the management, if the end users are opposed to the new application there is a heck of a fight to make it happen. Users who are forced to use a new application they dislike have many ways of showing their displeasure, from simply blaming the application for mistakes to losing passwords and putting in incorrect data.

If you recognize that there is potential hostility to a new application, you must identify the people most affected and do what you can to make the application work well for them. This may mean cutting back on the functionality! It is easy to assume that the more functionality, the better, but sometimes functionality benefits one group of people at the expense of another by making them do extra work. A classic example of this is CRM—customer relationship management—applications. Time and time again, CRM applications have not delivered the hoped-for benefits [26]. The root cause is hostility toward the CRM application from the sales force because it means extra work for them, and it means their handling of their accounts is more visible to senior management. Some of the advice to make the most of CRM applications applies to all applications, namely:

- Train your end users properly. Don't just train them in data entry; train them in how to make the best use of the system, and explain why it is designed the way it is.

- Tweak the application after rollout to make it better, using feedback from the users.

- Make sure the application is being used to bring maximum benefit to the organization. If the end user is forced to gather a lot of additional data, make sure that other parts of the organization use it and demand that they prove to the organization how important the data is.

Ideally, you should consider the rollout and business change issues when developing the context design. One worthwhile analysis of the context design is to look at the impact of the application on the workload of different user groups and consider what is needed for rollout and training.

There is a temptation for senior managers to use the introduction of an IT application as a crowbar to force change in an organization. Making change happen is one of the most difficult tasks in management, so the temptation is to force the change through by making the old way of working impossible. This might be done by taking away the application that supports the old way and introducing a new application that supports the new way. The problem is that the new application must work extremely well because every weakness will be seized upon as a reason not to change.

Technical Design Problems

Since large projects are often about the delivery of an application that supports large numbers of users, there is a high probability that there will be demanding performance, availability, and security requirements. We discuss how to attack these targets in Chapter 10. What I want to discuss in this section is why some projects don't tackle these problems well.

One reason is the huge range of alternative software products. Choosing among them is not made any easier by the knowledge that once you have selected a product you are stuck with it, because the cost of rewriting using another product is enormous. For Web application development you have a choice of languages: C, C++, C#, Java, Ruby, Go, PHP, Perl, and many others. If you decide on Java, you have to choose a Web application server; alternatives are WebLogic, WebSphere, Tomcat, JBoss, Jetty, GlassFish, and many others. There seem to be more and more options every year. Simply keeping abreast of all the developments takes a great deal of effort. I, like most programmers, have given up; I work with a narrow range of software—mostly chosen by accident—and I haven't the faintest idea whether it is the best. (On the other hand, I am confident it's not far off the best, and the best changes every year in any case.) The fact that programmers understand only a small subset of possible development choices often does not stop them from pontificating and expressing trenchant opinions on the desirability of this or that software product. Get together a group of IT professionals and you can almost guarantee that any choice of software will be controversial. There are people who seem to know all about all available software products, but since they can't possibly have used them all, I always wonder if their knowledge is more than skin deep. Choosing software is not easy.

As an aside, an IT department should actively try to build the skills of the organization by every now and then setting a programmer the task of trying out a different product and presenting the findings to the team.

On a large project with demanding requirements you are likely to find your choice of products severely restricted because many software development products have been designed to make it easy to write small applications quickly and don't have the features to tackle high-volume, high-availability applications. The following are some of the facilities you might need:

- Running with a database that spans more than one disk drive. In other words, the volume of I/Os is too great for one physical disk.

- Running on a clustered configuration because it exceeds the limits of what can be run on a single processor.

- Running 24 by 7. For instance, this means there is no time in the day or night to take offline backups. You may want to run some applications every day and night of the year—in other words, there is no time window in which the application can be taken offline to install a new release.

- Batch programming to do time-triggered applications like interest accrual. The batch programs must be scheduled, some in sequence and some in parallel. If you have a sequence of programs and the first one fails, you may not want to run the other programs in the sequence.

- Very high availability—in other words, the organization really wants the application to run nonstop.

- Remote disaster recovery backup site.

- The ability to build high levels of security to hold secure information such as personal information, financial information, or state/business secrets.

- Dark room operation—in other words, integration with systems management products so errors in both the system and the application software can be reported to some remote operations workstation.

Often you find that while the product does not support these facilities directly, they can be built with additional programming. Where software products do support a facility, they may support it in such a way that you have to do the programming yourself. For instance, the product may support clustered configurations but only certain types of clustering from a few named hardware providers.

Some of the code written to support the technical design may be code called on every input message. Examples include code for security monitoring, code for error detection and reporting, and code for capturing performance statistics. This is why demanding technical design can lead to a large increase in the time taken to program every task as discussed in the section on cost estimation in the previous chapter. The skill of the technical designer is in part to make programming the screen input as simple as possible by gathering together all system-handling parts in one place and making it easy for the application programmers to write their code.

I know only one way to sort out the technical design, and that is to try it out. This should happen in two stages. The first is experimental. Don't take just one product but two or three and implement a simple application in each. Then take the needed facilities from my list and add other facilities I have forgotten to mention. Also take out the items you don't need. Think how you could implement the remaining features in your list. Talk to the vendors and other users of the product and see how they think the problems should be solved.

The second stage is to start programming the technical environment for real and testing it under load.

Ideally all of this should be done before you start writing the application code—the code that implements the end user interface. Sometimes the ideal can't be done, but management must be aware that application code isn't stable until the implementation of the technical design is stable.

Large projects have often run into problems because they have not done any exploration or any early product testing. Instead, they have accepted the software vendor's word that the product can achieve everything they need. What the software vendor says is often true but only so long as the software is structured in a certain way. For instance, the software vendor may be assuming that the application does not rely on session state data being held in the server between messages. (Session state data is explained in more detail in Chapter 10.) If the programmers have not built the application with this constraint, it may be a long job to change their code to meet the performance objectives. I am not accusing the software vendors of being misleading here; it is simply that there can be dangerous misunderstandings. You may have two questions—Does the software support a throughput of X, and does it support sessions?—and the answer to both might be yes. Unfortunately the answer to the question of whether it does both at the same time might be no. The purpose of the exploratory prototype is not only to find out if the software works but also to find out if it works the way you intend to use it.

Often, of course, if you find out it does not work well the way you first expected to use it, the best solution might be to change your design to use it in a different way. For instance, at first you think you need session state data, but you might find a solution that does not.

But hang on—why can't we rely on industry benchmarks? There are industry benchmarks available that prove that some software products running in some configurations are capable of truly amazing performance feats. The trouble is that the benchmarks are highly unlikely to implement anything close to what you need. A throughput benchmark will not implement high-availability features such as switching to a disaster backup site and will not implement high security such as using encryption. Furthermore, the benchmark applications are very simple, and additional complexity, like additional indexes in the database, always adds overhead. The answer is to test your application.

One of the reasons why exploratory technical designs are not done is that the project is put out to bid to a third party and the third party has cut its costs to the bone to win the contract. While the third party may have the expertise to develop a good technical design, it may not use that expertise on your contract. The third party may assume that it can just wing it. Which leads us to the next area where large projects go wrong: procurement of third-party application development.

Procurement and Outsourcing

Using a third party for application development often makes sense. Imagine an organization that needs an IT department of 100 to run its IT systems and do regular maintenance but needs an extra 200 for a couple of years to develop a large new application. It stands to reason to contract the work to an outside organization, if only for the difficulty of hiring so many people with the requisite skills. Naturally, when an organization hires a third party to develop an application and it goes wrong, the organization blames the third party.

I have no reason to doubt the skills and integrity of the employees of consultancies, systems integrators, and outsourcers. Many people believe that it is not so much the people as the procurement contract itself that encourages bad behavior. Most of these criticisms have been aimed at public-sector contracts which are to some extent influenced by the rules for contracting defined in legislation in many countries, including the United States and the members of the European Union. The rules are designed to encourage value for money and prevent kickbacks. A small observation: it seems that IT contracts and defense system contracts are particularly prone to overruns, and I wonder why this is. Is it technical complexity or is it the stakeholders not knowing what they want?

Historically many contracts have been fixed price and, so long as the vendors can say that they can do the task in hand, have been awarded to the lowest bidder. Obviously, the vendors want to be the cheapest, which leads them to take two actions:

- If there is any ambiguity in the contract, they assume the least-cost option.
- They look for ways to earn outside the contract bid, for instance, by charging a great deal for changes to the contract and for areas outside the contract like training and maintenance.

The outcome is often confrontational and legalistic.

The other common way of writing a contract is cost plus. The idea is that the contractors are paid their expenses and get a guaranteed profit margin on top. The danger here is that contractors, who are looking to maximize their profits, may look for ways to drag out the work.

Learning from Civil Engineering Contracts

The civil engineering business has struggled with contract issues for years, and perhaps we in IT have something to learn from them. What follows is a bit of a diversion from the main thrust of this book, but I think it is instructive in this context.

In the UK there are two main kinds of contracts for construction work called JCT (Joint Contracts Tribunal) [27] and NEC (New Engineering Contract) [28]. JCT was first published in 1931 and is the old-style form of contract, full of legalese, but now fully supported by a body of case law. The latest version was in 2011. NEC is the newcomer and was partly written because of dissatisfaction with JCT. In particular, the authors wanted to escape from the confrontational relationship between client and contractor. It was first published in 1995 and is written in plain English, not legalese. The latest version is NEC3, published in 2005, but there are additions to cover recent changes to the law. The NEC has a wider scope than JCT, covering professional services, for instance. According to what I can see on the Web (so a big pinch of salt, please), JCT is still more commonly used, but NEC has been used in some big contracts, including the London Olympics.

One interesting feature of NEC is that it allows for five different kinds of payments, not only fixed price and cost plus, but also sharing the losses from cost overruns and the gains from early delivery.

However, the biggest difference, I think, is characterized in the NEC's promotional literature as "stimulus to good management." This covers a range of practices designed to persuade clients and contractors to solve problems collaboratively. I discuss two of them here:

- **Project management.** NEC is focused on project management top to bottom. The observation from one of the NEC authors is that in the old system (presumably JCT) "as soon as the contract was signed you lost control." Under

NEC a contractor must provide a "programme of works"—in other words, a project plan. As the project progresses, the contractor must record progress against the plan and deviations from it. Subcontractors of subcontractors must also be contracted by an NEC contract so the project plan spans from top to bottom.

- **Problem resolution.** In NEC if contractors want more payment, they must raise a Compensation Event. However, before raising a Compensation Event they should have raised an Early Warning notice, and if they haven't, the project manager is entitled to treat the Compensation Event like an Early Warning, which means that the project manager is entitled to look for alternative solutions. The project manager is also committed to raise Early Warning events if he or she sees something that might cause a delay, increase cost, or impact the work of others. Furthermore, everything is time constrained—there is a maximum number of weeks between all the steps. The aim is to ensure that the project accounts are complete at all times and there are no nasty surprises when the project is finished from contractors claiming extra fees.

Before I get carried away and tell you everything is rosy, I should point out that NEC is not without its critics. A judge complained about the contract being written in plain English—good heavens, it is even written in the present tense! There are warnings that if you go into an NEC contract you had better get some training as it is different. Others warn that trying to take an NEC contract and slipping in some JCT clauses is a road to legal confusion. The main criticism seems to be that NEC can be unduly bureaucratic, especially over the management of Compensation Events.

We can learn from this experience:

- It is hard to manage subcontractors without having a solid design. This is discussed in the next section.

- Find a way to have overarching project management top to bottom. Having the subcontractor present a project plan is a good start.

- Find a way the subcontractor can benefit from the upside as well as suffer from the downside.

- Communication is key.

However, it seems to me that the successes from using the NEC contract show that there is a different way; it is possible to run a project in a manner that is not antagonistic at every turn. If civil engineers can do it, I don't see why we can't do it too.

Outsourcing Design and Implementation

But there is a big hurdle to overcome: achieving a stable design has historically been a major issue with IT designs. As we have discussed earlier, the design cannot really be considered stable until at least the context design and the technical design are done. Furthermore, the technical design can be validated only by testing. Without a stable design a detailed program of work is more or less impossible. As a consequence I don't believe that it is possible to do context design or technical design under fixed-price contracts. As pointed out earlier, NEC does allow for cost-plus contracts, so it may still be possible to have an overarching contract like NEC on the whole process. You can time-box the early design—in other words, have the designers do what they can in a fixed period of time with the expectation that they won't finish—and then negotiate extensions if they need it.

However, I do believe that implementation design can be fixed price.

If I were running a large organization and felt moved to start a large IT project, I would feel uncomfortable contracting out the context design. The reason for my discomfort is that, however good the designers, they are not responsible for the roll-out of the application into the organization. The managers who are going to drive through the business change that comes with the new application need to hear the issues and concerns of the people providing input into the design. Thus, while a third party can provide expertise and maybe process leadership, the content of the context design is the responsibility of the organization that has the problem the project is trying to solve.

The contract for the technical design should include the testing—in other words, a trial implementation, ideally a trial implementation that becomes a systems test system. I suspect most organizations expect the hardware and software vendors to do any trials for them, and probably for free. This is a mistake as it will guarantee that the vendor will have a vested interest in downplaying difficulties. The vendor will want the simplest configuration needed to win the business and have the organization pay for any "surprises" that come about later. For instance, it might be desirable for a system to have a monitoring feature to help debug the application. As this is not directly implementing some business functionality, it is unlikely to be in the requirements list. Hoping a vendor will implement the code for features like this for free strikes me as optimistic to say the least.

It is common in big-project development to have one external vendor develop the requirements and another build the application. In terms of the six-box model, this is illustrated in Figure 4.1.

If you compare this diagram with Figure 3.1 in the previous chapter, you will see a major problem: the implementation vendor is not in a position to give a firm estimate of time and money because the technical design has not been done.

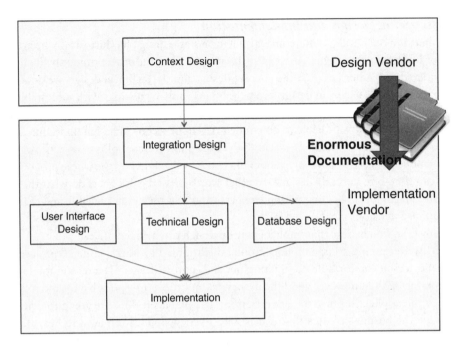

Figure 4.1 *Design Vendor and Implementation Vendor*

Given all these problems, it is hardly surprising that projects using outside vendors are often doomed.

I am not an expert in contracts, but it does seem to me that it is time for a major rethink of contracts, possibly along the lines of NEC but at any rate inspired by NEC, to find ways of encouraging collaboration. Second, it is clear that plans for using contractors should be intimately linked to a model of development, which of course in my view should be the six-box model.

Can Large Projects Be Avoided?

Whenever your organization is thinking about embarking on a large project, it should ask itself whether the project can be avoided by splitting it up into a series of more manageable smaller projects.

Many organizations have existing applications that do most of the functionality of the proposed new application. A more gradual approach to replacement is to first migrate the existing application to an SOA because adding features to SOA applications is much easier. What you are trying to achieve is illustrated in Figure 4.2. The diagram shows two configurations. In one there is a large monolithic application. By defining services the application can be split into more manageable parts. The other configuration shows many independent small applications. The issue here is that you want to integrate the applications, for instance, to support businesses better, and possibly to share databases when they have data in common.

In both, moving to an SOA requires turning the core of an existing application into a service. The next step is to change the old applications such that they have the old user interfaces but in the body of the program they call the new service. Put another way, the starting point is to insert some middleware (illustrated by the double-headed arrow in Figure 4.3) into the middle of the program.

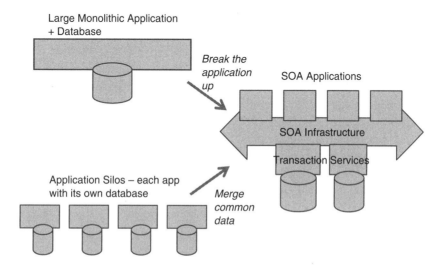

Figure 4.2 *SOA Configuration*

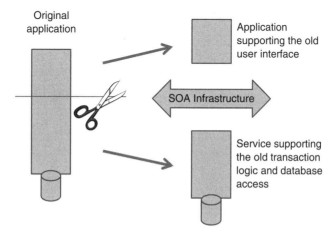

Figure 4.3 *Moving to SOA*

Once the existing application is converted to an SOA equivalent, a replacement front-end application can be written, existing or new applications can call the back-end service, and the back-end service can itself be rewritten or enhanced. All of these projects are relatively independent of each other since they rely only on the stability of the interface.

Deciding what functionality goes into the transaction services and what data tables go into which database is most easily done if you have a context model.

But in spite of this, people have many reasons for still wanting to do large projects:

- It is a genuinely new application area. Genuinely new application areas are rare today, at least large ones are. But they do still exist, I suspect more in government than in private industry.

- The changes are so pervasive—they claim—that it is much cheaper to do it all at once. In business, changes rarely are pervasive. I was struck recently when traveling by air that although the airline online systems have changed a great deal to handle online check-in and so forth, the overall flying experience has changed little in 30 years. You still wait in line, wait for loading, get packed into a long thin tin tube, and get served by harassed-looking airline staff. If the business changes piecemeal, why can't the application supporting the business change piecemeal? The answer is that it can.

- They think it will take too long or cost too much to do it piecemeal. That's the way it looks before the true cost of a large project becomes apparent.

- They want to use the new application to force business change. We have already discussed how risky a strategy this is.

- They think that if they do the project piecemeal, they will never fully get rid of the old application. A bit subtle, this one—and I don't think many people would admit publicly that this is their strategy. It may be true in many cases, because if you move bits of functionality out of the old application, you may be left with a rump of an old application that works just fine and supports part of the business that doesn't need changing. Thus there is no motivation to change it. Well, does it matter? Is it so bad to leave the rump of the old application around? If it is so bad, at least there is not much to rewrite.

- They are an external company doing the work and they want one big job, not lots of small ones. No one will admit to this reason either.

I suspect that sometimes the underlying drive to do big projects comes from two fears. The first is that IT applications somehow decay over time, so they have to be rewritten to take them back to pristine form, from which they start to decay again. The second is that the business will never invest in change if the justification for the change is only technology improvement; thus the first step of moving to an SOA is forbidden.

The first fear is bizarre. It is true that *knowledge* of an application decays if the application is not being changed on a regular basis, but rewriting an application costs far too much just to refresh the knowledge. It is also true that programmers put kludges into applications to make temporary fixes that become permanent. That can be fixed by management driving a culture of keeping up the code quality. It is also true that fashions for programming languages and technologies come and go. To illustrate how decay is not inevitable, consider some of the big important computer programs like operating systems and database systems. They don't decay over time. In fact the opposite happens; it is only because they have been used over a long period of time that each new version can be based on a predecessor in which the software is stable and functional. However, the feeling of software decay persists. Look at this sentence from the *Economist* magazine (December 14, 2013, p. 35) talking about (in disparaging terms) a new UK government welfare application: "Some £40m ($66m) spent on software has been written off and another £91m will be out-of-date within five years." Out-of-date within five years? What on earth does that mean? Does it mean it won't be supported? If so, I don't believe it. Or does it mean that programmers will refuse to write in the language? I don't believe that either. Some would say that applications written in COBOL on mainframes have been "out-of-date" for 30 years, but the applications are running fine and my guess is that many of them will be still running in another 30 years' time.

The second fear—that businesses won't invest in nonfunctional change—is not at all bizarre. The notion that you should spend a portion of your IT budget simply to improve the applications for the sake of making them faster, more secure, more resilient, and above all more responsive to change does not exist anywhere as far as I can tell. It is so different from the aircraft business, where, say, a Boeing 747 built today is very different from a 747 built 20 years ago. The airline industry frequently introduces new versions simply to update the technology. We don't do this with IT applications; we have an attitude of if it works, don't touch it. In the long run, this attitude is a mistake.

Concluding Remarks

Large IT projects are notorious for overruns, being over budget, and not satisfying their business management. I looked at four reasons why this might be:

- **Context design problems.** The requirements have been gathered, not designed. This is much more likely to be a problem in a large project because the context design is that much bigger.

- **Lack of end user support.** There is a temptation for the designers to listen to the stakeholders from management rather than the end users, and there is a temptation for management to use a new application to force business change. But if the end users aren't behind the application or at least neutral, they can cause enormous problems.

- **Technical design problems.** Changing the technical design halfway through a project can be very costly in both time and money. Since large projects often have demanding technical requirements, projects should ensure that the design is right. The way to ensure that it is right is to test it at the start of the project instead of at the end.

- **Procurement and outsourcing.** Many large projects are implemented entirely or in part by external contractors. If the relationship with the contractor is poor, problems may be exploited for financial gain or simply not reported in a timely fashion. Part of the solution is to understand that the different designs need different styles of project management.

The alternative approach is to avoid doing large projects when possible, which can often be done by using an SOA approach. The hurdle is psychological; management must invest in the old applications to turn them into SOA applications, a first step that has little obvious business benefit.

My final point is to keep business management engaged. The business managers have to take responsibility for the requirements and for the rollout. They have to understand the design approach taken, they must realize the impact of this on project management, and they must realize when estimates can be accurate. They must also understand the importance of keeping the end users on board. Above all, they must be active participants in the project.

This chapter concludes the opening series about the whole of context-driven design. The next series of chapters look at the context design, the user interface design, the database design, and the technical design in more detail.

Chapter 5

The Relationship with the Business

This chapter and the next are about context design. This chapter is mainly concerned with how you identify the application design tasks and understanding the dependencies between the tasks. It also considers the wider subjects of aligning the application with the organization's strategy and understanding how senior management views the application development. In the next chapter we will look at the detailed specification of the task. If you like, this chapter is about trying to please management and the next is about trying to please the workers.

There is plenty written in books and papers about how to gather requirements. You can do interviews one-on-one or collectively, face-to-face or remotely, maybe have a brainstorming session, read existing documentation, research technical and marketing trends, and/or find out what competitors are doing. This is not the focus of this chapter; on these subjects I have little to add to what has already been written. Instead of discussing how you should talk to management, this chapter is about what you should talk to them about.

First, I step back a bit and discuss business processes in general since it is vitally important to understand how the tasks underpin the processes. However, business process analysis does not suit all parts of a business, and I discuss this after the section on business processes. This is followed by two sections—"The Need for a Wider View" and "Applying the Business Strategy to Application Development"—that discuss the aims of executive management and how these should influence IT development. Finally, I look at how this top layer of the context design can be analyzed.

Understanding Business Processes

A process is a description of all the steps that are taken to produce an outcome. The outcome can be any of a wide range of things—for instance, a product delivered, an IT application developed, a service provided. As a programmer you are probably familiar with processes in the context of development methodologies and project management methods, and you have probably realized by now that a process description can range from being very prescriptive to being very loose. An example of a very prescriptive process is manufacturing something; all the steps and the ordering of the steps are exactly defined and repeated accurately for every item. An example of a very loose process is making a sale; the steps and their order are poorly defined, and only the outcome is clear.

Both sales and manufacturing are part of an overarching process from sale to manufacture, to delivery, and to billing; thus you can have processes embedded within processes.

Processes are often illustrated with a process diagram. The example that follows is inspired by the struggles my wife and I had persuading the water company to mend a leak outside our house. A man came to investigate, discovered there was a leak, and decided to ignore it. I complained again, and this time the man came and sprayed blue paint on the cover to the stopcock. The man raised a new work number—a number to identify the job. Nothing happened. I complained again, and this time not only did the man paint the cover to the stopcock blue again but something happened—some days later another team came to dig a hole, fix the leak, and fill the hole. A few days later they were followed by yet another team to put the pavement (that is sidewalk in American English) slabs back. The process is illustrated in Figure 5.1. The outcome from the process is a mended water pipe or stopcock.

The rectangles mean "Do something"—these are called activities. The rhombus is a decision point. The arrows show the flow from one activity to another. The solid circle is the start, and the circle within a circle is an endpoint. Activities or decision points joined by a line can take place immediately one after the other, but often a line means a delay. The delay could be because

- There is one person whose job it is to do the first activity in a sequence while there is another person whose job it is to do the second activity in the sequence, as in the separate team in my example to fix the pavement/sidewalk.

- The process is waiting for an external event like a stock item being replenished. In our example an event was me phoning up and asking what had happened, but it didn't so much as kick a process into action as start a new one.

- The process is waiting for a resource. In our example, waiting for a resource would be waiting for a team to be assigned to the job.

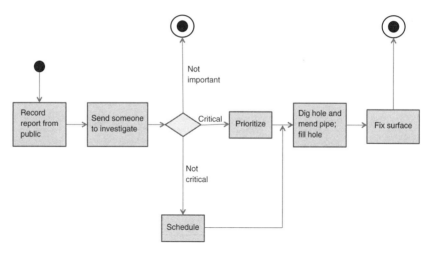

Figure 5.1 *A Process Diagram*

The process shown in Figure 5.1 would be a lot more complicated in practice. For instance, the team fixing the breakage may discover they can't do the fix—they need to call in some extra help. This in turn may mean that the schedule for upcoming jobs needs to be rearranged.

For developing a context design you need to convert a process view into a task view. This is illustrated in Figure 5.2. Recall that a task is one person doing one thing at one time. Some of these activities are done by teams, but only one person in the team actually reports what is going on as far as the IT application is concerned, and that person is going to report only that the work is completed or the work has not been completed. Note, too, that I have drawn a thick line to the Schedule Teams task. This is because I am assuming it is automatic, and the line represents a message sent from one task to another. It is not included in the Investigator task because it need not be done immediately while the investigator is waiting.

What is apparent from Figure 5.2 is where the delays are, because except for the automatic scheduling task, any lines that leave one task and go into another indicate a delay of some sort.

For each task you must answer the question, "How does this task start?" In this example, the Call Center task is started by a customer phoning the call center. The Investigator task, however, is started by an investigator reading a list of what incidents need visiting and going to investigate. Thus, from the IT application's perspective, the Investigator task needs to be broken down into two tasks: (1) Look at the list and decide what to do, and (2) Report on the investigation. Likewise, the Fix Pipe task is also two tasks: (1) Find out what fixes are scheduled today for my team, and (2) Report the progress of doing the fix. Figure 5.2 is wrong; we should redraw it showing the additional tasks as in Figure 5.3.

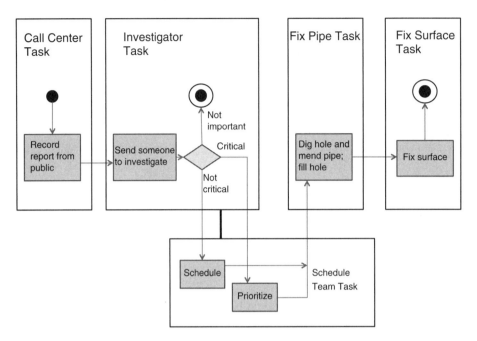

Figure 5.2 *First Draft of Mapping Tasks onto a Process*

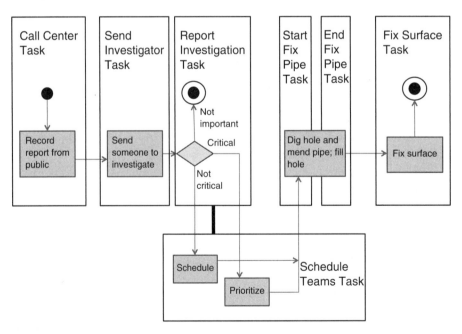

Figure 5.3 *Second Draft of Mapping Tasks onto a Process*

The next stage is to look at the data needed to make this process work. There is clearly a Work Items table that stores all reported incidents and the progress toward fixing them, and a Schedule table that assigns the teams to the work items. There may be three Schedule tables, one for investigators, one for pipe fixers, and one for surface menders. I am going to assume that investigators schedule themselves; for instance, each investigator may have an assigned geographical area. I have also renamed some of the tasks to make the names more meaningful. The result is a context design that looks like Figure 5.4.

If you were to discuss this context model with business management, I think you would find something to change. For instance, there is a discussion to be had around what happens if a team sent to fix a pipe fails to fix it or simply runs out of time. When they report their status, it is apparent that there is a possibility that another team may be sent to help them out or that they will take longer and other work items will be delayed. Perhaps the Report Pipe Fix task should also send a message to the Schedule task. And what happens if a team does the Find Pipe Fix Assignment but forgets to do the Report Pipe Fixed task? You don't know whether the pipe is fixed

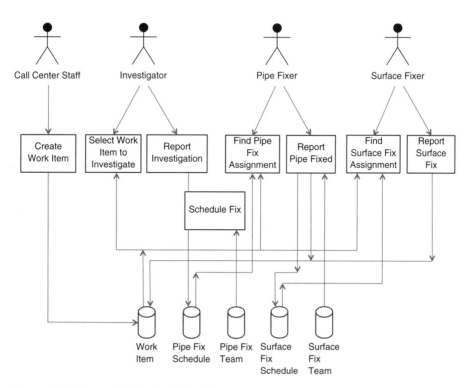

Figure 5.4 *Context Design for Fixing Pipes*

and the team forgot to report the fact or they never did the fix. Forgetting to report back on actions taken is especially likely soon after the IT application is rolled out, so if the system makes a mess of handling it, the application could quickly gain a reputation for poor quality.

Even without modifying the process it is clear that the context design is incomplete because no tasks put data into the Pipe Fix Team table or the Surface Fix Team table. Thus we need some additional tasks, which are illustrated in Figure 5.5. Note that some of these tasks may cause the schedule to be changed, so perhaps they should also send a message to the Schedule Fix task.

The fact that I have ended up with two context designs for different parts of the application is typical. Basically, the problem with all diagrams for IT applications is that they quickly become too busy. I could have drawn everything on one large piece of paper, and sometimes it is fun to do so, but in practice I usually find it is easier to draw several diagrams. I call these separate parts common purpose groups. It is worth showing how the common purpose groups interact. This can be done diagrammatically, as in Figure 5.6.

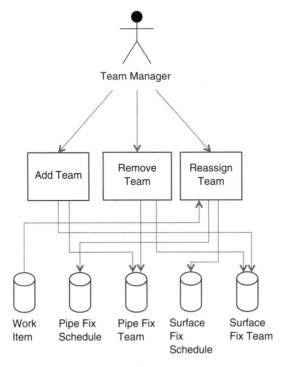

Figure 5.5 *Context Design for Fixing Pipe Management*

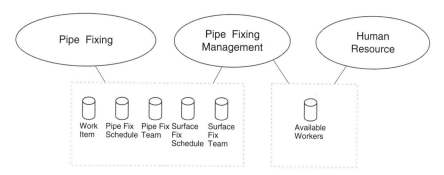

Figure 5.6 *Common Purpose Groups*

I have tried to show some of the thought processes involved in turning a business process model into a context design and have shown that as you do so you identify more and more tasks. Many business analysts are comfortable with process diagrams and will want to do the analysis in detail before identifying the tasks. That is, of course, no problem; it's up to them. If process optimization is done well, it can seriously improve the performance of the business by eliminating delays, detecting errors early, and finding and fixing bottlenecks. Whatever the complexity, a context design is a check on the business process analysis since it puts the focus on how the data supports the business process and who does what, which are two important points that are not obvious from looking at a process diagram.

As mentioned earlier, some business processes are not represented well in process diagrams. This is sometimes because they are too unstructured, but it may also be that the ways their activities interact don't fit well with the conventions of the process diagram. I understand a process diagram by imagining a token going through the diagram rather like a train going on model train tracks. The problems come when the token merges or splits. For instance, take police incident reporting. It looks like a classic process where an incident is reported and acted upon, but several people may report the same incident, and sometimes the reports make it look as if there are two or more incidents. When the police realize there is only one incident, the incident records are merged. The opposite can happen; a car crash simultaneous with a robbery might start off as one incident and later be handled as two. In any event, taking a task view of the process is sometimes easier than drawing a process diagram.

Often, too, a process diagram is incomplete. This is commonly true for handling errors. As noted earlier, it is common that business process diagrams are simple when everything goes according to plan but complex when it doesn't, like an order for a discontinued product or a piece of equipment breaking down. What often happens is that the error handling is handed over to a human. There is nothing wrong with that, of course, but you need to consider two points:

- How does the person handling the error get access to the data needed to understand the problem?

- When the problem has been fixed, what needs to be updated in the database to ensure that other tasks don't leap into action and do something silly? For example, if you cancel a delivery and ask for a repayment, you don't want a demand for money to follow in three months' time.

Business process analysis is not my expertise, but my advice is to remember that the purpose of the process is the outcomes. It is always worth thinking about the outcomes. For instance, what are the outcomes of a police incident management system? First and most importantly, one outcome is to send resources to an incident to stop something bad from happening, but there are other outcomes—gathering information that may go forward to a criminal prosecution, helping liaison with other emergency services, pleasing the statistics gatherers, and helping to reassure the public (not to mention the voters). Put like that, it is quite a daunting list. Against this must be balanced the organization's concerns—efficient use of resources, speed of process completion, avoidance of errors where possible, and speedy and accurate handling of errors where not.

When It's Not a Process

While business process is an excellent place to start in developing a context design, many business functions don't easily fit into the process mold. They could be one-task processes, such as using an ATM to withdraw money from a bank account; or they could be too vague, such as management tasks; or they could have outcomes that are too poorly defined, such as whatever the outcome is for a personal assistant doing his or her job well. So how do you capture all the tasks when there aren't any nice, neat process diagrams available?

In what follows I give three answers to this question, though I suspect there are others that haven't occurred to me.

Business Services

An alternative way to look at the business is as a provider of services, essentially asking the question, "What business services do you want to provide and to whom do you want to provide them?" An online banking system is an example of a service. Within a service, you need to break down its functionality by asking, "What are the requests?" For an online banking service the answer might be to move money between accounts, make a payment, change personal information, open a new account, and so on.

Don't confuse a business service with an application service as described in Chapter 2, "A Hierarchy of Designs." A business service may not have an IT element at all. Cutting hair is a business service. An application service is an IT application— it is 100% IT.

Within a business service there may be processes. Within a banking service, for example, there is a simple process for handling standing orders. It consists of three activities: creating a standing order, paying a standing order, and canceling a standing order.

And the opposite applies; you sometimes see services embedded within a process. These can be thought of as internal business services in contrast to external business services, which are targeted toward the business's customers. For instance, in our process example you can treat scheduling as an internal business service to the process. You elaborate an internal business service just like an external business service by asking, "What are the requests?" Think of some in our example:

- The investigator will find a problem and make a request to the scheduler for a fix team to be sent and at the same time define the size of the problem, the urgency, and whether any special equipment is required.

- The fix team may come along, suck their teeth, and say, "We can't fix this," and then will set up a different job profile, for instance, asking for some extra equipment.

- Alternatively, the fix team may run out of time and tell the scheduler that they will finish the next morning and all other jobs will be delayed.

- Management may tell the scheduler that one team is disbanded or some equipment has broken down.

Thus you have all these different demands coming at the scheduler from all directions, and the scheduler has to deal with them. These requests end up being implemented as tasks or being called within tasks.

Business services sometimes are completely automated and convert to application services. However, note that you should identify all the requests before even considering how much of the service can be automated.

Resource Management

A common situation is managing a resource, which I touched upon in Chapter 2. You can view resource management as a kind of business process, but frankly it is easier to go straight to a task description. For instance, to illustrate how a police car is managed, you might show a diagram such as Figure 5.7.

In reality, I suspect there are many more tasks in this example—perhaps for managing call signs or cleaning the car.

The key elaboration step is to identify the possible states of the resource. In the patrol car example the states might be Being Commissioned, Available, In Use, In Maintenance, and Damaged Needs Assessment. For each state there needs to be a task that puts the car into the state and a task that takes it out of the state.

Managing resources is something that might happen within another process. We have seen an example. To distribute a customer's order, the system might use one of the organization's trucks. The trucks need to be managed. Thus several tasks in the distribution application—Allocate Driver, Report Incident, Make Truck Available— will also be some of the tasks that manage the truck resource. This example illustrates that if you start discovering tasks by looking at a process, you can find yourself discovering more tasks when you find a related or overlapping process, and if you were to let this discovery continue, you can end up finding a vast number of tasks. At some point you have to draw a line and stop, but you need to go a bit beyond the core area you have been sent to explore because that will raise important questions about integration with other applications and databases.

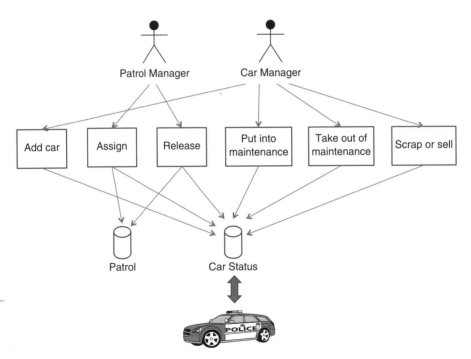

Figure 5.7 *Tasks Associated with a Patrol Car*

Reviewing and Monitoring

Another area where process diagrams don't fit well is in applications that review and/or monitor something. (Again, you can probably draw a process diagram to represent this situation, but in my experience it would add very little.) Examples are personnel reviews, plan reviews, and monitoring machinery. Project management software fits in here, at least in its status-reporting aspect.

Some questions to think about include the following:

- Should you monitor by review or by event? Reviews are done on a regular basis irrespective of whether anything of note has happened. Event monitoring is entirely reactive.
- What are the escalation procedures?
- Who can see what data?

This last point is important. Reviewing and monitoring are done by management, and management is organized into hierarchies. Everything a manager sees, his or her boss wants to be able to see, and so on up the chain of command.

Many review applications take input data from other applications and are used for management reporting, which we will discuss in the next chapter.

The Need for a Wider View

The previous two sections are about the practicalities of identifying the tasks, but the context design must address a more fundamental question: "Does the application satisfy the needs of the organization?" In Chapter 4, "The Problem of Large Applications," I discussed two studies showing dissatisfaction with IT project delivery. The studies didn't agree; the study that asked the project managers recorded a much higher level of satisfaction than the one that asked the management. I know of no study that explores this discrepancy, but there is one straightforward explanation. The project managers believed the projects were a success because they delivered what the stakeholders asked for, but the business manager didn't think the projects were a success because they did not deliver what the business wanted.

In this section and the next I explore the gap between formal requirements and what the business actually needs. Even if a context design satisfies its identified stakeholders, it may not satisfy the business needs. It may be that

- It is too expensive
- It breaks the law

- It is contrary to the organization's direction and strategy

- One or more of the stakeholders have their own agenda and are pushing the development in a direction the rest of the business dislikes

- By the time the project is completed, the opportunity it is meant to exploit has gone away

But why should IT application designers worry about any of this, and, if they think an IT project is setting off in a direction not entirely compliant with the direction of the organization, is there anything they can do about it? There are three reasons why an IT application designer should be sensitive to the wider needs of the organization:

- The designer is contracted to the organization as a whole, not to the people within the organization. The designer's duty is to the organization.

- The success of the project impacts the designer's reputation. Imagine a prospective client visiting your current client. I don't think what is written in the contract will have any bearing on what your prospective client is told.

- The designer has responsibilities to society as a whole. That means he or she should not aid and abet illegal activities. Arguably the designer should also not develop applications that are unethical but still legal, but I will leave that discussion to others.

Taking a wider view of the organization should not be a problem during context design because the size and shape of the project are not clear. However, I suggest that you ask more than one person to explain what the business as a whole wants out of the project.

In practice, sometimes a person you would like to talk to makes himself or herself unavailable. Thus, everything that I write in this chapter should be tempered with the thought that some clients are a dream to work with and some are just difficult.

So given that you think you should be conscious of the wider concerns of the organization, how do you act differently? You should do the following:

- **Look for gaps.** Look for gaps in the requirements as defined by the stakeholders. Eliciting what people hope for from an application is not a one-way listening process. You must respond, ask questions, even challenge. You really want to get insights into what they are thinking, not only what they want in the specifics, but also what their long-term aims are.

    One of the ways of broadening the input to the design is to increase the number of stakeholders. If you ask a manager the question, "Who are the stakeholders for this project?" you are likely to be told only of the potential users of the application or their representatives. In other words, the interpretation of the word *stakeholder* is narrow. You should look beyond this to the wider number of stakeholders. Besides direct users of the application— typically, the workers and their managers—there are also indirect users of the application such as the consumers of the data created by the application or people who work in a follow-on business process activity.

Senior managers often assume that junior managers are eager and able to explain the organization's long-term objectives. Well, maybe, but they often do so with a unique slant of their own.

- **Provide guidance for hard-to-document requirements.** Very few business managers know how to specify the requirements for an IT development project. But even if they have some experience, there are some areas where there are difficulties. In other words, they need guidance. One example is security. When clients say they want good security, do they mean security against a casual hacker or security that would not look out of place for the inner sanctums of the Department of Defense? Partly because the notion of "good security" is so unclear, security experts ask different questions: "What are the threats and what damage is done if there is a security transgression?" Another example of hard-to-document requirements is the "look" of a Web site. If clients say they want to look modern and youthful, do they mean a clean look, a trendy look (e.g., all the text in lowercase), and lots of primary colors, or would they prefer something dark and edgy?

- **Be conscious of what senior management thinks of the project.** The senior management perspective may be different from the local perspective. You want to know if managers are so unhappy that the project is likely to be canceled or undergo wrenching change. Sometimes you see a project that does not have the support of a large section of the organization. Of course, that may be because the application supports controversial internal changes. But it could be that the organization is just not fully committed to the program of change. What you might do in this case is to bring forward a release date and rejig what features are implemented in each release.

- **Try for transparency.** You want to ensure that a wide range of people know what is being planned so they can have their say. Transparency can be hard; for some reason people in business delight in secrets, even completely unnecessary secrets. They even try to keep secrets from their management; for instance, sales people keep a tight hand in negotiating their quotas, and projects are notorious for large slippages when they are nearing their finish date. You should try to involve everyone who you think needs to know and ask them to identify others. It has been observed that projects work better with senior management support. This is when you need it, because when someone suggests you don't involve this group or that group, you can politely reply that this is a decision that belongs to senior management.

- **Look for creative solutions.** Someone should look beyond the narrow requirements of the application to see if more can be done to meet the business goals. The successful online companies show this well. Amazon is always telling you what else to buy. Facebook is always trying to get you to add more information to your profile.

In a nutshell, the context design designer needs to be business aware.

Applying the Business Strategy to Application Development

Often you hear that the application development is in support of the business strategy. However, there are many approaches to business strategy [29], and it is often far from clear what the business strategy is. Instead of asking what it is, it is easier to ask what it does. The answer is that the strategy is meant to guide

- **Investment decisions**—where to expand and where to contract, for instance
- **Product decisions**—what products and services the organization supplies
- **Program decisions**—plans to change what people do in the organization

It is this last one that is particularly difficult and, unfortunately, particularly involves IT. It is worth noting that often the real strategy is not written down (or at least not so that the context designer can see it) and may even be contradicted by the published strategy. For instance, a business may say it is going after high-value customers but is in fact saving money in such a way as to deter high-value customers.

Sometimes you will find out that senior managers aren't wholeheartedly behind your project, maybe because it is a pet project of only one of them and the others would rather see the money spent elsewhere. In this case it becomes even more important to understand where most of the benefits lie, which parts of the application are welcomed by everybody, and which parts are more controversial.

In the previous chapter I wrote that during context design you should take the trouble to understand the fundamental business requirement. From this you need to create a list of the benefits and risks of the project.

You can take this a step further. For each of the benefits you can list the functionality that supports that benefit and then assess each one against the following criteria:

- The need for speed of development
- The balance between cost, performance, and availability

- The degree to which the application is experimental
- How long it will take for the business benefits of the application to materialize
- The need for security
- Whether the application has an impact on the customers' and the internal users' perception of the organization's culture
- Whether the application is supportive of changes to the organization's culture
- The degree to which the application is expected to change in response to changes to the business
- Whether the application supports a learning organization

Occasionally, considering these points will lead to reassessment of some of the application's functionality. More commonly, it will impact how you package features into releases, how you do the rollout, and how you manage the development project.

These points are further explained in the following subsections.

Speed of Development

The obvious way to speed up development is by cutting back the functionality or delaying some functionality by putting it into a later release.

An extreme way to speed up development is by releasing a version that cannot scale sufficiently. In a start-up company this may well be the optimum strategy because the business is strapped for cash and wants to exploit an opportunity before others do. Of course, the business may end up implementing the application twice—once with a slow version to start with and then with a fast version for when the company has grown sufficiently that it needs it.

In practice, projects attempt to speed up development by cutting back on testing. This is almost always counterproductive.

Cost versus Performance and Availability

The requirements for performance and availability are set by the needs of the organization, but sometimes you can compromise. For instance, peak performance may be needed only a few times per year, and the organization may be willing to live with a slow response time during this period because the cost of the additional hardware is too painful (perhaps they are hoping hardware prices will fall, making it possible to improve performance in later years). Another example could be related to availability; while it may be desirable to wait only a few seconds to switch to backup hardware after a fault has occurred, it may that a one-hour delay is tolerable.

Experimental Business Programs

The application may support a new method of working. For instance, it may support a new kind of maintenance contract but the business isn't sure how many customers will take the new option. In extreme cases, you may want to manage the new business stream rather as if it were a start-up company.

How Long Before the Benefits

Some applications have an indirect influence on the bottom line. For instance, they may improve the customer experience or reduce the number of manufacturing errors. The organization won't see monetary gain from the application until sales improve through increased customer satisfaction. It could be that there is no increase in sales because the application simply enables the business to keep up with the competition. Senior management may feel that developing the application is just the cost of staying in business, but sentiment can move against such applications because it's so hard to put a figure on the benefits. You should try to find ways in which the application itself can help measure the benefits, such as providing a simple report on how many manufacturing errors or reworks are done.

The Need for Security

The question is whether the application makes it more or less likely that there will be a damaging security breach. Is the organization prepared to take the steps necessary to protect against incursions? For instance, a small organization may start keeping customers' personal information but have no idea that this needs a magnitude change in their approach to security.

Designing for the Existing Culture

The IT application can reinforce an organization's perception of itself. Aspects of the design that are affected are

- **The application access device.** Some organizations are happy with PCs, but others want smartphones, tablets, and so forth.
- **The screen design.** A conservative organization will prefer a design that is straightforward and businesslike. An organization that fancies itself as fashionable and cool will want something more edgy and, maybe, more fun.

An expert on screen design look and feel is invaluable for getting this right, but you should sit down with the screen designer and see if you have a common perception of what the business culture is and how it should be reflected in the design.

- **The degree to which the organization is willing to take risks on availability, loss of data, performance, and security.** A bank, for instance, will have higher levels of risk aversion than an online shopping site.

- **The degree to which the workers will be monitored.** Some organizations seem to distrust their workers, while some are much more relaxed.

- **Attitude toward security.** Good security requires discipline from the staff. Some organizations are willing to impose this discipline; others aren't.

Design for a Culture to Which the Organization Aspires

The IT application may be part of a program for transforming the culture of the company. You can build an application that tries to show the values of the culture to which the organization aspires, making it more slick and fashionable, for instance. But it is easy to make an IT application that is bureaucratic and tedious; there is a tendency for IT applications to push the culture toward the bureaucratic and the authoritarian.

"Culture" may sound nebulous, or what we Brits would call "airy-fairy." But it can have a real impact on applications. In the previous chapter I discussed the difficulties of making a CRM application work well. One reason is that CRM applications work best in a culture that puts an emphasis on a disciplined approach to sales, "doing things by the book," if you will. Many sales teams aren't like that. They are results driven and secretive. I remember being told that "loose talk costs quotas"—the game being that you want to exceed your quota so you should hide a few potential deals from your manager during quota negotiations so they aren't included. In this kind of culture, CRM applications face an uphill struggle to work well.

Senior management may be hoping that introducing CRM will change the culture. Experience shows that this doesn't work unless the new IT application is introduced as part of a bigger program of change that includes such elements as training and perhaps a reorganization. From an IT designer's point of view, you want to see senior business management involved in the rollout and fully aware of the task ahead of them. The IT designers should ask themselves what they can do to make the application easier to sell.

Allow for Changing Plans

One of the common complaints about IT applications is that they are hard to change, and therefore they can make it hard to change the business.

If the change is anticipated, it can be accommodated, but this can be taken too far. It takes longer to develop an application that supports not only existing business processes but future business processes as well. It is also more difficult to design. Thus you pay a price for making it easy to implement an anticipated change only for the change not to happen. Instead, a change is made elsewhere in an area where stability was anticipated.

You should discuss with the stakeholders the likelihood of change, where the change is most likely to materialize, and how to manage change.

Support a Learning Organization

Sometimes a few small changes to an IT application can greatly assist organizational learning.

The application's help system can provide guidance on doing the job as well as on the details of the user interface.

There can be a built-in way for people to provide feedback. The feedback can be extended (if you dare) to allow users to report constraints—things that make it difficult for them to do their job—and techniques that make doing their job easier. Occasional surveys can be built in.

You can build into an application code to monitor how users use the application. At the very least you want to know what features the users use and what features they ignore. In an online shopping application, you can monitor how long they take, whether they abort tasks halfway through, and what products they look for. You can monitor how people seek help from your organization and perhaps provide more ways for customers or employees to give their input. There is no point in doing any of this unless you use the input to make changes. If you do make changes, it is a good idea to advertise the fact to make the users feel listened to.

Non-Business Applications

In this section I have been writing in the main about businesses. What about government departments, the military, and all the other non-business users of IT? There are of course huge differences. They are not allowed to go out of business, and rather than pressure coming from the competition, it comes from politicians and public scrutiny (in democratic countries at least). But the pressure is real nonetheless, and everything I have written in this section applies to them. Strategy and planning might be more top down than is typical in commercial organizations, but they have a culture, which may be in need of change, and they need to be better at becoming learning organizations.

Analysis

Three categories of analysis are done at the task dependency level. The first is a simple check on whether the process is well formed. The second is an analysis of the dependencies, and the third is an analysis of the objectives.

At the back of this book is Appendix A, "Context Design Checklist," that provides a checklist of all the different kinds of analysis. The list is structured a bit differently from the following discussion because there is overlap with some analysis points discussed in Chapter 6, "The Relationship with the Users," which looks at task analysis.

Is the Process Well Formed?

This is simply a check that the process diagram hasn't got errors. For instance, all boxes must be connected. Processes mostly have one good endpoint but maybe several error endpoints. You need to ensure that the process ends up on only one of the expected endpoints.

Processes often have loops and therefore could in theory last forever. How long a process should last is always a good topic for discussion with users because it will almost certainly lead to a discussion of what monitoring of the information is required. The monitoring information should not only tell us why something is not being done in time but should also, if possible, give an idea of where the delay is.

How the process handles errors is important. The key question is whether it handles all the errors. Handing an error over to a person to decide what to do is acceptable, but that person must have all the information needed to make a decision, and once a decision has been made, the system should be able to enact a change that does not spoil the integrity of the process. For instance, if an order is canceled in whole or in part, the money is refunded.

Dependency Analysis

In dependency analysis you need to investigate at least the following:

- Task flow
- Data on tasks

- Tasks on an external channel

- Data on an external entity

- Overarching integrity constraints

These are described in more detail in the following subsections.

Task Flow

Task flow can be analyzed as a task outcome diagram. An example is shown in Figure 5.8, which illustrates a series of tasks associated with picking goods from a warehouse so that they can be packed and delivered to customers. The complexity arises from what happens when there aren't any of the ordered goods in stock. Each box is a task with the task name at the top and a list of outcomes. Each circle is some data passed between the tasks. The data shown is not all the data shared by the tasks but only the data that is used to drive the next receiving task. Attached to each outcome is one of the following:

- **A line to a data object that is read by a follow-on task.** We are not capturing all data updates but only the ones that are used to control the process. There is flexibility here. One outcome may have a line pointing at two or more data objects (e.g., the "Partial success" outcome in Picking Done in Figure 5.8). One data object may have more than one follow-on task (e.g., "Pending picking list" in Figure 5.8).
- **An "R."** This means redo the task.
- **An "End."** This means there is no follow-on task.

There are two failure outcomes you must think about:

- The IT application has failed, for instance, through a hardware or software failure.
- The end user for the task has left the task before completing it.

For all the tasks in the example, both of these failure outcomes result in a redo, so they have been merged into one line.

The purpose of the task outcome diagram is twofold. One purpose is to ensure that the tasks truly do support the process. You want to ensure that every path in the process has a corresponding path in the task outcome diagram. Also, you want to ensure that you don't have any lines dangling in thin air, and this is a check on the

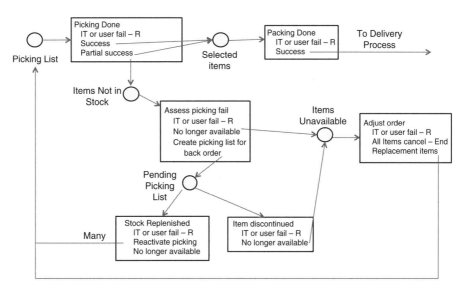

Figure 5.8 *Task Outcome Diagram*

completeness of the process. The second purpose is placing a requirement on the low-level designs. In the next chapter I will describe writing task descriptions, and by reading those you should be able to figure out how all the lines are implemented.

Earlier in this chapter I mentioned that you can think of process diagrams as tokens running on a network made up of activities, decisions, and connecting lines, analogous to trains running on a model railway track. I also said that this becomes harder to understand when the tokens split or merge. Figure 5.8 is an example of this. In the order-processing process, the tokens are—unsurprisingly—the order forms data, but one order might split into many parcels for delivery; some of the parcels may be delayed waiting for stock to be present; and some of products ordered may be canceled. The task outcome diagram is sometimes an easier way to understand what is going on than a process diagram. For instance, in Figure 5.8 we see that the order is converted into a picking list, but if some of the items aren't available, a new picking list is created and put into a pending queue waiting for stock to be replenished. Also, we see that either while building the new pending picking list or later when examining the pending list, the application might find that a product has been discontinued and hence the picking list is modified or canceled.

Task outcome diagrams aren't only useful for tasks that participate in processes. Tasks that are used to manage resources can also be drawn this way. For business service tasks, they are less relevant as most of the tasks won't have lines to other tasks. If they do, you may have uncovered a small business process (like the online banking standing order process I mentioned previously).

Data on Tasks

Data depends on tasks simply because every entry in a data table must be created in some task somewhere, used by some task somewhere—or copied to an information analysis system—and deleted or archived by another task.

If data is used in a process but not created by the process, it must be created before the process is used.

Tasks on an External Channel

Sometimes a service is called directly by an external channel, for instance, in an automatic response to a text message. Sometimes a task or a service sends a message to an outside channel. The issue that needs to be explored is what needs to be done to tie the output to an external channel to the input from an external channel. Suppose the application is sending a purchase order to another company. It may send the message that holds the purchase order but then get a message back that says yes or no. The application must realize that the yes or no applies to a particular purchase order and no other.

Data on an External Entity

Some data tracks the status of an external entity. Resource handling is one example (refer to Figure 5.7)—entries in the Car Status table must reflect the current status of a car. Resource handling is not the only example. Customer data tables also track an outside entity, in this case a person or an external organization. If the person has a new address, you want the customer entry for that person to be updated, which means there should be a task somewhere that does the updating or perhaps a service that is called from many places.

Overarching Integrity Constraints

It is useful to document rules about the process or service. For instance, in a bank account one rule should be that the account total equals the sum of all debits and credits. This means, for instance, that if you pay interest on the account, there is a credit record created for the interest payment. Banks' accounting rules insist that where there is a credit on an account, there is a debit on another account. Thus when the bank pays you interest, there is a credit on your account and a debit on the bank's account, and if someone transfers money from another account belonging to another bank, there is a debit against the other person's bank.

In order processing, there should be an overarching integrity constraint that all items in the order should be paid for, and there should be no payments for extra items. This might sound so basic as to be stupid, but it is not so easy to enforce when you consider refunds for damaged products and cancellations. Another overarching integrity constraint is that orders must apply only to products that are currently being sold. In other words, when the company decides to withdraw a product for sale, it should immediately stop taking orders for that product.

In our pipe-fixing application, there should be an integrity constraint that all reported problems are either rejected or the pipe is fixed. In other words, it is unsatisfactory to leave the job partially done.

Objectives Analysis

Clearly the new business processes supported by the application should help achieve the overall business goal. But in addition, there will be more mundane objectives. These mostly fall into five categories: usability, improved efficiency, risk, reduced cost, and customer service.

- **Usability objective.** In the context design you are not at the stage of looking at screen layouts and detailed usability issues, but you are at the stage where you can ask the simple question, "How much work does the user have to do?" This is enormously important for usability. The technique to check usability is to look at each user group and examine what the new system makes them do. If users of a task have to input data, the questions are where the data comes from and how easy it is to acquire.

- **Efficiency objective.** Efficiency and usability often go hand in hand. However, besides workload, other aspects of efficiency are reduced delays, reduced errors, and increased consistency.

- **Risk.** A new application may introduce new risks. The risk could simply be the impact of application failure. Security risks may be introduced, such as the possibility of theft of personal data.

- **Cost objectives.** During the development of a context design, you will have noticed that the solution to problems of completeness or consistency is often to add extra tasks. When a new way of working is proposed, it is often the case that no one has anticipated these extra tasks. The question that arises is whether the new way of working is really as efficient as it first seemed. In reevaluating efficiency and cost, people may realize that another solution is better.

- **Customer service objectives.** It is always a good idea to look at a proposed improvement from the perspective of the customer. Does it make things better for them or worse?

Concluding Remarks

You can view the functional design of a system as consisting of three layers. There is the layer described in this chapter, which has to do with identifying tasks and understanding how the tasks fit together to help the business work. The next layer is about the details of the task, and the third layer is the user interface design.

In truth the process layer—the layer described in this chapter—is more about business design than it is about IT application design. However, the IT application designer must understand how the tasks fit together because, as we noted before, this information is essential for being able to manage change requests. A good context designer will be a business partner rather than simply a passive note taker and will help business management achieve its goals. That said, many business managers will find the creative part of thinking about a new application much more exciting than ensuring that the solution is complete and consistent, so the other role of the context designer is to keep everyone grounded.

I have discussed several techniques for analyzing task dependencies. Often the resolution of any problems discovered lies in the task detail description, which we will discuss in the next chapter. While I have described the design in three layers, I see the two layers of the context design being done at the same time. Using the warehouse picking example, if you are discussing this with the local expert, you wouldn't confine yourself to a discussion of the task dependencies. You would discuss both the task dependencies and the details at the same time. You would draw a context diagram and a task outcome diagram, document the task details, and then go back to the expert and say, "I think you told me this." And maybe you say, "By the way, we have a problem here [pointing at the diagram]—this outcome doesn't seem to lead anywhere." This mixing of the task dependencies layer and the task details layer is why there is one context design, not several levels of design. Actually, when you talk to people you are likely to be told things that are input to all levels of design, not to mention much else besides that is completely irrelevant. The framework I discuss in this book is a means to structure this information and to analyze it.

Chapter 6

The Relationship with the Users

In Chapter 5, "The Relationship with the Business," I discussed identifying application design tasks and the dependencies between tasks. In this chapter I discuss how to specify the details of a task. When identifying tasks and their dependencies, designers need to talk to subject area experts and senior managers; for task details they also need to talk to the application's end users or, more precisely, the end users' representatives.

This chapter has four parts. The first is about adding detail to the tasks, in other words, giving each task a text description. The second is about the different kinds of users an application has and how their needs differ. The third is about analyzing the context design, and the fourth is about context design reviews.

Adding the Detail

There are two reasons why it is important to add detail to the list of tasks defined by analyzing the task dependencies. The first is to verify that the tasks support the process. Recall the task outcome diagram in the previous chapter (Figure 5.8), and look at the top left-hand corner where there is a data structure called a Picking List. Do we need a picking list? Why not use the order forms directly? If we did so, we would have to accommodate the situation of a customer ordering ten gizmos when only five are available. We could put on the order line the number of items that had actually been picked. This would mean that the Picking task would have to look at the orders and present a list of all orders that have an order line in which the number picked is less than the number required. But some of the "unpicked" are unpicked because the

129

items are being reordered, and we don't want the picker to look at these orders. And we need to allow for items lost in delivery, so perhaps we need another count for the number of items delivered with all its attendant complexities. It is getting awfully complicated, which is why I went for the other design—having a separate Picking List structure. What I want to emphasize here is that actually both context designs are viable, but whichever one we choose, we have to make sure the details are right so that the overall business process works correctly. Deciding whether or not to have a Picking List data object is the design hypothesis. Working out the detailed task description is the design elaboration.

This leads to the second reason for task descriptions, which is that the designers to come, in particular the user interface designer and the database designer, need the detailed information.

The detailed description of the context design consists of the following elements:

- Tasks
- Task fragments
- Common purpose groups
- Data tables
- Messages
- User groups
- Security threat model

User groups are just a list of users, and their only job is to ensure that when I mention a user somewhere else I can cross-check the spelling with the user groups list.

The security threat model is described in Chapter 12, "Security Design."

This leaves tasks, task fragments, common purpose groups, data tables, and messages, which I describe in the following subsections. These are followed by a section on nonfunctional requirements and a section on who uses the context design.

There is nothing fancy about these descriptions. They consist of an element name under which are headings, and under each heading there is a list of points.

Naturally, comments can be put alongside any heading or point in a context design document. I suggest that you keep the comments short, and if you have nothing to say, don't say anything. For instance, don't make comments like "Account balance—this is the balance of the account." The context design details document is not only the output from the context design, it is also a working document and as such will for much of its life be incomplete. Being short and concise is important, and you need to be able to write notes to yourself or to other designers like "More to come" or "Must review with James."

Task Details

The information needed to define each task is the following:

- What the trigger for the task is, that is, what makes the user start doing the task. Some tasks are triggered by a message sent from another application. Some tasks are triggered by a time (e.g., paying monthly interest on an account). Some are triggered by a user logging on to the application and being given a list of jobs that need doing.

- Who the user groups for this task are.

- What data is displayed. Often users will need some data before they can do anything.

- Outcomes. What data in the database is created, updated, or deleted. What messages are sent.

- What messages are received.

- The task fragments that are included. Task fragments are a way of sharing task details across many tasks.

- A short narrative description of the task in numbered steps.

- The rules the task obeys. These rules may end up being implemented in the user interface, in the program code, or in the database.

- Notes. This is the place to put information you have been told when building the context design that will be useful for others in the project team.

- Review. This is a note to the designers and implementers about which stakeholders take a special interest in this task and want to review the implementation.

- Uncertainty. A measure of how certain the stakeholders are about all of this information.

If there is no information to add under one of the headings, leave it out.

Here is an example of a task description of a familiar online shopping task:

```
User: Customer.
User device: Web.
Started when: anytime driven by the customer. Need 24 x 364.
Data display:
    Product information—codes, price, whether it is an external
        vendor.
    Product category hierarchy for searching.
    Current promotion code—code, discount, conditions.
```

Customer—list of credit card numbers and delivery addresses
used by the customer.

Outcomes:

Alternatives

Purchase made: Order and Order lines records created.

No purchase made: no updates

Failure/timeout: no updates

Plus optionally

Update customer profile:

Credit card record created and/or deleted.

Delivery address record created and/or deleted.

Narrative:

1. Customers select products to buy and when they want to buy
they go to the next stage (called checkout).
Searching is by keyword and category.

2. Many customers won't buy and will exit at this point. If
they continue they must be logged on. They may be logged on
already.

3. Checkout: any order:
   - Specify the quantities.
   - Choose delivery addresses from list or add new one.
   - Choose method of payment—PayPal or credit card.
   - Edit or delete entries in credit card list.

4. Submit: Payment checks—PayPal or credit card payment.

5. Order processing:
   i.   Order entered in database.
   ii. Order line entries that are handled by external vendors
        must be sent to the external vendor while the line entries
        that are handled internally must be sent to company's
        dispatch system.

Rules:

- The order can be canceled anytime up to the completion of
  payment.
- Products are completely defined by their codes—for instance,
  if two products have different colors but are otherwise
  identical, they have different codes.
- Products must not be available to buy if they are
  presale or discontinued.
- No delivery is made until the payment is confirmed.
- If a credit card date has expired, ensure that it is
  amended before use.

Notes:

- Must ensure that customer payment data is secure.

- The task to edit the customer details—for delivery
  address list and credit card list—can be called at
  any time while the customer is logged on.
- Ease of use and convenience for the customer are paramount.
Review: the user interface design and implementation must be
  reviewed by marketing.

There are several points to highlight in this description. The first is that it is compact. It consists largely of headings and lists underneath the headings. Where the lines are numbered, the order is important. Where the lines are preceded by bullets, the order isn't important. There is no attempt at descriptions and little opportunity for creative prose. (You might be forced to put all this information into a *functional specification* or a similar document, in which case you might have to write executive overviews, descriptions, and much else besides. Personally I see little point in any of this, but it pleases some people.)

An overall glossary of business terminology is often useful as an adjunct to the context design, especially if you are new to the business area.

Many methods say who the owner of a task is, who the author is, when it was written, and where the information came from. I don't do any of this; it seems to me to be more an exercise in establishing who is to blame than a way to move the design forward.

You will also probably have noted that there is a small bit of redundancy. The list of data displayed and outcomes might be obvious from the narrative and rules. The reasons I have both are:

- The task description is often written incrementally, and I find I often list the data displayed and outcomes before I write the narrative.

- It allows the narrative to be shorter, if only because you don't have to say, "Display this data."

- The data displayed and outcomes is very useful for the database designer and anyone checking dependencies between task and data.

- It provides an analysis check on the task description: are all the data updates listed in the narrative, and are there additional data updates in the narrative that are not in the outcomes section?

You will see from this example that to explain what the task does I use both narrative and rules. I find this combination works well. Narrative is good at explaining any natural ordering of the actions. Rules are good at explaining what is not allowed to happen. Try to use the rules as much as possible; they give the user interface designer much more freedom to create something special. They also encourage you to think about rules that apply to more than one task and cross-application integrity checks.

You want to be sure that the narrative is not too prescriptive. Because it is a list of steps, there is a temptation to just add to the list when you think of something else that must be done. You should always think about the order in which the steps should be done, and if there is no particular order, don't give them one. Try to give the user interface designer as much flexibility as possible by imposing as little order as possible.

This example also shows how some important decisions are pushed down into detailed design and implementation; in this example, the product search facility is one of the most visible and important parts of the application, and all the task description says is that the customer selects a product by keyword and category and that marketing will review the user interface design and implementation. In the context design the idea is to explain what happens, not how it happens.

Another example of this principle is that while it says what data is displayed, it says nothing about in which narrative step the data is displayed. This is because saying so would be too prescriptive. For instance, while it might be necessary to display the list of delivery addresses during checkout, customers may also want to see them when reviewing their customer profiles.

The product search is key to the success of this application. I have mentioned before that prototypes and experiments are useful for technical design, but sometimes they are useful for functional design, and this may be an instance. Again, it is all about closing down the uncertainty and making sure as early as possible that you have a viable solution.

One way of thinking about writing a task description is that it should look upward; that is, make sure the task description supports the process. One analysis technique is to cross-check the tasks against the task outcome diagram described in the previous chapter (Figure 5.8). Put another way, the context design should not look downward; it should not do the user interface designer's job.

This simple task description will be converted into several screens, but this is the job of the user interface design.

In the context design, the fields on the screen or in the database are not defined in full, but some fields are necessary to mention in the narrative or rules simply to make a meaningful description of the proposed activity. For instance, it is difficult to describe online banking without talking about how much money is in an account.

What about inquiries—tasks whose main purpose is to display information? I use task descriptions for these as well. They usually don't have a data update section, but they might if data is being saved for later analysis or search and formatting criteria are being saved for running at a later time. They often don't have rules, but they might because the rules may say who can see what data.

Task Fragments

Task fragments are simply a way for several tasks to share the same logic. For instance, we may define a task fragment called Customer Online Banking, and then define two tasks:

```
Web Banking:
   Include Customer Online Banking.
   User device: Web browser.
Phone Banking:
   Include Customer Online Banking.
   User device: mobile phone app.
```

The format of a task fragment is exactly the same as that of a task. When a task fragment is included, all of its contents are added to the task description, just as if you copied the text from one to the other. (In the example, the Customer Online Banking fragment should not have a user device heading.)

The only exception is the narrative section. You may want to say at which point the narrative of the fragment is processed. For instance, for phone banking you may put:

```
Narrative:
   1. Collect information about location and ask additional
      security questions if the location is unusual.
   2. Include Customer Online Banking steps.
```

I suggest that you don't have a complex interleaving of task fragment steps; it's difficult to understand and to review.

Often you will find that you start by having a task fragment shared by two different tasks but over time the task descriptions diverge. As the design progresses, the task fragments become smaller, and you end up cutting and pasting the text from the fragment into the task description and modifying it there.

Common Purpose Groups

Common purpose groups are a way of grouping tasks, usually because they share much of the same data or they provide facilities for many of the same users. Common purpose groups are important simply because in a large application with tens or hundreds of tasks, they provide a way of organizing large amounts of information. It is especially common that several tasks have the same or similar data display needs, and with common purpose groups this can be defined once. Thus the context design can be made more compact. An example is Web banking.

Common Purpose Group: Web Banking

```
User: Customer.
User Device: Web.
Data Display:
   Accounts . . . that belong to the customer. For each:
      Transactions . . . for the last five years
      Standing orders on the account
      Direct debits on the account
      List of payees set up for this account
      Customer details . . . that belong to the customer
Tasks:
   Make payment.
   Move money between accounts.
   Set up standing order.
   Etc.
```

The task definitions are assumed to inherit all the specifications from the common purpose group. (And for the theoretician, no, I don't allow a task to belong to more than one common purpose group. This is not an object-oriented-like inheritance mechanism; it is a grouping mechanism.)

Data Tables

In addition to data tables in the task description I also list the data tables. This is partly to ensure that I can cross-check the names of the data tables in the task description to make sure I haven't called the same data table two different names in two different places. But for each table I add

- A list of any attributes that are mentioned in other context design text. Again, this is to ensure that I have been consistent about using the same data attribute name.

- A list of *data bags*. All the other data attributes I haven't described are conceptually put into a data bag. I can then say a task updates any of the attributes in the bag without having to spell out what they are.

- Any rules that apply solely to the one table. This is so that the rules need to be stated only once and not in every task that uses the table.

The concept of data bags needs explanation. In the context design I don't define all the data attributes for every data table. That is the job of the user interface design and the database design. Some data attributes are important, and they are listed. For instance, it would be hard to explain what a bank credit does without mentioning the account balance. But it is often the case that there are many other data attributes that are just descriptive. They may be given data values when the data object is created, they may be updated at any point, and they are read. But as far as the business processes are concerned, they are just passive containers of information. It takes time to finalize what descriptive data attributes are needed, and I don't want to spend this time during the development of the context design because there are too many uncertainties about what will happen to the project. So I lump all these data attributes into this notional data bag, which allows me to say that the bag is updated or displayed without having to worry about the structure within the bag.

Why there might be more than one data bag is described later in the chapter in "Data Used by Other Applications."

Messages

Messages are described similarly to data tables:

- Sent by: task or external entity.

- Received by: task or external entity.

- A list of attributes in the message that are mentioned in other context design text. This heading and the next are the same as for data tables.

- A list of data bags in the message.

- Reply messages: One or more messages may be expected as a reply to this message. For each reply you need to specify:

  - A list of attributes

  - A list of data bags

- Integrity: The underlying network may break—that is a fact of life. Message integrity is about what you want to do about it.

Message integrity needs additional explanation. There are two aspects of integrity that must be defined. First, do you want to guarantee that the message is delivered? That sounds like an odd question, but there are applications—such as a stock market update being sent every second—where timeliness is more important than guaranteed delivery. The second aspect is that if the message is delivered, do you want to guarantee that the receiver receives it only once? This too may sound odd, but normally the technique to guarantee delivery is to resend the message if there is any doubt whether it arrived. This may mean multiple copies of the same message arriving at the destination. In most circumstances you want guaranteed delivery and for the message to arrive once and only once. For this reason, if the integrity is not set, this is what the designers should assume by default.

Messages specified in the context design are always send and forget (also called deferrable), meaning that the sender does not wait for a reply. Other modes of messaging you may know about, like client-server where the sender waits for a reply, are always modeled in the context design as part of a task. It is up to the integration designer to decide to put part of the task logic into a separately callable service. If you see some logic that you want to share across tasks, put it into a task fragment.

In Figure 5.4, I showed the Report Investigation task sending a message to the Schedule Fix task. It was designed this way because the Schedule Fix task does not have to happen while the Report Investigation task is going on. When it comes to defining the actual Schedule Fix application, it could be decided that the scheduling is a nightly batch run. In practice I find that messages are rarely defined in the context design, and when they are, they are usually related to sending data to systems outside the scope of the context design.

Nonfunctional Requirements

These are performance requirements rather than what the application does in support of the business. Some people prefer the word *qualities*. There are many potential nonfunctional requirements [30], but I think the most important for IT applications are

- To do with speed
  - Response time
  - Response variability
- To do with scalability
  - Number of messages it can process
  - How much data it can hold
- To do with availability
  - Planned uptime
  - Unplanned downtime
  - Disaster recovery capability
- To do with maintainability
  - The quality of the information captured when there is a fault and the ease with which the fault report is routed to the right person
- To do with reliability
  - Number of faults found in a time period
  - The time taken to fix a fault

- To do with manageability
  - Effort needed to keep the application running
  - Effort needed to learn to operate the application
  - Effort needed to install a new version of the application
- To do with security—discussed in Chapter 12

The fact that there are so many possible nonfunctional requirements means that it is easy to go overboard defining each requirement with great precision. This might be important for contractual reasons but is rarely worth the effort otherwise.

In any event, there should be a base level of nonfunctional requirements for all the applications in an organization. Additional requirements should therefore be necessary only to define more exacting requirements that exceed the base level. The exception to this rule is the scalability requirements, which are unique to every application.

Thus nonfunctional requirements fall into three groups:

- **Organizational nonfunctional requirements.** These are typically ones having to do with systems administration and maintainability, but also minimum levels of security, response times, and availability.
- **Application-wide nonfunctional requirements.** These typically have to do with availability and data size.
- **Task nonfunctional requirements.** These are typically related to volume metrics.

I prefer not to specify the nonfunctional requirements for individual tasks but to specify them for groups of tasks. In most applications there is a group of tasks that require high performance and high availability and a (larger) group that does not, in particular, management reporting.

The question on breaks in service needs qualifying. There are four points that need to be clear:

1. How often can you tolerate breaks in service? It is possible to configure a system so there are no single points of failure, but let's be frank: most problems are caused by software problems and network problems.

2. If there is a break in service, how long will it be before serious pain sets in? Many applications can be down for a few seconds without anyone caring much. However, if an application is down for an hour, pain may set in.

3. How much planned downtime can be used for taking backups and updating the software version?

4. If there is a disaster (e.g., fire, flood), how long can the business tolerate the application being unavailable?

In addition to performance metrics, the technical designer will also need to know about the security requirements. Chapter 12 provides details about security requirements, but to give a flavor of the subject, the information needed includes

- The business risk of data falling into the wrong hands.

- The business risk of someone performing an unauthorized task.

- An answer to the question, "Against whom are you protecting the application?" (Or, put another way, "Whose are the wrong hands?") In particular, is it external people or internal people?

- Who in the organization is going to administer the security?

As discussed later in Chapter 12, business management needs a great deal of guidance to develop a security plan for a new IT application development.

Who Uses the Context Design?

When you write a context design, you should keep the readers in mind.

The user interface designer is interested in all parts of the task description.

Database designers need to look at the task descriptions, but their focus is largely on the data display and outcomes sections. That said, the narrative and rules often help the database designer understand the meaning of the data and identify data attributes.

It is also a good idea for technical designers to understand what the application does and, in particular, why and in what way it is important. However, they need some additional information. They will concentrate on the nonfunctional requirements.

All of the information in the completed context design should be reviewed by both the business managers and the application, database, and technical designers. You want to use diagrams backed up by text. I find it is fine to use presentation software like PowerPoint. You may be required to put all the information into a document as well, in which case you will probably have to pad it out with executive summaries and some general background explanation.

Who Are the Users?

The previous section gave you an idea of what the output from the context design exercise is. So how do you set about developing this output? Clearly, one starting point is the process layer description discussed in Chapter 5. However, while that gives you a good idea of the wants and needs of the people who are operating the process, there are many more people affected by the application. You must consider these people as well; they too are users of the application. So, who are they and what do they want from a new application?

I identify five categories of users. There are people

- Using the application to do work.

- Using the application to monitor the people doing the work.

- Using another application that uses data generated by your application. For example, an order delivery application relies on information gathered by an order entry application.

- Using the data generated by the application to do business analysis such as understanding which products are being sold to which customers.

- Doing application administrative tasks, such as assigning new users.

Each of these categories of users has different requirements and, as we shall discuss in this section, they may be contradictory.

Since it is unlikely that you will be able to talk to all the people who will use the new system, you have to talk to their representatives. Unfortunately, representatives might have their own agendas. Often the representatives are *analysts*, by which I mean they come from a planning department and might not have a true idea of the concerns of the workers. Sometimes the *workers* are the public at large, and what they want and how they will use the application is guesswork, ideally informed guesswork.

In general terms, what users want from an application is for the application to

- Make their work easier

- Not make them do work they don't want to do

- Perform well and reliably

- Look good

I suspect that this list is in priority order.

To understand the first item in the list, making the work easier, it is important to check whether the application replaces an existing application and to ensure that all its features are considered for the new application; they may not be implemented, but they must be deliberately set aside and not accidentally ignored. Also try to find an opportunity to watch the existing application in use because then you can ask what the users like and dislike about it.

You need to be wary about the second entry in this list: not making workers do work that they don't want to do. Managers and business analysts are forever requesting information about anything and everything. This is a common complaint in the public sector; the police complain about the amount of information they have to document for an arrest, and social workers complain about the information they must enter when they meet a client. Sometimes gathering information is important, but you should be aware that requesting too much is a recipe for turning a simple, streamlined application into a large, clumsy application. Senior management might prefer the cheaper, streamlined application, and the workers certainly will. This tension between different groups of users is what I meant when I wrote that different user groups may have contradictory requirements.

The message from the preceding paragraphs is that gathering requirements is very error-prone. It is easy to miss something, easy to misunderstand, and easy to be directed along a line that is not in the organization's best interest. The approach I recommend is to design a solution, review it with stakeholders, amend it, and review it again. And perhaps repeat the amend-review cycle a few extra times. People are better at criticizing than creating, and it is easier to see what someone else has forgotten than it is to remember everything yourself. Thus you should expect that at least during early reviews, people will ask for radical changes—in fact, expect as much input during the review as when you first visited the main stakeholders and asked for their requirements.

In the rest of this section I examine the five user categories: process operations, monitors, users of the data, data analysis, and application administration.

There is another category of users I don't discuss here, which is the team that has responsibility for the application's future. I have noted a few times that while I don't think application designers should try to second-guess the needs of the organization, I do think that they should look beyond the immediate release, putting in facilities to gather statistics on how the application is being used and giving the users opportunities to give their feedback. It could even save money if you realize that implementing additional features on a part of the application no one uses is not the best use of resources.

Business Process Operations

These are the people moving the business forward. They are the people working in the business processes or services. They may be internal staff or customers using online applications. Examples are the people submitting orders, making deliveries, checking guests into hotels, taking out money from an ATM.

Often these people are quite lowly in the business (even if they are the business's customers). But for the IT application developer they are important because how well the application works impinges directly on the efficiency of the organization; also, however lowly they are, if they don't like the application, the application is in trouble. I discussed this point in Chapter 4, "The Problem of Large Applications."

Monitoring by Management

The managerial oversight of processes or services will want information about the operation of the process or service. The information can be classified by how quickly it needs a reaction. I split it into

- Alerts
- Performance metrics
- Trends
- Comparison
- Word searches and other nonmetric displays

Alerts

Alerts indicate that something has happened and may need an immediate response. One question you need to answer is whether you are willing to wait for the alert to be sent when the receiver next logs on or you need to send the alert immediately. If the receiver is logged on, it may be acceptable to put the message up on the next screen the application sends. If you need an immediate response, the application may have to send a text message or e-mail.

Performance Metrics

Performance metrics are there to answer the question, "How is the business operation going now?" Some performance metrics are often cumulative; for instance, a sales person will want to know how many sales he or she has made this quarter and how this compares with the target. Other metrics are running averages (e.g., the average over the last month) and lists of best and worst cases.

For performance metrics to have meaning to the business, they should be focused on tasks and business processes. Example process and task questions are

- How often is the process started?
- How often does the process take an error path?

- How often is the process aborted?
- How long does the process take?
- How long does a process wait for a resource to become available?
- Where are the delays?

The business might also want additional money-focused questions and geographical or product line splits. In our example in the previous chapter of a pipe-fixing process the managers are likely to want to know the following:

- How long is it between a report of a problem and the investigator coming?
- How long after a team takes an assignment do they report a fix?
- How many times does the fix team not complete a fix?

It is useful for a context designer to know the kinds of questions a typical manager asks, partly because a big warning sign should switch on in the designer's brain if the stakeholders are not asking for this information. The most likely reason is that the stakeholders have simply forgotten, but an alternative explanation could be that the stakeholders are assuming this information will be magically provided even if they don't ask for it.

Some metrics are easy to gather in the IT application, but in my experience it is often the more difficult metrics that are of greater interest. For instance, in our pipe-fixing example a couple of interesting questions are:

- How many times does an investigator report that no fix is necessary, only for it to be reported again and fixed later?
- How many times does a fix fail?

You can envisage the scenario of the pipe-fixing organization reporting a low average time to fix incidences because their investigators are closing jobs when they don't think the break is serious enough to warrant fixing.

Sometimes organizations focus on proxy metrics. A real metric is a direct measure, such as the number of rejects in a manufacturing production line. A proxy metric is an indirect measure, such as using the number of times a customer starts the checkout process but does not finish it to measure ease of use. Often there are many proxy metrics for the same factor. Thus for ease of use you might measure the number of times the session is aborted, the number of times help is requested, the number of times the user revisits the same screen, the number of errors the user gets when filling in a form, and many other measures. None of them accurately measures ease of use, and it would be excessive to measure them all. Another example is that in many organizations it is important to know if customers like or dislike the product or service you offer. A proxy metric would be to measure repeat business (though if the organization is a hospital, that might be a negative metric rather than a positive metric!). A real metric would be an answer to the survey question, "Do you like the product?" But the answer might be yes and there is little repeat business, which hints that the question is not useful. Perhaps the real question should be, "What do we need to do for you, the customer, to buy our product again?" When having a discussion with managers, always try to find out why they are asking for certain information; there may be a better solution for what they want to do.

Trends and Comparisons

Trends and comparisons supplement performance metrics; managers want to know if parts of the business are improving or falling behind and how the market is changing.

I am making a distinction here between the data reports that are done by an application with programmed code and data analysis done on data extracted from database or databases, for instance, extracted into a data warehouse. There is not a hard dividing line between the two approaches, but here we are focusing on predictable reports for line management. This issue is discussed further in the section on data analysis in this chapter.

Once you have decided to report on the trend and/or comparison within the application, you must decide on basic questions:

- How far back in time do we go? This directly impacts the size of the database.

- What level of detail is needed? Do you measure sales performance by groups, by product, by product range, by person?

- Should the information be displayed on a screen or loaded into a spreadsheet, a document, or other formatted file?

You have to be careful not to make the reporting part of the application overly complex and difficult to understand. I generally find that a good plan is to aim for a small number of key reports and then provide facilities to download additional data into a spreadsheet.

Loading data into a spreadsheet always raises a security issue because spreadsheets have a habit of going astray. One solution is to anonymize sensitive data, but in a short list of customers, for instance, you can often guess the customer from the data. It is better where possible to provide totals and percentages rather than individual customer names. This may still give enough information for a malicious person to figure out some sensitive customer information, but it is much harder. At some point, you have to trust people. If they genuinely have a need for the information and have been taught how to look after it, you should give it to them.

Textual and Graphic Displays

Textual analysis of information is becoming more and more common. Organizations are allowing their customers and employees to record comments or complaints. Besides simply reading these or counting them, what else can be done with this mine of information? One answer is to provide word searches or word counts. I suspect there will be more and more products that help you deliver this functionality into your application. Another nonmetric display that is becoming increasingly popular is linking your data to, say, Google Maps. I have done some work drawing diagrams from information, and I think this will become a more common way of displaying data.

Managing Excessive Reporting Requirements

You can see from this discussion that it is easy for managers to ask for more and more data. But the more data that is gathered, analyzed, and displayed, the more the application grows in complexity. More data gathering is likely to be a performance hit on the application, and there is a danger that users will become irritated by being asked to provide all this arcane information. It is also the case that many times, metrics are put into an application that are hardly ever used. If you have worked with senior managers, you are probably familiar with them deciding that they really want to know this or that metric because they are convinced it will shine a spotlight on some aspect or other of the business. But when the metric is provided, they find it does no such thing.

Thus there is a real temptation to indulge in some overengineering by putting every last suggestion into the requirements list. In theory the designer must decide for each suggested inquiry or report whether the information is

- Crucial

- Useful and likely to be used often and by many

- Just simply a nice-to-have

In practice, the designer will have difficulty resisting suggestions from senior managers, especially since often these senior managers will have been identified as important stakeholders. I suggest three ideas to counter such tendencies:

- As mentioned before, aim for a few key reports, and then provide the option to download the raw data, perhaps refined through some simple selection facility, for users to manipulate to their heart's content on their PCs.

- Discuss staged releases. Most stakeholders will like to have the application delivered earlier by delaying some features until later releases. By having a discussion about what feature goes in what release, you can avoid giving the impression that someone's bright idea is, in your humble opinion, totally pointless.

- Another technique for prioritizing management metrics is to introduce the concept of a dashboard. A dashboard is a single screen or part of a screen that gives managers some key information. By talking about dashboards, you are challenging them to restrict their view to what really matters.

As a designer, you also sometimes face the opposite problem: managers will struggle to find the key metrics. I find that in most applications there are only a few key questions for which managers would really like answers, namely:

- Are people doing their jobs properly as asked?

- Can the process or service be improved?

- Are the resources used in the business (e.g., people, equipment, backup services) too few or too many?

- Who are the easiest and/or most profitable people/organizations to sell to?

Unfortunately these questions are hard to answer, so the search starts for proxy metrics. But they are good questions with which to start a discussion.

Data Used by Other Applications

Besides managers of the process or service, there are other parts of the organization that may have an interest in the data collected by the IT application. Take product data as an example. Some of the information is used for the online product description, some of the information is used to tell the dispatchers the dimensions and weight and other special requirements for dispatching the product, and some of the information is used for product build or procurement. I have drawn this diagrammatically in Figure 6.1.

As noted before, I don't define all the data attributes in the context design but put all the undefined attributes into a data bag. Figure 6.1 illustrates the need to have multiple data bags. The Description data bag is used by the product brochures and online Web sites, the Packing Info is used by the distribution applications, and the Financial Info is used by the billing system. The concept of data bags allows me to design the application without worrying about some detail. In this example I can still design—and in fact do a great deal of implementation for—the application to create the product data before I know what information I need for, say, product

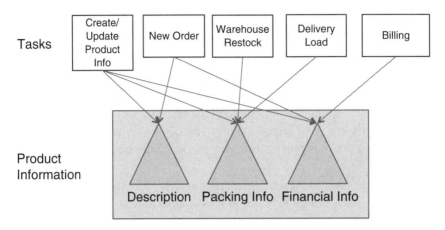

Figure 6.1 *Data Bags for Product Information*

distribution. Data bags allow me to discuss data ownership and design responsibility issues without getting lost in the detail.

The job of defining the content of the data bags falls to the user interface designer and the database designer.

When the attributes of the record are defined, it may be that a single data attribute belongs to more than one bag. For instance, there may be dimension data in the product display information that is also used by the warehousing system. For this reason, while different business managers will need to specify the data they need, the job of coordinating the input should fall to the database designer.

It is likely that an application that provides data and an application that consumes data won't be written at the same time. Thus if you are designing an application that provides data to another application that is also being rewritten, you have to find out both what the existing application wants and what the future application will want. If you are designing the application that consumes data, you have find out what data is available, and if that data is insufficient for your needs, you might have to persuade other people to change their IT application. A little senior management support greatly helps in any such negotiation. This point emphasizes the need for a context design—it is something to show people early on to explain your needs.

Data Analysis

Analysts who want to use data provided by an IT application is the final category of application users we listed earlier. They, or their IT representative, are likely to want to extract data from your application's database and put it into a data mart or data warehouse, or just into their spreadsheets.

When should a report or analysis be offloaded from a production database rather than examined in situ? This can be a difficult decision to make. Here are some of the criteria for making this decision:

- The degree to which the queries are unpredictable. Unpredictable queries need specialized query and data analysis products.

- The degree to which the queries are large. Large queries soak up processing and memory and if run on the production machine will destroy its performance.

- The degree to which the analysis needs data extracted from more than one database.

- Who wants to see the analysis? If they are not line managers who are often logged on to the production application, there is a good case for offloading the data if only for security reasons.

- By offloading data you have to be sure you are not introducing additional security problems like revealing personal information or secret product information.

Once it has been decided to load the data on another machine, there are several other issues to discuss:

- How timely do the data analysts want the data to be? Do they want it in real time or is a delay acceptable?

- Do they want all the data or just a sample?

The field of data analysis, data warehouses, and the data structures needed to support good searching ability is a specialized subject of considerable complexity. It is beyond the scope of this book, so I leave the discussion there. If you are interested, have a look at "Data Warehouse Tutorial" [31].

Data analysts may want to see the context design. If they don't, one wonders how else they are going to understand the meaning of the data they are analyzing.

Application Administration

Application administrators may be needed to do the following:

- Create new users for an application and remove users who no longer need to use the application. This may be a job for human resources, but in my experience it is normally given to a random person in the operations department. It should be given to someone who knows the users.

- Check the security logs to see if there have been problems. This may be a centralized security administration function, or the person may only look after the security of a single application. The problem is that you need to find someone who is interested enough to do the monitoring.

- Start batch processing runs. You should endeavor to make all batch runs start automatically.

I am assuming that database backups and system performance monitoring are done by IT operations, but there is a hazy area where some jobs could be done by either. Application administrators may also do business operations like

- Run regular reports for management

- Load data into the machine on a regular basis (e.g., a table of currency exchange rates)

- Copy data from one machine to another

These kinds of jobs, if done incorrectly, can lead to major application failures. For instance, if you load the wrong exchange rate file and business is done based on it, the organization could lose a lot of money. Furthermore, because the jobs are routine and often boring, they are often assigned to junior staff who have little idea that what they are doing is important.

There are several actions to take to alleviate any problems:

- Where possible, automate—in other words, eliminate the job.

- Analyze the jobs to check the consequences of their not being done or done incorrectly, and try to build checks in the application to ensure that they are done on time and correctly. For instance, put a date in the file of exchange rates, so the system can do a check. It's not a foolproof check, but it is better than nothing.

- Keep a log of what has happened.

- Try to build application logic that can undo work that is done incorrectly because of wrong files being loaded.

Ultimately the application may depend on the diligence and integrity of a few key people. It is important to understand whether this is the case. In short, management needs to know the risks associated with an application.

Analyzing the Context Design

In Chapter 1, "Introduction to Context-Driven Design," I wrote about the four steps for design: understanding, hypothesis, elaboration, and analysis. In context design the hypothesis is the process layer. Elaboration is both writing the task detail and considering all the users of the application, which should lead to the definition of many more tasks. So what about the analysis?

Analysis of the context design is done before presenting it to stakeholders. This way you involve them in finding a solution to any problem you discover. Thus if you have several reviews and you are making many changes to the design between reviews, you will need to do the analysis several times.

The range of analysis can be illustrated by the table in Figure 6.2.

This shows simply that you can look for ways to analyze each element in the context design in terms of completeness, consistency, and effectiveness. I will use this structure to discuss the analysis techniques.

The process layer analysis is discussed in the previous chapter. All the analysis questions are also listed in Appendix A, "Context Design Checklist," albeit in shortened form.

Process Layer

The process layer checks were described in Chapter 5, but since some of them are reclassified to fit with the scheme illustrated in Figure 6.2, I thought it worthwhile to

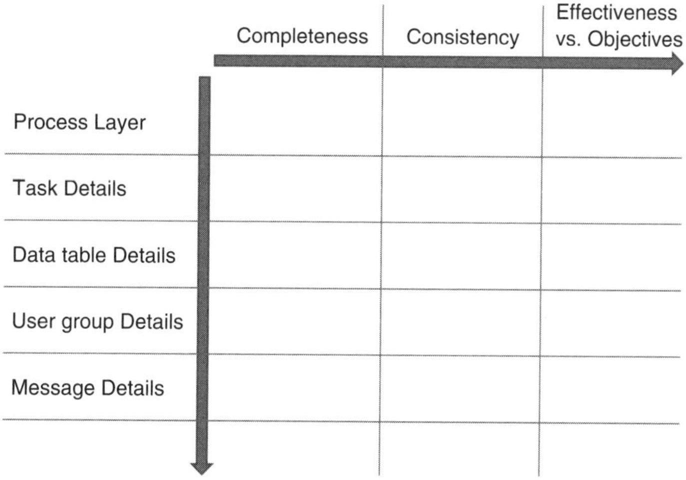

	Completeness	Consistency	Effectiveness vs. Objectives
Process Layer			
Task Details			
Data table Details			
User group Details			
Message Details			

Figure 6.2 *Analysis Opportunities*

repeat them in note form here. Process layer analysis is about whether the overall shape of the application is right.

Completeness analysis for the process layer includes the following:

- All errors are handled. Some errors will be explicitly handed off to humans, in which case you must ensure that there is enough information to handle the error. If after handling the error the process is resumed at some point, the data must be set up to move forward in the process correctly.

- All process activities have all needed tasks defined. In other words, the mapping from process diagram to task is correct.

- Tasks are identified for all resource state transitions. If a state transition on a data object has been identified, for instance, in a resource management application as illustrated in Figure 5.7, there must be a task that handles it.

- Tasks exist to handle message replies. If a message is sent and a reply is expected, there must be a task to handle that reply.

- Tasks are identified that ensure the accuracy of data that is tracking the state of external entities. For instance, if there is a data table that tracks customer details, there should be tasks to update the object, and the tasks must be assigned to user groups that are likely to know about the change of details.

- Data table objects are created, used, and deleted or archived. Every data object must be created somewhere before it is used and deleted or archived when it is no longer used.

Consistency analysis for the process layer includes the following:

- Process diagrams are well formed. There must be a flow from start to end. The process diagram must not have endless loops and must not have activities or conditions that are not implementable.

- The process diagram and the task outcome diagram must match. In other words, the flow from task to task in the task outcome diagram must be consistent with the flow between activities in the process diagram. All outcomes from a task must be handled.

- Process integrity constraints are enforced. An example of a process integrity constraint is in an order-processing application where payments must match deliveries. It is especially important to analyze the maintenance of integrity in error paths.

Effectiveness versus objectives analysis for the process layer includes the following:

- Are the business objectives achieved? Since the process layer is about functionality, only functional objectives can be tested here.

- Is work needlessly duplicated?

- Are errors handled automatically where possible?

- Is the business process optimized? You should look at the time taken to do the process and the best place to handle errors.

- Does the IT application open up a new business risk? It might be holding excessive amounts of personal data.

- Do the IT costs and time frame targets look achievable? Of course, you can't answer this question fully, but you can have an idea of whether it is a large, complex application or something straightforward.

- How is the customer affected by the new application?

Task Details

Task details analysis looks into the tasks and checks whether they implement the process layer requirements.

Completeness analysis for task details includes the following:

- All referenced data tables exist, all referenced user groups exist, and all referenced messages exist. This is largely a check on the spelling!

- All outcomes defined in the process layer are implemented. It is especially important to check that the error outcomes—application failure or a user abandoning the task—are handled.

- All tasks have the data to do their job. The rules and steps will rely on data either from the database or from the user. Is the data ready to be used when required?

- All tasks are started. For instance, if the task is started by a user, there must be a user group defined for the task.

Consistency analysis for task details includes the following:

- The steps implement the outcomes. This is a check on whether a step is missing.

- The steps and the rules do not contradict each other.

- The steps and the rules do not contradict the data table rules.

Effectiveness versus objectives analysis for task details includes the following:

- Work is not duplicated. It is quite easy to accidentally check something at the start of a task and then check it again later.

- Task step order is not unnecessarily prescriptive. Often you imagine how a task is done and write it down, and only when you look at it again do you realize that some of the steps could be done the other way around. You want to write the steps in a way that has the minimum of ordering defined to allow maximum flexibility to the user interface designer.

Data Table Details

The data table details analysis is about checking that the data supports both the process layer and the task details.

Completeness analysis for data table details includes the following:

- All data attributes are mentioned in one or more of the task descriptions. If not, why are they there?

- Before a data attribute is used, it must be given a value or the task must be able to allow for a null attribute.

- Rules in the data tables must not be replicated in the task details. This is a check on overcompleteness rather than completeness, but it is worth checking to protect against accidental contradiction.

Consistency analysis for data table details includes the following:

- Data table rules must not contradict each other.

- Are the rules sufficient? The question is whether the task details narrative and rules make assumptions about the nature of the data that are not enforced. For instance, if a task expects to find a data object using a key, the key value must be unique to that data object.

- Data table rules do not contradict task rules or steps.

- If a data attribute references another data table object, that object must have already been created.

Effectiveness versus objectives analysis for data table details includes the following:

- Could one or more of the data attributes be calculated from other attributes? For instance, do you really want to hold data about people that tells you the country they live in as well as their address?

- Is the effort of acquiring the data worth it? Marketing would love to know details about each customer, such as age and profession. If the application demands that data is input, will it be input accurately, and will it put customers off?

User Group Details

I can't think of any test for completeness and consistency for user groups, mainly because I don't record additional information about them. But there are several tests on the effectiveness versus objectives. These include the following:

- Can such people be identified in your organization? You might identify some specialist knowledge worker. Do you have any in your organization?
- Are users being asked to do too much? Are they being asked to do too many tasks and are the tasks too laborious?
- Do the users have the information they need to do their tasks? Are the users being asked to gather a lot of difficult-to-acquire information?
- Are the tasks allocated to a user group compatible with the users' job descriptions? Is the set of work assigned to one user group compatible with the division of labor in the organization?

Message Details

As noted, messages are rarely defined in a context design, but if they are defined, they had better be defined correctly.

Completeness analysis for message details includes the following:

- The message must have a valid sender and receiver. This is a cross-check on whether the sender and receiver are valid task names and whether the task details also know about the message.
- Does all message data have a source? The data in a message must be acquired from the data accessed by the task or from the user of the task.

Consistency analysis for message details includes the following:

- Is message integrity necessary? There are three questions here: What are the consequences of losing a message? What are the consequences of sending the same message twice (because the sender is uncertain whether the first message got through)? And what happens if the receiver cannot process the message (e.g., it contradicts some task rule)?

Effectiveness versus objectives analysis for message details includes the following:

- Are the messages unnecessarily large?
- Would it be better to put the message data into a data object and store it in a database?

Reviewing the Context Design

Developing the context design is an iterative process. This process is illustrated in Figure 6.3.

You must first listen to people to find out what they want. This is the requirements-gathering stage. How you do this is up to you; in addition to having one-to-one meetings you may read existing documents, send and receive e-mails, have brainstorming workshops, and view existing applications. With the information you gather, the next stage is to come up with a design. This means go through the steps, create a design hypothesis, elaborate in order to meet all the requirements, and analyze. The design should be reviewed. Expect the first cut of the design to be incomplete and ideally to have identified inconsistencies. The purposes of the review include

- Correcting the design
- Changing the design to meet the reviewers' aspirations better
- Finding out who else to meet with to fill in any gaps

If there are gaps to fill, go back to the requirements-gathering stage and go through the design again. If there are just flaws in the design or a redirection needed, go back to the design stage.

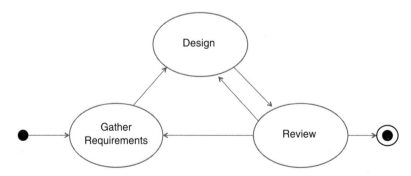

Figure 6.3 *Iterative Context Design*

In the rest of this section I discuss reviews.

Reviews are much more potent if you can represent the designs visually. The primary diagrams for the context design are context diagrams as shown in the previous chapter (Figures 5.4 and 5.5). The diagrams show the relationship between user group, task, and data table. However, these diagrams do not show all the relationships between the tasks, and they do not show the details of the task descriptions. Additional information about task relationships can be shown using process diagrams (e.g., Figure 5.1) and the mapping from process diagrams to tasks (e.g., Figures 5.2 and 5.3). Showing the relationship between tasks and outside entities like resources is also useful (e.g., Figure 5.7). You should be creative—try to show all task relationships in some diagram or other. You should also show a task outcome diagram (e.g., Figure 5.8) because it bridges the gap from the process layer to the task details.

In addition to showing diagrams, you will need to take at least some of the stakeholders through the task details.

One way to review the context design is to take the stakeholders through the analysis described previously in the "Analyzing the Context Design" section. Many of the analysis points—especially on completeness and consistency—you will have already fixed before showing the design to the reviewers. You will, however, need to highlight any changes you have made and explain why you have made them. The analysis points on effectiveness are worth a discussion. You may have views on how to improve the application, but the stakeholders may prefer a different way to achieve the same aim. Sometimes because there is more than one way to solve a problem, it is good to show reviewers some alternatives. You should try to engender the feeling among the stakeholders that it is their design and you are not trying to impose a design on them.

Reviewing the context design is not an exam; you want a lively discussion and a fair consideration of the alternatives. A simple way of provoking thought and comment is to look at the context design from a series of different perspectives, such as these:

- **Process perspective**. The point of a process is to create an outcome. The question to address is whether the IT tasks assist in creating this outcome and whether there is a better way.

- **Service perspective**. Is the application providing a service? If so, what is the service and is it provided in a manner that is useful and enhances other business operations? Are there gaps in the service being provided?

- **User group perspective**. What does each user group do? Are we making their job easier or harder? Are they being overburdened by too much work? Do they have the information they need to do the tasks? Are they trained?

- **Data perspective.** Who needs the data? Where is the data created? Is it deleted or just stored forever? Where does the information come from?

- **Resource perspective.** Are there resources in the outside world that need tracking (e.g., Figure 5.7, tracking patrol cars)? How are resources managed?

- **Manager's perspective.** Are the right management metrics being gathered?

- **Objectives perspective.** Why is this application being designed? What are the organization's aims and objectives for the application and are they being met?

- **Change perspective.** What parts of the application are likely to change in the future? Should we make provisions for the changes or not?

- **Security perspective.** Discussed in Chapter 12.

It is OK to review a context design before it is finished. Sometimes you want early agreement that you are going in the right direction. That said, many organizations will want a formal signoff of the context design.

Concluding Remarks

This chapter concentrated on the detailed description of the tasks. It outlined how the detailed description should be structured and summarized the range of analysis techniques that can be applied to the design.

The user interface design, database design, and technical design will provide further checks. I will describe the allocation of tasks to applications in Chapter 7, "The Relationship to Other IT Projects."

As a final comment, you ideally want the stakeholders to take ownership of the context design because implementing it often means imposing business change on the organization. It is the stakeholders who must drive that change, so they have to feel comfortable with the direction taken. The role of the context designer is as facilitator with the stakeholders and coordinator of the overall detailed design.

Chapter 7

The Relationship to Other IT Projects

In this chapter I discuss integration design—the placing of tasks into applications and services and the placing of data tables into databases. Recall that in Chapter 2, "A Hierarchy of Designs," I defined applications as separately implementable projects in the sense that each project produces new versions of working code out of sync with other projects. Recall too that I defined three kinds of applications:

- Online applications or simply applications
- Batch applications—typically applications that are run on a regular basis such as every evening
- Service applications or simply services—applications called by other applications

The design for each of these can proceed relatively independently from the others. Thus while integration design covers the same range as context design, user interface design covers a single application. Of course, this means that user interface design does not exist for a batch application, and for a service application the closest equivalent is the description of the programmatic interface—the users are the program, if you will.

Please note that while these categories of applications are valid and useful, they do not mean that an online application cannot be implemented using many separately compiled components, which of course need a programmatic interface designed for them. The application designers may decide on a tiered implementation and put a network between the tiers. Designing such a programmatic interface is more or less identical to designing the programmatic interface for a service application. The important point about service applications, in contrast to callable runtime components within an application, is that they are designed and implemented separately from other applications. The reasons for having a separate project are:

- The flexibility of separate development outweighs the additional complexity of managing releases at different times.

- The service will be used by more than one other application or service and hence cannot have synchronized releases with both of them.

In practice this means service applications typically implement a nontrivial amount of task logic.

In this chapter I include four sections. The first, "Integration Design," looks at integration design in a greenfield situation, where you have maximum flexibility to split up the context design functionality into separately implementable chunks. The question is, What is the best way to do this?

The second, "Services Interface Design," is about a related question: How do you design a reusable service interface? As noted previously, this topic is also of interest for component design when it is needed within an application.

There is a high probability that your new IT application will do one or more of the following:

- Replace all or part of an existing application

- Integrate with an existing application

- Integrate with an application that is already in development

- Use an existing database as is

- Use an existing database but also require changes to that database

- Integrate with some existing IT infrastructure service like single sign-on

This means that your new IT application development not only has end user stakeholders and business manager stakeholders but also has stakeholders who are other IT project managers and IT designers. The third section, "Existing Applications," is about integration with existing applications.

The fourth section, "Looking Back at the Design Process," is about how designing with existing applications—or applications from third parties—changes the design process. In particular, you may need to analyze what exists before developing a context design for the new applications.

These last two sections spill over into the subject of IT architecture. I have a short discussion of enterprise architecture in a box because I think you might be interested, but it is not the topic of this book.

Integration Design

In this section I discuss the assignment of tasks to applications or services and the assignment of data tables to databases. I have split this section into "Applications," "Services," and "Databases."

Applications

The argument about having a few large applications or having many small applications has been running in IT for as long as I can remember. It sounds cynical, but I think it is largely correct to say that what has happened in the past is that one large project leads to one large application, not many small applications, and one small project leads to one small application, rather than adding to an existing large application. You can find two organizations in a similar line of business, one with a few monstrous applications and the other with a highly fragmented IT application portfolio.

Third-party vendors are making their applications larger and larger; they use functionality not only as a means of boosting their competitiveness in their core market but also as a means of encroaching on other markets. While there are clear core areas like finance, sales, manufacturing, distribution, order processing, and human resources, there is overlap between them. Thus the use of third-party vendor products by itself pushes IT practices toward larger, more integrated applications.

Large applications have several disadvantages:

- Fault fixes and new features may be delayed because there is a long, complex procedure for testing the application and releasing it into production.

- No one person understands the application. There may need to be an internal triage mechanism to route a problem description to someone who can fix it.

But having small applications may also be a problem; for instance:

- Dependencies between applications are harder to manage than dependencies within applications.

- Triage to find the right person to fix the application is also a lot harder because operations lose track of who is responsible for what, and there is greater scope for people to point fingers at other applications or services.

I suggested in Chapter 2 that the basic logic of placing tasks into applications is as follows:

- Different end user devices call for different applications. For instance, Web browsers and smartphone apps should be in separate applications even if they are meant to do exactly the same thing. This relates back to our definition of an application. Dealing with different technologies typically requires different development teams and different operational management teams. But also you should note that the functionality of applications on different devices tends to diverge as there are demands to do more on one platform than on another.

- All tasks used by one user group should be put into one application. The justification is ease of use—you can look at the work done by one person and have a perspective on that person's workload.

- If a single person is likely to belong to two related user groups (like sales person and sales manager), add the tasks together to form the application. The justification is likewise ease of use.

There may be reasons why the application needs to be broader than this. But if you find yourself facing pressure to create large applications that cover a wider range, perhaps you should wonder whether you have defined too many user groups; in other words, you have split the user population too finely. However, if you feel the application is becoming too large, there is another solution, which is to make the application do little more than handle the screen interface and put all the data handling and business logic code into services.

Applications may be developed centrally but installed in several geographical locations. These constitute one application to my way of thinking because there is one development and support team. Sometimes you have essentially one application at different locations but tailored to suit local conditions. This may be because of legal differences in different countries. But it may also be simply left over from a recent merger. These are separate applications because they have separate development and support teams.

Services

In Chapter 2 I suggested that these could be the reasons for putting code into a service:

- The code is used by many applications. You will often see this correspond to context design task fragments included in many tasks.

- You want to run the code on many servers, either for performance reasons or to provide backup.

- You want an additional security barrier between the user-facing server and data-facing servers.
- You want to have several small projects in place of one large one.

The middle two of these reasons are discussed in more detail in Chapter 10, "Technical Design—Principles." The only point I wish to note here is that the technical designers should be involved in the integration design. And while we are on the question of who should be involved, the integration designer must talk to the project manager to discuss the last point on this list—creating services as a technique to divide up the work.

The list of reasons for defining a service is not complete. We tend to think of services as having a request/response interface, meaning that the caller cannot complete its task until the service has responded, even if the response is merely an "OK" or error result. But there are other kinds of services that are receivers of a send and forget message, meaning that the sender of the message is not expecting a reply. Such services can be thought of as automated tasks; often these services implement work that used to done by a person but are now fully automated.

One of the most common reasons for defining a service is when common functionality is required by two or more end user devices. In some businesses like banking people often talk about many *channels*. When you hear this word, you have to be a bit careful because there is ambiguity between usage channels (e.g., IT end user devices) and marketing channels. Banking is a classic example of many channels (of both sorts). An account debit service can be called from an ATM, a branch bank teller, within check processing, a credit/debit card transaction, a direct debit instruction, a SWIFT international money transfer, and so on.

These are common and in practice clear-cut reasons for defining services, but there are situations where it is not so clear-cut. There are many possible solutions, and they depend very much on the idiosyncrasies of your application. In general terms, it is worth considering the scenario illustrated in Figure 7.1.

The idea here is to organize your applications according to the needs of your users and to organize the services according to the needs of the data. Thus Service 1 is devoted to all the processing concerned with Data Tables 1, 2, and so on. Some data tables are used by more than one service, and that is done because some code, servicing one task, touches a data table that is otherwise accessed through another service.

This kind of application architecture works if you can truly identify neat packages of functionality that touch only certain tables. Actually this is common. Suppose you create a table as in Figure 7.2 with tasks in one dimension and data tables in another. What you see is typically several clusters of tasks and data. It makes sense to implement a cluster as one service. However, it is also likely that the user groups cluster in exactly the same way, so we end up with one application calling one service.

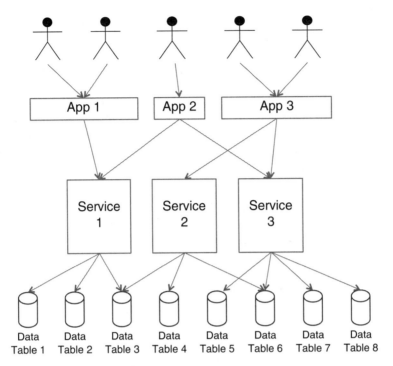

Figure 7.1   *Possible Service Configurations*

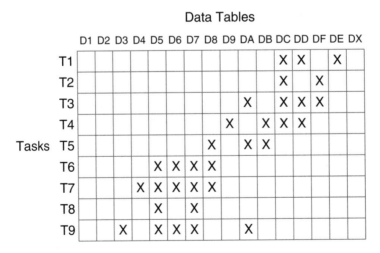

Figure 7.2   *Task versus Data Table Clustering*

Data Tables

Tasks	D1	D2	D3	D4	D5	D6	D7	D8	D9	DA	DB	DC	DD	DF	DE	DX
T1											X	X		X		
T2												X	X			
T3									X		X	X	X			
T4								X		X	X	X				
T5							X		X	X						
T6				X	X	X	X									
T7			X	X	X	X	X									
T8				X		X										
T9		X		X	X	X				X						

The conclusion is that there is no one easy answer—there are trade-offs. This is a typical situation that calls for a design, so I suggest you use design techniques. First, understand what you are trying to achieve. In particular:

- Do you need a complex architecture for scalability, resiliency, and security?
- Do you need to split the work among different development teams?

Second, have a hypothesis—deciding on the basic shape of the solution. Third, elaborate; decide where all the narrative and rules in the context design are implemented. Finally, analyze; look for instances of closely coupled code needing two services to implement it. In particular, try to avoid more than one service being involved in a single transaction.

Databases

Many organizations are rather fed up with large, complex databases because operations and administration are harder and the consequences of getting it wrong are so much greater. So is it possible to break up a large database into several small databases? If we could, when one database is offline the other services could still work unimpeded.

Look again at Figure 7.1, and ask if instead of having one database, there were three databases, one for each service. What could go wrong? Look at Data Table 3, which is shared by Service 1 and Service 2. First note that if Service 2, say, reads and updates two databases—one for Data Table 3 and another for Data Table 4—then Service 2 is likely to be unavailable if either of the databases is offline. This kind of defeats the purpose of splitting the database.

Sometimes the only reason why Data Table 3 is being accessed by Service 2 is to maintain referential integrity because there is an attribute in, say, Data Table 4 that refers to the key of a row in Data Table 3. Often the value of this attribute is in the input message to Service 2, so the only worry is that if the row in Data Table 3 is deleted, the attribute points at nothing. You may know that rows in Data Table 3 are never deleted, or you may be willing to have a message sent to Service 2 if a row in Data Table 3 is deleted, which gives Service 2 the opportunity to fix up any referencing attribute. What this complicated discussion points to is that the problem of splitting the database is often less formidable than it looks on first inspection, but you have to look at the detail.

An alternative, more general solution is to replicate Data Table 3. In the rest of this section I discuss data replication.

Data replication is common and an effective solution to many problems. Suppose, for instance, that the database services a single supermarket or a single school in a chain of schools. The main advantages of distribution are

- **High performance**—the database is small and the network is local.

- **Reliability**—the application does not rely on an Internet connection or any other wide-area network connection, and if one server fails, it has only a local impact.

The main disadvantage is operational; for instance, introducing a new version of the application is much more complicated when there are many distributed servers to upgrade, and local operations are likely to be of mixed quality. With the low cost, high reliability, and good performance of many cloud solutions, many of the old reasons for having distributed applications like this go away, though my personal experience of the Internet does not lead me to have great confidence that a network connection will always be there.

Many distributed applications have some data that is shared with the center. For instance, in supermarkets product information will need to be loaded from the center on a regular basis. This does not necessarily invalidate a distributed solution if the shared data is read, not updated, by the distributed application and the data can be copied from the central server in a controlled and regular manner. For instance, I expect that it is possible to load supermarket product data to a local supermarket server well before actual items of the product are sent to the supermarket for sale.

But what about situations where you want to have separate databases that have some element of shared data? For instance, in a business, customer data, order data, and product data are all likely to be particularly pervasive, but you might still want separate databases for order entry, distribution, marketing, and finance. In financial businesses, the accounts tables are used by many applications. We don't want to end up developing one giant database that supports most of the applications and cuts across many departments because such monsters are hard to understand, hard to change, and hard to manage.

One answer to this question is to put commonly shared data into a database of its own and have the applications access two or more databases. This is probably best done by putting the data behind a service interface so that the database schema can be changed without impacting other applications. This is illustrated in Figure 7.3.

The downside to this approach is that having one copy of the data may introduce a bottleneck in the application and a single point of failure. This will be particularly severe if the applications need to access the database over a long distance. Large organizations are likely to have more than one data center, so any application not in the same data center as the shared data will have to access the data over a network link. If for some reason the network link is down or the shared data service is down, all the applications using the service will be unable to run. A further difficulty comes when it is necessary to synchronize updates across multiple databases. This can be done using two-phase commits, but two-phase commits introduce inefficiencies. It is better, where possible, to send an asynchronous message (such as with message queuing) to the service to update the shared-data database. This is illustrated in Figure 7.4. This diagram shows local applications being updated before the updates to the Product database are processed. The question is, Does the delay to updating

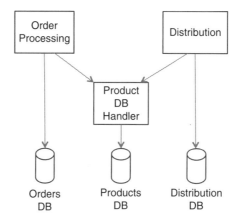

Figure 7.3 *Multiple Database Access*

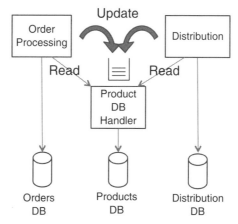

Figure 7.4 *Using Asynchronous Updates*

the product database matter? It may not if whatever attribute is updated is not immediately needed by any of the other applications. To give an example, suppose the order and delivery applications are recording in the Products database the number of orders for the product and the number of deliveries for the product. It really does not matter if the updates to these counts are delayed by a few seconds.

The alternative to having some single copy of the data is to control the duplication of the data. There are several ways of doing this:

- **Broadcast read-only data**. We met this option in the supermarket example where the shared data was the product information. This works best if you can send updates to the shared data before the data is used. Message queuing is a way of sending the messages. This is illustrated in Figure 7.5.

- **Pass-through**. The data can be updated by one application and then passed to another. For instance, the data from an order entry application can be passed to a manufacturing database, which in turn passes it to a warehouse database, which in turn passes it to a billing database. This is illustrated in Figure 7.6. Pass-through is what you get if you implement the process workflow unthinkingly. In our order-processing example it suffers from the problem that it is hard to discover what has happened to the order because you can't see how far in the chain it has been passed along.

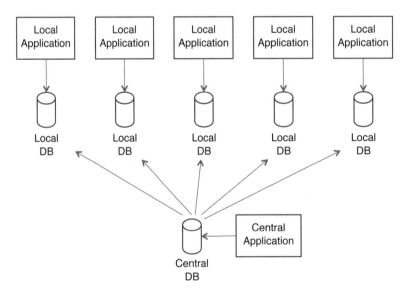

Figure 7.5 *Broadcast Updates*

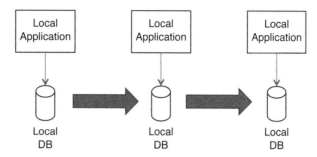

Figure 7.6 *Pass-Through*

- **Check-in/checkout.** I expect many of my readers are familiar with the concept of check-in/checkout in the context of IT application development. A programmer may check out a file of code and has exclusive rights to update that file before checking in the file to make the new version available to others. However, the same idea can be used in other contexts with data records rather than files. For instance, in the order-processing application there can be a central order database, and instead of pass-through of data from order entry to the manufacturing database, the data can be checked out to the manufacturing database and checked in when manufacturing is finished. This is more complicated than pass-through, but it has two big benefits. First, only the data that is needed can be checked out, which helps stop prying eyes from seeing information they should not see, and second, there is one place to look to find out what has happened to the order.

- **Data warehouse and data mart.** The data may be copied from a production system (or many production systems) to a data warehouse, possibly being reformatted in the process. It may be copied again to a data mart. As discussed in the "Data Analysis" section of Chapter 6, "The Relationship with the Users," there are several reasons for all this copying, but the main one is to have an efficient platform for doing complex queries and analysis of the data that does not impact production performance.

In all these solutions the data can be reformatted as it is passed from one application to another. This is a huge advantage; in particular, it helps to keep sensitive data away from servers that have no reason to see the data.

Those of my readers who are up on the latest trends will no doubt be wondering why I haven't discussed *eventual consistency*. The idea of eventual consistency is that you can update duplicate data as you like and then fix any inconsistency issues later. The Web is groaning under the weight of presentations, blogs, and papers expounding the wonders of eventual consistency, and the subject has been given a veneer of intellectual respectability by the introduction of such terms as CAP (Consistency, Availability, Partition tolerance) theorem and BASE (Basically Available, Soft state, Eventual consistency). What none of these presentations, blogs, and papers seem to mention is:

- Eventual consistency is hard and sometimes impossible.
- Living with inconsistency is a business decision.

I discuss this subject in more detail in Chapter 9, "Database Design."

Because as soon as we move away from a monolithic database we have possible timing problems and consistency problems, the strategy for multiple databases must be checked against the context design. And sometimes you will want to change the context design to make the implementation easier. Don't be afraid to discuss these issues with the stakeholders; just paint some scenarios for them. Often business people will be willing to trade some minor inconsistencies for a cheaper, faster implementation.

Services Interface Design

The effectiveness of services is intimately linked to their interface. You must try not only to have each service implement a clear, coherent, well-bounded set of functionality but also to ensure that the details of the service interface—how many messages are needed to do some work and the content of the messages—are good for all users of the service. This is the topic of this section.

Let us suppose that in the context design there is a task fragment described as follows:

Service: Create New Order
```
Data read:
   Products (for prices)
Outcomes:
   Create order and order lines.
   Failure/Timeout - no updates.
Narrative:
   1. Create a new order.
   2. Calculate price.
   3. Route the order to the right delivery database.
```

```
Rules:
    • Each product has only one price but a percentage discount
      can be applied to the total order.
    • Delivery prices are stored in the Product database or
      calculated from other information stored in the Product
      database.
Notes:
    • Delivery price is currently not stored in the Product
      database.
      Issue that must be resolved.
    • To have different prices for different channels, the
      product must be loaded twice into the Product database with
      different product codes.
```

The fragment is used in a Web server application, a mobile phone application, a workstation application supporting call center staff, and an application running in a shop, so we decide to implement it as a service.

In the user interface design for a service, a description like that for creating a new order can be split into a series of function calls, each call with input and output data parameters.

Designing the interface to a service requires some careful thought. The two extreme positions are

- **Giving the server the data it needs in small chunks.** This would be suitable for an end user device that has a small screen and will allow only small amounts of data to be input in one go.

- **Giving the server all the data it needs in one large data message.** This would be suitable for a message sent electronically from another company.

Look again at the sales order service example. Business often wants to treat different end user interfaces in different ways. For instances, discounts may be available on the Web and not available in the shops or vice versa. Processing the payment will definitely be different; over the Web the payment will be through PayPal or a credit card processing service, while in the shops the payment will be money in the till. If the order is from another business and is taken by a sales person, it could be that the payment is delayed until after delivery. Hence we have several applications providing the user interface and one back-end service for creating the order data and ensuring that the order is passed on to the delivery or manufacturing applications. With all the different ways of creating an order, the fundamental question is, Is there a single common interface for all the different applications, or does the service need to provide separate interfaces tailored for each user application?

The following subsections tackle these points. The next subsection discusses how to write a service interface and the one after that discusses reusability.

Service Interface Definition

Let us take for our example an order clerk inputting the data from a paper form cut out from a catalog and received by mail. The best interface to the underlying order-processing system might be this:

- Create a new order—the server should return an *Order ID*.

- Add an order line using product code, quantity, and Order ID. This could be repeated many times.

- Submit the order (after the payment has been done) using the Order ID and payment reference.

- Delete the order (if the payment failed) using the Order ID.

This dialogue is illustrated in Figure 7.7.

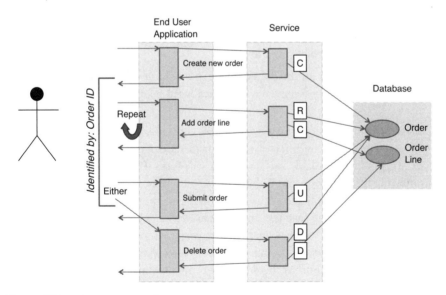

Figure 7.7 *Order Processing Flow*

This diagram is roughly based on UML sequence diagrams. It reads as follows: Time goes down the page. Processing elements are represented by rectangles, the stick person represents the end user, and the ovals on the right are database records. Lines represent data messages being passed from one processing unit to another. The "Add order line" call can be repeated any number of times, and at the end of the dialogue the user chooses to submit or delete the order. The lines to the database records are annotated with the letters C, R, U, or D—create, read, update, or delete. The bracket with the text "Identified by: Order ID" indicates that the client needs to hang on to the Order ID for these calls to work as the Order ID ties the input messages to the order in the database.

This is meant to be a working diagram, in other words, something to discuss rather than formal documentation. Because it is informal, I haven't tried to specify a standard for it, and if I find I want to express something that isn't in the standard repertoire of diagram elements, I invent something new on the spot.

Actually, if you compare this diagram with the task fragment described earlier, you might be left wondering how the calling application asks the service to calculate the order's monetary total. Just because it is a separate step in the task fragment narrative does not mean it must be a separate function call. The total to date could be provided in the output message from every "Add order line" call. But an additional function call may be a better approach if you want the "Create new order" service to calculate discounts.

The diagram should be supplemented by text, which I call the logical service interface. As always, the text is the formal description and the diagram is a suggested way of communicating the text to reviewers. The text rather differs depending on the nature of the service.

I identify four kinds of service interfaces:

- **Deferrable** (from the caller's point of view this is often called *send and forget*). The message sent to the server can be delayed by the system if the server is not ready to receive it. An example is e-mail. This is appropriate only if the sender does not need a reply from the server.

    All the other service interfaces are request/response service calls, which means the client must receive an answer before it can complete whatever it is doing.

- **Uses session**. The service interface relies on underlying session software where the server knows about the client and can hold onto data on behalf of the client. For the new order example this would be different from Figure 7.7 because there would be no need for the client to pass the Order ID back to the server—the session would tell the server that the input came from the client and would be able to look up the Order ID from its internal tables.

- **One-shot**. The sender sends a message to the service and receives a reply (which may or may not have data). Server functions can be called anytime in any order. There are no dependencies between them. An example might be a service that provides the current exchange rate between two different currencies. The "Create new order" example could be implemented by a one-shot call if all the order information, order lines included, was included in the input message.

- **Uses identifier**. This is like the example in Figure 7.7. Some of the calls rely on one or more data values generated by the server—the Order ID in the example—and passed back to the server on subsequent calls.

(For the technical among the readers, *deferrable* can be implemented by message queuing. You can implement request/response by message queuing if you set up a message queue for sending the replies. *Uses session* would rely on software such as Remote Procedure Calls. *One-shot* or *uses identifier* could use a REST— Representational State Transfer—protocol. REST puts the identifier data in the URI, the Uniform Resource Identifier, which is the extended Web name, the domain name plus the local names. Perhaps I should have called the uses identifier interface the representational interface, but while "uses identifier" is less elegant I think it tells you better what it is about. The implications of these kinds of interfaces for scalability and availability are discussed in Chapter 10, "Technical Design—Principles.")

A service can have multiple interfaces, and each interface can be of a different kind (in theory at any rate, although it is kind of clumsy to implement in practice). For instance, a service providing exchange rate conversion may have another interface for loading the conversion factors.

For a deferrable service the logical service interface considers a list of the functions to call, and for each function

- A description of the input data.

- A description of what the function does. This is best done in a manner similar to task details with sections:

  - Narrative

  - Rules

The narrative and rules can usually be copied from the context design.

For a one-shot service you need the same functions except in addition you need a description of the output data.

A uses identifier service has a sequence of calls as in the example in Figure 7.1. A text form of this example is as follows. The ID (unless it is set to "nil") is data held by the client (that is the program making the calls) passed by parameter to the server.

Service: Create New Order

```
ID = nil
   Create new order.
      Input: customer name, delivery address, e-mail
      Output: order no.
      Narrative
         1. Create new order.
ID = order no.
   Add order line.
      Input: product code, quantity
      Output: total money in order
      Narrative
         1. Create an order line and attach to the order
            identified by the order no.
         2. Update the total money in the order.
      Next state: order no.
   Submit
      Narrative
         1. Send order identified by the order no. to the
            delivery application.
      Next state: nil
   Cancel
      Narrative
         1. Delete the order identified by the order no.
   Next state: nil
<<Timeout/Abort>> . . . as Cancel
```

In "Create new order," the return value is the order number, which is used by subsequent calls to identify the order. I don't include the order number in the input data as it is a given.

Note that in the "identified by" data interface you also need to specify what happens if the sequence of calls is never completed. There are two main reasons why it might not be completed: the calling program could fail, or the service could fail. I record what to do if the calling program fails under the <<Timeout>> heading, and I record what to do if the server fails under the <<Abort>> heading. What you put under the heading is like other function calls, though of course there aren't any parameters. In this case for both Timeout and Abort, I have specified that the Cancel function is called.

This style of describing the interface can be extended for more complex scenarios. We could have two levels of identification, for instance, identifying the order line if you want to delete it. However, in general I suggest that you try to keep the interface as simple as possible.

Describing a session interface is more or less the same as an identified by data interface, except instead of writing `ID = order no.` I suggest you write `Session data = order no.`

Many developers don't bother to document a logical service interface and instead rely on programming it. A logical service interface is useful as it helps delineate exactly what the service does, which allows sensible discussions to take place on whether all the functionality is provided and whether the service design is good. I recommend publishing a logical service interface within the development team as the effort is negligible and if it prevents misunderstanding or bad design, the gains are enormous.

Designing Reusable Services

So how can a service be made reusable? Let's take the example illustrated in Figure 7.7 and see how different ways of creating an order work. First an extreme—an order over the Internet from another business (i.e., a B2B message) in XML format. This can be provided by another interface to the service, or it can be provided by another service—a gateway service if you will. I prefer the second solution because the service is external—its users are outside the business—which means that it will have different security and management requirements. In any event the interface is stateless, and its input parameter is the XML message. While this is completely different from all the calls in Figure 7.7, it is easy to envisage how the XML service can be implemented by taking the XML message apart and converting it into calls as in Figure 7.7; in other words, the new function takes the XML message and calls "Create new order," "Add order line," and so on.

What about reusing the New Order service for a Web order application? Here the details of the order are specified by selecting items and putting them into the online shopping cart. You could use the service described in Figure 7.7 to implement the shopping cart. When the first item is added to the shopping cart, a "Create new order" function would be called. The order number could be stored in a cookie. When additional items are added to the shopping cart, the "Add order line" would be called. There would need to be additional functions to list the current order contents and to delete order lines. The disadvantage of this approach is that it is quite common for users to fill a shopping cart and then not go to checkout, in which case the order would sit in the database and never be submitted or canceled. In other words, the Timeout would be common, and you would have to purge the Orders table of unfinished orders from time to time.

Alternatively, the shopping cart data could be stored somewhere else, perhaps even in the Web browser's cookie. In this case, the checkout process would be rather like the B2B message described earlier; in other words, the call to the order entry service would be right at the end when the customer submits the Web order.

The Web application also must handle online payment. The "Submit order" call in the service must not be done until the payment is complete. Note that users often abort the payment, again leaving the order in limbo, so again there would have to be some kind of housekeeping process to throw away unfinished orders.

Thus the service as specified has turned out to be rather flexible and largely for two reasons:

- It has functions that can be easily assembled into what you need.

- It does only one thing. It does not handle payments, and it does not handle shopping carts.

Although additional interfaces have been created internally, they work largely by calling one or more of the basic calls, packaging them up if you will. When looking for reusability, it is useful to identify basic steps and then assemble them as needed.

A possible solution is illustrated in Figure 7.8. This shows both the integration design and the implementation. The integration design is the simplest statement of the problem. The services user interface designer has worked with the technical designer to put in additional one-shot services to resolve any issues the technical designer may have about performance and switching to backup. The shaded rectangles behind the applications are meant to indicate servers. In other words, the

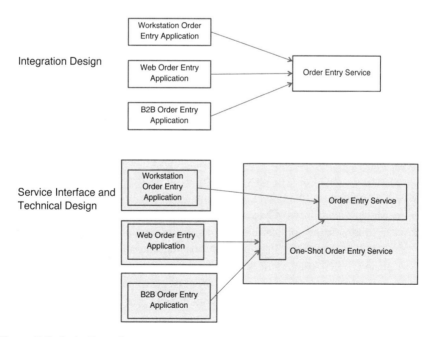

Figure 7.8 *Order Entry Services*

connection from the applications to the services goes over a network, while the connection from the one-shot service to the order entry service is in the same server.

This solution is, of course, one of many. The important points are, first, keep the integration design simple so that the detail designers can look at several solutions, and second, the designer of the service interface must work with the technical designer to reach a conclusion that is good for both. Of course, the service interface designer and the technical designer may be one and the same person or team.

Existing Applications

As pointed out in the introduction to this chapter, rarely do you do a large application design without having to consider existing applications. The first problem is finding them. This is discussed in the first subsection. Other subsections discuss replacing existing applications and fashioning services from existing code, which is often the best way of replacing old applications in a stepwise fashion rather than all at once.

Knowing What Is There

Before designing integration between your new application and existing applications and databases, you must first find them and second figure out how much overlap of functionality there is between the proposed design and the existing implementations. This is surprisingly difficult.

The complexity of large IT systems is astounding. Organizations often have a thousand-plus applications, some of them replicated over many locations, a thousand-plus database tables, hundreds of servers, and many machines of various antiquity keeping the business going. Simply knowing what everything does, how services and databases are used, and which users use which applications is a major undertaking. Mostly what happens in practice is that knowledge of what an application does is held in the heads of the old-timers in the IT department. If you are lucky, there will be someone with a title of something like application architect or enterprise architect who has made it his or her purpose to pull all this information together.

You can subdivide the applications and databases into large functional areas such as finance, HR, order processing, distribution, manufacturing, and so on. But you have to be aware that some data is shared across functional areas (especially customer and product data) and that business processes can span functional areas. Thus integration is not necessarily confined to one of these large functional areas. However, in spite of this, subdividing into functional areas is a big help. In terms of context modeling, a functional area is like a big common purpose group—one that is made up of smaller common purpose groups.

I have in my past had *architect* somewhere in my job title, but in spite of that, I have often been puzzled by what people who call themselves enterprise architects or IT architects or *something else* architects actually do. It is not necessarily their fault, and my personal opinion of why IT architects of different descriptions struggle to find a role is because the notion of context design is not ingrained in IT people's thinking. My take on this is that there are two distinct functions in this *architect's role space*; one is to look after the context models and the other is to oversee the technical designs. In the remainder of this section I discuss the first of these roles and show how it helps the application designer with the integration problem.

Recall that I defined the words *context model* as the description of what existing applications do, and *context design* as the description of what you wish a new application to do. The key to understanding what an application does is to reconstruct its context model.

Thus a context model has the same kinds of design artifacts a context design has, namely:

- User groups
- Tasks
- Data tables
- Messages
- Plus, where appropriate, business processes and other diagrams to indicate dependencies between tasks that are otherwise not obvious. These can be illustrated by task outcome diagrams.

You also need an integration model for the existing applications and databases. You need to know what applications, services, and databases there are, how they are connected, and how they relate to the context model.

So imagine that you have two context models and you want to know if they overlap. They can share user groups, but the user groups might be given different names, or the user groups in one model might be subdivided whereas that is unnecessary in the other model. They can have similar tasks. It could be that the tasks are actually the same but some detail has been forgotten in the specification of one of them. It could be a subtle difference and you need to figure out what the source of the difference is. An example is order entry; one application may handle order entry for hardware products and the other for a consultancy service. They will have similarities but distinct differences as well; for instance, the payment of a consultancy service is unlikely to be before delivery of the service. Likewise they may have similar data tables but in different databases, or they may actually share some data tables.

In the discussion about context design I have suggested that there are two levels of description:

- The process layer—the relationships between tasks
- The task details layer

The first of these levels is sufficient to tell you if two context models/designs overlap, but it is not sufficient to understand the degree of overlap between applications. For this you need to know the task details. Since building context models for existing applications takes considerable time and effort, I suggest that once you have identified an area you wish to change, you do the process layer context model of the existing applications, but only do the task details layer when you need to understand the details of the overlap.

If your organization is a merger of earlier organizations or has different departments that have been allowed to do their own thing, you may find a large—not to mention confusing—degree of overlap.

In summary, the role of the *context model architect* or whatever you want to call him or her (or it could be a team) is

- To maintain the application and database portfolio
- To keep all context models reconstructed from existing applications and context designs for new applications
- To engage IT management in developing a view of how the portfolio should change, in other words, which common services should be developed and which applications should be removed
- To assist application designers in identifying the applications and databases with which the new applications should be integrated
- To assist application designers in identifying which existing applications and databases should be partially or wholly replaced by a new application

This means that when you are developing a context design, the context model architect must be heavily involved in this stage of assigning tasks to applications.

Replacing Existing Applications

This section is an aside on the context model architect's biggest problem: what can be done with old, complex applications.

There are two main reasons for replacing an old IT application. The first is to replace the technology because it is old. It is hard to build a business case on changing technology just because it is old; you have to prove that it is more expensive, less reliable, or has some other problem to make a business case. The fact that so many mainframe applications, written in COBOL or PL/1, still exist hints of the difficulty of making this business case. Some organizations have reached the point where the people who understand the old applications are retiring but the organization still won't rewrite them in newer technology. Sometimes there is no change until the organization is forced to make a change, such as when the old software no longer runs on modern machines or uses technology that is no longer supported.

The second reason for replacing an old application is that new functionality is required. It is rarely cheaper to redesign and rewrite an IT application if the only requirement is to add some functionality. It is only when something fundamental changes that it becomes cost justified to replace the old application.

What tends to happen is that there is never one point at which the business can see that it is cost-effective to replace rather than extend an old application, but looking back, you realize that if you had rewritten the application, say, five or ten years ago you would have saved a great deal of money in the intervening years.

To add insult to injury, there are many instances of organizations that try to rewrite applications and fail. Applications grow over the years, and a well-used old application that has been extended and altered for over 20 years will be large, complex, and difficult to understand. Replacing it in its entirety is a large project, fraught with pitfalls.

Some organizations have avoided the problem of old applications by using two techniques, either singly or together. These are:

- **Surround the old application.** Essentially this means using some software that gives the old application a modern service interface. For example, an old transaction monitor such as IBM CICS can be given a Java interface.

- **Offload the data to another machine.** This is most widely done in the context of developing a data warehouse, but it can be done to provide any management report.

In my humble opinion neither of these strategies is ideal in the long term. Take the example of banking systems.

When banks first implemented computer applications, they developed COBOL batch applications; see Figure 7.9. This diagram shows money transactions being captured on tape, merged, sorted (to be in account number order), and then applied against a master tape which holds the bank accounts. The net result is a new master tape.

After many years this application was converted to a database application that replaced the master tapes with a database. But a problem arose with debit cards and ATMs; it was necessary to stop account holders from taking large quantities of money out of their accounts in the time period between batch runs. The solution was a *pseudo updated account* that kept a running total of the account totals. This is illustrated in Figure 7.10.

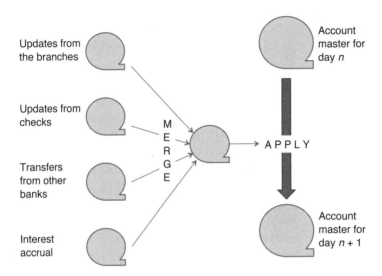

Figure 7.9 *Original Batch Banking Application Much Simplified*

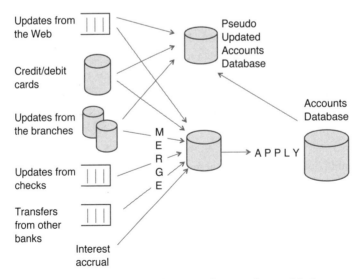

Figure 7.10 *More Modern Banking Application, Also Grossly Simplified*

Every time the batch run was done, the pseudo updated account had to be reloaded because many account updates such as check processing never went through the pseudo updated account.

This is where many banks are today (early 2015). Many of the programs are big COBOL programs that have bits dating back 40 years. Clearly using a surround strategy or an offload strategy won't address the problem of an old, complex, barely understood program.

So how does the bank move on from here? The obvious answer is to merge the pseudo accounts with the real accounts—make the bank a proper real-time bank. The difficulty is that once a day the bank must count all the money in its accounts to see if the total covers the loan book (because, of course, the bank is not allowed effectively to print money by lending out more money than it actually has). Thus there is embedded in the bank's procedures a daily cycle, and the assumption of this daily cycle is that there is a time when accounts aren't being updated and the bank can calculate its own accounting totals.

A modern way around this difficulty is to create a mirror clone of the Accounts database and use this data as the daily snapshot for all the banking checks. Thus a step-by-step strategy for updating a banking application might go like this:

1. Change all the old batch applications so they update the pseudo updated accounts as well as the original accounts. As they migrate over the different sources of bank updates, the pseudo updated accounts will become more and more accurate.

2. When the pseudo updated accounts are 100% accurate, change the account reporting programs to use the pseudo updated accounts.

3. Stop updating the old database.

To summarize, there are four strategies for handling existing applications:

1. **Replace**—risky because of the poor record of large application development

2. **Surround**—limited functionality and does not reduce or simplify the existing application

3. **Offload data**—limited functionality and does not reduce or simplify the existing application

4. **Step-by-step move**—requires a willingness to change existing applications

The key information you need in order to choose among these options is the context model of the existing application, because that tells you how the information hangs together from a business perspective. It will tell you where common service functions are likely to be found and whether the applications are highly integrated or stand-alone.

Fashioning Services from Existing Applications

I discussed turning old applications into SOA applications in Chapter 4, "The Problem of Large Applications," where I rather blithely suggested snipping the old application into a front-end application and a back-end service. There was a lot of detail skated over in that discussion.

Recall that earlier in this chapter I discussed what makes a reusable service, and the key points were:

- Define a set of simple functions with a clear purpose to each.
- Where possible try to ensure that the functions can be called in any order.
- Define a service that has unity of purpose.

One of the issues with old applications that makes them hard to understand is the lack of unity of purpose; particular features of the program are often dispersed around the program rather than all being in one place. An example of the kind of changes you may need to make is illustrated in Figure 7.11 where code A calls code B

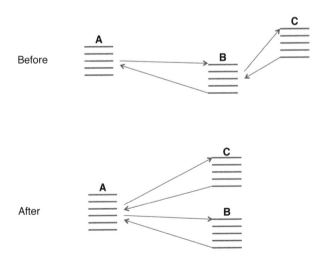

Figure 7.11 *Example Code Restructuring*

which calls code C, whereas you want code A to call code B and code C. An instance would be that code A is for creating a new order, code B does the actual submit code, and code C handles payment details. As I noted before, different kinds of order processing have different payment requirements.

Many organizations are very reluctant to make changes to existing code to clean it up and prepare it for cutting out good reusable services. On the other hand, operating system vendors and database vendors have been much more prepared to make large changes to their code base to support the evolution of their products. My suspicion, for what it is worth, is that tidying up an existing application's code in preparation for splitting it into services is much less work than is commonly supposed. There are several reasons for my belief. First, searching large program source code is so easy these days with the tools at our disposal. Also, there is usually someone in the organization who knows how the program works, so a good understanding of the large program's structure is within reach. Second, the advantage of working on existing programs is that the testing and installation procedures are all there.

If you are prepared to change existing code, the way is clear. The steps are:

1. Look at the old code and identify functionality that would make good services.

2. Design the new services.

3. Restructure existing code so that the code for the new services is all in one place, albeit still in the old program. Test this newly restructured code.

4. One by one, for each new service take the code out of the old application and replace it with a service call. The service itself can be created by either reusing the old code that did the same thing or rewriting it. Test each time.

5. Rewrite the remnants of the old application, making the new code call the new services.

6. As you provide each service, you may want to redesign the part of the database it uses and sometimes create separate databases or indeed merge databases that should be together.

You are then in a position to create new applications using the newly created service. Alternatively, you may rewrite the remnants of the old application which will be smaller and easier to understand. In a large old application, you may find yourself doing this several times, in other words, carving off several different services from the one code base.

Using Context Models to Analyze the Application Portfolio

I discussed the use of context models in helping define the integration requirements. I want to point out that context models are sometimes useful as an aid for analyzing an organization's use of IT.

When a context model has been built, you can ask all the analysis questions described in earlier chapters. Questions that are particularly pertinent for analyzing suites of applications are the following:

• Who is allowed to see which data tables?

• Is the same data being collected by more than one application?

• If data is copied to another system, is there a master/slave relationship built up to ensure that it remains current? Does it matter if the data gets out of sync?

• Is unnecessary data being collected? Is the data collected somewhere else in the organization?

• How many applications does one person have to use?

• How do we ensure that one person can use only the applications that his or her user group membership dictates?

If flaws are found, fixing them becomes something to consider when working on the IT strategy.

Looking Back at the Design Process

Integration design done well and consistently across the organization has significant business paybacks:

• It improves data accuracy, which is typically done by keeping one primary copy of information with possibly a number of consistent copies. Data accuracy helps avoid business errors and reduces duplication of effort.

• Integration often helps business efficiency by supplying data fast to the people who need it.

- An integrated IT infrastructure should have fewer IT assets as it eliminates duplication.

- In the long term it reduces cost because shared services are written only once.

But taking into account existing applications may not only change the implementation but also change the business design. It can do this in several ways:

- **By providing a much cheaper option.** It may be that integrating with an existing application is quicker but is functionally different. Management may decide that while the existing way is suboptimal, the cost saved or the speed to market makes all the difference.

- **By changing a business process to piggyback on work done elsewhere.** For instance, if company A merges with company B, and A uses external carriers to deliver its products while B uses its own in-house distribution service, it may be better for A to start using B's in-house service.

- **By forcing the application design team to understand additional points they had not considered.**

There is an underlying question lurking in the background to all of this discussion: How do IT application development projects start? Often development starts not as a brand-new idea but as a request to change an existing application. I have so far described development this way:

Idea ⟶ business analysis ⟶ do context design ⟶ build context model of existing applications ⟶ change context design ⟶ do detailed design and implementation

In fact it is often closer to this:

Idea ⟶ build context model of existing applications ⟶ business analysis ⟶ do context design ⟶ do detailed design and implementation

There can be any number of variations on these patterns such as parts being done in parallel.

This fluidity is something the application designer has to live with; you cannot be too rigid about methodologies and the *right way to do things*. But it is a problem familiar to traditional architects and civil engineers. Often they are designing extensions, not new builds, and their first step is to put the design of the existing buildings into a computer modeling package. In a similar way, context model architectures, or whatever you want to call them, develop context models for existing applications before designing the new application extension.

Concluding Remarks

This chapter is about integration design and service interface design. A major issue is the relationship between the new application and existing applications. It may be that the best way to deliver the functionality of the context design is to extend an existing application. Alternatively, you may need to replace all or part of an application. It is likely these days that you will have to integrate with an existing application by calling a shared service, by being called by the old application, by sending data, or by sharing a database.

A major problem is understanding which applications overlap or impinge on your proposed new application. An extensive use of context modeling is useful, and I suggest a preliminary analysis that explores how tasks depend on other tasks and on data, and how different user groups use different tasks. This should be enough to establish whether applications do overlap in functionality. If they overlap, you should do a detailed analysis of the tasks to establish the differences between them.

I also discussed the issue of incorporating existing applications into the design by turning them into reusable services. This is easier than rewriting the existing application and less risky. It provides a better foundation for moving forward than surrounding strategies or data offload strategies.

I wrote at the beginning of this book that one of its aims was to have application development work to enhance the overall architecture of the IT applications. This chapter is largely about where in the development this should be done. How effective this is depends in large part on how well the IT architecture is managed. If there is strong IT architecture leadership, over time the IT assets will become more efficient and more effective.

The following chapters describe detailed design, starting with user interface design.

Chapter 8

User Interface Design and Ease of Use

This chapter and the next two are about detailed design, the three boxes in the middle of the six-box design (illustrated in Figure 2.1). The assumption is that the context design is done and therefore the tasks, user groups, and data tables have been described, and the relationships between tasks have been documented. The integration design has also been done, the tasks have been assigned to applications and services, and data tables have been assigned to databases. The user interface design applies to a single application.

From now on, down the boxes so to speak, the applications and services can be designed separately from each other with only a loose degree of coordination. If that turns out not to be the case—in other words, designers and implementers keep finding that they need additional features put into other applications and services—the way the context design has been split into applications and services in the integration design is probably at fault. It may be necessary to rethink the split and possibly merge some applications and services.

The user interface design may apply to an application that will be run in a portal or be called from within an internal or external Web site. This may dictate how security sign-on is done, and it may dictate some of the look and feel of the application. I leave the area of logons and home screens or portals to the technical designers. In user interface design I specify nothing about security logon except that it needs to be done.

The three detailed design exercises are to some extent connected. In particular, the user interface design and the database design must be coordinated to ensure that all of the detailed data attributes are identified. But all three detailed design exercises can be started when the context design is finished; the coordination between them is best done when there is a first-cut design for each of the detailed designs.

This chapter is about the end user part of the user interface design. If the design is for an application service, the equivalent of the user interface design is the service interface design. This was described in the previous chapter. This chapter is about designing to create a good user experience.

You can't create a good user experience unless the application does something the user wants to do. The context design should take care of this. Furthermore, users have a strong preference for applications that have good speed and reliability. It is the job of the technical design and the implementation to make sure that will happen.

The user interface design is about the logical user interface—it is about what the screens do, not about the details of what they look like. The reasons I make this split in screen design between logical and actual are:

- The logical design directs the attention of the reviewers toward how the user interface works without the distraction of the screen look and feel.

- The person designing the look and feel will be in a better position to do a great job when he or she sees the logical user interface.

- The look and feel can best be done when there is working code. With Web technology you can create a Web site and easily change its look and feel using the CSS (Cascading Style Sheets) files without changing the code.

This way of working has worked well for me in the past. I bring in a graphic designer to make the application look great when there is enough to show the graphic designer core parts of the application working. That said, it is often useful to bring in the graphic designer to review the user interface design. The user interface design tells the graphic designer the size of the project and its major challenges. The graphic designer should have some insight into what makes an application easy to use.

The body of this chapter is about ease of use. But before I discuss ease of use, the "Logical User Interfaces" section focuses on how to describe the user interface design. The "From Tasks to Clicks" section is about the issues of transforming task descriptions to user interface descriptions. And after the section on ease of use, there is a discussion of a topic that is easy to forget: "Transaction and Task Integrity," which describes maintaining the integrity of the tasks and processes through a hardware or software failure. I included this in this chapter because it is a check on whether the user interface design is complete. I also have a small section at the end called "The User Interface Design and the Other Detailed Designs," which discusses how user interface designers must work with the database and technical designers.

Logical User Interfaces

A logical user interface for a single screen tells you

- What data is displayed

- What data is input

- What commands there are and what those commands do to retrieve more data, update the data, and/or send messages to other applications

- How task integrity is maintained

- How to traverse to another screen

What it does not do is show the actual screen layout.

The way I do logical screen design is to write a document with lots of indentation. I showed a diagram for the logical user interface in Figure 2.8, but I suggest you don't actually draw it until the design is ready for review.

Here is an example logical user interface:

Application: Web Banking Application

```
Common Functions:
   Logout
   Change personal details—go to Personal Details screen
Screen: Home
   Display:
      List of
         Account Name—go to Account Details
         Monies in account
         Action on item: Payment—go to Pay
Screen: Account Details
   Display:
      The name of the account
      List of last 10 transactions
         From name if credit
         To name if debit
         Reference text
         Credit or debit amount
         Account running total
      Input data:
         Month range (for Show earlier transactions action)
```

```
          Actions:
             Show earlier transactions—go to Transaction screen
             Make payment—go to Pay screen
             Add new payee—create new payee record, go to Payee
                Details screen
             Change payee details—go to Payee Details screen
             Change standing order
          Integrity:
             A: All updates handled by database transactions
             I: Ensure that user cannot log on from different devices
                at the same time.
   Screen:  Transactions (like Account Details screen but all the
      transactions are for an earlier month)
   Screen: Pay
      Input data:
         Select from list of payees
         Amount
      Actions:
         Pay—go to Pay Confirmation screen
   Screen: Payee Details . . . etc.
```

Reading downward, the first line is the name of the application. The line below "Common Functions" is for actions that are on every screen. As noted earlier, I don't include anything about the logon as that is taken care of in the technical design. Otherwise, the file consists of a list of screens, and for each screen the text displayed, the data displayed, the input data, the actions, and a note on integrity. On a Web screen an action is normally implemented by clicking a button, but it is possible to implement it by using a link or some JavaScript, which is why I use the word *action* because it is nonspecific. Where the actions update the database rather than just going to another screen, I put in some text like this:

```
Action Pay—use Payment task rules, go to Payment Confirm screen
   if succeed, Payment Error screen if fail
```

Most of the details of the actions I document by cross-referencing the context design rather than writing them out again.

The integrity section is described in the "Transaction and Task Integrity" section, but just so you know: *A* stands for "atomicity" and *I* stands for "isolation."

There may also be notes and additional help text not illustrated in the example.

The basic headings of "Text," "Display," "Input," "Actions," and "Integrity" provide the skeletal structure of each screen specification, but the details are described freely. This is not a formal language, or at least the formal parts don't extend much beyond the headings.

The main reason why I like to use text documents rather than diagrams is that I can edit them easily. This is important because I can *play* with the design, trying out different options without feeling that I am spending time drawing and redrawing or rewriting code.

When the design is finished, three quick checks can be made:

1. Ensure that for all the text such as "Go to [screen name]" the screen name actually exists.

2. Ensure that all the tasks and all the narrative and rules in the task documented in the context design have a home somewhere in the user interface design.

3. Ensure that all the data reads, creates, updates, and deletes documented in the context design also have a home somewhere in the user interface design.

The main analysis of the application design is to develop scenarios for how the interface might be used by different user groups. At each step of the scenario you need to ask these questions:

- Is there sufficient data for users to do what they want?

- Is there additional data that would make the job easier?

- Are we forcing the users through additional screens or clicks that don't add much value?

- What happens if there is an error?

The last of these points is discussed in more detail in the "Transaction and Task Integrity" section later in the chapter.

It is of utmost importance to review the application design with the stakeholders. I suggest that you start by explaining where you are in the project and then talk them through the relevant bits of the context design—in other words, the tasks implemented by the application. I would then take them through a scenario, introduce the screens that will be used in that scenario, and discuss each in detail. I would then show other scenarios and discuss any screens not already presented. Try to persuade them to express their own ideas. Make it clear that radical change to the design is OK; only your pride is at stake.

There is a chance that the review of the user interface design will find fault with the context design. There are several reasons for this:

- The stakeholders have changed their minds.

- The stakeholders misunderstood the context design.

- Because we are moving closer to the implementation, the stakeholders may bring along people who are closer to the actual work and who know in detail what the organization does at the moment. They bring up issues that were forgotten.

- The context design has errors.

- The context design is overly prescriptive (for instance, has unnecessary ordering in the narrative section) and the user interface designer wants to achieve the same aims a different way.

You as a designer must be mentally prepared to accept this; go into a review meeting expecting change. Make sure the context design designer is there. Design is an iterative process, and the whole purpose of having a context design and a user interface design is to drive through the iterations and not to worry if you have to go around the whole circle again because the investment in time and effort has been minimal. Also, making changes to the design as a consequence of a review helps engender ownership of the design on the part of the stakeholders, which will help smooth the path during the actual rollout.

The user interface design documentation is used not only by stakeholders for review but also by programmers for implementation. It is possible that the programmers will find a problem with the design, in which case the user interface design may need to be changed. In most cases, the changes will be small. When the project is finished, the user interface design can be thrown away. Everything in it should be available in the user documentation, but perhaps that is hoping for too much.

From Tasks to Clicks

One of the questions about context design is why have a user interface design step at all? Why not let the programmers look at the task descriptions in the context design and program directly from those? I have already given two answers to that question: the design will be more effective for the user if it is designed as a whole, and review by the stakeholders is a good check on the context design. If you let the programmers design the user interface, it will, in all probability, be done in an ad hoc manner, likely by taking one task at a time. The user interface for later tasks will then probably be designed—if *designed* is the word—by lashing it onto whatever happens to be already implemented. Put bluntly, programmers who are under pressure to code as fast as possible will get it wrong. There is a fundamental reason for this: the transformation from task descriptions to user interface is neither obvious nor trivial.

Let us take an example: filling in an expense form to be reimbursed for business expenses. It is a very simple application and consists of essentially four tasks: Submit Expenses, Approve Expenses, Pay Expenses, and Expense Reporting. The Approve Expenses and Expense Reporting tasks are only for managers. Since we want to allow saving expenses and submitting them later, we also add a task for Save Expenses. There will also be a separate application that uses the same database for auditors. The Pay Expenses task is a time-driven task because it is done automatically once a week or once a month and has no user interface.

If you made a direct conversion from tasks to user interface, you would have a menu on the front page of the application with four options, one for each of the tasks, like this:

```
Screen Home:
   Actions:
      Submit expenses—go to Incomplete Expenses screen if there
         are any, or to Submit if there aren't.
      Approve expenses—go to ApproveList screen—only if manager.
      Expense reports—go to Report screen.
Screen Incomplete Expenses:
   Data input:
      List of incomplete or rejected expenses:
         Week start date
         Action on item: go to Submit screen.
   Action:
      New expenses—go to Submit screen.
Screen Submit:
   Data input:
      Week start date
      Table of items
         Expense category (e.g., meal, travel, accommodation)
         Description
         Date
         Amount
         Action on item: delete—delete the item and redisplay.
         Action on item: update—go to Item screen.
      Total
   Actions:
      Add item—go to Item screen.
      Submit
      Save—puts the expenses in the incomplete expenses list.
      Cancel
```

```
Integrity
    A: On time-out, roll back to last saved copy.
    I: Each input is associated with a user.
Screen Item: . . .
Screen Report: . . .
```

Do you really want this? At the very least you want the users to see the latest expenses they have submitted so they know which weeks they have done and which ones they haven't done. Maybe it would be much better to show a table on the home screen like this:

```
Screen Home:
   Display:
      Table of recent and partially complete expenses
         Week start date—go to Submit screen (if not submitted)
            else go to Inquiry screen.
         Total amount
         Status—values are: Partially complete, Submitted,
            Approved, Rejected, Paid.
         Action on item: update—go to Submit screen. Allowed only
            if not approved or paid.
   Actions:
      New expense form—go to Submit screen.
      Expense reports—go to Report screen.
      Approve expenses—go to ApproveList screen—only if manager.
Screen Submit: . . . As before but additional action—
   Save . . . save input without submitting.
Screen ApproveList: . . . shows list of expenses to
   approve . . .
Screen Approve: . . . shows details of the expense and the option
   to approve or reject (with comment).
```

The user could then select a week to work on.

But hang on—what about multiple currencies? Maybe you need a separate form for each currency and the table has a column for currency.

And what about proof—bills, receipts, and invoices? Let us suppose the employee must supply an electronic copy of each bill and receipt, either by passing on an electronic copy (e.g., from an e-mail) or by scanning in the documents. But the bill might span multiple weeks, and parts of the bill (e.g., a hotel bill) may not be reclaimable. So it might be a neat idea to have a task to *add a bill* as well as a task to submit a week's worth of expenses, and in the task to identify all the expense's line entries and explain them. The auditor's application will need to look at this data. For the auditor it would be neat to display an expenses claim on the left side of the screen and display the bills one by one on the right-hand side, and if we are being really sophisticated, we could highlight the line entries in the expense claim when the bill is displayed. Hang on a moment—this would be a neat feature for everybody. Therefore, let's merge the auditor's application with the expense claim application.

This is an example of feedback from the user interface design to the context design, something I have mentioned several times. The programmer may also want to make a comment; he or she may want to insist that the bill be in .jpg, .gif, or .txt format.

We aren't finished with the front page of the expenses application. As well as having a table of expenses by week, we may want a table of bills that we are going to claim. But for managers we also want a table of expenses that need approval. Our design now looks like this:

```
Screen Home:
   Display:
      Table of recent bills
         Date added—go to Update Bill screen.
         Description
      Table of recent and partially complete expenses
         Week start date—go to Submit screen if not submitted
            else go to Inquiry screen.
         Total amount
         Status—values are: Partially complete, Submitted,
            Approved, Rejected, Paid.
         Action on item: update—go to Submit screen. . . .
            allowed only if not approved or paid.
      Table of expenses to approve
         Name
         Week start date
         Amount
         Action on item: go to Approve screen.
   Actions:
      New expense form—go to Submit screen.
      New bill—display short dialogue to upload electronic copy
         of the bill and go to Update Bill screen.
      Expense reports—go to Report screen.
Screen Submit: . . . as before
Screen Approve: . . . shows details of the expense and the option
   to approve or reject (with comment).
```

```
Screen Update Bill:
   Display:
      Date added
      Table of items
         Date
         Description
         Amount
         Action on item: Update—use input data below. . . .
            Available only if the associated expense report has not
            been approved.
      A copy of the input document
   Input data:
      Description
      Item date
      Item description
   Action:
      Add new item
      Save item
      Delete bill and all items
      Save bill and all items
```

Finally, managers may have a budget for expenses. It would be neat to display on the front page the cumulative amount of expenses for their department for the reporting period (e.g., month or quarter) and where they are with respect to their targets.

Putting this all together, we have defined a lot on the front page, perhaps too much. Maybe we should display the important information and leave links to the rest. Observe that even in this simple application there are big decisions to be made that go way beyond what is specified in the context design.

You can characterize the kinds of changes I have discussed in this example as moving from a *task-focused* design to a *data-focused* design. In the former the tasks are highlighted on the front page. In the latter, the data takes center stage.

Finally, in this example there is a wider question. The expenses application is built on the notion of a hierarchy of management. Everyone except the CEO has a boss who approves their expenses. This hierarchy of management is the same hierarchy of management that is used for personnel reviews, maybe for project reviews. In all these applications you want managers to see downward all the data from their staff and, if the staff members are managers as well, their staff's staff, and so on down the hierarchy. But (in most organizations) employees aren't allowed to see their bosses' expenses. So suppose we have two applications with the same management information; we must decide in the integration design whether to merge the applications, have them share a common database, have both call a common service, or transfer the management hierarchy data from one database to another.

I have spent less than a day thinking about this example and writing the words (though probably a half day changing it when I came to review the text). Of course, it would take much longer to draw some diagrams and to explain the design to the stakeholders, leading to a final decision. This is time well spent as the final design puts the programmers on the right path. If the programmers know exactly what they need to do, you will be surprised by how fast they can work.

Ease of Use

Ease of use is critical to the success of an application. It is hard to define and hard to measure, but we all know it when we see it, and we certainly know it when it is awry, although one person's easy-to-use application may be another person's nightmare.

You cannot just let ease of use emerge through the brilliance of the programmers. It must be designed, and the main place to try to do it is during user interface design.

Why is it that some applications are loved and some are loathed? The *look and feel* of the application has something to do with it for sure, but it is far from the whole story.

But first, what can *look* and *feel* achieve? The *look* refers to the visual aspects such as typeface, images, and positioning. The *feel* refers to how buttons, menus, and so forth work. The average programmer, in my experience, builds Web sites that look like a complete mess. It is instructive to compare, say, Amazon with your local builder's rental shop Web site. It is difficult to get the look right, but getting it right does not necessarily mean a design that has "art school" written all over it. You do see Web sites that combine elegance and good looks with an almost complete inability to do anything useful. You also see Web sites that frankly look a bit clunky but work really well. There are aspects of the visual design that help users and have little to do with the overall look. These include putting important information in prominent places, highlighting most commonly used buttons and links, and avoiding too much clutter. For customer-facing Web sites, the graphic design is important as it makes a statement about your organization.

This section is all about all the other aspects besides look and feel that make a user interface easy to use. So what are they?

- **Function**—doing what the users expect and ideally a little bit more to exceed their expectations

- **Information**—providing users with the information needed to do their jobs and the search facilities to find the information

- **Navigation**—guiding users to the right page for them to do what they want to do

- **Text**—giving pages, menu titles, links, button titles, and so forth the right text to help users understand what each page or action does
- **Help**—the additional information needed to guide users

In this section I have included subsections on all of these points, and I end it with three subsections. One is on the notion of "Intuitive and Likable Applications," which looks at the subject from a different angle. This is followed by a section on "Ease-of-Use Design." Finally, there is a section on "Monitoring Ease of Use," which is about improving the ease of use after the application has been released.

Function

There are several points that make applications just a little bit easier to use. The points I make are not a complete list but rather something to get the thinking process working.

- If users can't complete a task (e.g., they need to ask someone for advice), allow them to save what they have done so that they don't have to retype it all again. Make finding the saved information easy.

- Try to ensure that they don't have to visit the same page twice. This is one of the underlying reasons why shopping carts work so well—users can fill the shopping cart even if they haven't committed to placing an order. Without a shopping cart you may visit a page once while browsing and again to place the order.

- Ensure that users don't have to write anything down to remember it. This is the other reason why shopping carts work—users do not have to write down the product codes in order to submit an order.

- Validate data early so that users have not done much work before they realize there is a problem. Likewise, if some data is required, check that it is present as early as you can, or put the required input data field near the top of a form so the user is more likely to fill the field in.

- Where possible, let users select data rather than type it. I used to work for a company in which, because the sales staff typed the customer name, there were multiple records for each customer, each with a different variant of the name, including misspellings and abbreviations.

- If some action is irreversible, make sure there is a confirmation box. In other words, make it hard to do the action by accident. On trading floors (for stock and shares, etc.) there is an expression, a "fat finger trade," which is a trade where the trader accidentally added an extra 0 or similar. The application should have a confirmation box if the value is high and maybe for a really large amount, a signoff from a manager.

- When creating a new record, I find it better to have one button called something like Create New (which blanks out the input fields) and another button called Save rather than having buttons called Create and Update that both update the database using whatever data happens to be in the fields at the time. This is slightly harder to program but seems to confuse people less.

- If the application can't complete the task, don't force the user to do additional work. I once went to book a train journey online and the application forced me to enter a lot of personal data. Once that was finished, it took me back to the earlier screen and told me I couldn't book online because it was too near the departure time.

Information

One of the ways to make an interface more efficient for users is to show them the information they need before they ask for it, on their home screen, for instance.

A few management statistics or alerts on the home page may also be useful, but I suggest you don't display figures just because you can. Give users information that might provoke action, like the list of expenses that need approval in the previous example.

As noted in the section "Function," people may have saved incomplete work. They need to be made aware of what is saved but not completed when they log on. Also in many applications, the task the user is doing is part of a sequence of related activities. For instance, in a maintenance application, there may be many actions and records that all have to do with one customer, and the user will want to see a list of these displayed when next dealing with the same customer. Another example is selling; knowing what has recently been sold to the customer is of interest if you are talking to that customer again.

Many applications need a searching facility; for instance, in an online buying application you may want to give customers help in finding a product. There are various well-known ways of searching—finding by category/subcategory, finding by producer, and partial text search. What is more often forgotten is searching using other relationships between products; for instance, to find the right model of ink cartridge for your printer it would be nice to be able to input the model number of the printer as well as the model number of the ink cartridge.

Navigation

Many Web sites have a menu at the top of the page or on the left-hand side; links embedded in the text; links and buttons at the top or bottom of the page for signing on, logging out, and so forth; and maybe some extra links in a box on the right-hand side of the page, normally for providing shortcuts. In non-Web applications, you can throw in links that come from pressing the right-hand button of the mouse as an extra source of complexity. Users can find the profusion of links quite perplexing.

There is a convention that is worth following, which is that you should be able to get everywhere in an application by using the menus, and the additional links are shortcuts. An advantage of this convention is that the menus tell the user the scope of the application. One of the most frustrating things to do on a Web site is to search for something that isn't there. I expect we have all done it at some time or other. Knowing what the Web site or application cannot do is important.

Sometimes the interface is such that you must select some data before going to the page that does some action on the data, and this is an exception to the principle that all screens must be findable through the menus. In order to retain the idea that what you can do from a page should be as obvious as possible, if data has not been selected, you should still show the commands, perhaps in gray.

My particular *bête noire* is menus that not only show you a submenu when your mouse hovers over a menu item but also go to another page—a page not in the sub-menu list—if you click on the menu item itself. Hovering over a menu item should tell you what you can do from that menu item, either with an explanation or with a list of submenu items that cover the whole ground.

The advice I have gleaned from papers and articles is that a menu structure should take you everywhere in a maximum of three menu clicks. In a large application or Web site that may mean a large number of submenu items. The advice is also that the application should make it clear where you are in the navigation. Some Web sites do this with a bar across the top of the screen underneath the menu, like this:

Home > Top menu selection 1 > Next menu selection > The name of this screen

But I observe that this is not common. I expect that is because most graphic designers think it looks ugly.

Text

The effectiveness of menus and links is crucially dependent on the text in the links and buttons. Writing the text is one of the most difficult parts of creating a user interface. I was involved in a Web site for a church, and they wanted a menu item that people would use if they wanted to ask the church for a wedding, baptism, confirmation, or funeral. So what heading encapsulates these services in one or two words? *Occasions* is the word they used, which I didn't like, but alternatives like *Rites of Passage* or *Special Services* aren't much good either. I suggested they use *Weddings* and the other services as submenu items under the *Contact Us* heading on the assumption that someone wanting to ask the church about one of these services would be drawn there in any case.

Help

Help comes in many forms: a link to a special Web page, text that is displayed when your mouse hovers over an item, or simply explanatory text on the page. Help text can be associated with an item on a page, or with the whole page, or can be general explanatory text about the system. My personal feeling is that the least useful help text is the most common, which is help that explains what the whole page is about. More useful to my mind is an overview of the whole system (with diagrams, please) and text that explains single items. A glossary is also useful in some applications.

There is help text that exists on separate pages that supplies information about the purpose of the application, definitions of terms, and details of how to fill in the input data fields. The user interface design should tell you how to access this text but not the text itself. This can be done later.

Whatever you decide on help, you should not rely on help text to solve all your ease-of-use problems. You should remember that many users will simply ignore the help text and just guess.

Another form of help you should consider is whether to allow the user to ask questions. Many selling applications on the Web offer the opportunity to chat with someone, though I notice that many support applications seem to be going in the opposite direction—trying to deter you from talking to anyone by demanding that you look at the FAQs first and a list of known problems second.

Intuitive and Likable Applications

People often say that one application is intuitive and another is not intuitive. An intuitive application is one that works the way the user expects it to work. Whether an application is intuitive or not depends a great deal on the past experience of the person using the system.

There was a time when users had widely different experiences with different styles of application user interfaces, but today people are so immersed in Web and phone technology that selecting a set of conventions that most people will understand is straightforward. It is worth studying applications you like and applications you don't like and asking yourself why you have come to feel this way. Put another way, it is worthwhile for application designers to try to improve their skills in designing easy-to-use applications, and one way to do this is to nurture a critical attitude toward other applications.

Difficulties come when the application is going to be used by the elderly or the disabled. How to provide a successful interface for these groups is beyond the scope of this book.

Some applications use special devices, and these have special challenges of their own. For instance, what do you think about the controls for your central heating system? And do you have a digital alarm clock that is also a radio? How easy is it to program for a different time and different radio channel? Perhaps it is me and my advanced age, but I find these devices astonishingly unintuitive. Obviously these devices have problems inherent in the fact that they have a small screen and few buttons. Most designers of these products have grasped the idea that they need to establish a convention for setting values (e.g., the temperature or time), and normally they provide one button to move to the next item to set and two buttons to set the value—one to move the value up and the other to move the value down. But then they add extra buttons, and they don't make it clear where you are in the command sequence, and the labeling is awful, and so on.

As an aside, if you are looking for a good exercise on ease of use, take a manual that documents, say, a central heating control and try to design a Web interface or mobile interface that has the same functionality.

However, being intuitive is not the same as being likable. For an application to be liked, I suggest it not only must be easy to use but also do the following:

- The application should be useful. This is an obvious point, but if you are thinking of engaging customers, it is worth reminding yourself of it from time to time.

- The application should not be annoying—also an obvious point, but surprisingly often ignored. Annoyances can be as simple as having to scroll down to find the next screen button.

- Data should be consistent across the organization; if two different applications display the same data, it should have the same value in both places.

- Text and button labels should be consistent.

- The application should be efficient. By this I mean that it is straightforward and quick to do the tasks the user needs to do. It means few clicks to get to the screen you need. It also means displaying the information you need so you can make a decision early.

- The application should tell you early if it cannot do something. For instance, a shopping application that tells you that something isn't available only when you try to buy it is a pain.

- The application should make it clear if you have done something. If you are waiting for your payment to be cleared, it should be evident that the application is waiting rather than having you guess whether you clicked the Proceed button.

- Sometimes the reason an application is slow is because of the Internet or the person's PC is a tad ancient. In this case, people are going to press the same button twice or press a Cancel button. Your application should not do something stupid in these cases.

- The application should be acceptably fast. By "acceptably" I mean users should never feel they are waiting. I have noticed that many Web sites are slow these days because they want to play some stupid video.

- The application should be reliable.

Except for the last two, the place to discuss and resolve these issues is during user interface design. The importance of these issues is another reason why the application design does not define the look and feel.

Ease-of-Use Design

Let us look at designing for ease of use by going through the design steps: understanding requirements, choosing a design hypothesis, elaboration, and analysis.

Understanding Requirements

The requirements are about understanding the users. The context design should tell you about the different user groups, what tasks each user group needs to perform, and what data they need to perform the tasks. What it won't tell you is the skill level of the users and the terminology that they use in their day-to-day work.

One way of estimating the skill level is to understand how often an individual user uses the application. If the answer is once per month, you should expect that the users will need considerable guidance. If the answer is many times per day, the users will appreciate fast links to the common tasks.

Choosing a Design Hypothesis

There may be many kinds of design hypotheses if only because there are many different kinds of user devices, most with their own quirks and styles of working.

But taking a Web application as an example, I suggest that the three most common questions your design hypothesis should address are:

- Is the design data-focused or action-focused? This was previously discussed in the expenses example.

- To what degree should explanation and general information be embedded in the application?

- Should the users need to be steered along a narrow path of options, or can they have the full range of options presented to them up front? It may be possible to do both by having a list of shortcuts somewhere on the home screen.

In user interface design more than the other designs I suggest that you try out two or more hypotheses by partially elaborating the design in enough detail to give you an idea of how they would work in practice. A discussion of the options with one or more of the stakeholders would be good.

Elaboration

Develop the logical user interface design as described earlier. Three quick checks were listed in the section "Logical User Interfaces." These checks are about ensuring that the interface is consistent and complete. Do these checks.

The other area of elaboration is to think through the implication of a failure. This is discussed in more detail in the "Transaction and Task Integrity" section.

Analysis

The user interface design should be reviewed by stakeholders, but as always you want to do the analysis before the review.

The main analysis I suggest is simply to go through each task scenario twice, once as if by an experienced user and again as if by a naïve user. You may need to find a naïve user and take him or her through the design to experience the truly naïve mindset. For the experienced user, the main point to examine is how many links, how many buttons to click, and how many fields need to be filled in. For the naïve user, the primary point to judge is whether there is sufficient guidance to lead the user to the correct result. You must assess not only the ability of the user to do the job but also the likelihood that he or she will be misled or distracted by other text on the screen.

Another test is to imagine yourself in the place of a user who is looking for something that isn't there. The first question is, "Is this likely, and why might it happen?" The answer to this question should provide a range of scenarios. For each scenario you need to examine how you can prevent it. One of the problems with many Web sites and applications today is that everyone is expected to behave like a marketer and to be relentlessly positive. Sometimes the easiest way to steer a user in the right direction is to say, "We don't do this," but unfortunately people are averse to being so blunt.

It's clear that thinking through who your potential users are is something that many Web designers completely ignore. I've recently had a reason to investigate an open-source content management product, so I looked at their Web site to find some basic information—what it does, how it works, and whether there are restrictions on where I can host my Web site. After a considerable amount of searching and some looping around to find myself back at pages I had visited before, the only introduction I found was in a list of online courses, the latest of which had been given over one month previously. This kind of experience is all too common, and I find that open-source products in particular are prone to be missing basic overview information. It does not take long to think of a few user profiles of likely users of your application, and just thinking of them leads you to see your application from a new perspective.

As an aside, content management applications are a good example of the difficulties of ease of use. In my experience the structure of the products is easy to use; the difficulties lie mainly in understanding what they can and cannot do and the jargon. The product I was looking at used words like *taxonomy* and *widget* in ways outside of their day-to-day meanings.

The classic way of testing ease of use is to have a usability lab. Here you run one or several versions of the user interface and watch people use it. You want to see where they run into trouble and how fast they find the action they want to perform. Unless you are prepared to wait until the end of the application development, the only way to do the usability tests early is to write a prototype application. I think it is fair to say that very few application development projects do usability testing, mainly because of the extra expense it incurs. The organizations that do have usability labs are large software vendors with big budgets for whom usability is a key marketing point. (Oddly, one way of improving usability would be to stick to the same user interface for release after release. Since some vendors are forever changing their user interfaces, I suspect that marketing is trumping usability.)

There are other options. One is to run a paper test early in the design. A paper test has the screens drawn (typically roughly sketched) on pieces of paper. Instead of using a workstation, users are presented with the drawing of the home screen, say what they will do, and someone acting as the application gives them another drawing representing the screen to which they have traversed. The advantage is that it is quick and easy and you can do it early in the design. At least it makes a change from endless PowerPoint presentations.

Monitoring Ease of Use

Application development teams often have a regrettable attitude of *chucking the application over the fence* and running away from it. Outsourcing either internally or externally tends to reinforce this attitude. However, one of the best ways to achieve great ease of use is to listen to the users. To do so effectively you must make it easy for them to supply the information. This can be done in the application itself in two ways:

1. Provide a feedback facility where the users can comment on any aspect of the application, for either good or ill. This will work well only if you show the users that you are listening to them, either by responding directly to the user making a comment, or by summarizing the input you have received and publishing it to a wider audience, perhaps by using a blog.

2. Monitor the application by recording the path through the program of a random selection of users. You can record how long they took to make a decision and see if they seemed to loop back through the screens with the symptoms of someone who didn't know what they were doing.

For either method, every month or so the development team should look at the comments and the paths captured and plan changes.

Transaction and Task Integrity

Almost all of the preceding discussion has assumed that the application works perfectly. But what happens when the server fails, the software fails, the end user device fails, or the network fails? Task recovery is dependent on database recovery, so first I need to explain some background on database applications that might be well known to many of my readers.

Database applications move forward in transaction steps. A transaction is a group of database update operations (insert, update, and/or delete) that either must all be done or none of them done. For instance, in a banking transaction you must create a record of the account change (the debit or credit record) and must in the same transaction update the account total, and in most cases there are accounting totals to be updated; all of these actions must be done or none of them are done. If the transaction supports this notion of all or nothingness, we say it is *atomic*. Of course, a transaction might fail when only some update operations that make up the transaction have been done, in which case during database recovery the updates that have already been done are undone. We call this *rollback*. The atomicity of a transaction makes it possible for a programmed transaction to support *consistency*. Consistency is defined by the business; it is the proper execution of all the rules and narrative in the context design description.

We also say a transaction must be *isolated*, which means that the database updates must happen as if nothing else is happening to the database at the same time. To see why this is important, think of a transaction that takes 100ms (let's call it transaction A) being processed at the same time as several transactions that take 10ms (let's call them transactions B, C, and D), which finish before transaction A. There are all sorts of possible problems, such as:

- Transaction A might create a reference to a record that transaction B deletes. The reference is now pointing at nothing!

- If both transactions A and B update a total and A reads the total before B but then updates it after B, then B's update of the total has disappeared from the record.

- Transaction C might update a record that transaction A later reads, but transaction C might abort and the update is rolled back. We say that transaction A has read a phantom copy of the record—some data that came into existence and quickly disappeared again.

Without isolation transactions B, C, and D might invalidate the consistency of transaction A. In practice, isolation is usually enforced through locking—transactions will wait for a data row to become available. (This is all done by the database software.) Thus if transaction A has read or updated a database record, it locks the record so that if transaction B later wants to update the record, it must wait for transaction A to finish.

Finally, transactions must be *durable*, which simply means that when the transaction has finished, the updates are really done. In practice this means that we can be sure that the updates are or will be written to durable media like disk. In a high-performance database only the change log is physically written to disk before the transaction is committed since that holds enough information to reconstruct all the other transaction updates.

Atomicity, consistency, isolation, and durability make up the transaction's ACID properties.

Transactions can apply to pieces of software other than database systems. Writing a message into a message queue often needs to be done within a transaction, which means that if subsequently the transaction aborts, the message is not sent.

As I wrote earlier, many of you already know all this well. However, what is less well known is that while IT applications move forward in transaction steps, businesses move forward in task steps, and tasks can be made up of several transactions. This means that a business requires that a task be atomic, consistent, isolated, and durable. An obvious solution is to make the task a single transaction, but because humans are involved in the decision making, a task will often take several minutes rather than a few microseconds, and to lock out data for so long would most likely kill performance. Furthermore, you have to allow for the fact that people might start a task but then go off to lunch and finish it when they get back or, even worse, start a task but are then interrupted and leave the task forever unfinished. We need another way to ensure that the task is consistent, building on transaction consistency but not assuming that transaction consistency solves all the problems.

Usually the solution is simple. Suppose there is a warehouse application and workers are picking orders from a list to make up a package. We can make the task isolated if we can stop two workers from picking the same order at the same time. A solution is to make the worker select the order and mark it before going to pick the stock. Someone who then tries to select the same order will be notified that it has already been assigned to someone else. You can consider this application as using another variation on the check-in/checkout protocol; the users are reserving something to work on, doing whatever they have to do, and finally releasing the data—after it has been updated—for someone else to work on. There is always an additional issue with a check-in/checkout protocol. What happens if the person who has checked out the data forgets about it, leaving the data in limbo and untouchable by anyone else? You need an additional management facility first to see who has had data assigned for an excessively long period of time and then to take it away.

Another example of a task that takes more than one transaction is a long form. You will be familiar with these from paying for your purchases online. You usually go through several steps: check that the order is correct, fill in your delivery details, fill in your credit card details, and confirm. At the end of each step the data is updated on the database, but nothing will happen to the order until it has been confirmed. It is possible for several days to pass before each of the steps is completed. This can be handled so long as you can ensure that the order is updated only by the person who first created it. The ACID properties are ensured by the rule that a single person (or the proxy for the person, such as an e-mail address) can work on only one order at one time, and by the fact that the final submit is done under the control of a single database transaction.

When a task is made up of multiple transactions, it is almost always possible to define it like a check-in/checkout protocol. The first step is to assign a data record to a user, and the last step is to release the data so other users can work on it. It becomes complicated when other data is updated during the task. In the warehouse example, when an item is picked from stock, there may be an update on the system to reduce the number of items left in stock, and maybe the new level will dip below a threshold so that a reorder of the stock is automatically initiated. But what happens if the item is returned to stock because something happens and the order is canceled? The application should ensure that the stock level is incremented again, but the stock reorder may be harder to stop. The designer must consider such scenarios, and let's face it, unless the item is very expensive, the probable outcome is that the decision will be to let the reorder proceed.

This is an instance of another point: while a task should obey the ACID properties, sometimes we can relax the requirements because the business consequences are not severe. However, analyzing what is needed to implement the ACID properties for a task leads you to identify what happens if it goes wrong, at which point you can decide whether you care or not.

With all transactions you must consider the possibility that the transaction will complete on the database but the system will fail before the message is sent to the user. A bad scenario is when the user needs a document printed and the task fails after the database was fully updated but before the document is printed. It may be necessary to have a reprint facility whereby the output is resent. Naturally you have to ensure that the output is sent only to someone authorized to receive it, which could be the person who first asked for it or a manager.

Note that although this chapter is about end user interfaces, a similar problem applies to services. A transaction will take place within the service call, so it is possible for the system to fail after the transaction has committed but before the client application has received the output message. If it is really important not to lose this data, you can put it in a message queue and synchronize writing to the message queue with the database transaction. Otherwise you may want to write an additional service function that returns a copy of the last data sent.

The user interface details described earlier in the chapter had a heading called "Integrity." This is where you tell the programmers how the task integrity is managed and what they have to do to maintain it. For convenience I repeat the example here:

```
Integrity
      A: On time-out, roll back to last saved copy.
      I: Each input is associated with a user.
```

The idea is to describe how integrity is maintained using the headings A, C, I, and D. In practice C and D do not need documenting, and of course if a screen does no updates, an integrity heading is not required.

As we have seen, task integrity builds on transaction integrity. Similarly, process integrity builds on task integrity. I discussed process integrity in Chapter 5, "The Relationship with the Business," and showed an example of a task outcome diagram (Figure 5.8). Task outcome diagrams are the main tool for analyzing process integrity. Even at the process level the concepts of atomicity, consistency, isolation, and durability come into play. For instance, I likened a process diagram to a model train going around a model train track; isolation means don't let the trains get mixed up. A real-life example of task or process isolation going wrong is delivering an order to the wrong customer.

The User Interface Design and the Other Detailed Designs

The user interface designer cannot work in complete isolation. In addition to taking input from the context design, the user interface designer needs to talk with the technical designer and the database designer.

The technical designer should provide input for the service interface design, especially in answering the analysis questions on recovery, performance, and so forth. Also, if there is a decision about whether to use any special end user devices (e.g., a device with a small screen), this should be decided by the user interface designer and the technical designer. The database design should provide input on the actual data attributes of the data tables. The application designer and the database designer will often work together to identify the detailed structure of the data input and output in the screens, but there will be data that will be used by other applications, and it is the database designer who must have ultimate control of the data design in the databases.

The project manager must ensure that everyone is working together. Having frequent short meetings of all the designers is probably the best approach.

Concluding Remarks

Designing for ease of use is difficult, mainly because there are so many aspects of the application that come together to create a good or bad experience for the user. At the context design level you need to ensure that the tasks are doing what the business needs and that the users are not being laden with too much (or too little) work. The technical design ensures that the applications perform and are reliable. The database design should ensure that there is data consistency across the organization and that the same data is not input into many applications. But the user interface design is the linchpin for achieving good ease of use.

It is important that the user interface be designed as a whole, not designed in little bits incrementally. There are plenty of bad Web sites around, even from seriously techy companies, that amply illustrate the perils of ad hoc Web site development.

Designers must put themselves in the place of the users of the application. They must also consider all kinds of users, in particular users who are just starting out using the application and users who are experts.

This chapter has some hints on what makes an easy-to-use application. This is far from a complete list and is biased by what I like about some applications and hate about others and by what has worked for me. There is extensive literature on ease of use, albeit mostly about graphic design.

This chapter also discussed the user interface aspect of transaction and task integrity, in other words, the impact of a failure on the user. The reason for discussing it in this chapter is that the user interface design is the major document for briefing the programmers on what they need to do.

Designing for ease of use is something all the designers of the application must think about and think about frequently. It is another of the important aspects of design that are hard to specify in formal requirements. Thus if you have outsourced user interface design, you must have a plan for reviewing the ease of use. You must also be convinced that the designers are flexible and responsive to user concerns. Unfortunately, many designers take criticism of their designs as a personal affront. If this is a problem, one way to counter it is to insist that the designers present two logical user interface designs. As the section "From Tasks to Clicks" showed, this can easily be done with little impact on total project duration. It also helps considerably that changing the user interface design does not mean rewriting code as it does in many of today's design methodologies.

Chapter 9

Database Design

There are whole books written about database design, and I cannot hope to give you all the information you need to become a fully fledged database designer. My intention in this chapter is to tell you enough about database design for you to work well with a specialist database designer. To this end I try to give some insight into how database design has developed and what issues database designers face. I also want to emphasize the importance of having central oversight of data. Data is an organizational resource that should be controlled like any other valuable organizational asset, so even if you are designing a small database that you think is going to be used by only one stand-alone application, you should still work with the knowledge and support of the central database design team.

This chapter has five sections. The first is about database design and the practice of database design. The second is about database design theory. This section also addresses the question of whether the theory helps you become a better designer. The third is about the potential for conflict between database designers and programmers. This is followed by a short section on database access services which are commonly promoted by the programming fraternity. Finally, there is a section on NoSQL, which offers an alternative approach to traditional databases.

Database Design

Data is stored in a database only if it means something. I have seen very little discussion in the literature about the meaning of data, but to my mind it is fundamental and guides database design.

Data can mean several things:

- **External tracking.** The data tracks some state in the outside world, for instance, customer names and addresses. The implication is that there must be mechanisms in place to keep the data as accurate as possible but always with the knowledge that the outside world may have changed and no one has had the opportunity to update the data to keep up with the change.

- **Internal tracking.** The data tracks some state in the organization, in particular, the state of a business process. A difference between this and data used for external tracking is that the data must always be accurate because it is the only record the business has of where it is in each ongoing process.

- **Internal entity.** The data is a business object (the terminology is a bit clumsy but I can't think of anything better). An example is a bank account. Once upon a time, bank accounts were records written in big fat ledger books. Today the only record is the record in the database.

- **Summaries and indexes.** The data is used for searching or analysis and is a copy of other data or is a consolidation of other data (such as totals, averages, maximums). It is important that the copied data be synchronized and that the consolidated data be accurate.

- **Internal IT.** The data helps make the IT systems and applications work and has no organizational meaning outside of the IT systems. Examples are security logon name and password and performance monitoring data.

As you can see, the notion of consistency and accuracy is different for each of these categories of data. Furthermore, there is no notion of consistency and accuracy unless you consider how the data is obtained, managed, and used.

Understanding the meaning of data is crucial when analyzing the context design. Looking at each category of data, we can list what needs to be done:

- **External tracking.** There must be tasks to create the data, update it, and delete or archive it, and there must be good reason to think that those tasks are doing as good a job as is needed to keep the data in the database in sync with the outside world.

- **Internal tracking.** Each time the status of a process changes, the data must be updated to reflect the change without fail.

- **Internal entity.** As in the previous case, this data must also be 100% accurate.

- **Summaries and indexes.** Every task that changes underlying data must change these data tables as well.
- **Internal IT.** That's up to you.

The context design identifies the data tables with the exception of the internal IT tables. I have described context design data tables as being tables of data objects. Speaking for a moment to those who understand database jargon, I call them data objects because while developing the context design, we have no way of knowing whether the data objects are in first normal form. A data object representing a product, for instance, may have a complex structure. The important point to remember (for those who are not database experts, too) is that context design data tables may correspond to several data tables in the database design.

During context design we may also, as mentioned before, identify a few of the attributes because that comes about naturally when describing what tasks do. But you are unlikely to identify all data attributes because the purpose of many attributes is simply for information; in other words, they are not used in the application to do anything except be stored in the database. I handle these in the context design by introducing the notion of a data bag. A data bag holds a data attribute and allows us in the context design to describe data attributes being updated and moved when we don't know the details of what the data attributes are. The database designer must work in conjunction with the user interface designer to fill out the definition of the bags and hence complete the attribute description of the data tables. Many of the data bag data attributes will be identified only by the stakeholders telling the user interface designer that such-and-such a screen needs to display such-and-such data. Often there is a business decision to be made here; the more attributes there are, the more effort is required to fill them and the greater the likelihood that they will be filled incorrectly, but the additional attributes can be used for searching and analysis. It was also noted in Chapter 6, "The Relationship with the Users," that data is passed from application to application, and this data is often described in the context design as being a data bag because the context designer does not know its structure (see Figure 6.1). The database designer must find out the data attributes in these bags, too.

If there are several data bags in a data object (as shown in Figure 6.1), when the database designer comes to identify all the attributes in the bag, he or she may find the same attribute in more than one bag. For instance, a data object representing a product description might record the product's weight, but the delivery application also needs that information. The database designer needs to confirm that the attributes are the same and, if so, put only one attribute in the completed database design.

Of course, while it's fine to have data bags in the context design, the database designer has no such luxury; the database designer needs the detail, and that might mean looking at existing database structures or talking to other application designers because the reason the data attributes were undefined was that they were used by different applications. In this case, the database designer needs to tell the user interface designer what fields to put in the screens.

Defining attributes becomes particularly difficult when the same data table is used by different departments and one wants many detailed attributes while the other wants a few general ones. I once wrote an application that stored information about business methods (the plan was to disseminate this information throughout the business in order to promote best practices), and for each method there were 20-plus data attributes: Name, Status, Owner, Investor, UpdateDate, Symptoms, ImpactMoney, RootCause, ConfidenceOnRootCause, Solution, ResidualImpact, Implications, and many others. (I don't know what they all meant either.) What would have happened if another department objected to this approach and wanted only six attributes? If the department that loads the data wants 20 attributes, that is normally not much of a problem. You may have to reformat the data to present it to the department that wants six, but they can often live with more data than they need. But if it is the department that loads the data that wants only six attributes, conflict will arise and the database designer is unfortunately stuck in the middle. You may be able to develop an application that allows minimal data to be input but encourages the user to add more, the way Facebook is always prodding you to add more personal information to your profile.

A more subtle problem arises when one word is used by two departments with two different meanings. This can happen to attributes with general names like Status or Comment, but I have seen examples of two departments having technical definitions of the same word with different meanings. Perhaps the equitable solution is to qualify the term in some way so both departments can carry on using their term as a shorthand. Thus we might have in a product data object two Status attributes that we end up calling Design-Status and Marketing-Status. But before naming the attributes, the designer has to notice that there are two attributes, not one; it is easy to leap to the erroneous conclusion that two people are talking about the same thing. For instance, in a warehouse and distribution application the dimensions of a product would be the dimensions including all the packaging. But a customer would want to know the dimensions unpacked. One diagnostic of attributes being different is that they are set or used in two different places.

Different words can be used for the same concept. Since the user sees only the name of the data on the screen, this is not necessarily a problem. Again, the bigger difficulty is the database designer realizing the state of affairs. Attributes are often updated in only one or two places and usually by the same business unit, which will tend to use the same jargon word for the attribute's name. Hence, one diagnostic for two attributes being in fact the same is that only one of the names is updated.

Some attributes are calculated values (sometimes called derived values). For instance, from length, width, and height you can calculate volume, and from share price and dividend you can calculate yield.

In order to detect all these problems, the database designer must pay close attention to where all attribute values are created, changed, and used, not only which tasks do what action, but also which user groups do what action. If the pattern is odd in any way, further investigation is needed.

Another area of design difficulty has to do with null attributes. A null attribute is an attribute without a value. There can be many reasons for the lack of a value:

- **Membership of a subclass.** For instance, suppose we have a table of people in a school system. Some people will be teachers, some parents. A parent who is not a teacher will have all the teacher-associated attributes set to null because setting a value for them has no meaning. (This example is discussed in relation to Figure 9.1.)

- **Value not known.** A data object representing a person may not have an address attribute set because the organization does not know what it is.

- **Value does not exist.** On the other hand, if a person really is living in a cardboard box on a street, the address value does not exist. If the data is being used to track a process, it could be that the step in the process that sets the attribute has not happened yet. For instance, in data representing an order, the delivery date will only be assigned by the distribution application. (And maybe there should be two delivery dates—planned delivery date and actual delivery date.)

- **Null has some special meaning.** If the record is there only for the benefit of the programmer, it can mean something special. For instance, if the IP network address of a table of devices is null, it could mean the device uses dynamic IP assignment.

No database system to my knowledge makes distinctions among these kinds of nulls, which is probably just as well as sometimes you don't know why the value is missing. For instance, the data can come from a customer filling in a form who has left some boxes empty.

The subclass point needs more discussion. Programmers will be familiar with the concept of subclasses from programming, but unfortunately there are as many different concepts of subclasses as there are programming languages that support them. Some of the conceptual issues are discussed in the next section; here I want to discuss some practical points. Let us start by looking at an example: teachers, parents, and people (see Figure 9.1).

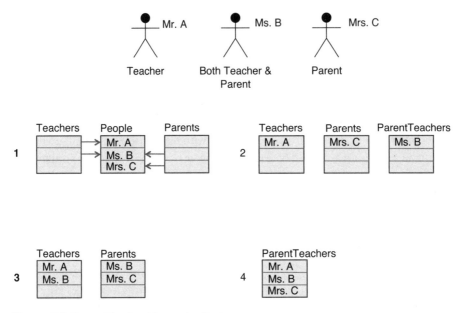

Figure 9.1 *Parent-Teacher Alternative Designs*

Teachers and Parents are People. You can store them in the database in several different ways, and they differ in the amounts of data and schema duplication and the complexity of the program finding and updating the information. (For those uninitiated in the database priesthood, a *schema* is a definition of the structure of the database. For instance, it defines the names of the tables and the names and the type—number, text, date, and so on—of the columns in the table. The words *column* and *attribute* are used more or less interchangeably, but strictly speaking a column is like a column in a spreadsheet and an attribute is the value at the intersection of a column and a row.) The different solutions to the Teachers/Parents/People design, numbered 1 to 4 in Figure 9.1, are as follows:

1. **Three tables:** People, Parents, and Teachers with a link from Parents to People and another link from Teachers to People. The People table holds the basic information about people common to everyone like name and address. There is no duplication of either the schema or the data.

2. **Three tables:** Parents, Teachers, and ParentTeachers and the People information are separately stored in each of the tables. If someone has an entry in the ParentTeachers table, there is no entry for that person in either the Parents or the Teachers table. The ParentTeachers table has the parent information, the teacher information, and the people information. There is no duplication of the data but a great deal of duplication of the schema information.

3. **Two tables:** Parents and Teachers with People information stored in both. For a parent-teacher the people information is duplicated in each table.

4. **One table:** People table with attributes available for parents and teachers. The parent attributes are null if the person is not a parent, and the teacher attributes are null if the person is not a teacher.

Which one is best? Number 1 is the *purest* implementation since it has the least duplication of data and schema information, but the two-table solution (number 3) is the easiest to program, and since parent-teachers are not that common, it is not that inconvenient either. An additional factor to consider is that you may want to hold different personal information about parents and teachers. For parents you may have only one phone number, for instance, while for teachers you may have several.

Note the factors used to make the decision. Duplication of data is one issue; in our example, if someone's address changes, the question is, "How many tables need to be updated?" Another issue is duplication of schema information; in the two-table solution we have to ask the question, "Do we have to keep People information in the Teachers and Parents tables in sync?" In all probability there will be different screens for updating the Teachers and Parents data, hence this solution relies on the application user to remember to update both tables. The third issue is ease of programming. The three-table solution with a ParentTeachers table (number 2 in the list) is dreadful in this regard because for many actions we have to search two tables. The one-table solution is not great either as we often have to search the one table for teachers only or parents only, and to simplify this code we will probably end up adding an extra attribute to indicate whether the entry is a teacher, a parent, or both. A final factor is efficiency. The three-table solution requires a join between the Teachers and People tables whenever we want to display a teacher's name. Let's be honest, though—given that we are talking about only a few thousand records at most, the chances are no one will notice the efficiency gains of moving from one solution to another.

Differences between subclass hierarchies are not the only areas of conflict where one department will want one table and another department will want two. A common situation is where one attribute of a table could be used as a key to another table. Suppose there is a school application for managing pupils that has a table in it for Forms in which there is an attribute called FormTeacherName. (I am assuming all pupils are assigned to a form even if they are not doing the same set of subjects as every other pupil in the form.) If this application is merged with another application that manages the school's timetable, this application might have a table for Teachers that has much more information in it than just the teacher's name. When the merge is done, instead of the Form record having a

FormTeacherName attribute it has a FormTeacherRef attribute that is a reference to the Teacher record in the Teachers table. In database jargon, an attribute that holds a name is converted to an attribute that holds a foreign key (a reference to a row in another table).

This example is still simply an example where one department wants more information than another, and in general that can be easily accommodated so long as one department does not expect the other department to provide the additional information. The greater problems are detecting and resolving differences of opinion about the meaning of data. This is best explained with an example. I once extended an existing application that handled business operational reviews to handle personnel reviews. My stakeholder's idea was that each person should be assigned a role, and associated with each role would be a pro forma review structure—in other words, the list of all the different review criteria by which members of the role would be assessed. I am used to the word *role* being used in an IT context where a single person can have multiple roles. My stakeholder was adamant that a person could have only one role. What if a role is called *manager*, I said, and the boss wants to change the pro forma review structure to add a new measurement criterion for all managers? Surely you want someone to be both a manager and, say, an IT application developer or a sales person. He said that in that case you specify a new measurement criterion and you develop a system for copying that criterion to multiple roles. This would allow you, he pointed out, to be flexible in applying the criterion; even general management criteria should not necessarily be applied to all managers. For instance, a business may decree that all managers should be competent on the CRM application but then realize that if someone is simply managing the business's real estate this is silly. So I agreed to put that in—he was the stakeholder, not I. It is easy to imagine that instead of him and me it could be one department and another department and the database designer would be in the middle.

The important point of this example is not that he was right and I was wrong or that I was right and he was wrong; it is that the structure of the data depends on what you want to do with it. The database designer must figure out if there is a real case of conflicting visions from the cases where names are changed and one department simply wants more detail than others. Real conflicts can usually be resolved by explaining to one group of people what the other group is thinking; the one group will either be happy to go along with it or point out some flaw in the other's thinking. In the latter case, you go back to the other department and explain the alternative design and why it's important. In very rare cases, you can't find a common view and you will have to ask senior management to resolve the problem.

Database Design Theory

It might seem odd to discuss theory after discussing the practice, but the reason is, to put it bluntly, that I have long thought that database theory tackles the problem of database design from the wrong angle. Database designers like to study the data outside the context of the applications, which, as I hope is clear from the previous section, makes little sense. But knowing something about database theory helps in two ways: it provides some analysis techniques to check whether the design works, and it helps when there is conflict over data structure to analyze precisely where the conflict lies.

Before I describe more traditional database theory such as normalization, I think it will help some of my readership if I discuss the differences between a programmer's view of data and a database designer's view of data, in particular, why have I used the words *data table* rather than *class*. For the next few paragraphs I am going to assume you understand object-oriented (OO) programming concepts, so if you don't, please skip them. Alternatively, the concepts are explained in "Introduction to Object Oriented Programming Concepts (OOP) and More" [32].

Both objects and database table rows have attributes and a hence need some other structure—called a class in the case of objects or a schema in the case of database tables—that defines the name and the type of each of the attributes. The difference is that when you define a table in a database schema, you get not only the description of the attributes but also a container of rows. Put another way, to convert a table into the equivalent program structure you need both a class and a variable, which is the set of objects of the class; for instance:

```
table Person { string name; date born; string address};
```

becomes

```
class Person { string name; date born; string address};
set<Person> personset = new set<Person>();
```

The programming way of doing things is more flexible because an object of class `Person` is not confined to a single variable; you can have `personset1` and `personset2` if you wish. The reason why I do not think this feature is sufficiently important to be used in the context model is that most tasks start with finding an object, and having objects of the same type spread over multiple variables just adds complexity to no advantage. Some programmers might be thinking at this point that sometimes it is useful to put objects into other types of collection variables such as queues, ordered lists, or stacks rather than a set. For instance, when a warehouse application wants to list the orders that it needs to service, it wants the orders in an oldest-first order—in other words, the orders should be in a first-in, first-out (FIFO) queue. The trouble is that in real-life systems there are errors, and these other kinds of collection variables don't handle them well. For instance, if orders cannot be serviced because stock is unavailable or orders are canceled, maintaining the order of the queue programmatically becomes more difficult. It is easy enough to replicate the effect of a FIFO queue by recording the date and time the order was made and then searching for the oldest incomplete order. In general, it is more flexible to represent any ordering or object state using data attributes like date and time, rather than putting the object into collection variables.

As every programmer knows, in OO technology you can have classes that are defined as subclasses of other classes. A subclass allows you to define a new kind of object by adding attributes to its parent class. Classes also define functions, and a subclass can override the code in the functions as well as add new functions. Here are some points worth noting:

1. An object cannot change class, even to a subclass of the object's class (at least in every programming language I know about). For instance, if you define `ReleasedProduct` as a subclass of `Product`, you cannot convert a `Product` object to a `ReleasedProduct` object. The nearest you can do is create a new `ReleasedProduct` object and delete the old `Product` object, remembering to fix up all the references pointing at the `Product` object to point at the new `ReleasedProduct` object. This is so clunky that almost everyone would simply put all the additional attributes for the `ReleasedProduct` in the `Product` class.

2. The attributes and operations available in an object of class C are also available to every object of class D if D is a subclass of C. In a type-checking language, you can use an object of class D in a parameter whenever an object of class C is defined as the parameter's type.

3. Not all subsets are subclasses. Some subsets are merely objects that obey a certain condition; for instance, a square is a rectangle that happens to have equal-length sides. It makes little sense to define `Squares` as a subclass of `Rectangles` unless `Squares` in your program for some bizarre reason have additional attributes or operations.

4. Just because some code can be reused does not make it a good candidate for a subclass. For instance, we could have a class called `Square` with one attribute—height—and we could define a subclass of `Square` called `Rectangle` and add a new attribute—width. The reason why this is bad is because of type checking; every parameter that matches to a `Square` will also match to a `Rectangle`.

5. Some programming languages support multiple inheritance (subclasses that have more than one parent); most don't. One reason for this is that the programming language's syntax has to set some rules on multiple inheritance that are far from obvious. For instance, it must resolve issues like this: if A inherits from B and C, and both B and C inherit from D, are there two copies of D's attributes in A or only one, or is this "diamond" structure disallowed? There are a lot of people who say that multiple inheritance should be banned, but I have seen it used well (e.g., the WTL class library [33]).

6. Class libraries—collections of predefined classes—are used to define reusable code. Class libraries come in various styles. In some, a class implements lots of features and the programmer is expected to use only a few of them. In others, there are many more classes and each is more specific in its functionality. Some use templates and supply "building block" classes (my words) to allow you to assemble functionality by using multiple inheritance [33].

So why don't I use the programmer's way of describing data for the database? One reason is that the restrictions I've listed are more serious for databases than for programs, as my example of the `ReleasedProduct` class shows.

Another reason is that object design introduces irrelevant questions. Let us suppose you want to make the context design object oriented. You could do this by associating every task with some data. Sometimes this looks like a good idea—for instance, you can say an *account* object supports the *debit* task. But sometimes you have a choice of objects, and you get into a ridiculous discussion about which object takes precedence. Thus you *assign* a *course* to a *teacher*. Is *assign* a task defined for the *course* class or for the *teacher* class or even for a *course-teacher* class? Of course it doesn't matter, but now you have three alternative designs for exactly the same problem that, when implemented, could end up with exactly the same code. In other words, you are being forced to make a decision when no decision is necessary.

But a more important reason for not having an OO angle on design is the confusion between object models and semantic models. A *semantic model* is the notion of structuring the data in a way that corresponds to how information is structured in the real world. Let us see how this can be done.

Think of all the words we use to describe the information in an application, and then think of how the words are related to each other. We can say that Teacher is a Person, Parent is a Person, a Person has a Father and a Mother who are also Persons, a Classroom is part of a School, and a School has many Teachers. The words *is a*, *part of*, *has a* are relationships that bring structure to the information. If you pick up a textbook on programming, you will as likely as not find that the class-subclass relationship is explained as a way of modeling *is a* relationships. This is misleading. While a subclass can be used to model an *is a* relationship, often it is not, and sometimes it contradicts an *is a* relationship. We have seen one example of this already—not all subsets make good subclasses (point 3 in my previous list—a square is a rectangle). Another way of looking at an *is a* relationship is as a classification hierarchy. However, you can frequently have multiple classification hierarchies. For instance, if the objects are vehicles, you can classify them as trucks, tanks, sedans, SUVs, motorbikes, and bicycles, but you can also classify them by where they can go—off-road, on-road, flying cars, cars that are boats. A third form of classification could be power unit—electric powered, diesel powered, gasoline powered, and human powered. The only way of modeling multiple hierarchies using subclasses is to have multiple inheritance, such as defining a `dieselpoweredSuv` and a `gasolinepoweredSuv`, because the rule is that you can create an object only with one named class or subclass. It does not take long for the number of combinations across multiple hierarchies to become unmanageably high.

Taking a semantic approach to database design by trying to understand a semantic model of the information used in a business can be a fruitful exercise, and I think it is something we tend to do instinctively, I suspect because semantic relationships are hardwired into our understanding of the real world in some way. But there is a small danger and a big danger. The small danger is that classification is not an exact science. For instance, you define a bicycle as a two-wheeled vehicle without an engine and along comes an electric bicycle. The big danger is not knowing when to stop. I recall looking at a catalog of a company that rents equipment to builders (concrete mixers, diggers, etc.), companies (trucks, portable air-conditioning units, etc.), and gardeners (mowing machines, seed drills, chain saws, etc.). At one end of the scale you could build a database that has only one class—catalog entries. At the other end of the scale you could build a database that has numerous subclasses—for instance, *catalog-entry*, *builders-tools* subclass of *catalog-entry*, *diggers* subclass of *builders-tools*. It makes sense to go into fine subdivisions only if you hold different data for each subdivision. Unfortunately, when you are just thinking about data separately from thinking about the application that uses the data, it is easy to imagine that there might be different data for each subdivision whereas in fact there isn't.

We are kind of going backward in time in this survey of database theory. The object-oriented approach was the latest. Its selling point has been the close match between database and programming language, but at least as far as I can tell, it seems to have made few inroads into the relational database consensus. Semantic database systems were researched mostly in the 1970s and 1980s, and I think produced many fruitful ideas that went nowhere. I worked on a semantic database system called SIM for Burroughs (which later became part of Unisys), and I know from experience that we couldn't sell it.

Relational database systems have dominated since the 1980s, and I think the main reason is that they seem simple. The relational model is normally described as having tables, rows, and columns, rather like spreadsheet tables. It is more complex than that. There are

- **Primary keys**—one or more columns whose values uniquely identify a row.
- **Foreign keys**—columns that hold a primary key of a row in a different or the same table. Foreign keys implement a one-to-many relationship between the row that holds the primary key and the row that holds the foreign key.
- **Domains**—usually not implemented—define the set of values from which the column values can be taken.
- **Constraints**—like uniqueness, required (a row must have a value in a required column), and check clauses (such as a parent's age must be greater than a child's age).

The relational data model has always been promoted as having a design methodology soundly based in normalization. Normalization is a way of detecting anomalies in the structure of the database. Suppose you have a table that is a merge of the Course and Lesson tables, like so:

```
Table LessonAndCourse {Lesson code, Course name, course info,
lesson info}
```

The anomalies are:

- **Create anomaly**—you can't create new course information without creating a lesson at the same time.
- **Update anomaly**—if you want to change the information about a course, you may have to update all the lesson rows that belong to that course.
- **Delete anomaly**—if you delete the last row of a lesson for a course, you also delete the course information.

The way normalization is done is to look at the attributes. To my mind this makes normalization a good way of checking a database but not a tool for designing one, because instead of starting from tables and populating them with attributes, it starts from attributes and splits them into tables. However, that makes it a good check on the correctness of the database design. In particular, the issues it identifies are real, and even if you decide not to fix them you want to know that they are there.

I am not going to describe the concepts of normalization in full as there are many other textbooks that do that in detail. But I hope to describe enough to show that it is useful. Imagine a table with attributes A, B, C, and D. Normalization looks at every pair of attributes (AB, AC, AD, BC, BD, CD) and asks whether one attribute is fully functionally dependent on the other attribute. If A is fully functionally dependent on B, then:

- If B is null, A is null.

- If in one row the value of B is x and the value of A is y, then in every other row in which the value of B is x the value of A is y.

If A is fully functionally dependent on B, let us write it as A $\longrightarrow$ B. Essentially normalization is about arranging the attributes into tables in which all the attributes are fully functionally dependent on one attribute. That one attribute is the primary key for the table.

That is the simple story. The primary key could be a compound of two or more attributes, as in

$$A \longrightarrow \{B,D\}$$

Furthermore, you may have a table with several alternative keys—known as candidate keys—any of which can be used as the primary key.

So what does it all mean? Let us step back a moment and discuss keys and relationships. A *key* is some data that identifies a row. Keys must be chosen carefully. For instance, people are normally identified by their names, but of course several people might have the same name, so in databases people are often identified by their Social Security number or similar. This is fine until you find someone who does not have a Social Security number, such as a foreigner. Even if the person does have a Social Security number, you may not know it. Looking again at our school example which holds information about people, parents, and teachers, you may find that you know the teacher's Social Security number, but you don't know the parent's Social Security number. In practice the world of business is full of invented primary keys, like product code, catalog number, customer number, and account number. Any candidate key must

- Never be null

- Always be unique (every row in the table must have a different key from all other rows in the same table)

- Must never change in the lifetime of the row

If there are a number of candidate keys, you would normally choose the shortest or the most memorable. In addition to primary keys there are foreign keys that as noted previously can be used to build relationships. For example, in our school database we could have tables:

> Subject—attributes are Subject Code, Subject Name, Head of Subject
>
> Course—attributes are Course Code, Subject Code, Teacher
>
> Lesson—attributes are Lesson Code, Course Code
>
> Teacher—attributes are Social Security Number, Name

The first attribute of every table is its primary key. All the attributes ending with *code* have invented values. Head of Subject in Subject and Teacher in Course are foreign keys pointing at a teacher, so they might contain the Social Security number of the teacher. The Subject Code attribute in the Course table and Course Code in Lesson are other foreign keys. What we have here are the following relationships:

> Subject to Course: one to many
>
> Course to Lesson: one to many
>
> Subject to Head of Subject: many to one (it could be one to one, which you can ensure by specifying that the Head of Subject attribute is unique)
>
> Teacher to Course: one to many

In other words, primary key attributes have two roles. One is like any other attribute—it is a value that conveys information. The other is to identify the row. Because of this, it is extremely inconvenient to change the value of the key because you have to change all the values of its foreign keys. Some database designers will split this dual role by having a separate generated primary key—for instance, a simple integer that increases by one for every new row (many database systems have a feature that implements this automatically) which is set when the row is inserted into the table and never changed. This used to be called a surrogate, but these days it is more likely that you will hear people call it an object identity. Whatever it is called, its function is to identify the row without having any additional meaningful value. Such a feature is especially useful when other candidate keys are long or have multiple parts. There are differences of opinion here; some database designers think all key values should carry some meaning.

Database systems should support an important integrity constraint called *referential integrity*, which essentially is about ensuring that foreign keys are always valid. There are two possible implementations: either a row cannot be deleted if a foreign key references it, or all foreign keys referencing the deleted row are set to null.

It is sometimes nice to draw these relationships in a diagram. There are several different diagrammatic conventions, three of which are illustrated in Figure 9.2. These are

1. **Crow's feet**—the "feet" parts indicate many.

2. **UML**—the asterisk indicates that there are many rows at the other end of the relationship.

3. **Entity-relationship diagrams**—relationships are represented by rhombuses.

An important part of database design is checking whether the relationships are correct. For instance, are all courses associated with only one subject? If not—for instance, some introductory courses could be shared across several subjects—the

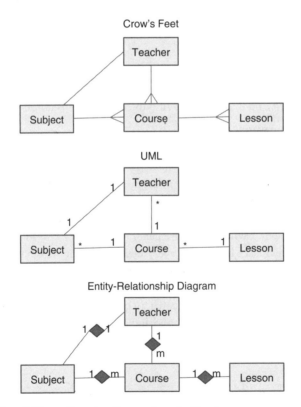

Figure 9.2 *Three Different Drawing Conventions for Databases*

relationship between Subject and Course is many to many. Can one teacher be head of subject for only one subject? If not, the relationship between Subject and Head of Subject is many to one. And so on—for every relationship you should try to think of counterexamples and ask whether they can happen.

The relational data model implements many-to-many relationships as a separate table. Thus if more than one teacher can teach one course, you might have

```
TeacherCourse relationship table - attributes are: Teacher
number, Course code
```

This is a table that has two attributes, both of which are foreign keys, and the two attributes combine to form the primary key of the table. Many-to-many relationships can have attributes; the attributes tell you something about the nature of the relationship. (Arguably one-to-many relationships can have attributes, too, but since they can be stored in the table with the foreign key, they don't look any different from any other attribute.) Attributes of the TeacherCourse relationship may describe what role the teacher plays in delivering the course.

You can have ternary relationships as well. They have three foreign keys in the table. An example would be StudentCourseTeacher, which matches a student to the version of the course taught by a particular teacher. A ternary relationship has three parts to the key, each of which is a foreign key pointing at a row in a table. Ternary and higher-level relationships are rare; they are often two binary relationships mashed into one table. For instance, if a student is assigned to a course without being assigned to a particular teacher who teaches the course, the data is better expressed as two tables—a StudentCourse table and a CourseTeacher table. (For those interested in relational theory, let me show off my knowledge by noting that the normalization technique of testing for fourth normal form is in reality a convoluted way of checking that a ternary relationship is better implemented by two binary relationships.)

The previous section was a discussion of subclasses. Normalization (and relational theory in general) says nothing about subclasses. If you work through a normalization exercise where subclasses—often called subtables in relational databases—exist (e.g., the PeopleTeacherParent table), whether a subtable will be identified as such will entirely depend on whether it happens to have a key. If People, Parents, and Teachers all have the same key—Social Security number, say—normalization will not split the tables at all. But if teachers have their own key—a special teacher number, say—the normalization will split off a Teachers table. Database designers tend to split out each subclass as a separate table to avoid nulls. (As an aside, SQL has flaws when handling nulls, mainly to do with the fact—OK, this is going to get complicated—that any expression in which a variable is null returns undefined,

which if used in a WHERE condition acts as if it were false. Thus "SELECT *
WHERE (X = 3) OR NOT (X = 3)" will not return any rows where X is null. The
consequences of this are beyond the scope of this book.)

Can normalization go too far? Many programmers dislike the fact that normalization fragments large tables into many smaller tables. This means they have to write
SQL statements with lots of joins in them—which frankly should not be a problem for a professional programmer who should know SQL data access statements
in detail. There may be, in a few rare cases, performance problems from having to
process a lot of joins, but that aside, my sympathies are with the database designers. Programmers are often looking at the data from the narrow perspective of one
application, and when you merge the data structure from many applications, frag-
mentation ensues, as illustrated in the example of FormTeacherName becoming
FormTeacherRef as described previously.

Sometimes, however, an unnormalized row structure is preferable. The check
whether it is acceptable is to look at the create, update, and delete anomalies listed
earlier. For instance, let us look at the Students and Parents tables; programmers will
often want to store parent information—say, name and telephone number—in the
student record, which implies duplication if there are two or more students at the
school with one set of parents. But in these days of divorce, remarriage, and so on, it
might not be such a bad idea to allow parent information to be associated with each
individual student.

In conclusion, you can ignore a rule when you know the consequences and are
prepared to live with them. What the normalization and relationship analysis techniques described here give you is help in finding design issues and understanding
their consequences.

It is often good practice to denormalize data when copying it to a data mart/
warehouse where it is used for searching. Of course, if you are not going to update
the data but only search it, update anomalies are not a concern.

Another case where an unnormalized structure may be better is when there is a
list of data for one data attribute. Relational database theory says nothing about
how complex the data in an attribute can be, so there is nothing in theory that stops
a data attribute from being a data structure of arbitrary complexity. It's just that the
database will retrieve and update the whole attribute as a single unit. This might
be fine for some big chunks of data like images. The issue comes when you want to
break apart the data attribute and search on part of the value. For instance, suppose
you want to allow an attribute in the Teachers table to have a list of phone numbers.
The database system will probably not allow you to do this directly, but you can subvert the system by declaring the phone number to be a string of characters and putting in a list of phone numbers separated by commas. The problem is then answering
the query, "Find a teacher who has the following phone number." If this is an important query for you, it's best to make a separate table of teacher phone numbers.

Database theory does provide insights into the deeper structure of the data. However, database design is not an abstract exercise; it is intimately concerned with how the data is used and how the data has meaning in the outside world.

Programmers versus the Database Designer

Often the relationship between programmers and database designers can be described as prickly. In this section I want to explain why there is conflict in order to help chief designers and project managers resolve any tensions that might arise.

The fundamental reason behind the conflict is that programmers and database designers have different objectives. Programmers would often rather do any database design themselves as it is quicker, partly because having someone else brought in to oversee part of the design will always lead to delays, and partly because database designers always seem to make the databases more complicated and more difficult to program.

Database designers, on the other hand, feel that programmers don't understand their concerns and don't seem to understand that other people use their data. Database designers are also concerned about the accuracy of the data and the control of data as a business resource. By accuracy I mean not only that data is consistent (e.g., the product code in an order form identifies a real entry in the table of products) but also that the data is correct (e.g., the name of a person recorded in the database is really that person's name). By control of data as a business resource, I mean ensuring that the data is accessible to the people who need it and not accessible to the people who don't.

The management of data is important to an organization, so it would be rather nice if programmers and database designers didn't argue. So why do they argue? It boils down to the fact that programming an application with due concern for the data takes time and effort.

Let us take an example, illustrated in Figure 9.3.

Suppose in our school database we want to record what subjects a teacher teaches. A simple solution would be a text field in which people would add a list of subjects separated by commas. In the corresponding database there could be one data attribute that would be a string containing the list of subjects. This solution is really simple to program. Now along comes the database designer, and he or she wants a separate table for Subjects and a table, TeacherSubject, to represent the many-to-many relationship between teacher and subject. There are advantages to this structure, such as:

- The user does not have the opportunity to mistype a subject's name.

- You can much more easily do searches to find out all the teachers who teach a particular subject.

- The database can be integrated with a timetable application.

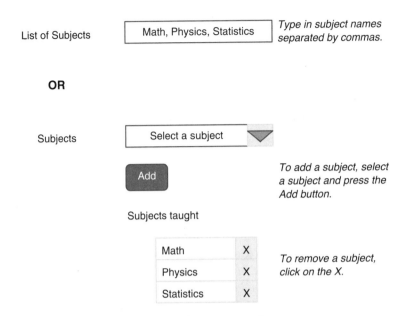

Figure 9.3 *Two Designs for Assigning Subjects to a Teacher*

But to program this new design properly, instead of having the user just type a list of subjects separated by commas, the programmer must do something like this:

- Create a drop-down list of subjects populated from the Subjects table.
- Create a button to put the currently selected item from the list and the teacher into a new row in the TeacherSubject table.
- Define a list of subjects that the teacher teaches and display it on the screen populated from the TeacherSubject table.
- Put an X against each row in the subject table to delete the entry.

This is a great deal more code than just a text field.

Let us extend this example and look at adding a new teacher record (Figure 9.4).

To add a new teacher, we press the New Teacher button, which blanks all the fields. We then put in the new data and press Save. Logically what is happening is that we are creating a new record when the New Teacher button is pressed and updating the record when Save is pressed. However, suppose the database designer has made the Name attribute required in the database—a logical move since you don't want an unnamed teacher. Now if the programmer tries to create a new record when the New Teacher button is pressed, the program gets an error because the Name attribute is not set. A solution is to delay creating a new record in the database until the

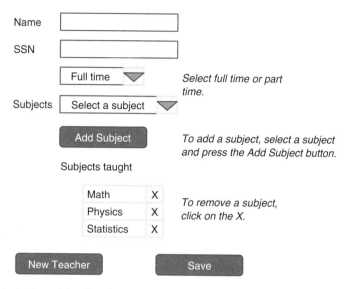

Figure 9.4 *Adding a New Teacher*

Save following the New Teacher action. This is not hard to program, but there is a problem: what about our old friend the Add Subject button? The TeacherSubject row cannot be created because there is no teacher record and therefore no teacher primary key.

There are several solutions:

- Create a dummy record with, say, ". . . no name . . ." in the Name field. You will be surprised how many ". . . no name . . ." teachers accumulate in the database because someone has pressed Add Teacher and not followed it by a Save.

- Disallow Add Subject until a Save has been done. This might mystify the user.

- In the Add Subject code, do a Save action automatically. If the user has not filled in the Name field, the error might be puzzling. (This is the solution I usually deploy because chances are that people will add a name before adding a subject simply because they fill in the fields on the screen from the top downward.)

- Build the entire new Teacher row and TeacherSubject rows in a programmatic data structure and add the TeacherSubject rows during the Save action. (This is arguably the ideal solution but is more complicated to implement.)

The programmer is likely to turn on the database designer and suggest that the Name attribute should not be required. However, this is rather like the ". . . no name . . ."

scenario, and the database will clog up with Teacher rows caused by pressing Add Teacher and not following it up with a Save. This shows that the required integrity constraint is not really a check on the end user; it is a check on the programmer.

Database integrity checks are important. My message to programmers is (and I am one myself): Please remember that there is one thing worse than a program failing or indeed a database failing, and that is updating the database with bad data. That way you have corruption in the database. If it's your job to fix the corruption, you have two large tasks: finding the source of the corruption and fixing the bad data. Even worse, other programs may rely on the database not being corrupt and will create more corruption or cause the program to fail. Such problems can be hard to pin down, let alone fix. So sorry, programmers, you should listen to the concerns of the database designers and find program solutions to whatever they throw at you.

Database Access Services

Because of the conflict between programmers and database designers, many programmers think you can and should hide the database access by creating a series of object-oriented classes that encapsulate all the database code. There are products in the marketplace that help you do this by generating a class library from a SQL schema. Some of these products allow you to specify more complex mappings than simply one SQL table equals one OO class. The question is, Should you use such products, and if so, how?

The reasons for having such an object library are:

- Most programmers don't have to understand the database or even SQL. This reason worries me. Personally, I think programmers should understand the database structure; they should be proficient in SQL and they should have a good understanding of database performance characteristics and availability features, even if they don't use them.

- Even if they do understand SQL, the syntax of using an OO interface is so much better than the function calls to SQL that it makes it worthwhile. I personally use the SQL-to-LINQ mapping if I am writing a C# database program these days simply because the code is so much easier to understand and maintain.

- You can change the database structure, and most programmers don't need to know. If the change is trivial—like renaming a column—this is true, but for more complex changes, as illustrated in the second design in Figure 9.3, the structure of the database and the design of the user interface go hand in hand.

- Implement a cache. It is common for there to be some tables in a database that just provide lookup codes (for instance, for airports, LHR is London Heathrow, JFK is New York Kennedy). These are small amounts of data that are read often and updated rarely, so there is a considerable performance benefit from having them in memory.

- There are some things that SQL does not do well. I once wrote a program a major part of which was handling an organization's management structure. Managers of managers, and so on, form a hierarchy, and SQL is clumsy at handling hierarchies, so I read the entire hierarchy into memory and handled it outside the database. This is cache as well, but it provides additional facilities over and above simply reading and updating records.

- If you are implementing one of the data copy schemes described in Chapter 7, "The Relationship to Other IT Projects," you can hide the complexities of the replication behind an object interface.

The last three points illustrate what to me is a general principle: putting a database behind a service interface works well when the program code in the service interface adds value above and beyond what the database provides.

However, some people go further. They implement what is called a *domain model*. In essence this is about creating an OO database design and implementing it as a class library. They then map from the classes to SQL, assuming they are using a SQL database. There are several things wrong with the idea. The first is that, in my humble opinion, as explained early in this chapter, OO classes are not ideal for defining databases. They are great for programming, but the reason has to do with how OO concepts extend classical programmatic type matching and how overriding promotes abstraction. Don't let people tell you that OO classes provide a natural way of modeling real-world data structure semantics because they don't. The second reason I dislike domain models is that it seems silly to design the database twice, once as an OO model and again as a relational model. Not only is this more work, it is also dangerous, because the reason why a relational database is designed as it is often has to do with how the data is used by other applications. The temptation with domain models is to design for one application only, and the danger is that the database may be incompatible with other applications, as discussed previously in the section on database design.

In summary, there are many good reasons to give a SQL database an OO veneer, and if you can add some selective caching and/or additional database management functions to the objects, that is even better. But don't do an OO design of the database and then try to map it to a relational database designed by others.

If there is a problem with mapping object design to database design, there is another approach, and that is not to use a relational database.

NoSQL

As I write this book (in 2015), the latest hot trend in data management is NoSQL. I have heard that NoSQL stands for "Not Only SQL," but since I am not sure there is a NoSQL product that supports SQL, I think "No SQL" seems equally appropriate.

There are several different kinds of NoSQL products, but basically there is a range from ones geared toward searching documents through ones geared toward rowlike data as in a conventional database to ones geared toward network data. (The latter, called graph databases, store their data in nodes and connections.) However, to my knowledge none of them has a schema.

Recall that a database schema describes the database structure, and not having a schema means you have to define the structure of the data at the time you add the data to the database. This has many consequences, one of which is that it takes the control of the database out of the hands of the database designer and puts it into the hands of the programmers.

How you add structured data depends on the kind of database. Document NoSQL products store structured data documents in formats like XML and JSON that combine data values with data descriptions. Table and Column NoSQL databases define the name of the attribute at the same time as the data values. For instance, instead of a SQL statement like this:

```
SqlCommand  cmd = new SqlCommand ("Insert into person (Name,
        Age)" +"values('Fred', 21)", con);
cmd.ExecuteNonQuery();
```

you might have to use a statement like this (this is Java for DynamoDB from Amazon):

```
Item newperson = new Item().withString("Name", "Fred").
        withNumber("Age", 21);
Persontable.PutItem(newperson);
```

Graph databases have predefined nodes and edges (connections between nodes), but you can add data attributes to nodes programmatically much like I have added data attributes to a data object in the preceding example. I think two points should be made about the programmatic interface to NoSQL products. The first is that they are not wordier than a typical SQL program (except perhaps if you are using a SQL-to-object mapping product). The second is that every NoSQL product's programmatic interface is different, and not only different in trivial ways but different in fundamental approach. Once you have chosen your NoSQL product, your application is locked into it.

So what do you miss by not having a schema? Schemas in databases have three main roles. One is that the attribute names (Name and Age in the preceding examples) need be stored only once, not for every row. That used to be a big point many years ago but is not so important in these days of massive disk drives. The second role of schemas is to define integrity constraints like uniqueness, referential integrity, and check clauses. The NoSQL answer to this is that these constraints are better implemented in program code. As noted in the section "Programmers versus the Database Designer," in practice database integrity checks are backstops; just because the database checks the integrity does not mean the programs chuck any data they like at the database. The programs ensure that the data given to the database already complies with the integrity checks. There may be the occasional exception to this, especially with the uniqueness constraint, but in general that is how it goes. Thus having the data integrity imposed by the program code rather than the database does not make much of a difference—until, that is, the program or the database changes. Or another program is written to use the database and the programmer hasn't understood the database constraints. As noted previously, the practical role of database constraints is to protect the data against programmer incompetence. So the NoSQL programmer has to be careful, especially if many programs use the same database.

The third impact of having no schema is that it makes complex queries difficult to implement. In particular, very few NoSQL products support joins. I am not going to belabor this point, mainly because I have a sneaking feeling that the technology in this area will change enormously over the next few years and anything I write will look foolish.

One of the impacts of having no schema is that if your database structure changes, you can just start adding data with the new structure. There is no requirement to change your existing data. This could be a good feature in some scenarios because there is no downtime for reformatting existing data and it is easier to maintain a historical record of exactly what data was put in the database. But it requires careful programming. Obviously if something like product data exists with product data objects in several different structures with similar but slightly different attributes, you have to program with care to handle them all. The biggest danger is new applications that look at old data, because if the data objects exist in five different structures, the new application programmer may have been told about only four of them.

In my opinion, the main problem with not having a schema is not having a schema designer—in other words, the database designer. Of course, you don't have to get rid of the database designer, but the temptation is there. I expect that in practice NoSQL databases aren't shared among many applications, but instead any data needed by another application is extracted, reformatted, and sent on its way. Some of the ways this could be done were outlined in Chapter 7. But as I explained in the section in this chapter on database design, one reason for having database designers is to understand and resolve the problems of different parts of the organization having different data structure requirements. If you add in the notion that data structure will evolve over time and objects with the old data structures might be still around, the need for some careful control of data becomes more important, not less important.

One of the motivations for developing NoSQL databases is to handle truly enormous databases. Both Google and Amazon provide NoSQL databases as part of the supporting software in their cloud offerings. They want you to run your applications on their platform, and they want to make the database aspect of your application as easy to use as possible, which in part explains why it is attractive for them to provide a database with no schema. Using these databases is rather like being given a small corner of an enormous database to work in where all the administration and recovery are handled for you.

Truly enormous databases need to be distributed; they simply don't fit on one machine. Besides being enormous, the vendors want their databases to be forever available and thus want to duplicate the data. If you duplicate data across many machines, there is always the chance that the network between the machines will be broken or just clogged up with data transfers and for a short period of time is unusable. In a conventional database you would normally have one copy as the primary and one as the secondary, but the NoSQL vendors want to do better than this and allow updates to both sides of the broken network. The idea is to sort out the consistency issues when the break is mended and the sides merge. This idea is known as *eventual consistency*. (To bring you up-to-date with the buzzwords, a broken network like this a called a partitioned network. The idea that there is a trade-off between consistency and partition tolerance is known as CAP theorem—Consistency, Availability, and Partition tolerance—and a database that supports eventual consistency is said to support BASE—Basically Available, Soft state, Eventual consistency. Well, they've got all the big words sorted out, so the software should work, shouldn't it?)

Let us look at an example. Suppose we have a bank and in either partition a single account is updated. The bank account starts off with $1,000 in it, and

- In partition A there is a debit of $800 from the account, leaving a total of $200
- In partition B there is a debit of $700 from the account, leaving a total of $300

Now the partitions are joined, and there is an attempt to establish eventual consistency. Option 1—the simple way—is to use the latest value for each attribute. This will be a total of $200 if the latest is the update that came from partition A and $300 if the latest update was in partition B. Clearly the total should be minus $500, so this is not good.

Option 2 is to replay the transaction program codes. Thus the input message for the transaction in partition B is processed to the database as left by partition A and the logic of the transaction—including subtracting $700 from the account total—is done. But suppose there is a rule that any withdrawal that takes the account into negative territory is denied. This would mean that the replay of the second withdrawal will fail!

A third option is to look at the details of the operations on the data attributes and process those; in other words, don't process after images, but process a subtraction. This is hard to implement. No database that I know of allows you to update an attribute by adding or subtracting; you do the adding and subtracting in the program code and only put the answer in the database. Furthermore, this is a very simple scenario; the transaction might take the input data from the database and pass it through an arbitrarily complex algorithm before updating the database again.

A fourth option is that the transactions might be replayed, not using the original code but using special replay code that doesn't have the check in it. But suppose this is done and the end result of the eventual consistency is minus $500. The business might not like this at all. There may need to be special procedures to tell the customers that they have sinned and special charges applied for the privilege of being told they have sinned. (That's how banks work where I come from.) Many people have pointed out that banks do have similar procedures to allow for excessive ATM withdrawals. Somehow I don't think bank executives would appreciate being told that they have to have another business procedure to accommodate a lack of consistency in the IT application. This is what I meant when I said in Chapter 7 that eventual consistency is hard and that living with it is a business decision. As pointed out in Chapter 1, "Introduction to Context-Driven Design," when you design anything, you make assumptions about the performance and integrity of the components. If those assumptions turn out to be false, you have to redesign at the higher level. Eventual consistency is just such an assumption breaker.

But as always, there are database access patterns that can easily accommodate eventual consistency. For instance, inserting new data objects is no problem so long as there is no limit to the number of new data objects and there are no uniqueness constraints that cannot be handled with a partitioned database. It is the update transactions that read information in the database (like the account total in our example) that are most likely to have problems.

There are businesses that will tolerate inconsistencies. Airlines often overbook flights because they know some people will cancel.

I was once at an organization that had a database failure and didn't want to wait for the recovery (this was a long time ago). So I fixed up what I thought was an inconsistency in the data and switched off the bit in the control file that forced recovery to happen. The database ran for a while, but then another data inconsistency was found and I had to do the whole process again. And it happened again. The moral of this story is that while the business might be willing to live with inconsistency, the software might not be.

To conclude this section, NoSQL databases are here to stay, and I would consider using them in certain circumstances, especially if I were writing an application that the client wanted to run on an Amazon or Google cloud service. But you have to be sure that the application designer understands all the consequences.

Concluding Remarks

In this chapter I discussed the practical issues of database design, concentrating on resolving differences of opinion between different departments that share data. I also discussed some theoretical approaches to database design. Understanding the theory I believe helps you find weaknesses in the database design. However, the key to effective database design is understanding how the data will be used. It is the usage of the data as well as where the data comes from that gives the data its meaning.

The last portion of the chapter discussed how different database designs have very different impacts on programming. Programmers must understand the database and understand the intentions of the database design. I think programmers will warm to NoSQL databases, and I discussed some of the advantages and some of the dangers in the ideas that have been implemented in these databases.

I hope that context-driven design will resolve many of the tensions between programmers and database designers because of its insistence that the database design be done early. I fully expect that some programmers will go ahead and implement their own database design instead, but there is a simple solution to that: install only the official database schema on the systems test machine.

Chapter 10

Technical Design—Principles

Technical design is a specialist's subject, and I anticipate that many of my readers are generalist application designers or project managers. This chapter's primary aim is to help the generalist understand the issues and problems the specialist faces. The main body of the chapter discusses the principles of IT application performance and availability. The chapter's secondary aim is to advocate a practical, hands-on approach to technical design. While specialists might skim over the principles part with a critical eye (possibly a very critical eye!), I hope they fully engage their brains in the second part of the chapter.

The first two sections are about performance. The first is about performance in a single server and the second about performance across many servers. I then look at the subject of resiliency. Another topic that deserves a "principles of" section is security, but that topic is contained in Chapter 12, "Security Design." The final two sections are about the process of technical design. The first of these sections is about testing and benchmarking, and the second is an overview of how to tackle technical design in the round.

In this chapter and the next I mention some software products. However, my aim is not to promote or endorse any vendor's products. The reason for mentioning them at all is that I find myself saying that products exist to do such-and-such, but it seems a bit odd if you don't follow it up by saying what any of them are. I have two reasons for not endorsing any products. The first is that I have not done the enormous amount of work needed to be unbiased. The second is that whatever I say today will be out-of-date tomorrow.

Many applications don't need high performance or high availability. In those cases, the technical design may be trivial.

If you ask business managers for requirements for performance, resiliency, and security, more likely as not they will tell you that they want fast response times, scalability to many times the initial application size, 100% availability, and absolute security. In practice you can meet good performance goals, good availability goals, and reasonable security for not a lot of effort and at a reasonable price. What they don't understand—and lack of understanding here has been exploited by parts of the IT industry to overconfigure their solutions—is that trying to achieve those last few fractions of a percentage point improvement in availability, or trying to boost the performance from, say, 30 input messages per second to 300 input messages per second, or trying to put in a high level of security that would be appropriate for the Department of Defense, costs huge amounts of money and effort. Setting reasonable expectations and guiding business managers in the trade-offs among cost, time, and performance are things professional designers should do as part of their professional duty. I discuss this at the end of this chapter in the section "The Technical Design Process."

I begin the discussion of technical design principles with the principles of high performance on a single machine.

Principles of High Performance on a Single Machine

These days most of the discussion about high performance is couched in terms of using multiple machines, but you cannot understand the issues of extracting performance out of many machines if you don't understand how to achieve good levels of performance from one.

The difficulty of achieving consistently high performance is rooted in the mismatch of performance in the various parts of the machine. Consider:

- Fast processors are measured in gigahertz. Thus a 3GHz processor does three operations every nanosecond (10^{-9} second).
- RAM access time is typically tens of nanoseconds. When you add in the time dealing with the memory logic and the memory bus, you will find that the time taken for a processor to read memory is typically over 50ns. In other words, to access memory in RAM the processor must wait for a time in which it could have performed 150 or more operations.
- Disk access time is measures in milliseconds. Top-end disks take an average of 4ms to position the read heads in the right place and then, on average, have to wait half a rotation for the data they want to be under the head. A 3GHz processor could do 12,000 operations in 4ms. SSD (Solid State Disk) is perhaps 10 times faster but a good deal slower than RAM.

These figures are roughly right in 2015. If history is any guide, all these speeds will increase, but the ratios between them will hardly change at all. Very roughly there is a ratio of one to hundred(s) to thousand(s) between processor, memory, and disk.

There are two techniques to overcome these enormous wait times:

1. **Cache.** Cache is memory, and the idea is to avoid using slow data retrieval by already having the data in the cache. Disk I/O is reduced either by using buffers in the RAM or by having some cache RAM in the disk's controller. RAM access is reduced by having superfast cache memory in the processor, sometimes on the same chip as the processor itself.

2. **Multithreading.** This exploits the idea that while one program is waiting for user input or an I/O to finish, the processor can work on another program. There is direct overhead in switching to another thread, but also extra overhead incurred by the fact that other threads' data and code are less likely to be in the processor cache! But if a single I/O is going to take as long as 10,000-plus cycles, there is opportunity to do a great deal of work.

Multithreading is the technology that underpins multiprocessing, that is, several processors working on the same workload and sharing the same memory. Essentially, the several processors are all looking for threads to process.

Let us now examine each in more detail.

Cache

Figure 10.1 illustrates how cache works. Say the processor requests one word of memory (e.g., 32 bits worth). The cache address lookup will either find the data in its fast memory or retrieve it from the slow memory.

If you have some small amount of data that your program uses over and over again, cache will work wonderfully; the data will be in cache and the processor will have much quicker access to it. On the other hand, if your program is reading and writing an enormous array of data starting at one end and going to the other, cache won't be that affective because each chunk of data is being used only once. Between these two extremes there is a very large and very gray area in which it is hard to predict exactly how much cache will help. There are many questions of detail. Some important ones are:

- How big is the cache? If it is one-tenth the size of main memory, then if all the data access was random you would expect a cache hit ratio of one-tenth. But programs aren't like that. They have parts that are used only once and parts that are used all the time. That highly used part is called the *working set*. If all of the working set fits in cache, the performance is great. If it doesn't, performance can trail off a lot or a little—it's program dependent.

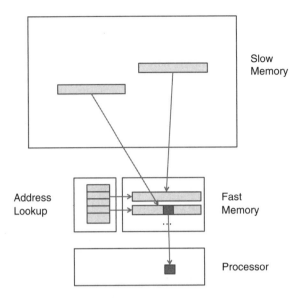

Figure 10.1 *Cache*

- How granular is cache memory? Think about the address lookup for a moment. For every chunk of memory in cache there must be an address to look up. If the chunks are one word long, then for every word in cache there is an address in the address lookup. If the chunks are eight words long, then for eight words in cache there is one address in the address lookup—thus proportionately much less of the chip real estate is devoted to holding addresses. But if the working set is scattered over memory—a word here and a word there—eight-word chunks may mean that lots of the data in cache won't be used. On the other hand, if the cache logic reads a chunk of memory and it is all going to be used, that's great—the cache has data stored in it before it is needed.

- How long does memory kick around in cache? When the cache is full, reading some more memory into cache requires overwriting existing cache data. You can just cycle through the cache, overwriting the cache that was put into cache longest ago, but a better design is to overwrite the memory that was last used longest ago.

- What happens if the data is updated? A simple design is to *write through*—write the updates back to the slow memory. A more sophisticated design is to let it kick around a bit in cache in the hope that additional updates will go to the same chunk of memory in cache and the updated data can be written to RAM in one go.

The hardware designer must balance all these factors. Cache design is a big factor in explaining why some superfast processors don't provide superfast performance, and it also helps to explain how a computer can be optimized for certain kinds of work, for example, games versus Web browsing.

Disk cache works in similar ways; the cache is RAM rather than fast processor cache, but it is still much faster than reading disk data. Database software will have a buffer pool of data read from the disk, and this is also a kind of cache. The trade-offs are similar to those in the processor cache. Randomly accessing data structures that are too large for the cache won't be very effective. On the other hand, if your program does a lot of work on pieces of data that are physically located near each other, cache might work well. An example is an index on an attribute that holds the date and time the row was created, because almost all new entries to the index will be to the last block of index, which is likely to be in cache. But cache has limited use when reading all of a large data structure sequentially. If you cannot fit the whole data structure in the disk cache or database buffers, you will find that you will fill it up with data that you use only once.

Because of the complexity, cache performance is hard to predict. Furthermore, as applications and databases grow in size and complexity, cache hit rates can suddenly deteriorate because the working set no longer fits in the cache.

When you optimize an online database application, you have to remember that most of the time the processing power is not being used to process the code in the application you have written but is being used instead to drive the database software, the network handler software, the Web server system software, and the operating system. Optimization is not only optimizing the application program but also economizing on the use of the system software. There are many techniques to optimize applications, but there are trade-offs all over the place, for instance:

- Adding an index may eliminate the need to search sequentially through a database table, but it will increase the load when adding a new row to a table.

- User-written cache may eliminate the need to read rows from database tables, but it increases application code complexity and the size of data variables. This was discussed in the section "Data Access Services" in Chapter 9, "Database Design."

- Having the client send and receive a few large messages in preference to many small messages will reduce the load on the networking software, but if you overdo it, you may find yourself sending a lot of data to the client that isn't used. An example of this is query results—sending ten results at once may be sensible; sending 1,000 is unlikely to be sensible.

Understanding the principles of performance helps you make good decisions, but computer performance is so complex and unpredictable you can only be sure by building the application and testing it under load.

Multithreading and Multiprocessing

Multithreading is the other important technique to speed applications up. The basic idea, as noted previously, is simply that when one program is waiting for something (like a disk read to complete or input from the network), the processor does work for other programs. Alternatively, the operating system can interrupt work on one thread to reassign the processor to work on another higher-priority thread.

(Terminology note: I have used the word *multithreading*, not *multitasking*. They are distinct concepts. A task is a running program, and each program has its own memory allocated to it. A task can have multiple threads, though it often has only one. Each thread can be executed independently. Multithreading in a single task is useful if you want to have one thread waiting for user input while the other thread is doing some background work.)

A balance must be struck between having too many threads waiting to be processed and having too few such that the processors have nothing to do. The main penalty of too many threads is that each thread consumes memory, especially if the threads belong to different programs.

When a process is waiting to be processed or simply waiting for any other reason, like waiting for input from a user or for a disk read, it may have some of its memory overlaid. That means part of its memory is written to disk to make room for another process to have more memory assigned to it. When the first process starts to be run again, it may find it has to read the overlaid memory before it can do useful work. If this happens too often, the processor can end up in a condition known as thrashing where it spends an excessive amount of time overlaying memory and reading back overlaid memory. Thrashing is disastrous for performance, but even small amounts of overlaying can cause a serious dent in overall performance.

Application servers—such as Enterprise JavaBeans servers and Microsoft's ASP—and mainframe transaction monitors—such as IBM CICS and Unisys TIP—help optimize memory by trying to run enough threads to service all the pending input messages from the network but no more. They also keep a pool of database connections open and reassign them to threads as necessary because database connections are large consumers of memory and opening and closing them is costly.

Multiprocessing—several processors processing the threads at once—works well only if there are enough threads waiting to be processed. That depends on the application having enough work to do, of course, but it depends too on the memory being big enough to run all the tasks it needs.

The performance improvement from adding processors is not linear—two processors do less work than one processor times two, and three processors do even less, and so on. The reason is mostly because if they are running threads that need to update the same words of memory, they have to do it serially. This is best explained by considering what happens if this is not enforced. Suppose there are two processors adding one to the same integer in memory. One processor will read in the integer, add one to it, and then the new value might hang around the processor's internal registers or it might hang around cache for some time. Meanwhile, the other processor reads the old value of the integer from memory and updates that instead. Chaos ensues. The solution is locks; one processor grabs a *lock* (locks are physically just a word of memory, but the grabbing of them and the releasing of them have special hardware support), does its updates—like adding one to the integer—and releases the lock. The action of releasing the lock ensures that everything updated in the processor registers and the cache is written back into memory. Some multiprocessor servers have shared cache and sometimes there are multiple levels of cache, but there is always some additional work to do when two processors need to use the same physical memory. You might think that the chance of two tasks wanting to update the same memory is remote, but in a transaction-processing application it isn't, mainly because the system software (database software, operating, and others) has a few important data variables that it is reading and writing all the time. These data variables are central to activities like memory management, controlling the disk I/Os, or buffer management in the database software. The slowdown from multiprocessing is why it is common to see servers with up to four processors but much less common to see servers with more processors than this.

For more than four processors there may be a clustered solution. There are many forms of clustering, but the basic idea is that each unit in the cluster has some private memory exclusive to the processors in that unit. There is then either some shared memory or some other way to synchronize work across the cluster so that it looks like one large server. Clustering is effective, but different vendors do it in different ways, and it only works well if not only the operating system but also the database system software and application server system software support it.

One of the main aims of optimizing an application is to have it running such that the only constraint on its performance is processing power. In a transaction-processing application you will need the facilities provided by application server software to run the application efficiently. You will also need to have enough memory to run enough programs without significant overlaying to keep the number of processors busy.

So assuming you have done all that, what can go wrong? Several things:

- **Database data disk I/O.** If your application is servicing ten transactions per second and each transaction does on average ten disk reads and writes, on average there are 100 I/Os per second. That is likely to exceed the capability of a disk drive (depending on how much the reads and writes are scattered across the disk rather than being all in one place). In high-performance applications you have to use many disks, possibly many channels to disk (each channel controls one cable going to the disk drives), irrespective of the fact that a single disk can hold gigabytes of data and might easily hold your entire database.

- **The database log.** This is another variant of the disk I/O bottleneck. For the database to be recoverable, a database log is maintained. The log has *before images*—copies of data before it is updated—and *after images*—copies of data after it is updated. The database log can be large and must be physically written to disk before the transaction commits. High-performance database software does *group commits*; it physically writes the logs of several transactions in one I/O.

- **Network messages.** The network capacity might not be enough to service all the network messages you want to send. Applications that use forms tend to send only small amounts of data to the browser in one message, although the number of messages may be very high if thousands of users are logged on. But the network can still be flooded by other Web sites that are sending enormous amounts of data back to the Web browser (for instance, by having advertising video clips).

- **Database locks.** Databases have read locks and write locks, and depending on the database software, a lock may control a single record or a block of records. If two applications want to grab the same record lock at the same time, one waits for the other. There are in practice lock *hot spots* in a database—data that is read or written to a great deal. Keeping statistics is an example; an extreme case would be keeping a count in the database of the number of transactions processed per day. There are internal locks like a lock on an index that is being updated. There can be contention for these locks, too. I mentioned that indexing records on the date and time of the record's creation is good for cache efficiency. Unfortunately it is bad for lock contention. A solution is to ensure that updates and reads to hot spot data are done just before the transaction commits so the index table is locked for as short a time as possible.

- **Application locks.** If the application has its own locks (for instance, as part of a multithreading implementation), there is also a possibility that the application will grind to a stop because it is waiting for a lock that is being held by another thread.

- **Deadlocks.** If program 1 locks records A and B in that order and program 2 locks records B and A in that order at the same time, they will be stuck—program 1 will be waiting on record B and program 2 will be waiting on record A. This is called *deadlock*. It can happen with non-database locks, too. Database software should detect a deadlock and abort one of the transactions. Deadlocks are typically not common, but they can be avoided if applications lock their resources in the same order (both programs 1 and 2 read records A and B in that order).

There are solutions to all these problems, but they require work. You can't just install any old application, buy more powerful hardware, and expect it to perform; you must tailor the parameters, tailor the hardware configuration, and maybe tailor the application code. However, observe that these problems don't become apparent until the transactions overlap in time; in other words, the applications are processing several transactions in parallel. For instance, if your transactions do about ten I/Os each, you can probably do several per second before there is any degree of overlap. There is a vast number of applications where the volumes are well below this level.

For a quick guess at how many transactions per second there could be, assume that each user is doing one transaction per minute and multiply that by the number of simultaneous users. This calculation probably leads to an overestimate as people don't work that hard. If you want a real example, observe people queuing at an ATM machine and time how long they take on average.

Note that if you do have a population of 120 end users and you know that each user does a transaction every two minutes in the busiest hour, you cannot assume that there is an even flow of transactions coming into the machine, one every second. Instead, there will be some busy seconds and some idle seconds. What should happen is that the input queues build up slightly during the busy seconds and are emptied in the idle seconds. But when the server load is increased, several bad things may happen:

- The transactions take longer because when they need the processor, the processor is more likely to be busy.

- If the transactions take longer, locks are held for longer and waiting for locks becomes more of a problem.

- If the transactions take longer, they consume memory for longer and it is more likely that some other process will have its memory overlaid.

- The queues themselves take memory, also increasing the likelihood of overlaying.

The net effect is that it is bad to run at a high level of processor utilization. How bad it is and at what level the utilization is critical seem to differ according to the workload and the operating system. Note that if in a workload there is batch processing in the background, a mix of short transactions and complex online queries, the cheapest solution may simply be to reschedule the batch run for a time of day when the other loads are light.

The main message I want to convey is that second-guessing the performance of an application before it is written is very hard. Fortunately for most applications, the performance requirements aren't onerous enough for there to be a problem. But for the few applications that have demanding performance requirements you must first have a design that is capable of high performance, and second test it under load to eliminate the bottlenecks.

Principles of High Performance on Many Servers

So what about some horizontal scaling (also known as scale-out)? If an application can run easily at ten transactions per second on one server, why not achieve 100 transactions per second by having ten servers? The simple answer is that while you can find solutions that allow you to have ten application servers acting as one (for instance, with the same Internet domain name), it is much more difficult to split the database across many servers. I am going to divide the discussion into front-end concerns—essentially how we can implement parallel application servers—and back-end concerns—how we can implement parallel database servers.

Front-End Parallelism

In this section I will discuss the configuration illustrated in Figure 10.2.

The question is, How can the application servers act as one? In Web technology, the domain name (that is the Web site name such as www.myapp.com) is resolved by a server known as a domain name server which converts the domain name to a network address (the IP address). It is usually one or a few specialized network machines called routers that take these messages from the Internet, and the router distributes all the input messages to the application servers. The simplest algorithm to do this is round-robin; the router just sends the messages to each server in turn.

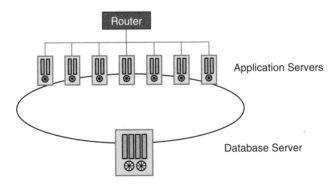

Figure 10.2 *Multiple Application Servers, Single Database Server*

But there is a catch: session data. Session data is data held at some time or all the time from when a user logs on to the application to when the user logs off or otherwise stops using the application. Session data has several uses, for instance:

- **Security**—it can be used to prove that the user has logged on and to identify the user. This is discussed in Chapter 12.

- **Screen traversal**—for instance, suppose you have a screen called "Fill in Complaint" which can be called from several other screens. When the complaint is filled in, you want to return to the screen you came from—session data can tell you what screen that was.

- **Capturing small amounts of data**—for instance, a shopping cart.

- **Ensuring that several screens in a series update the same object.**

- **Refining searches**—users may be searching a large table, and instead of forcing them to set up new selection criteria every time, it is more friendly to let them refine the last-used selection criteria. Thus you need to save the current search criteria for each user while he or she is using the application.

Session data can be stored in the server, in the client, or in both. In Chapter 7, "The Relationship to Other IT Projects," I defined four types of service interfaces. The same four types apply to the user-device-to-server interface. By user device I mean Web browser, phone, or workstation program—anything a human uses to access a server. Two of the four are session-less: the *deferrable* and the *one-shot* interfaces. Deferrable means that sending the message can be delayed because the user is not waiting for an immediate reply; the most commonly used technologies for end users that work like this are e-mail and text messaging. There are applications that accept e-mail or text input, but the input messages are typically very simple, like the one word *unsubscribe*. The one shot can be used easily from a Web browser; it's just a form you submit where there are no follow-on forms, so the Web server does not have to remember anything about the browser or the user of the browser.

In the old days, the *uses session* style of interface was the most common. Terminals attached to mainframes had an automatic session, and in the transaction managers of yore you could associate data with a terminal and use it to do all the things I listed earlier for session data. Sessions at the network level are still important. The TCP (Transmission Control Protocol) in TCP/IP is session software that can be used for program-to-program communication over the Internet. It ensures that if a message is split up into lots of little blocks that whiz through the network, the blocks are recombined into the same message at the other end without any missing or duplicate blocks. Web browsers use TCP, but the session lasts only while loading a single page, and from the programmer's point of view the Web is essentially session-less. But you can run a program over the Internet that uses sessions with software like SOAP.

So why not use session interface to support, well, sessions? The answer is that the session must have an endpoint that is a server, which means in turn that a configuration as shown in Figure 10.2 doesn't work.

That is not quite true; you can use session software in a configuration like Figure 10.2 so long as you terminate the session at the router and not at the application server, but that tends to put a bottleneck on the router. Besides which the router may not support the software to terminate the session properly, so to take this approach is likely to mean putting in an application server at that point, which is a lot bigger and more expensive than a simple router.

So we are left with the *uses identifiers* kind of interface. In this style of interface, the server sends some data to the browser and gets the data back on the next input message. (The example given in Chapter 7 was of the server returning an order number that was used in subsequent updates to the order.) There are several ways of implementing this with Web browsers, some of which are illustrated in Figure 10.3:

1. **Use cookies.** Cookies are files stored on the browser machine that are set by information from the server and included in all subsequent input messages to the server.

2. **Put the data in the URI.** This is illustrated in Figure 10.3. The URI string www.mywebsite/order/123 consists of two parts: the domain name, www .mywebsite, and the session data, order/123.

3. **Use an input parameter.** In the example in Figure 10.3, we could replace the text www.mywebsite/order/123 with www.mywebsite?orderno = 123.

4. **Use a hidden field.** There can be fields you don't see as well as the fields you fill in on a form. This is useful for the server application to hide information that it can use on the next input.

Figure 10.3 *Browser Session Data*

So how does this help implement the configuration illustrated in Figure 10.2? Look at Figure 10.4. So long as the identity being passed between browser and server matches an object in the server, you can go through any number of intermediate servers. Furthermore, you can have several identities in several servers. You could, for instance, have one identity (e.g., the order/123 used previously) to identify an order on the order server and another identity (e.g., user Fred123) to identify a user on the username server. But also note that you can put the data object in the intermediate servers, so long as you replicate the data accurately across all the intermediate servers.

So is there a preference for any one of the mechanisms of holding identity data in the browser? It mostly comes down to security. When a user logs on to an application, the browser needs to hang on to some user identity so that in all subsequent inputs the server can identify who the user is and check whether that user is still logged on. There is a whole range of security pitfalls in this scheme, which I will discuss in Chapter 12; however, to make a long story short, you probably need to encrypt the user identity and in many applications encrypt the whole message. If you are encrypting the user identity, it is safest to put it into a cookie or as an input parameter (option 3 in the preceding list). Encrypting parts of a URI (option 2) is sometimes a bad idea because you may want to use the URI for routing to the right application or server. The other approach is to encrypt the whole message, which can be done with standard technology like TLS (Transport Layer Security). However,

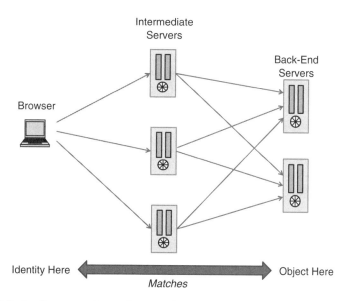

Figure 10.4 *Configurations Using the Uses Identity Interface*

encryption uses keys and lots of processing power to encrypt and decrypt. You don't want to burden your back-end servers with decrypting anything. Thus you want to push encryption to the intermediate servers or to the router. With TLS you will probably configure a boundary router or server which on one side is attached to the Internet and uses TLS and on the other is attached to a secure internal network.

European Union and Cookies

An aside about cookies: In the European Union it is now compulsory for Web sites to tell users that they are using cookies, and the obvious inference to draw from this is that cookies are "bad." Actually cookies are fine for session data. However, cookies can also be used by sales and marketing Web sites to monitor how you use the Web. How bad that makes them is controversial, to say the least.

I am conscious that this discussion is becoming more and more technical and esoteric, so I am going to leave it at that. This is why you need a technical expert to help you sort out your parallelism strategy. Let us now leave the front-end performance concerns and look at the back-end performance concerns.

Back-End Parallelism

In Figure 10.2, the database is put in a dedicated database server. The reason is simple: it is hard to coordinate the writing of data to a single file from multiple servers. But using a single database server may create a bottleneck because in a typical transaction-processing application the database is a major user of disk I/O and processing power. Furthermore, you have to be careful about the network traffic between the application servers and the database servers. You don't want separate network messages for every database command as that would enormously increase the load on the database server. Figure 10.5 illustrates this point. For one input and output message per transaction there are several database commands. Thus by having the database commands sent over a network—a technology known as *remote database access*—you greatly increase the network overhead. Thus you end up either writing shared services to run on the database machine or using database procedures—which from a design perspective amounts to more or less the same thing, albeit using different technology. Of course it depends on the nature of the workload, but don't be surprised if you have to configure a database server at least half the size of the server you would have configured if you had put all the load onto one server. To make a

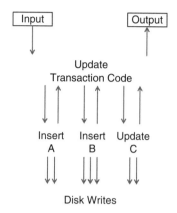

Figure 10.5 *Distribution Points in a Database System*

dramatic improvement using many servers running in parallel you have to find a solution to running the database across several servers.

Let us examine two possible solutions. One solution is to duplicate the databases. There are features in some database products that let you do this—in prescribed configurations at least—but they work well only if the number of reads to the database is far higher than the number of writes. The reason is that the read commands can be done on any server, but write commands have to be done on all copies of the database. As Figure 10.5 shows, there are often several disk writes for each database update, and thus sending all the writes over a network is expensive, and many times more expensive than updating on a single machine. Thus updating a duplicated database entails a big overhead, which will smother any improvement you see if the updates are frequent.

But there is another option: you can duplicate the database without using special database features and simply ensure that all update transaction inputs are copied and sent to all copies of the database. This is illustrated in Figure 10.6. You can build an update transaction duplicator using middleware such as message queuing and broadcast all updates to all databases. You would use message queuing to help ensure that all update transactions are processed in the same order on all database copies. However—since we are trying to solve the problems of a high-performance requirement—we may need many programs to empty the queue on each machine. If so, there is always the possibility that the transactions are not processed on each machine in exactly the same order. The fact that the order matters was discussed in the section "Transaction and Task Integrity" in Chapter 8, "User Interface Design and Ease of Use."

Let us look at an example. Suppose the database being duplicated supports an order entry application. For the vast majority of update transactions there is no

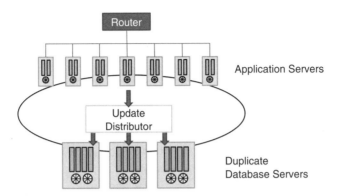

Figure 10.6 *Duplicate Database Servers*

problem because each transaction is about an order, so even if you process the order update transactions in a different sequence, there is no cross talk between the transactions, and they will not be muddled up. But how about the allocation of the order number itself? If this is done within the transaction code, there is a possibility that the same transaction running on different machines may generate different order numbers. This will cause serious problems. In other words, the design for a distributed solution may have dependencies on how the application is programmed. Technical designers must have faith in the programmers—or program the important code themselves.

When you are considering these kinds of designs, it is good to think of some extreme events. For instance, suppose one of the servers is running slow or has stopped (for instance, the database log file could have run out of space on disk).

As a general observation on the design thinking process, note that I have considered extremely unlikely events. This is good practice in IT design, not only because it's nice to get everything right, but also because if your application is doing, say, one million transactions a day, extremely unlikely events have a habit of becoming rather common. I remember finding an operating system bug once that was two lines of code the wrong way around, but it mattered only when two threads hit the same code at the same time. Fantastically unlikely, you might think—but it happened, and it happened often enough for the company to fly me out to find out what was going wrong.

A second solution to the distributed database conundrum is to distribute the databases according to data values. This is illustrated in Figure 10.7. The illustration assumes that the data being distributed is the accounts data as in a bank, but in another application anything could be chosen—product number, customer number, and so on.

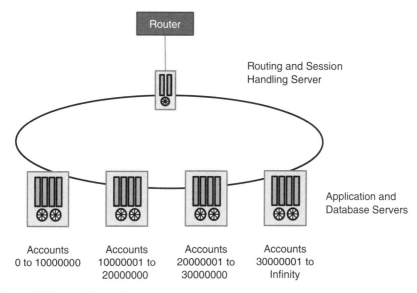

Figure 10.7 *Distribution by Data Value Range*

If you distribute data by value, you have to consider what to do with all the other data; for example, in a bank with account numbers used for distribution you must consider all the non-account tables. You can duplicate these tables as in the previous solution, or you can put them in another server. (Ideally you won't need to update two databases in one transaction. It can be done with distributed transactions, but the danger is that you will nullify all the performance and resiliency gains of spreading the work across multiple servers.) The problem with distribution using values is finding ranges of data values that give you something like an even balance across the database servers. As illustrated in Figure 10.7, the workload on each server could be very uneven. Early accounts tend to be older accounts so they might include many inactive accounts. Somewhere in the accounts might be a very heavily used account like one used by a large company. You could consider instead of data ranges having a lookup table in a routing and handling server. This could take the account number and look up in a table to find which back-end server must process the transaction. An advantage of this approach is that you can, over time, move accounts from database to database to rebalance them across the servers.

In conclusion, if you need to distribute the database, you need to design very carefully. Beware of sales staff or systems integrators waving their hands over problems.

In practice the best solution may be to mix and match. Suppose you are building a large, Web-based shopping site. You probably have a large number of users who are just looking; hence there is a large volume of product browse queries and a smaller—but maybe still large—number of buying transactions. Let us have many servers handling the product browsing and one server handling the product purchases. How can we ensure that the product browse databases don't specify a product that isn't available on the product purchase database? It's simple, actually: we do product additions first on the product purchase database and product deletions last on the product purchase database. What about changing the price? We could do a similar trick: making increases to the price last on the purchase database and making something cheaper first on the purchase database. Another option is to ensure that the last display before the user commits to buy uses prices taken from the purchase database information. A third option is to store the price in the shopping cart data.

The two examples shown Figure 10.6 and Figure 10.7 are two of many solutions. There are almost always many solutions that are specific to the application. What you have to do is think creatively. Put another way, you need a design hypothesis and you need to go through the elaboration step to check that it meets all the requirements.

When you are elaborating your design hypothesis, there are several points you must think about:

- **Timing problems**—whenever you have data duplication, you need to consider the order in which the data is updated.
- **Session data**—where can the session data be stored?
- **Availability requirements**—I discuss these in the next sections.
- **Security requirements**—discussed in Chapter 12.

And finally, it helps if you have thought of a couple of design hypotheses because they help you clarify the pros and cons of each solution, and often you find that the solution you finally implement takes ideas from both designs.

Principles of High Resiliency

There are several goals that broadly fit under the overall heading of resiliency:

- **No data loss.** If there is a failure, you don't want to find that work done on the database has disappeared.
- **Availability.** You want the application to be up and running as much as possible. Some applications must run all the time, though usually there is some time (Christmas, for instance) when a new version of the software can be introduced.

- **Disaster recovery.** There are two categories of failure, one that affects the local system (for instance, a software bug or hardware failure) and one that affects the complete data center, like a fire or a flood. The latter failure can be mended only by switching to a disaster backup site. Organizations are usually prepared to live with significant downtime in the event of a disaster, but for organizations that cannot run without IT the cost of downtime rapidly escalates. However, it is common to find that in the event of a disaster, the backup machine is too small, is running an old version of the software, or is not configured correctly, leading the organization to spend days with the application offline.

Recovery can be broken down into a four-step process:

1. Detect the failure.

2. Plan what to do.

3. Recover the data.

4. Bring the backup copy of the application online.

It is the last two steps that are normally thought of as "recovery" and are well understood and well supported by database and operating system software. It is the first two that need discussion.

There are many kinds of failure that can cause an application to stop:

- **Hardware failure**—for instance, processor failure, memory failure, or disk failure. Some memory failures are transient (without error-correcting memory, cosmic rays can switch a bit on or off occasionally), but mostly the machines die unless they have built-in redundancy. Old mainframes from 20 years ago had excellent redundancy and coupled with mirror disk would normally carry on through any single-point hardware failure. For a cheap server the only solution is to switch to backup hardware.

- **Data center failure.** This can be catastrophic, like a fire, or it can be temporary, like a power cut. If catastrophic, the only solution is to switch to a backup data center, of course. Transient failures can be very transient; many data centers have backup power, for instance.

- **System software failure**—for instance, a fault in the operating system or database management software. The symptom is usually the server stopping. Ironically, many of these faults are timing problems, and the problem does not reappear after the restart.

- **Application software failure.** Application programs can stop by doing an invalid operation (e.g., divide by zero), but they can also go into a loop which is much harder to detect quickly. Even worse, application faults can cause bad data to be written to the database or sent back to the user, and this is even harder to detect. Switching to a backup server rarely solves any of these problems, and often since the same input data is processed on the other machine, the application fails again.

- **Network failure.** This can usually be solved by switching to a backup server in another part of the country.

- **An application is too busy and slows to a stop.** As I previously noted, when an application has too much load thrown at it, it often slows down so much that it is indistinguishable from a stop.

- **Running out of a resource**—for instance, the database runs out of disk space to write its log. The application may be just waiting, doing nothing.

- **Operational problem**—for instance, the application-monitoring software reports an error that does not exist.

- **Application deliberately stopped.** It is very rare to find an application that can do even a partial software upgrade without a halt in service.

Whenever there is a failure, someone or some automated management software must be notified. This normally relies on an *agent* program running in the box that runs the application. An agent program monitors one or more resources and reports back to the manager. But if the box fails, the agent fails with it. Therefore, there must be another mechanism to detect that the hardware and system software are running. This is normally done with a heartbeat; on a regular basis the manager software sends a message and listens for a response. It is analogous to the manager asking, "Are you there?" and the agent replying, "Yes, I am." If the agent fails to reply, the manager knows there is a problem. However, the problem could be that the network between the manager and the agent has failed, not the server. Furthermore, even with an agent some application failures are hard to detect such as a loop in an application. This is especially true with a multithreading application because only one thread may be looping and hence only one user is hung waiting forever for a response. Detecting the difference between a performance-related slowdown and an actual failure can be hard as well. What is enormously helpful is to be able to monitor the application performance from the end user perspective as well as to report failures. For instance, if you have a display of a count of the input and output messages and the average response time over the last few seconds, you are in a good position to tell the difference between a slowdown and a stoppage.

When it comes to planning what to do about failures, there are two strategies. One is to collect information, think, and work out how to recover. The other is to switch to a backup system and try to figure out what happened later. If you are looking for very high availability levels, you will probably go for the second strategy—switch first, then think. As I have noted, some reasons for stops are not fixed by switching to backup. Thus to really make the switch-first strategy work well, the designers and programmers must try to ensure that there aren't any application failures or operational cock-ups. Which means that there is an onus on exhaustive analysis and checking.

If an organization really takes recovery seriously, it should switch from the main production system to the backup system regularly just to prove that it can be done.

If there is an incident, there needs to be a postmortem. You need to know why it happened and what could have been done to prevent it.

One of the biggest failures happened in June 2012 at the NatWest bank in the UK, caused by a software upgrade that went wrong [8]. Testing and configuration control are some of the most vital aspects of building highly available systems.

The Need for Testing and Benchmarking

I hope it is clear from the previous discussions that to develop an application that has high performance, fantastic availability, and great security requires

- A deep understanding of the principles

- An understanding of the technology you propose to use

- Some creative thinking to devise a good solution

Even with all this knowledge and skill, sometimes it is hard to predict how the solution will perform in practice. There is a straightforward way to ratify a solution: do some experiments.

A corollary to this is: don't believe industry-wide benchmarks. They are a guide—and a guide only—to relative performance, not absolute performance. Likewise, don't believe sales persons and don't even believe that just because organization Z can build an application with the technology you are being urged to use, you can do the same. It could be that the few extra integrity checks and consistency requirements in your application nullify the reason organization Z is getting high performance. The only way you can have confidence in the performance of your application is to try it out.

If an IT department is considering some new technology, it will usually try it out before embarking on a major development. This will typically involve little more than installing it and writing some small programs to test the various features. There may be a small performance test as well. The idea is to understand the technology and see if it is suitable for general use. This kind of casual test is good for the first objective of understanding the product but poor at figuring out if it is good for a particular project. Often organizations evaluate technology by using checklists— answering the question, "Does it have this or that feature?" They often use checklists without consideration of whether the feature is useful or whether there is an alternative design to meet the same need. Checklists are never a substitute for thinking and designing. A large project will probably need technology from several vendors, and the issues are often less about how good each product is and more about whether the products work together to achieve what you want to achieve. My advice is that IT departments should do exploratory tests but only as a first look, to see whether the product works. You should go into exploratory testing with the mindset that only half of the products you test will actually be used.

IT departments sometimes do benchmarks but often only halfway through a project when they realize there is a performance problem. Benchmarks are expensive because as well as the system under test there often needs to be a system that is doing the testing, for instance, a system emulating many users across the Web.

I suggest that you set up what I will call a *skeletal application*. I suggest too that you do not develop a throwaway prototype but rather the real thing. Second, I suggest that you develop it like a benchmark—you implement another system to put load on the application. What you are developing is the first cut of the systems test framework. To start with you have stub code for the application and stub code driving the test. As the application is developed, the stubs are replaced with real code and the tests are refined to be more realistic. The purposes are

- **To test integration.** Make sure all the software you use can work together.

- **To test performance.** You may find bottlenecks that you can't afford to fix in the test configuration.

- **To test recovery.** Find ways of emulating hardware failure and put deliberate bugs in a stub to emulate an application error. In addition to testing the software's ability to recover you also need to test the operational procedures.

- **To examine the system for security problems.** Also to test security monitoring.

- **To test functionality of the application code.**

I urge three points. First, build the skeletal code early in the project. Ideally it should be done before the programmers tackle the actual application code because that will save time. It will also help size the final project for delivery time and cost. But above all, to my mind, it will give the technical design team time to try out options and to change their mind. You can start building it after the context design is finished and even before any configuration management software has been chosen because version control and management can be applied later on.

Second, test early and test thoroughly. Give the application a proper thrashing. Do things like have a competition for people to break it. Many projects leave issues such as availability, security, and systems management on trust and don't test them at all.

Third, experiment. Try out alternative designs and try out alternative system products. As the application develops, experimenting will become more and more costly as there will be more code to change. In my humble opinion, people start projects too fast and make too many key decisions without considering alternatives or thinking deeply about them.

The Technical Design Process

As mentioned in the previous section, I think it is best to go straight from technical design to technical implementation because the best way to analyze the design is to test it for real. Thus the first-cut design can be no more than a swift sketch, perhaps presented to management for review. As the framework programming progresses in tandem with the development of a comprehensive test environment, problems will be identified, and it is likely that the design will be radically altered. A further review is needed of the completed technical implementation, largely to convince management that the tests are adequate and the application passes the tests. When the design is finished or nearly finished, a short document and/or presentation is developed for the benefit of the application programmers who need to know where their code fits into the application technical design. It may be beneficial to bring an application programmer into the team (or for the technical design team to do some of the functional implementation) to test the technical design to ensure that it does support the application code successfully.

There is another audience for the technical design, which is the computer operations and administration department. You need to tell them what you expect of them. The tests should establish the size of the servers needed to provide the right level of performance, and with input from the operations department on operating costs, it should then be possible for IT management to establish the purchase price and the runtime costs of the application. At that point, coupled with the development cost estimates, it is time for a full management review of the project. Sometimes the project is canceled at that point. Sometimes a major redesign is called for. Alternatively, the implementation phase may be rescoped to spread the costs.

Thus the outputs from the technical design and implementation are

- **Code**—an implementation of the common system parts of the application

- **A test environment for systems testing**

- **A document/presentation for application programmers**—to tell them how to implement the application from a technical point of view

- **An operations plan**—a list of requirements for the operation and administration of the computers and the network

- **A sizing of the complete configuration**—to establish the purchase and run-time costs

So how do you develop your first-cut technical design? The first step toward developing a technical design is to understand the requirements. You need to understand the following:

- How many users are there and where are they? What is the balance between users inside the organization and users outside the organization? This will tell you about the network requirements.

- What are the tasks that are done most often? Normally there are a few tasks done in large numbers and very many that are done in small numbers. A rough idea of the complexity of the commonly used tasks is worth knowing.

- What services are defined and what kind of integration requirements do they have? In particular, you want to know whether a service call is deferrable—in other words, can be delayed—and whether it is provided externally to the project—for instance, if it already exists.

- What are the availability requirements? What is the cost of downtime? Also, should special steps be taken for disaster recovery, or put another way, what is the cost of a few days' downtime?

- What are the security risks? Who would most benefit from stealing the data? Who would most benefit from the system being down? Who would most benefit from using the application illicitly? I discuss security more in Chapter 12.

The second step is to define the design hypothesis, which is the hardware configuration, the choice of software, and the outline of the framework, which are discussed in Chapter 11, "Technical Design—Structure."

The third step is elaboration. The elaboration has two parts. First is a quick analysis to review the requirements to see how they can be met. The second is to write down (in a document or a presentation; I prefer a presentation)

- How the application can grow with more users
- How timing and consistency problems are overcome
- How the application recovers from a failure
- How disaster recovery works
- How security risks are mitigated
- How security is monitored
- How the application is administered by operations
- How new versions of the application are put into production

Keep the documentation short; for a simple project it is OK if it is one page. The primary purpose of elaboration is to help ensure that everything has been thought of. Writing the documentation is itself an aid to thinking, but its primary purpose is for review and for explaining the application's technical design to the programmers.

The final step is analysis, which in this case is the implementation of the skeletal application as discussed in the previous section.

During any of these steps beyond the first one you might find that the design is inadequate and go back to an earlier step. In particular, you may iterate over the last two steps a few times as you discover and fix holes in the design.

The technical design will not work unless the computers and network are up to scratch. The technical design team needs to make their requirements explicit on

- Operations and administration requirements (e.g., backup frequency)
- The size and number of servers
- How they are connected
- The network bandwidth
- The disk space that the application and database will need

Operations will no doubt have opinions on where the servers should be installed, the vendors, and the adequacy of the existing computer rooms. They may also demand (rightly) that the application be integrated with the organization's preferred systems operation and security management systems. The technical design team should include the operations department early in the design.

Similarly, the technical design team will need to talk to the security department to tell them of their requirements, to hear the security department's requirements, and to reach a common agreement on security features and security administration.

The technical design is reviewed not only by technical experts but also by the business. After the elaboration step you should be in a position to do a first-cut estimate of the production costs (including the cost of the systems test configuration). The project manager should also be able at this point to estimate the development costs. Naturally there may be a delay from finishing the design and having the cost estimates because you may be negotiating with the vendors. It is quite possible that you will be told to go away to find a cheaper solution. A smart strategy is to present two or more alternative designs with different price tags. This will provoke discussion and help bring to the fore the real concerns of the business. There is a trilemma here, a three-way trade-off among

1. Cost

2. Speed of implementation

3. The two quality attributes of scalability and availability

For instance, this means that if you go for low cost, you will have to sacrifice either or both of speed of implementation and the *-ility* attributes.

Sometimes the answer to the business need is not to sacrifice formally any of the goals but to cut the project deliveries into phases. A later delivery may be a performance upgrade timed to coincide with the installation of more hardware. You want a technical design to ensure that planned changes to the hardware and software configuration do not require changes to the application code.

Finally, you will also need to explain to the programmers how the code they write fits in with the technical design. A presentation of the technical design is useful, but what they will use more than anything else are example implementations.

Concluding Remarks

There is a vast number of small applications that do not have demanding scalability and availability requirements for which the technical design will be trivial.

There are various choke points where the technical design becomes more and more complex. These are points like the number of I/Os per second exceeding the capacity of a single disk, or the amount of processing power needed exceeding the power of the largest server. You need to identify these choke points early and develop a design to overcome them.

There are three levels of complexity:

1. The application can run on a single server. Both the application and the database can fit happily on a single server. Software vendors provide many solutions for this configuration and the technical design issues are well understood.

2. The application can run with a single database server. This is the configuration illustrated in Figure 10.2. There are complexities with ensuring that sessions are handled properly, but there is plenty of knowledge and advice to call upon.

3. The application has such demanding requirements it needs to duplicate or distribute the database servers. Not only are there the difficulties over sessions, but you have to employ some creativity to find an effective solution to dividing the work across several database servers.

In all these configurations the need for an effective resiliency design may introduce an additional dimension of complexity.

This chapter was about how to tackle demanding performance requirements. I tried to do it in a software-product-neutral manner by drawing out the principles that underlie many different implementations.

The complexities are such that the best way to see your way through to a working design is to test it and test the options. The later part of the chapter was largely about how this should be done. I encourage project teams to make a serious attempt to tackle the technical design early on and build test configurations that can prove the performance and the resiliency and can also evolve into the systems test configuration. This is in contrast to many projects today that tackle performance and resiliency issues after a great deal of the functional code—the code implementing the business functional requirements—has already been written. Of course, for small, undemanding applications that is fine. But for large, demanding applications it can be disastrous since it leads to a big redesign in the middle of the implementation.

This chapter was largely about satisfying demanding nonfunctional requirements. The next chapter is about using technical design to make the programmer's job easier.

Chapter 11

Technical Design—Structure

In the previous chapter I discussed one of the aims of the technical design, which is to ensure that the throughput requirements, the availability requirements, and the security requirements can be met. But there is another aim, which is to make the implementation as easy as possible without compromising any of the other requirements. This is the topic of this chapter.

The decisions that impact the ease of implementation and, for that matter, the ease of subsequent support are as follows:

- Deciding which programming language to use.

- Deciding which framework to use.

- Deciding how to use the framework. Even for a simple application there are decisions to be made, such as which file directory structure to hold your program source files, what to call the classes, where to put common code, and so on.

- Deciding whether to extend the framework, and if so, how.

- Implementing common functionality.

Discussions on each of these decisions constitute the body of this chapter. There is no section about deciding how to use the framework because that is framework specific. I have included two sections at the beginning of the chapter, "Program Structure" and "What Is a Framework?," that provide background for the rest of the chapter.

Program Structure

I start by discussing general program structure because program structure helps explain frameworks.

I think it is fair to say that programmers have struggled to represent program structure in a way that is meaningful and useful. Since the program structure is the high-level program design, the implication of the previous sentence is that we don't have a well-established way to represent and discuss high-level program design. As mentioned in Chapter 3, "Reusing Existing Methods and Practices," in the section "Working Software over Comprehensive Documentation," there are numerous ways of representing aspects of program logic diagrammatically. The problem is that most of them represent small-scale aspects of a program, such as how object attributes point at other objects; they don't represent large-scale program structure. For instance, you can draw a diagram showing how functions call functions by drawing the functions as rectangles and representing function calls as lines between the rectangles. Furthermore, some of the functions handle input from the user or input files, so if you draw these at the top of the diagram, you will see something that looks a bit like a hierarchical design. So why don't programmers do this much? Simply because it is not useful; it does not help you think about the problem at hand. It is the end point of the design, not the starting point. So what is the starting point? Obviously, programmers start thinking about writing a program somehow or other. It is rather odd that this fundamental subject is so little talked about. In this section I will give you my answers to these questions, but because the subject is rarely discussed I am not sure how my experience relates to other people's experience.

One of the more obvious goals of high-level design is to bring together the code that handles one aspect of a program in one place. Furthermore, you want to *encapsulate* the code so that you can change how this part is implemented without changing the rest of the program.

When I started programming, the words programmers used to describe these ideas were *modules, interfaces, cohesion,* and *coupling.* The words are still used today but much less than they used to be. A module is a part of a program hidden behind an interface. The interface—in the C language the interface is usually implemented as a separate file—consists of a collection of function headers (sometimes called signatures) and variables. A function header is the name of a function and its parameters, in other words, a function without the implementation code. Inside the module there can be other data variables, other functions, and the implementation of the functions in the interface. The interface is what other parts of the program use when they need the module. The data variables and functions inside the module are said to be hidden because they can't be used from code that is outside of the module.

One of the questions that programmers have to answer is whether two modules should be merged or a single module broken up. The words used are *cohesion* and *coupling*. They are kind of the same thing viewed from opposite angles. High coupling means that two modules use each other a lot and have a large number of dependencies between them. The definition is a tad vague but gets over the general idea of stickiness. In other words, if two modules have high coupling, you should think of merging them into one. High cohesion means that a module can't easily be broken apart into smaller modules. Low cohesion means that the module can easily break into two or more modules. Put another way, if you have low cohesion in a module and you break it into two modules, the two modules will have low coupling.

But as I said, the definitions are vague, there is no exact measure of cohesion and coupling, and it is not inconceivable that one programmer will measure a module high for cohesion while another will measure the same module low.

Modules have been superseded by OO classes. Classes support the same notion of encapsulation but are more flexible. However, classes are often small, and a not-huge program can easily have 100 classes or so. Classes are too fine a level of granularity to represent a high-level design. What can we do? We can try to reintroduce modules where a module is a collection of tightly coupled classes, but to be honest that does not help me think about design either. Again, it feels to me like an end result of thinking, not a tool for helping me think.

What I do is look at the information flow. I want to split the program up according to the big steps of how information is transformed and stored. I want to be able to explain in simple terms—preferably in a single sentence—what each step does. I can explain this best with an example, and for this I have chosen a program that I am sure most of my readers know about but are unlikely to have thought about how it's implemented: a compiler. Here are the basic elements of a compiler:

- **Tokenizer.** The purpose is to split the source text into words, numbers, strings, and symbols (e.g., >= may be one symbol) while ignoring comments in the source code.

- **Grammar.** The purpose is to scan the source, using the tokenizer, check for syntax errors, and build the dictionary and the statement and expression handlers.

- **Dictionary.** Its purpose is to keep track of all names.

- **Statement handler.** Its purpose is to hide the statement data structure that provides an internal representation of the program.

- **Expression handler.** This is a tree data structure to represent arithmetic, boolean, and string expressions. Instances of this data structure are incorporated into the statement handler.

- **Optimizer.** This traverses the statement and expression data structures, changing them to make them run faster.

- **Code generator.** This turns the statement and expression data structures into code.

These modules are of very different kinds. Some of them simply hold data, such as the statement handler and dictionary. Some of them hold data but also do some processing. The expression handler is an example since it must resolve operator precedence (to handle the fact that in an expression like $A + B * C$ the multiply must be done before the add). Some of them do not hold any data but transform data from one form to another. Representing the transformers as arrows, the data holders as rectangles, and files as cylinders, I can illustrate this design in a diagram such as Figure 11.1.

I think of diagrams like Figure 11.1 as representing the deep structure of the program.

Clearly some of these elements have strong interdependencies between them. For instance, if-statements contain expressions, and expressions that contain variables have pointers to elements in the dictionary. In fact the three elements—expressions, statements, and dictionary—are hopelessly tangled. This is one reason why using modules to describe large-scale structure breaks down—the modules are too big. It is better to look at these data structures as objects, almost as if they form a mini internal database. I would supplement the diagram with a structure diagram of the objects, or (actually more commonly) I would just write out the classes in source code files with their important attributes.

Let's bring our compiler up-to-date. We may want to compile for different hardware platforms. That's easy; just change the code generation module. We want to

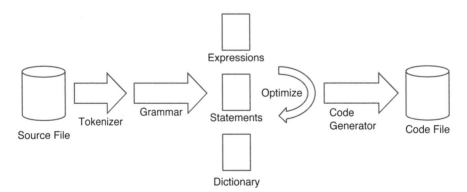

Figure 11.1 *The Program Structure for a Compiler*

compile while editing, at least to report syntax errors in real time. This is much more difficult, but let's start by writing a few steps:

```
Start - do the compilation as illustrated in Figure 11.1.
Loop
    Accept input
    Move to line or insert new line
    Edit line
```

A bit of inspiration—also known as a design hypothesis—is required at this point. When the user goes to a new line, we want to undo all the compilation from that point onward. When the user has finished with the line, we want to redo all compilation from that point onward. So we need to keep tabs on where the line being edited is and where the corresponding place is in the expressions, statements, and dictionary data structures. But as I have pointed out, expressions, statements, and dictionary are muddled up together. The restart point is illustrated in Figure 11.2.

In this diagram little triangles that look like arrowheads indicate indexes into data structures. The circle represents a control element, which in this case implements the steps outlined earlier. Looking at the diagram, you probably are thinking, "How the heck can the line number correspond to a position in the expression/statement/

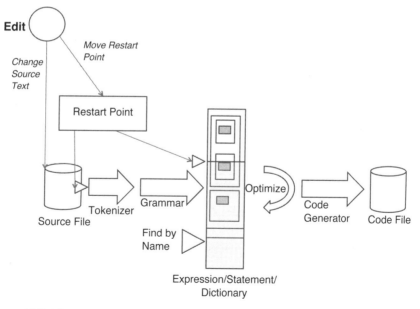

Figure 11.2 *The Program Structure for a Compiler with a Restart Point*

dictionary data structure?" In practice we may need to move the restart point a little way back so that it aligns, for instance, with the start of an expression. You may also have realized that there is some optimization in moving around the restart point; if the move is to a line after the current restart point, it is necessary to redo the compilation only up to the new position of the restart point rather than undoing and redoing the rest of the file. If you are feeling really clever, you might want to set up the undo and redo into a thread running in the background.

This is a complicated example, but it is a complicated problem and I thought that presenting a simple example—in other words, discussing a trivial solution to a trivial problem—would make the case unconvincing.

With the deep structure in place, the next step is to design the classes. Observe that the elements of the deep design don't correspond to either modules or object classes. The statements data structure does correspond nicely; we might have classes called `IfStatement`, `WhileStatement`, and so on, all subclasses of the `Statement` class. But the grammar and the code generation don't match any object. For instance, code generation is probably best implemented as an abstract function in `Statement`, which is overridden by functions that generate the code in classes like `IfStatement`, `WhileStatement`, and so forth.

I find that if I am looking at a program for the first time and wondering how it works, I have to reconstruct the deep structure from the code. This may not be easy, and I would love to find a way of expressing a program so the deep structure is readily apparent.

In summary, presented with an empty project file on which to develop your program, I suggest that you start by thinking in terms of the deep structure. This is the design hypothesis. From there you can start developing your class definitions, and this is the elaboration. People talk a lot about program style and patterns, but my experience is that the most important part of developing a good program is getting the deep structure right.

What Is a Framework?

What we often observe with these deep structures is that there are some parts that are added to over and over again. With the compiler it is adding new types of statements or, more precisely, new grammar elements. Say we are adding code to handle a for-statement. We would define a new `ForStatement` class, extend the grammar code to build it, and write the code generation function for it—and similarly for any other new kind of statement. In other words, there are definite places where code is added and the rest remains the same. This is the essence of a framework; it is skeletal code into which you can place functional elements, typically placing code in several places to achieve one function.

I want to persuade you that you should think in terms of frameworks rather than patterns. I admit it; I have a problem with patterns. The concept is an old one and it is powerful. The notion of a tokenizer in the compiler is an example of a pattern. The notion of layering as used to implement network software (e.g., link layer, network layer, session layer, etc.) is also a pattern. But patterns came to prominence when OO programming was becoming popular and programmers were struggling with the concept. In pre-OO languages it was all obvious; you started at the top and broke the problem down, step by step, forming a hierarchy of code. In OO you kind of start with the data structures, which feels like starting somewhere in the middle. Patterns gave a bit of guidance, but my problem with them is that they are far too low level and frankly trivial; they do not give any guidance for building a large program. For that you need the deep structure described in the previous section. So if you are a programmer, I suggest that you read the pattern book once and then put it on the shelf. Don't try to remember the patterns (I have been told that there are well over 100 patterns if you search the literature, so you are not going to remember them in any case) but instead try to hone your skills in assessing why something works and why something else does not. You will find that you will have no problem finding a solution without searching the pattern books, and when you do, you will already be halfway to understanding the coding implications and the pitfalls to avoid.

There are other kinds of patterns—sometimes called, to maximize confusion, architectural patterns—that do operate at a large-scale, structural level. An example, which we will look at later, is the MVC pattern. The problem in practice with those patterns is that the implementations are so varied that it makes a mockery of the notion that they all implement the same underlying pattern. But it is at this level of design that I suggest you should think about frameworks rather than patterns, because the main goal of having a framework is making it easy for the programmers by telling them what code they have to write to achieve some functionality.

Many frameworks are provided by software vendors. The frameworks are normally associated with a particular runtime product and a particular development product. Often as well as supplying skeletal code they generate code. For instance, Microsoft ASP (Active Server Pages) Web Forms generates C# or VB source code from the ASP files and knits it all together with a runtime framework that runs in the Microsoft IIS Web Server. You give each Web form a name, then write an ASP file and a code-behind file in C# or VB. The development environment converts the ASP file into an OO class, and your code-behind file provides code to process events associated with the Web form. It is a controlled and frankly constraining environment.

ASP Web Forms and JSP (Java Server Pages) are a bit passé these days. Programmers are more frequently using ASP MVC. This has a deep structure as illustrated in Figure 11.3.

MVC differs in that when you create a new Web page, you don't get the code-behind file but just an empty function. The *M* stands for "model"—which on the

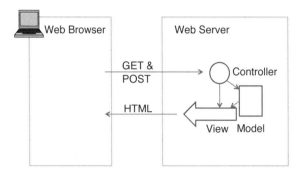

Figure 11.3 *ASP MVC Deep Structure*

face of it seems to be a fancy word for database—but if you consider how it is used, in my opinion at least, it is best thought of as a logical output file. The *V* stands for "view," which is for creating the output page, and the *C* stands for "controller," which takes the input calls from the end user and decides what to do with them; it would normally use the model to get the data and then call the view to send the output. It's a more flexible scheme than ASP Web Forms though harder to understand when you first try to use it.

The preceding was for illustration only; there are numerous Web application frameworks. Some of the other frameworks from other vendors work something like ASP Web Forms, and many more work something like MVC.

MVC

The concept of MVC was invented for Smalltalk, an object-oriented language that has its roots in the 1970s and 1980s and was designed for applications running on workstations. The idea was rather different from what I described (and some will argue that Web MVC isn't MVC at all). It is illustrated in Figure 11.4. It allowed for one model to have several active controllers and views. This makes sense if you are looking at the data in several different ways in different windows on one workstation (think of a text view and a diagram view). What you need in this instance is that if one window processes a command that changes the model, you want the other windows displaying the same model to be updated also. This is what the original MVC supported. It is hard to implement multiple views using a Web browser, so from here on, back to the simple Web MVC. The reason for this aside wasn't just to point out yet again how old I am, but to point out that the words *model* and *controller* come from a completely different context.

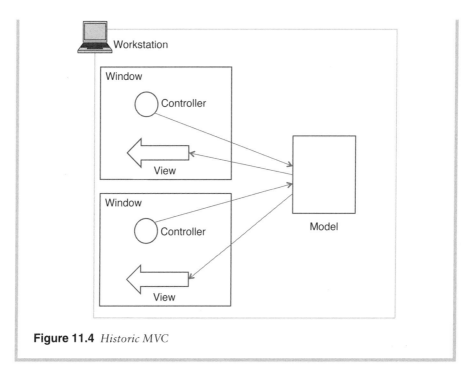

Figure 11.4 *Historic MVC*

Of course, it is fine to use a vendor's framework. The problem is that the vendor frameworks rarely cover all you need to cover even in a simple business application. Thus you need to extend the framework. Take, for example, the MVC pattern. Where is the business logic—in the controller or in the model? You can argue that it doesn't matter, but the words *controller* and *model* kind of imply that the logic should be in the controller. But let us suppose the technical designers want a two-tier solution—a Web server layer for handling the end user device, sometimes called the presentation layer, and a back-end layer for transaction and database processing. The reason for this decision is that one of the rationales for having tiers is so that you can develop another presentation layer for another type of device and thus can share the business logic. The answer is that the MVC framework applies only to the presentation layer; in effect the model becomes simply a means to access the other tiers.

But why be straitjacketed by the MVC model? Perhaps a better solution is illustrated in Figure 11.5; let us call it a CBDLV—Controller, Business logic, Database, Logical output, View—framework. I also invented another symbol for the logical output to indicate transferring a data structure across a network. One reason for thinking of a structure like this is that you might have another presentation layer that does not have a controller and a view.

No vendor implements all this to my knowledge (I am writing in 2015; I wouldn't be surprised if some full-range frameworks eventually appear because they are

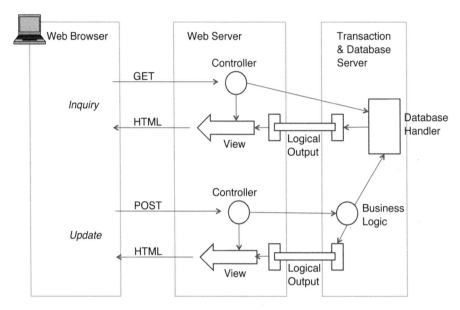

Figure 11.5 *A CBDLV Framework*

a great marketing tool). There are lots of Web application frameworks, a goodly number of frameworks for handling windowing applications on workstations, and I expect several for mobile devices, but few others.

There are some major decision points that impact the technical design of a Web application, namely:

- **Tiering**—discussed in the section "The Principles of High Performance on Many Servers" in Chapter 10, "Technical Design—Principles"

- **Use of JavaScript**—how much processing you want in the end user's Web access device

- **Security implementation**—in particular how sessions are handled

Each of these decision points can have a major impact on how code is written. You want a framework that guides the implementation programmers in how much or how little to use these features.

Choosing a framework is an important decision because it is hard to change. For example, I want to convert an application I wrote from ASP Web Forms to ASP MVC. In spite of the fact that the programming language is the same and the database design is the same, I reckon I will have to change 50% of the code.

The Variety of Programming Languages

Choosing the programming language is one of the decisions made during technical design. The choice dictates much in the development. Vendor-supplied frameworks are strongly linked to programming languages. In most cases, you have to decide the programming language first, and that restricts your choice of frameworks. In this section I want to step back and distinguish among compiled languages, interpreted languages, and scripts. I know for some of my readers this will be old hat, but for designers, project managers, and business people this is an area of great confusion.

Figure 11.6 shows the development environment for a compiled language.

Examples of a compiled language are C and C++. The source—simply a text file—is compiled into code. Maybe many source files are compiled into code and the small files of code are merged together (the technical term is *linked*) into a larger code file. The code file is moved to a system where it will run. It relies on an operating system to run it, but it might also need a Web server or some other container

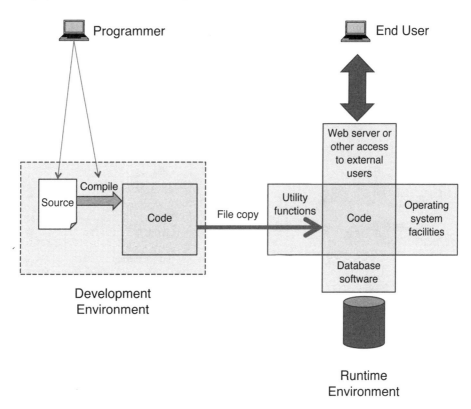

Figure 11.6 *Compiled Language*

or middleware. (The word *container* is not often used, but I mean some software that runs programs on demand and may manage other resources. A non-Web-server example is the CICS transaction monitor.) The program might also need a database system and some system-provided utility functions to do mathematical functions, date conversion functions, cryptography functions, and many, many other kinds of functions. These are usually provided in code libraries supplied by the vendor. The program may require configuration information set in the Web server or similar and the operating system.

Using interpretive languages is illustrated in Figure 11.7.

Examples of interpretive languages are Java and C# (although in Microsoft .NET, C++ can optionally be interpretive). The difference is that the source code is converted into a special bytecode (in Java this is called Java bytecode and for C# it is called CIL—Common Intermediate Language) that is interpreted by the virtual machine (VM). On the face of it this looks as if it just slows the runtime environment down, but many virtual machines these days do just-in-time compilation, thus converting each function into machine code on an as-needed basis.

There are two main advantages of having your program run in a virtual machine. First, the virtual machine can do more for you than the real machine hardware

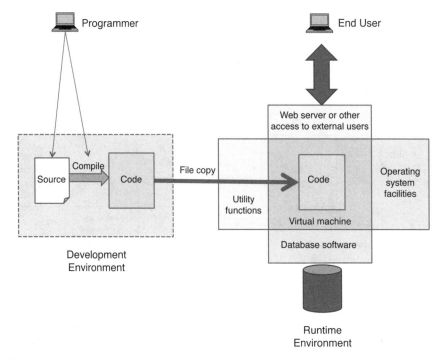

Figure 11.7 *Interpretive Languages*

does. In both Java and C#, the virtual machine looks after getting rid of objects that aren't being used. Deleting objects—either deleting them prematurely and thus having pointers pointing at random memory, or not deleting them at all so they consume memory unnecessarily and don't release resources like database connections—is a major cause of bugs in C++, so having it done for you is useful. Second, the virtual machine provides standardization. Different machines have different word sizes, different character sets, different floating-point formats, and so on. Different operating systems and system utility functions have different functions to call, different date formats, different multiprocessing facilities, and so on. With a virtual machine, all these differences are the problem of the implementer of the virtual machine itself. For the programmer, there is no difference. Java uses this standardization to run on different hardware platforms and operating systems. Microsoft uses CIL bytecode to allow different programming languages to be run together as one program.

The reasons why you might want to write a program in C or C++ are to write something that has very fast and predictable performance (the Java and C# automatic object deletion tends to be done in bursts) and to write system software like your own data management software. Many games and much real-time software (e.g., for avionics) is written in C++, but Java and C# are making inroads.

In a complex application, the development environment probably looks something like Figure 11.8.

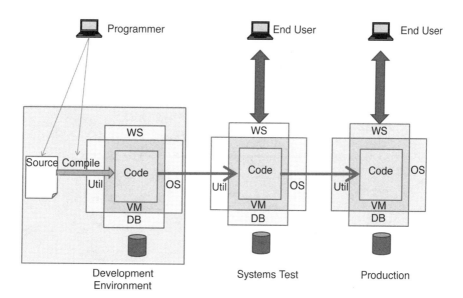

Figure 11.8 *Staged Development*

The idea is that the programmers test the unit they are developing—known as *unit tests*—on their own machines. These days you can run a test Web server and database on your workstation. You then move the new or updated unit to the systems test environment where all the units are gathered together and tested. Periodically the systems test environment is copied to production. This example is a simplification because it is best if configuration management and version control are keeping track of everything. You might have several versions under development at one time, and a bug on the production system may need to be fixed on more than one version.

This kind of heavy-duty development scares many people. The complete opposite is to develop using a server-side scripting language like Ruby, Python, Perl, Go, or PHP. This is illustrated in Figure 11.9. There is no compiler. The source code is loaded on the runtime machine and interpreted there.

The advantage of server-side scripting is speed of development. The main disadvantage is that the scripting language typically has limited features and won't scale well. There are many cheap Web site providers that allow you to put HTML Web pages and, say, PHP files in your Web site but do not support a full development environment like Java or ASP.NET.

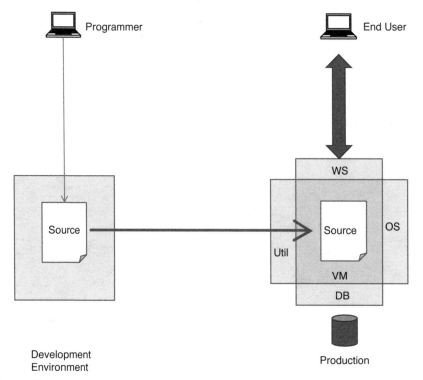

Figure 11.9 *Server-Side Scripting*

Frameworks are often integrated with the virtual machines, as described earlier with regard to ASP.NET. Except for the Microsoft frameworks that run on restricted hardware and software platforms, frameworks run with only one language. If you want to write in Java, you have many choices of framework, but if you choose another language, you typically have only one or two. Many of the arguments about the relative merits of this or that language are actually arguments about the relative merits of different frameworks.

Finally, there are languages such as JavaScript that run on Web browsers, and there are other languages that are designed to run in mobile phones. JavaScript is either embedded in a Web page or put in a separate file that is loaded to the browser. There is an increasing demand to do more on the browser and less on the server. The problem I see, however, is that JavaScript is a primitive language compared to most of the others I have mentioned in this section, and also that testing facilities are poor. Perhaps between the time I am writing this and the time you are reading it, new products will transform browser code development. I hope so.

Today programmers write in OO languages (at least for new applications), and probably the most popular are Java and C#, though C++ is common for more performance-critical work. But server-side scripting languages are also very popular, especially with organizations that don't have a history of Java or C# development.

I have to admit that I view the proliferation of languages with considerable foreboding; I suspect I am seeing the beginnings of the maintenance nightmare of the future. Capers Jones in "Jones's Law of Programming Language Creation" [18] reckons that two programming languages will be developed every month forever! Programmers are often obsessed with programming languages, and I sometimes suspect that there are programmers out there who see the invention of a new programming language as the acme of the profession; it is hard to explain otherwise why so many have been invented. And there is a view that the best programmers have many programming languages under their belt, and thus we find articles like "10 Programming Languages You Should Learn Right Now" [34]. I find this obsession profoundly depressing. What is particularly annoying is that the productivity of someone who knows a language well is an order of magnitude greater than the productivity of someone who has just learned the language; thus learning lots of programming languages is in reality a recipe for mediocrity. Furthermore, there have been many good programming languages developed in the past that are now almost invisible. Pascal and Eiffel were well designed, albeit short of features. I have a book on a programming language called Icon which incorporates some clever ideas, especially in the area of string scanning. And there are functional programming languages like Haskell and Miranda that take programming in new and interesting directions. None of these languages has had the popularity of the C language. I've never understood the attraction of C. A good goal for programming languages is to prevent or at least encourage you not to put bugs in your program. C is littered with traps that do exactly the opposite; what look like slight and obscure programming gaffes in the source code can bring the entire system crashing to its knees. History tells us that there is no correlation between the technical quality of a programming language and its success in the market.

Given the proliferation of languages, one would expect there to be a large body of research on which language is most effective. There has been very little, but there are reasons why quantitative research is hard to do:

- Programmers are much more productive in languages they know well. Basically you have to develop a style of writing in a particular programming language, and by default you tend to write in a style more appropriate to a language you know well.

- The best programmers are possibly an order of magnitude more productive that the worst programmers.

To overcome these sources of bias would require an enormous sample. The sad fact is that as an industry we know little about the real reasons for programmer productivity.

Choosing a Programming Language and Framework

So what language should you choose? I am not going to make a choice for you, because anything I say will be out-of-date in six months and would upset the quasi-religious fanatics who tend to dominate any discussion on programming languages. However, I now outline some factors that should help guide your decision.

The discussion that follows has six subsections:

- Choose a language that fits your organization's skill set.
- Choose a language that is appropriate for your application's performance goals.
- Choose a language that can meet your integration requirements.
- Choose a language that supports group working if needed.
- Choose version control software and project management software as well as a language.
- Choose a language that chimes with your development methodology.

Choose a Language that Fits Your Organization's Skill Set

As noted earlier, programmers are much more productive if they are working in a language they know and like. An organization should have a preference for either C# or Java and also select one or two (at most) server-side scripting languages. Programmers will also need to have expertise in HTML, CSS, and JavaScript for the browser side, and they may need some expertise in phone app development. They will also need expertise in SQL and will need expertise in all the old languages that were most likely used to build the applications that are running the business. That is quite enough.

Needless to say, a good IT organization should devote time and effort to keeping its programmers up-to-date and effective.

Choose a Language that Is Appropriate for Your Application's Performance Goals

Some of the techniques for high performance, high availability, and high security, discussed in the previous chapter, may be hard or impossible to program in some languages, especially scripting languages. Implementing programmable caching might be hard because of the difficulty of writing shared functions, and especially so if you need multithreaded programmable locks. Also, not all languages work well on clustered hardware configurations or with some of the large-scale database systems.

Several of the well-known Web sites started their implementation using server-side scripting and found that as they grew they needed something more. For instance, Twitter was originally written in Ruby but was rewritten in Java [35]. Facebook still uses PHP but reimplemented the VM to create something called HipHop for PHP, which instead of interpreting PHP commands converts them into C++ [36]. You have to have a large budget and the confidence that you can hire excellent programmers to take that approach.

Choose a Language that Can Meet Your Integration Requirements

It may be hard to program shared services in some scripting languages because the language does not implement callable program code. Also, using middleware may present difficulties, especially using message queuing. If the language can call a C++ or Java subroutine, it may have an escape mechanism to implement these extra features, but if it does not, you are stuck.

Choose a Language that Supports Group Working If Needed

One of the decisions you have to make as a programmer is how to split the functionality into programmable source code files.

To understand the problem, imagine a Web application that updates a database. Server-side scripting languages usually have one source file per Web page. A programmer will work on one or more files at once. What needs to happen is that when a programmer is assigned to work on one file, there needs to be some mechanism to ensure that no other programmer is working on the same file. A simple approach suitable for small teams is to write the file names on a whiteboard and indicate for each who is working on it. This works fine until someone wants to make changes to many files at once.

So let us consider the kinds of changes that may cause you to want to change more than one file at once:

- Technical design changes, like changing how session handling is done. These might mean a small change to all files.

- Database schema changes, like changing the name of a column. All files that use this column need to be changed. Changing the format of a column is likely also to affect screens that display or update the corresponding screen field.

- The same applies to any program variable that is widely used. You may think you can avoid this by hiding the usage of the variable with functions ("get" and "set" functions), but in practice, if you have a good enough reason for changing the variable's type, you usually want to change it everywhere.

- Changes to widely used functions. You may do something clever with dates and you want the same function called from several different places. If you change the function's parameters, you must change all the calls to the function.

- The change affects more than one page. For instance, you want one page to call another, but you want the called page to work slightly differently from before.

It helps if the common data and common functions are put into a separate file. It helps too if the technical design and the database design are done before programming begins. This won't eliminate technical and database changes but will reduce their occurrence.

Choose Version Control Software and Project Management Software as Well as a Language

For a large project, using a whiteboard to keep track of where you are in the project won't work any longer. The solution is to use version control software to track the source files and how they are bundled into releases, and to use project management software to track progress and tasks. Integrated development environments (IDEs) such as Eclipse for Java and Visual Studio for ASP.NET have good integration with such tools, but some server-side scripting products may not.

Choose a Language that Chimes with Your Development Methodology

I have added this point because there is confusion between the productivity benefits of the methodology and the productivity benefits of the programming tool. You can use an engineering approach to design using, say, server-side scripting and an agile approach using Java or C#. However, the people who use server-side scripting tend to use an agile approach, and many would claim that they go together. I disagree; I believe context-driven development can be used with any language.

A bit more history; this is an old argument. Prior to agile there was an application development methodology called RAD—rapid application development—and it was very much associated with what were then called 4GL products. (4GL is short for fourth-generation languages. Generations 1, 2, and 3 were machine code, assembler, and languages such as COBOL, Fortran, and Pascal.) Interestingly, even in the 4GL days, some organizations would try out a 4GL product and wonder why it didn't work for them. The reason was that they were not using RAD, but the question left hanging in the air, which I never did see answered, was whether the application development productivity advantages had to do with RAD or with the 4GLs.

Both RAD and 4GL went out of fashion, largely I think because they were overwhelmed by the tsunami of hype that hit the IT industry in the late 1980s and early 1990s around the C programming language (arguably a *3-minus* generation language), workstations, client-server technology, and, later, object-oriented languages. Eventually the ideas came back but this time renamed agile, and 4GLs came back, but this time they were renamed server-side scripting. While unquestionably there have been some impressive achievements using RAD/agile combined with 4GL/server-side scripting, in my experience such methods tend to push organizations in the direction of having many stand-alone, small applications, which is not always in the best interest of the organization.

Personally I suspect that the productivity advantages of server-side scripting are exaggerated. When I first wrote a Web application in C# and ASP.NET, I had a steep learning curve. I reckon on that first project it took ten to 20 days of struggle to master the programming environment, try things out, learn, and decide how to use the features. I like to think it would take someone less experienced even longer. Later the application was moved from a cheap Web provider that gave a restricted ASP.NET environment to another one that provided something close to a bare-bones server, albeit with ASP.NET and SQL Server software loaded. I then found myself struggling with learning how to set up the software, and that was another ten- to 20-day learning curve. It is these learning curves, and the sheer time spent researching all the options and choosing a way forward, that are so time-consuming and, to be honest, intimidating. Put another way, it is much, much quicker to get started on building your first server-side scripting application than it is to get started building one in

Java or C#. But once you understand the language, the framework, and the runtime software (and how to find answers in the documentation—I don't think I've cracked that one), after these initial hurdles, I am not at all sure there are productivity benefits. It is ironically the richness of features that necessitates so much research and decision making that is the time waster. Over time, in order to compete, the server-side scripting languages will be given more and more features and productivity will decline. Put bluntly, forcing programmers to make decisions slows down development. Which is why in context-driven development I want the technical designers—presumably the most technically savvy programmers available—to make the technical design decisions.

As an aside, strange to tell, I also found that some of the gizmos in ASP.NET didn't help productivity either. For instance, when I first started developing an ASP .NET application, I found some neat facilities for putting tables on a Web page (like the GridView controls). But I found that when I wanted to go beyond the canned solution, it became more and more complex. I found I was spending so much time reading the documentation and trying to understand the examples that I eventually thought it would be easier to build these tables myself from scratch. Which is what I did, and I found that it was straightforward and easy. I could then do what I liked and bend the application any which way I fancied. So now that is what I do, and although there is much more code to write, I can normally copy most of it from somewhere else and make the necessary changes; in other words, it is easy and fast coding—not a lot of thinking required. The point to remember is that judging programmer productivity by the number of lines of code they have to write is very, very misleading.

This does not mean that languages such as PHP and Ruby don't have their place. A Wikipedia article, "Programming Languages Used in Most Popular Websites" [37], lists what large Web companies use. Almost all of them use a server-side scripting language, but most also use C++ and/or Java. Every organization has some lightweight applications, and server-side scripting is ideal for them.

Extending the Framework

So you've chosen your programming language and you have bought a framework and possibly designed some extensions to support additional tiers; now what? Recall that in technical design we are trying to make the programmer's job as easy as possible, and the major way to do this is to supply a framework of code. The framework does two things. First, it tells the programmers where to put their pieces of code. Second, it provides the IT equivalent of the all of the application's plumbing and general housekeeping services.

In a large, technically demanding application you are likely to want to extend your framework to add features like

- Security monitoring

- Systems management

- Switching to backup

- Testing assistance (like recording and replaying input)

- Debugging assistance

The framework might look something like Figure 11.10. The gray boxes are extensions to the framework written by the technical team.

From the programmer's point of view, using a framework is rarely as simple as slotting code into place. The programmers must be educated in how to use the framework correctly. For instance, suppose the application supports two user groups, and some user groups have the ability to perform some additional actions the other ones don't. To code this, the programmer will have to find out additional information about the users such as what user groups they belong to. The code for finding the user group information should be written by the technical design team since it is intimately linked with other security code. The programmer will have to be told how

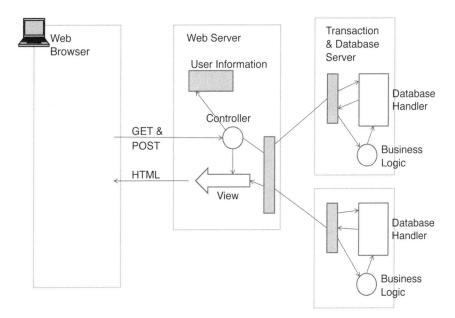

Figure 11.10 *A Real-Life Framework*

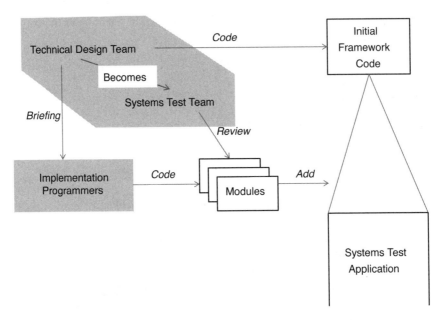

Figure 11.11 *Relationship between the Technical Design Team and Implementation Programmers*

to use this code. Another example is using middleware. Adding functionality is likely to mean adding a new kind of message layout for the middleware to send. The programmers need to be told how to do this, or whom to ask to do it for them.

You want to encourage a constructive dialogue between the technical designers and the other programmers. If the two teams aren't on speaking terms, the programmers will go ahead and reinvent the wheel. They will find their own solutions to problems, which in the long term may be incompatible with the rest of the application and in the short term will mean different teams solving the same problem. This is why I believe the technical design team should evolve into the systems test team. In this position they can review all modules as they are developed and can have ownership of the technical quality of the application. The relationship between the technical design team and the implementation programmers is illustrated in Figure 11.11.

I suggest that the technical designer should be involved in code reviews because the review of the programmers' code should be partly about the correct use of the framework. The code inspection needs to look for at least the following:

- Errors
- Security vulnerabilities

- Resiliency impact (e.g., if the strategy is to switch to backup, you need to be sure this is being implemented correctly)
- Possible performance problems
- The proper use of reusable code—see the next section
- Adherence to programming standards

The technical designer should be able to provide input on at least the first four. The code inspection will also help tell the designers that their design or implementation of the design could be improved. All code should be inspected, however well qualified the programmer, including, of course, any extensions to the framework.

Implementing Common Functionality

As noted in Chapter 2, "A Hierarchy of Designs," there are two sorts of common functionality: one has to do with supporting the framework and the design is largely driven by the nonfunctional requirements, and the other is to support functional code. Supporting the framework was discussed in the previous section; it is code to handle security, systems management, and so on.

Examples of the other sort—code for functional requirements—are

- Date and time handling
- Programmatic caching
- Having the application send e-mails or text messages
- Generating PDF files or Excel files

It is this that I discuss in this section.

The questions are:

- Who should write the common code?
- When should it be written: when it is first identified as a need or in anticipation up front?
- How is it designed?

On the first of these questions, it's worth pointing out that you can sometimes buy code (or find it open source) that does what you want. For instance, there is code available to help you generate PDF files. You will have to check licensing conditions, which is a subject way beyond the scope of this book.

To answers these questions let's lay out some of the issues:

- If programmers write one of these functions, they will often not tell anybody else. Hence the next time the function is needed, it will be rewritten by someone else.

- If programmers write one of these functions, it may be written in such a way that it can be used in only one context. For instance, if the function is to send an e-mail, some of the text of the e-mail may be embedded in the code in such a way that the code cannot be reused.

- If programmers are told to write a function to be used by many in unspecified ways, they are likely to overengineer the solution to apply to a wide variety of options, most of which will never be needed.

The key to resolving the problem is some management oversight. If you put into place a procedure for the systems test team to inspect the code, they can include checking for opportunities for reuse that have not been exploited.

I have often programmed what I thought of as a reusable function only to find when I came to reuse it (which sometimes is never) that it had to be rewritten for the new use. It is best to figure out exactly what a reusable function needs to do when you have two examples of wanting to call the function. Therefore I suggest the following:

- Have a procedure in place for publicizing within the implementation team all the reusable functions.

- As noted previously, as part of code inspection you should look to see if the code could be using reusable functions and isn't.

- If you know some functionality that will be used in several places, code it early but expect the code to change.

- Whenever someone wants to call a reusable function, he or she should have the right to ask for a change to that function.

There is a wider point. The implementation team should not only reuse functions, they should reuse ideas and reuse code. You want to build up a library of code examples, each one answering the question, "How do you do X?" There are plenty of snippets of reusable code on the Internet, but code that has already been written for your application in another place is likely to be more reusable than anything you find there.

Concluding Remarks

This is the second of two chapters about technical design, and I would like here to highlight some of the messages.

The first message is to experiment. If you think something can be done in such-and-such a way, prove it.

The second message is probably rather unwelcome to technical designers; I want them to stay on the project. I am happy for them to write some of the implementation code, but especially I want them to build and run the systems tests and to inspect the code.

I don't like gurus wafting in and out of a project; I like them to commit themselves to a project. I once worked on a project where I thought I had designed a technical solution that bordered on the genius, but then I left the project. When I returned a year later to see how they were doing, my technical design had been changed beyond repair, mainly under the influence of gurus who had never thought deeply about the problem and made ill-informed pronouncements that browbeat the project team into moving in poorly thought-out directions. In my experience, technical designs deteriorate as they are implemented unless someone takes responsibility for keeping the quality up.

I am conscious that much of this discussion has been about large, difficult applications, especially in Chapter 10. These are the kinds of applications where the problems are, but the fact is, a huge number of applications don't fall into this category. For instance, I might have seemed negative on, say, server-side scripting, but let me make clear that using server-side scripting products is fine for probably the majority of applications.

I also want to emphasize that even for large, difficult applications a multitiered solution isn't always the best solution. Often multitiered solutions got there by accident; the bottom tier is in fact an old application no one dares to change. If you are writing from scratch, sometimes a multitiered solution is best, but sometimes you can be creative in a different way, especially by looking at the alternative distributed data solutions discussed in the preceding chapter.

Finally, in any size of application, you should always be on the lookout for code that can be shared. The technical designer always has two objectives. One is meeting the nonfunctional requirements. The other is to make the implementation programmer's job as easy as possible.

Chapter 12

Security Design

I have put security design into a separate chapter because it is so pervasive; everyone must do their part, not only the development team but also the application administrators and the end users. Thus, while there may be someone with overall oversight of security, there is no one security designer.

In this chapter I discuss

- **IT application security principles**—some basic terminology and ideas.
- **The security component in each of the designs.**
- **Security programming.** Careless programming can open up your application to all kinds of security vulnerabilities.

There is a great deal of discussion and concern about IT security these days, some of it couched in apocalyptic terms like *cyber-war* and *cyber-terrorism*. It is undoubtedly true that there is a great deal of cyber-crime around. But if you look more carefully, you realize that most of it preys on the computer-naïve. This doesn't make it any more acceptable, of course, but it does hint that you can build a secure IT application and that the biggest weakness is people.

Organizations should undoubtedly be concerned about cyber-spying. Most of the attacks rely in the first instance on someone accidentally loading a malicious program on an office PC. An effective attack method is the *spear phishing attack*—people in the target organization receive e-mails that look as if they were sent by someone else in their organization whom they trust, and embedded in each e-mail is a file [38]. The file is a program that opens a back door to an external machine, which is unlikely to be the PC that is the source of the attack but some slave server working on the attacker's behalf. The program allows the attacker to snoop around, download additional programs, and upload data.

There are several defenses against these kinds of attacks:

- Educate the users not to be fooled by phishing attacks. Of course, someone in your organization may be working for the enemy, in which case this won't work.

- Set up the e-mail server to filter executable files. But it is harder to stop users from clicking on links and to detect links pointing at sites that deliver malware; clicking on such a link is referred to as a drive-by download. Most of the ways of doing this are blocked if

  - The PC software is kept up-to-date

  - The users don't do their day-to-day work under administrator privileges

  - Firewalls are switched on

  We are back to education again.

- Work with one of the expert security companies and try to find and eliminate any back-door programs as fast as possible. Of course, there is a time gap between a program being loaded and being eliminated.

- Ensure that PCs with access to the Internet don't have access to any sensitive data. Unfortunately, everyone wants access to the Internet these days, and people want to work at home, often using PCs loaded with sensitive data while being connected to the Internet.

- Ensure that sensitive data that users access is encrypted. For documents loaded on a PC, a keystroke-logging program could read the keystrokes and watch a password being entered.

- Try preventing the spy program from calling home. But some spy programs call home by pretending to be a Web browser, so to block them would be to block all Web access.

It is easy to encrypt database data, which makes it harder for spy programs to attack databases, and it is probably true that most of the damage done by these attacks has been from stealing confidential documents, not database data. However, some applications allow loading database data into spreadsheets, which opens up vulnerabilities all over again.

What this discussion illustrates is a major difficulty in designing a secure system: the weak point is the people. People often want to be trusting. If left to their own devices, they will happily give privileged usernames and passwords to friends and acquaintances and send confidential information to anyone who says they need it. The corollary to this is a point that is often overlooked: you should design a security system that *encourages good behavior*. In particular, the security should not make it difficult for people to go about their normal business because if it does, people will search for ways around it—and usually they will find them. For instance, they will phone their friend in another department and have him or her e-mail the information they need. You want to engender a culture where because everyone knows that the system allows them to see the data they need, any request to circumvent security is treated with suspicion. Put another way, too much security can be as bad as too little.

I am mainly discussing the security of Web applications in this chapter. This is because Web applications are where many of the difficulties lie. Applications that don't use the Web typically have a much easier security problem to solve.

IT Application Security Principles

The aim of security design can easily be stated: you want to control who can do what. Breaking this down into key points, we have:

- **Authentication design.** You want to decide how to identify the users and what proof they need to give to show that they are who they say they are.

- **Access control design.** You want to give different groups of users (or individual users) different access control privileges. Think of the set of all commands that are possible in an application. Each user group can use a subset of these commands. You may also want to control access to data. For instance, online banking customers have the same set of commands but are restricted to applying them only to their own accounts.

- **User administration design.** You need to decide how to add new users, remove users, add privileges, and take away privileges. You also need to decide who does the user administration.

- **Security protection.** You need to define how the servers are set up and programs are written so that they do not have security vulnerabilities that allow people to circumvent authentication or access control. You also want to protect against vandalism and resource theft—people maliciously making your application partially or wholly unavailable.

- **Security monitoring design.** You need to decide whether and how to look for attacks on the application and how to gather a log of an attack.

The IT application design team may not be allowed to do (or be capable of doing) all aspects of security design. Security protection in particular relies on server security, network security, and physical security, which are deeply technical subjects. Instead, the IT application designers will typically just place a requirement on the IT operations department to provide a secure system on which to run their application. If you are using a cloud vendor, much server security, network security, and physical security will be the vendor's responsibility.

Another reason why the IT application design team may not be allowed to do all aspects of security design is that there is a security department in the organization that will dictate parts of the security design, especially in the areas of authentication—perhaps using company-wide authentication mechanisms—security administration, and security monitoring.

In the rest of this section, I look at authentication, access control, user administration, security protection, and security monitoring in more detail, especially trying to delineate what is the responsibility of the IT application design team and what is the responsibility of others.

Authentication

The simplest and most common way of doing authentication is for the user to log on using a username and password. There are many objections to this scheme. First, passwords can, in practice, be easily guessed. The number of people who have a password simply called *password* is astonishing. This is why some sites force you to choose a password that is eight characters or more and mixes numbers, lowercase letters, and uppercase letters. Second, people end up with many passwords for the many applications they use, and as they cannot remember them all, they write them down. Alternatively, they use the same password for many different applications. Third, if someone is looking over your shoulder —or a keystroke-logging program is running, perhaps without your knowledge—he or she can see what you type. Banks seem to be more concerned about the last problem than many online (and well-known) businesses, probably because businesses are fearful of turning away the less-security-conscious customer, which, to be honest, is most of us. In my experience banks ask additional questions like, "What is your mother's maiden name?" and have partially blanked-out passwords where you supply only a random selection of three characters from the password. The reason for the partially blanked-out passwords is to create difficulties for keystroke-logging programs. The next time you log in, you will be asked for a different set of three characters, so the keystroke-logging programs must watch you log in many times before they can reconstruct the full password. Another way of making life difficult for keystroke-logging programs is devising a method of submitting the password by moving and clicking the mouse rather than typing, for instance, by supplying a keypad with characters randomly positioned. I use a bank that has gone a step further and given me a little electronic keypad gizmo that generates keys; again, the idea is to ensure that every login is unique, so someone who has watched you go through the process cannot repeat it (without stealing your gizmo). There is a great deal of research on biometric methods of authentication, so perhaps the problem will be more or less solved by the time you read this.

One of the most vulnerable areas of authentication is password recovery—in other words, the process that happens when a user forgets a password. The main questions are:

- How can you be sure you have sent the new password to the right person?
- How do you stop the password from being intercepted?

Some organizations think that sending the new password to an e-mail address is enough. Sending a text message is probably slightly more secure. Others will ask a question like, "What is your mother's maiden name?" and give you a password online or over the phone. Anyone who is serious about breaking into your account will know the answers to these questions. Yet other applications send the new password by mail or use a combination of methods—sending part of the password by regular mail and e-mailing the rest. While painful for the user, this is much more secure. What method is best, as always, depends on how secure you need your application to be.

One of the approaches to authentication for an application is single sign-on. The idea is that the user signs on once for many applications. Thus it is less of an issue with the user if the sign-on is a bit more complex than normal, and the user benefits from having to remember only one password. The downside is that if someone does find out a user's password, many applications are vulnerable, not one. Furthermore, there is a temptation to leave the PC signed on for long periods of time, which might give someone the opportunity to use your machine pretending to be you when you have left your desk to go to a meeting or out to lunch. You can do single sign-on over the Web technology known as OpenID [39], in which case there must be a Web site (typically Google or Facebook) that handles the sign-on. When the user connects to such an application, the application sends a message to the other Web site to be authenticated. The application receives a message back telling it whether the sign-on was successful or not. If you want to see an example of this in action, try logging on to stackoverflow.com, the useful site for answering programming queries. While OpenID is a sound piece of technology that works well and brings the advantages of single sign-on to the Web, if I were running a bank I would not trust that, say, someone's Google login was particularly secure. Part of developing a security plan for an application is balancing how much risk you want to take against convenience.

How Do We Identify a User?

In most applications with a sign-on you must have a username or e-mail address. The application will insist that the name or e-mail given be unique, by which I mean it has not been used before. For an application used only within a business you might be given a unique username. In Web technology you cannot prevent more than one person from using the same username and password. If an e-mail address is used, you cannot ensure that only one person uses that e-mail address on a regular basis, nor can you detect when a single person has multiple e-mail addresses. There are many people who do online banking on behalf of their elderly relatives, so even there more than one person can use a single account. Interestingly, if biometric authentication becomes prevalent, this will break down and organizations will have to decide if they want to allow more than one person to use an account.

Access Control

Once users are authenticated, they start a session. Session data was discussed in Chapter 10, "Technical Design—Principles" in the section "Principles of High Performance on Many Servers." In many applications—probably most applications—the program must take the user identifier supplied in the authentication process and from that find out what user groups the user belongs to.

Access control in an application is up to the application program. One of the confusions in understanding security is that operating systems, database software, transaction monitors, and Web server software all claim to do access control. They do, but only to a very limited extent, and they usually assume that one program is being used by one user, which is of course not the case for Web server applications.

Access control in applications is primarily about ensuring

- **Application access control.** Only a restricted subset of people are allowed to use the application.

- **Functional access control.** Within an application, members of certain user groups are allowed access to additional tasks. For instance, managers may have additional functions they can use. The best way of enforcing this is to make only the actions a user can do available on the screen. For instance, managers' Web pages may have additional buttons.

- **Data access control.** For instance, in online banking the data you see is restricted to the accounts you own.

Another form of access control described in the literature is security levels. This is the computer equivalent of having documents labeled *secret*, *top secret*, and so on, and the idea is that users have a clearance level that allows them to see documents up to a certain level. (They can write documents at a higher level of security than they can read!) I have never been asked to work on a system like this, and I have worked in some high-security environments like banks and law enforcement. One of the extraordinary aspects of well-publicized spy cases—for instance, both the Robert Hanssen and Edward Snowden cases—is the range and amount of material they managed to get their hands on. One is left with the impression that if the CIA did apply multilevel security, they didn't apply it very well.

However, I have been asked to implement complex forms of access control. As mentioned before, I wrote an application for logging business reviews where the access control rule was that managers could see all the data about not only the operations they managed but also all the way down the management hierarchy; they could see information down the hierarchy but not up the hierarchy.

User Administration

An application such as Facebook is largely self-administered by the users; users decide their own username and password. The same is true of online banking and online purchase applications, though for a bank there may be a delay between applying for online access and being given online access. But this is not true of applications that are internal to an organization. Typically, when people change jobs, they must be given all the access rights to the new applications they will be using and (this is the difficult bit) must have the access rights of the applications they used in their old job revoked. The big problem is that few organizations have the processes in place to do this job accurately and consistently. A common reason for this is that each application has a different person or team assigned to do security management.

User administration can be a source of security vulnerabilities. It is not so much the obvious vulnerability of the administrator assigning privileges with malicious intent; the underlying cause is much more often laziness, ignorance, or a naïve trust in one's fellow workers. I once wrote an application that was secure in almost every way, but I let the administrator set the initial username and password for a new user. The administrator devised a simple scheme to convert names and initials to usernames and passwords. Unfortunately, if you were assigned a username and password by this administrator, you could easily guess the rules to generate the username and password for everybody else. Users could protect themselves by changing their passwords, but how many people changed their passwords? Not a single one. What I should have done to make the application secure was to have the new user password generated randomly. Security solutions are often very simple; you have just got to know what the problem is.

Security Protection

The following is a list (undoubtedly a partial list) of ways security can be compromised:

- **Password stealing or guessing.** I discussed this point in the "User Administration" section.

- **Using an authenticated channel without the user's knowledge.** The idea is essentially to steal and reuse the session data. There are various protections against this. One is for the server to give the client a new session identifier on a regular basis. It is also important to close finished sessions. Unfortunately, it is hard to detect when a session has finished on the Web unless the user logs out. The only solution is to time out. This is why if you don't use an online banking application for a short period of time, it times out and you have to log back in again.

    A related danger is that a program running on your own PC could use your session behind your back.

- **Message interception.** Suppose you access an application from an open wireless Internet connection, such as in an Internet café. It is possible for others to make their PC the wireless hub and look at all the data flowing through the hub. The usual protection against this on the Internet is TLS or SSL encryption.

- **Accidentally providing a command in the application that doesn't check access control constraints.** This is a programming fault; again, it is easy to fix when you know it is there.

- **File transfer of data from the server.** The server is probably configured to support copying files to and from it (usually by using FTP, File Transfer Protocol) so that operations can load the application files and copy any error logs. The file transfer password must be secure.

- **Reading and/or writing data files or databases on the server.** Operations are also most likely to need to do this, if only to upgrade to a later software version. They must ensure that they do it securely. You can encrypt important data so that if the server is compromised, the data is still secure.

- **Installing and running a program on the server.** Similarly this is needed by operations, and they need to do it in a secure fashion.

- **Reading backup data.** The data in the database also exists in copies of the database made for backup. The solution is to encrypt the data.

- **The network being made slow or inoperable.** People with malicious intent may not want to spy but just cause as much inconvenience as possible. This is called a denial-of-service attack. It is up to your network security experts to fix this.

- **Servers being made slow or inoperable.** It may be possible for a malicious person to send many requests to the server to clog it up because the application is spending excessive time trying to respond to these requests. These requests are most likely to come from a user who is not logged on; thus every part of the application must respond very quickly to users who are not authenticated.

Some of these points are the responsibility of the IT application designer and some the application programmer, but many are the responsibility of operations or systems administration.

There are some principles to make it less likely that an attack is successful:

- Reduce the opportunities. Close sessions as soon as possible. Put enterprise servers on private networks, and force Web traffic to go through a Web server and maybe a few firewalls before it reaches the enterprise backbone network. If a server does not need a feature, don't make it available. Store passwords either encrypted or hashed. (A hash is like an encrypted form but condensed to a 32- or 64-bit number. This is good for passwords because you never have to convert the hash back to the actual password text.)

- Be careful how you encrypt. Don't write your own encryption routines; writing encryption routines that are robust is difficult and best left to the experts. Use seeds, which are random numbers used in the encryption to make it extra secure. If two identical pieces of text are encrypted using different seeds (which can be known to anyone), the result is two different byte streams. Anyone who sees the encrypted data won't know the two are identical.

- Think carefully about whether it is better to encrypt database data programmatically rather than encrypting the whole database. Encrypting the whole database is easier and protects against people reading the data directly or in the backup files, but it does not stop someone from running a database browser program that will show the data unencrypted.

- Ensure that access to servers or other components by systems management and maintenance is restricted because they are likely to use privileged passwords.

- Don't keep important passwords on any personal device—PC, phone, and so on. Spear phishing attacks are after them.

- Complexity is the enemy of security. If security management is complex, it is likely not to be done properly.

- Use security monitoring to look out for security vulnerabilities.

Security Monitoring

The purpose of monitoring is to detect either security intrusions early or attempts at security intrusions. If the intrusion is successful, you may be able to limit the damage and make a fix to prevent it from happening in the future. If the intrusion is unsuccessful, you may be able to see a pattern of attack and strengthen your defenses. In both cases, you may want to gather evidence for a successful prosecution. Another reason for monitoring is for peace of mind; if you are not detecting suspicious activity, at least your system has some level of security.

There is a great deal written about security monitoring and many products on the market, but few of the products address application monitoring; they are mostly focused on generic solutions such as monitoring PCs and server operations. Since this book is about IT applications, I am going to discuss only security monitoring for applications.

So what do you want to monitor? Here are some important user activities that might be worth monitoring:

- Security commands. Anyone adding a user or changing a user's privileges should be monitored. If someone steals the administrator password, you want to detect any damaging activity and change the password as quickly as possible.

- Inquiries that display sensitive data like personal information, especially if the inquiry has a facility for downloading the data to a PC.

- Login failures. The occasional login failure is only to be expected. It is a high volume of them that is suspicious. If there is a series of failures and then a success, you want to know the name of the user who successfully logged in. You might then send that user an e-mail and verify his or her identity.

- Several logins for different usernames from the same PC. But you may find that in some departments the secretary is doing all the work for several managers!

- Application-specific suspicious activity. You have probably met this already in relation to credit cards. A sudden spurt of spending, especially on high-value goods, or spending from abroad may trigger your credit card supplier to phone you up to check whether your card has been stolen. A simple check useful on many applications is to see if it is receiving commands sent at unexpected times of day or from abroad.

- Monitoring all the activity from one person or from a range of IP addresses. (The IP address from the Internet can often tell you roughly where the message is coming from. Look up *IP address location* in your favorite search engine to see how.) You may want to be able to switch monitoring on and off for a user who has aroused your suspicion.

When you monitor security commands, you want to record who is doing the command—the name the user logged on with and the IP address. If it is very important you might, as a further check, have your application generate an e-mail to the administrator to tell him or her that such-and-such command has been done.

There is no point in monitoring unless someone is reading the logs. The difficult part is producing pithy information for the administrator who reads the monitoring logs. You must build the monitoring software to focus on suspicious activity rather than just monitoring everything; otherwise the administrator will be flooded with information and do nothing.

The Security Elements of Each Design

Security design is not a separate box in my six-box model of design, and the reason is that it is pervasive. Unfortunately, as can be seen from the discussion in the previous section, it is pervasive well beyond the bounds of the application, and beyond what the IT application designers can control. What this means is that the designers should place requirements on the people who manage the IT infrastructure. Sometimes there is a security department that drives the security design from outside the IT application design team. The biggest danger of a security team is that they will demand that the security be overengineered. For instance, a bank may demand banking levels of security for an application that has few security dangers, such as an application that analyzes market information. In this section I look at each box in the six-box model in turn (except for implementation) and set out the security component of each. Implementation is covered in the next section, "Security Programming."

Context Design

The context design specifies the security requirements. It defines user groups and what each user group can do. This sets out the access control requirements. However, it should do more than this; it should also define the *threat model*.

I hope it is clear from the previous discussion that you can practically ignore security at one end of the scale, and you can go completely over the top at the other end. Also, if the dangers come from the public on the Internet, one kind of defense should be put in place, but if the dangers come from employees (e.g., as for an HR application), a different kind of defense is needed.

The starting point is to build a threat model. You need to describe the dangers of security being broken and in particular figure out who are the kinds of people or organizations that would most benefit from a breach of security. For instance, the sales records for a company that sells cupcakes might interest a competitor, but the biggest danger from such a release would be if the company was not living up to stock market expectations. However, if the company was not selling cupcakes but selling surveillance electronics, more people might be interested in who was placing orders.

A threat model consists of

- **Who.** Who is the threat? Example answers are kids, spies, fellow employees, competitors.

- **What.** What are you worried that these people will do? You may be worried about a schoolkid vandalizing the application, or about competitors and foreign spies trying to read information undetected.

- **Damage.** If the threat materializes, what are the consequences? Is it financial? Is it legal? Is it reputation? Is it competitive position?

Usually in an application some parts need only minimal security while other parts need high security. Personal information and especially financial information must be secure. Product information typically needs to be more secure before the product is launched than after. Before product launch the danger is competitors. After launch the main danger is probably vandals—someone rewriting the product description for a laugh. But you should also consider the danger of someone lowering prices behind your back. Thus the threat model may need to be repeated for different parts of the application.

An example of a threat model is presented here. The application is one I have mentioned before, which is logging operation reviews in a business. The application also allows employees to download their business plans for the operation.

Operational Review Application Threat Model

```
Who: External person with an interest in the company.
   Action: Reading organization plans.
      Damage:
         • If a plan can be seen as unethical, there may be a
           reputational risk.
```

- If the plan includes any change of land use, external
  groups hostile to the company's plans may be in a better
  position to oppose them.
    Action: Malicious damage.
        Damage: affects the ability of the management to manage.
Who: A competitor organization.
    Action: Reading organization plans.
        Damage: Increased competition by stealing ideas, finding
            product weaknesses, and identifying key customers.
    Action: Reading the management structure and personal details.
        Damage: Enhance their ability to find employees to persuade
            them to change jobs.
Who: An employee.
    Action: Seeing their boss's plans.
        Damage: Destroy trust in an organization. Poison the
            relationship between boss and staff.
    Action: Malicious damage—as before.

I think the threat model should be short. If you look for examples of threat models on the Internet, you will find guidelines that are much longer than the one I showed. There are several reasons for this. One is that they replicate a great deal of the basic information that we have already documented in the context design. If you are not using context-driven design, you should be aware that it is hard to develop a security plan unless you know what the application does. Another reason for threat models being large as currently written is that the scope is way beyond the application and includes data center security, server security, network security, and so on. Put another way, the traditional threat model is written after the integration and technical designs have been done. To my mind the threat model should be input to the security design as developed in the technical design. Of course, you could look at the context design and develop a threat model while you are doing technical design, but you want the stakeholders' input, and the best time to get it is when talking to them about application requirements and application design.

It is important that the application design team develop the security plan for the application and lay requirements on the IT infrastructure that are up to other groups to satisfy. I see it as a bad idea to mix application security with infrastructure security because one infrastructure applies to a large number of applications. In my experience very few security experts are application developers, and they tend to have an IT infrastructure view of the world. Generally speaking, that is not a problem (most of the issues with security are in the IT infrastructure), but both parties have to understand the demarcation line. Application security is responsible for putting procedures in place for users to be allowed to use the application and for ensuring access control within the application. Infrastructure security is required to ensure that there are no back doors, for instance, that the administrator password to the server is safe. The area of most overlap is authentication. The IT infrastructure managers may insist on certain authentication standards, especially if single sign-on is used, but they are not in a position to know who the users are.

To analyze the threat model you can ask a few easy questions:

- Does the data include personal data and, if so, does the threat model adequately express the risk of the personal data being stolen?

- Does the data include the company's sensitive data and, if so, what are the risks of it being stolen?

- Do any of the actions have monetary consequences and, if so, what is the risk of fraud?

In addition to the threat model, the other area of security analysis in the context design is a consideration of whether the grouping of users into user groups is correct. In zoology and other disciplines where taxonomies are developed, there are *splitters* and *lumpers*. The splitters like to split the categories up, while the lumpers like to lump the categories together. The same happens in context design; some context designers are splitters and will identify many user groups with fine distinctions between them, and some of them are lumpers who will define a few broad user groups. Security concerns help resolve how to divide up the users into groups. If two groups have the same security requirements, they should probably be merged. If one group has a wide range of security requirements, especially if it turns out that part of the user group has additional data access privileges, the user group should be split.

Some more specific questions are:

- Are there general data access rules that need to be applied across the whole of the application? I mentioned one earlier: managers see their team's data but not vice versa.

- Are user groups being given privileges they don't need?

- If users can only see data selectively, is all the data they need viewable? In other words, have you accidentally devised a system where some data is invisible?

In some applications, a security threat that is often overlooked is fraud. You should look at the tasks and examine whether there are temptations in them that might make them a target. For instance, suppose your application is about inputting new orders and it supports multiple currencies. If the order form allows you to put in your own exchange rate, there is a temptation to give someone an especially good discount by manipulating the exchange rate. This is best fixed by using an exchange rate supplied by someone else in the organization.

There is a final security question that needs to be decided in the context design: Who assigns users to user groups and who removes users from user groups? Context designers will often come across stakeholders who are more than keen to pass the responsibility to some other department or to give it to a junior staff member who has no reason to be particularly security conscious. If you feel uncomfortable about who has been given this responsibility, you should consider putting in monitoring code to look at how the facility is being used in practice. Perhaps you should provide an automatic management report as part of a business summary of application activity that lists the number of users in each group and how many have been recently added or deleted.

The threat model and the user group assignment should be understood and reviewed by business stakeholders. Please note that if you discuss user groups, threat models, and fraud with them, there is no complicated security technology to confuse them.

Integration Design

The integration design can help achieve security aims.

Security is a driver toward fragmenting applications and databases. From a security perspective each user group should only be able to use applications that give them the facilities they need and no others, and those applications should use databases that hold data that only services the needs of the application and nothing more. Taken to extremes, this is often impractical and unnecessary, but some judicious splitting to ensure that highly sensitive data is separated from nonsensitive data often makes devising a security plan much simpler. It also helps protect against an inadvertent error such as someone working on a mundane change accidentally exposing sensitive data to the wider world. For instance, in a warehouse application the only customer data that needs to be present is the customer's delivery address. Sometimes a similar application is used by two distinct user groups. An example is an application used by maintenance engineers to order new parts which, on security grounds, is useful to separate from an order entry application used by sales and/or customers. With a split application, there is no opportunity to have a new product sold at maintenance prices, and there is no opportunity for the maintenance engineers to see who bought what or to look at sensitive customer data.

It is easy for stakeholders (and many in IT) to think that all security threats come only from the end users. One area of vulnerability is the IT operations and infrastructure management. Large IT configurations have internal networks—maybe many internal networks. Someone with access to an internal network has much more scope for doing damage than someone without access to the internal network. It is not up to the integration designer to fix these problems, but it is up to the integration designer to establish the boundaries of each application and service, in other words, all the different ways data comes into or out of an application or database.

Many of these boundaries are about sharing data, either by sharing a database or by copying data from one server to another. Your application may be wonderfully secure, but if the data is copied to another application or data mart/warehouse for data analysis and the recipient of the data is insecure, the whole system is insecure. There needs to be someone or some group that has oversight of all the data in the organization to understand the security implications of data being passed around the system. This job is normally understood to be part of *data governance*. Today, many of the people who have data governance as part of their job specification have an impossible job because of the lack of context models in their organization.

Some data—like customer data and product data—is widely used, and different attributes of the data objects in these tables are of importance to different applications. This was discussed in Chapter 6, "The Relationship with the Users," in the section "Data Used by Other Applications," where I introduced the notion of data bags. This is the idea that data attributes are grouped because they are all used in the same way, and the usage of the data bag can be specified before you know what attributes are in the data bag. This is a useful concept when analyzing security. If a data table has several data bags, the chances are that they will have different security access rights for different user groups.

User Interface Design

Access control in applications usually translates into application code. When defining the end user interface, you don't ever want to send the user the message, "You can't see this data because you aren't allowed to." Instead, you simply want to ensure that seeing such data isn't a selectable option. It is an important security point that if users do not need to see some information, they should not even be told that the information exists. By restricting users to actions they are allowed to do, you are also simplifying the user interface for them.

The analysis of the user interface design should consider first whether the user groups can do all they need to do and no more, and second whether sensitive data is displayed.

Database Design

One database may be used by many applications. Furthermore, the data may be extracted from the database and either loaded into another application database or into a data warehouse or data mart system that allows for data analysis. As the data crosses these boundaries, so should data security. In practice this is hard because large organizations have so many applications—hundreds or thousands of them. Knowing about the security of all of them, especially without the assistance of context models, is hard if not impossible. In practice you are probably going to have to restrict your security analysis to key data like personal data and financial data.

You can show how data moves around the system by a diagram such as Figure 12.1. The thick line in the center represents a single data object for a single product. Thus it shows product data being created on the left-hand side and moved through the system (a bit like a process diagram but focused on a single data object). The product can be created in two places—internally or from an external supplier. When the product is released, the data is sent in three different directions—to the sales application, the distribution application, and the maintenance application. The idea of this diagram is to show all the tasks and the user groups that access the data. Of course, in a real-life example a diagram such as this would be much busier; you would need to draw a series of diagrams showing how the data object moves through time.

This diagram illustrates the challenge of data security since at each stage the data object has different user groups that need access, each of which should be allowed to see only a subset of the available data. Drawing the diagram is a technique for analyzing the data movement in the organization. For instance, just looking at Figure 12.1 helps answer the question, "What do you have to do to terminate a product?"

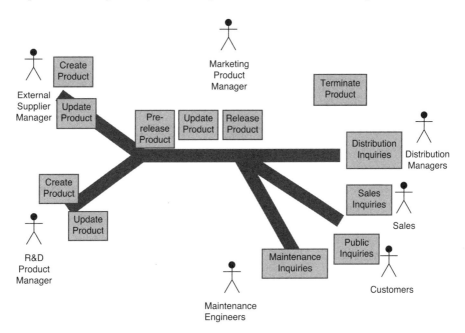

Figure 12.1 *Data Moving through the System*

If data is being moved around, you have the opportunity to take out security-sensitive fields or to anonymize the data. You should take this opportunity if possible.

Anonymizing data is not foolproof. For instance, if you make a customer name invisible, someone will often be able to work out who it is from the location. So even with anonymized data you may have to track who can see it and possibly put some processes in place that assert they are responsible individuals and not only do they want to keep the data secure but they also know how.

Technical Design

While the context design and integration design can be thought of as identifying the security problem, the technical design is the main point at which to create the security solution. The major task is to identify the weak points where a security attack might be aimed and to develop countermeasures. In security experts' jargon the weak points are known as *attack vectors*. Naturally the countermeasures should be commensurate with the risks identified in the threat model.

More specifically, the technical design must cover the following security points:

- **Authentication**. The technical design must describe how authentication is done. It could be that the solution is to use single sign-on, in which case there is not a great deal to do. There are dangers from password guessing and password stealing, especially during password recovery. These must be considered in the design.

- **Security administration**. I suspect mismanagement of user privileges is one of the major—and often unreported—sources of security failure. The context design should tell the technical designer who allocates and deallocates users to user groups. The technical design must give them the means to do so, and the programmatic interfaces so the code can figure out what user group the user belongs to.

- **End user vulnerabilities**. This is largely the exploitation of security holes created by programmers and is discussed in more detail in the section "Security Programming." Vulnerabilities are typically users pretending to be someone else or commands to the system that inadvertently can be done without first being authenticated.

- **Security monitoring**. The security-monitoring code must be designed. The security infrastructure team will probably tell you they can do extensive security monitoring. That may be true, but security monitoring of the application code can be much more focused, by which I mean it can monitor only what truly matters, and the data it can capture can be much more meaningful. In addition to monitoring end users, you should monitor security administration and authentication failures.

- **Server security**. If the server is insecure, all bets are off. This is a topic for discussion with the operations and IT infrastructure team.

So how should the technical designers approach a discussion with the operations and IT infrastructure team? To begin with, there are three points to establish. The first is whether the IT infrastructure provides some services the application should use, like single sign-on. The second is that you need to let the infrastructure team know whether there are unusually high security demands on an application, service, or database. Third, you need to tell them where the users are, the two extremes being people from the organization who are expected to be trusted and, at the other end of the scale, anybody on the Web.

Server security can be compromised in several ways, in particular by

- Finding the password for administrator and other operational functions (e.g., file transfer password)

- Exploiting a software security hole or poor server setup

- Writing code to become a middleware client, in other words, calling a service directly

- Reading backup files on another server

Fixing these holes is the job of IT infrastructure management, but the technical designer has to decide whether to build in additional lines of defense such as encrypting the database or putting security tokens in the middleware message. Security tokens are simply random values placed in a field in the middleware message that is passed from client to server. Their purpose is to identify the client and hence to stop any client that is not recognized.

It is just as important not to overengineer security as it is not to underengineer security. Recall the water pipe maintenance application I discussed in Chapter 5, "The Relationship with the Business." The threat from a breach in this application's security is what? If a wicked foreign government hacked the database to pull out a list of broken pipes in South West London, well, frankly, who cares? There is a threat from vandalism from a malicious outside person or, more likely, from a disgruntled employee, but if the whole application were lost, what would happen? Paper records would have to be kept, communication would be by phone, and probably pipes would still be fixed. There would be a serious drop in efficient use of resources and poor communication with the public (we hope—otherwise what's the point of the application?). More seriously, there may be a breakdown in the payment system to subcontractors. However, there is no need for military levels of security. If I were developing this application, it would not be security that would keep me awake at night.

Security Programming

All the good intentions in a security design can be undone by clumsy programming.

Most of the focus of this section is on Web application programming. That Web technology has so many exploitable security loopholes is not surprising; the Web was designed so scientists could share documents, and security wasn't part of the specification. Some of the exploitable loopholes are not that easy to understand, but fortunately you can at least find out what the common problems are and do something about them—and most of them are easy to fix. I recommend that every Web programmer have a good long look at OWASP (Open Web Application Security Project [40]). OWASP keeps a list of the top ten vulnerabilities, and the 2013 list—the most current one in early 2015—looked like this:

1. Injection

2. Broken authentication and session management

3. Cross-site scripting (XSS)

4. Insecure direct object reference

5. Security misconfiguration

6. Sensitive data exposure

7. Missing function-level access control

8. Cross-site request forgery (CSRF)

9. Using components with known vulnerabilities

10. Unvalidated redirects and forwards

I discuss these entries in a bit more detail, mainly to give a flavor of where vulnerabilities may be found and to consider how easy they are to fix. Some of the following points are technical, so you may want to skip the detail.

Some points in this list are essentially bad application design and should have been caught in the user interface design analysis. This includes number 6, sensitive data exposure, and number 7, missing function-level access control. The second vulnerability, broken authentication and session management, should have been caught in the technical design. The fifth vulnerability, security misconfiguration, is basically IT operations not doing their job correctly. Using frameworks like PHP and exploiting vulnerabilities that others have discovered in the framework is the focus of number 9, using components with known vulnerabilities. I hasten to add that I don't know of any vulnerabilities in PHP, and if there are some they may be fixed by the time you read this book. Again, that should have been considered in the technical design.

The rest of the vulnerabilities listed by OWASP are programming bugs. Injection attacks and cross-site scripting exploit the format of Web pages. To illustrate an injection attack, consider some program code that constructs some SQL text like this (the + sign concatenates the text strings):

```
Sqlstring = "SELECT * FROM PERSON WHERE Name = '" +
      nameinput + "'"
```

where `nameinput` comes from a field in a Web form. Suppose the user puts data into the name input field as follows: "Fred'; DELETE PERSON WHERE Name = 'David". When the SQL statement is used, the Person record with the name of Fred is found, but also a Person record with the name of David is deleted. There is a simple solution to this problem by using SQL statement parameters.

Cross-site scripting is similar but exploits HTML itself. A Web page is made up of tags that control how the page looks, and tags are delineated by "<" and ">". This vulnerability arises when what should be normal text has tags in it. It is made all the more dangerous by the ability of HTML to include JavaScript code. Suppose someone enters some text in an input field (like a comment on a product) and the text reads "blah, blah </p><script>alert('boo')</script>". Then, when the text is displayed by the application—and I mean when the application is used by any of its users—this script is executed, and a box appears with "boo" in it. Naturally the script can do something a good deal more damaging than go boo, like rewrite a link so that it takes the user to a different site or call a bad Web site directly. The solution is to ensure that any "<" and ">" characters in output text are replaced by the HTML code strings `&lt;` and `&gt;`. This tells the Web page to display "<" and ">" and not treat them as tags. Most Web application technology provides functions that make it easy to do this.

When you follow a link in HTML, a URI is sent to the server. (URIs were discussed in Chapter 10 in the section "Principles of High Performance on Many Servers.") Figure 12.2 shows a typical URI that might be used to retrieve data about a product with the code C9804.

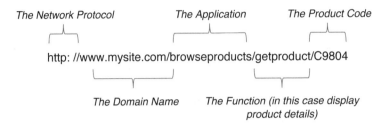

Figure 12.2 *A URI Example*

Now suppose that in addition to products that are available to the public there are products that are secret. They might have special prices or be available only to maintenance engineers. However, if someone happens to know the product code—or tries lots of alternatives—and if that person knows the format of the URI (which of course they do, having looked at it), they can access the secret product by using the same URI but change the product code. This is vulnerability 4 in the OWASP list: insecure direct object reference. There are all sorts of variants. The URI might be used only in internal redirects in the code (a way of routing to a different page from within the code), in which case we have vulnerability 10, unvalidated redirects and forwards. The fix is simply to check that a user who uses the `getproduct` function is logged on.

Look at Figure 12.2 again, but imagine that instead of C9804 being interpreted as a product code it is interpreted as a session identifier. If that were the case, anyone could type in the URI and the server would think the input came from session C9804. This is rather obviously dangerous, which is why most applications use cookies to hold the session identifier. However, cookies have a flaw; there is one cookie per domain name on a PC. Thus if you have two tabs in your browser, both running the same application, the server will think they are part of the same application. That's no big concern, you might think, but imagine that one of your tabs is running the application while the other goes to some malicious Web site. In the malicious Web site there is some script code that accesses the application running in the other tab—and this time it accesses it with the application's session cookie and has all your privileges. It could empty your bank account, for instance, without you knowing. This is called cross-site request forgery (number 8 in the OWASP list). There is again a simple solution. The server puts some random data in a hidden field in the output page, and when the command input comes, it checks that the same data is still present in the field.

Note that in all of these vulnerabilities, the solution is simple. However, some of them are quite devious, so a programmer who is not aware of the vulnerability may involuntarily allow it to creep in. So how do you ensure that programmers don't introduce the vulnerability? The simplest solution is code inspection; the code is checked by a security expert before it is put into the production system.

Note too that it is very hard to test for security vulnerabilities. Again, you can call upon an expert to try to hack your application, but there is no guarantee the expert will find every vulnerability. The literature talks about setting up honeypot machines, which are machines that look like they have lots of interesting secret information but are in fact fakes. You then watch people trying to access the data and investigate how they do so. I have never heard of anyone doing something like this for an application rather than for documents, but it's quite hard to find out what goes on in the world of security.

The conclusion is that you can never be absolutely sure your applications don't have a security flaw, which is why monitoring security is so important.

There is also another conclusion, which is that programmers should show a level of professionalism in the work they do. They should be aware of the main pitfalls, and it should not be necessary to ask them to code with security in mind, any more than it should be necessary to tell nurses to wash their hands.

Concluding Remarks

In this chapter I looked at the principles of application security and at the security design elements that need to be done in each of the boxes in the six-box model.

Most of the writing about IT security is either couched in general terms or is about infrastructure security, such as network security or server security. In my reading of the subject, there is very little written about application security. Unfortunately this has given the impression that security can be bolted onto applications late in the implementation rather than designing it into applications from the word go.

The context design and integration design are largely about setting the security requirements. The starting point is the threat model, which is simply a posh way of saying 'identifying what sorts of people and organizations you are worried about and why'. The integration design establishes the application boundaries and asks the question of whether there are wider security concerns like data that is secure in one place but has copies that are not secure somewhere else.

The user interface design shows how the access control requirements implied in the context design will be implemented, and the database design shows how the context design data access requirements are handled.

The technical design defines how user authentication will be done, possibly by using single sign-on, the details of which are implemented by another team. The technical design also designs how programs find out about users (e.g., find out the user group the user belongs to) and how security administration and monitoring are implemented. The technical designers must work with the IT infrastructure group and maybe implement additional server security like database encryption.

Poor implementation can undo all this good design work. Programmers must be security conscious and keep up-to-date with programming security flaws. Unfortunately, there is no good way I know of to test security. You can try hiring good people to behave like hackers, but I suspect the best you can do is extensive code reviews.

Just as I was writing this, early in 2015, a Russian firm, Kapersky, reported that hackers had extracted $1B from 100 banks. I was just about to write that applications can be secure—just look at the banks—when this happened. It seems to be that the initial entry point was achieved by our old enemy the spear phishing attack, but once inside the banks they ferreted out passwords and operating instructions. The vulnerability seems to have been operations and security administrators who should have known better.

In spite of this, I do think that applications can be made secure. (I'm not so sure about the security of documents, but that, fortunately for me, is not within the scope of this book.) I think this because

- Basic security of servers is solid.
- Encryption is essentially unbreakable (at least outside the security services).
- If good passwords are chosen, they are essentially not guessable.
- The main ways into a machine are well known and can be protected against intrusion. Writing effective monitoring code is not hard, and you can often catch intruders before any damage has been done.

The problems are people and organizations. A simple step is just not storing vital passwords on PCs, even PCs that are not on the Internet. Build your security design on the assumption that some idiot in your organization has let his or her machine be completely hacked.

I made some further points:

- Design security to face the real-life threats; you don't need military levels of security for most applications.
- The key to building good security is understanding where the problems are. Once you have identified a problem, you will find that the solution is often simple. Unfortunately, you can never say for certain that you have detected all the problems.

- You should always consider why an employee might want to subvert the security. Sometimes it is the easiest way to get the job done, like giving someone your username and password because you can't do what you need to do from outside the company premises. Try to design the application so temptation is not put in the users' way.
- If you can't protect, monitor. You should monitor insiders, such as operations and the security administrators, as well as outsiders; insiders may be trustworthy but, as our banking example testifies, they may have been hacked.
- A source of much bad security is poor organization. Someone must be responsible for looking at any logs. Someone must ensure that people who don't need access to an application any longer don't have access to the application.

Ultimately, security is about trust. You have to trust someone. If there is encrypted data, someone must have the key. Every server must have an administrator password; who has that, and is it kept safely? Every application administrator, setting up new users and allocating privileges, also has a username and password. That person may be very junior and not very computer literate—an ideal target for a spear phishing attack!

I was walking the dog once and saw some people open up a wine shop. I could see that to open the door required two keys, each held by a different employee. Stealing two keys from two different people is much more difficult than stealing one key. Inside jobs—theft aided by an employee—is much more difficult if two people have to be included in the plans. I suppose you could call this a kind of multifactor authentication, but multifactor authentication is a term usually used to describe using several methods to identify a single person (e.g., password plus answering a question). This is having one task done by more than one person. What struck me was that it is simple precautions like this that can make security much more effective.

Chapter 13

The Future of Application Development

This chapter, the final chapter, is mainly about three topics. The first is how context-driven design changes design today. The second is, assuming we live in a world where context-driven design is commonly used, how context-driven design will be improved by new tools and other resources. Third, in a world where context-driven design is commonplace there will of course still be many challenges left, and I thought it would be interesting to discuss these. I end with some concluding remarks to wrap up the book.

How Context-Driven Design Changes Application Development

Imagine you are starting a largish application development project and you are using context-driven design. What differences will you see compared to a largish application development project today?

To begin with, it won't seem like an application development project at all. A context designer or team is appointed and they develop a context design. Well before they are finished, the size of the project becomes apparent—in outline at least—and a technical designer or team is appointed. Furthermore, the two teams are small and self-motivating and need very little guidance. A project manager is appointed, but he has very little to do except organize review meetings. At this point the project manager does not know the size and scope of the development, so any planning is fuzzy.

It is not all smooth sailing. The context design team has found a flaw in its first-cut context design and has asked the stakeholders how it should be fixed, and an almighty row has broken out because two managers can't agree. But finally this is overcome and a compromise is reached. The project manager now prepares a first cut of the budget with the assistance of the technical designer. There is considerable sucking of teeth and quizzical looks all around, and it is pointed out that half of the application's functionality already exists in other applications.

All is not sweetness and light in the technical design team either. One of the team members wants to use some new technology, let's call it NL—New Language. However, the team is under pressure from management to use OL—Old Language. They are told to experiment and prove that NL can do the job. The designer isn't very happy with this; she is used to her word being taken as gospel. However, the rest of the team members are happy as pigs in mud, playing with the new technology. They are less happy when they develop a first-cut framework design and are met by a barrage of criticism, mostly coming from the IT infrastructure group and mainly about systems management interfaces and backup requirements that they haven't designed yet.

The context design team in the meantime is building context models for existing applications. Then the lead context designer, the project manager, and the lead technical designer get together, find somewhere quiet for a few days, and develop the integration design. It is decided to use some existing applications and to replace others. The original context design is reworked and reanalyzed to reflect the changes, and both the context design and the integration design are reviewed. The first-cut technical design is now ready, albeit with many loose ends like systems management interfaces and test harness implementation. A new cost plan is developed, and there is a major stop/go review. The review takes far longer than planned, partly because the two business managers who were arguing are still trying to push the organization in different directions, but eventually the plan is accepted more or less intact and the project is given the green light.

At this point, activity steps up and the project becomes much like a conventional project. The project has been split into several applications and services, and programmers join the team to implement them. A user interface designer is temporarily hired to help with the user interface design. The central database group provides assistance with the database design. Meanwhile, the technical design team is implementing the framework and the test harnesses. Some of the programmers join the technical design team to help write stubs and test code. There is a heart-stopping moment when the performance tests don't perform to spec and when a recovery test is a shambles.

Eventually the framework is robust, version control and testing procedures are all in place, and the user interface and database designs are ready for the first application and service. Early versions of some of the application functionality have already been programmed because they have been used to test the framework. But these now need to be revisited, and the full application implementation starts in earnest.

With all the designs in place, the actual implementation is much quicker than in traditional application development. The programmers know what they are doing, the procedures are in place, the test plans are in place, and the designs are there. There is little to hold them back.

Business management will see a big difference between a context-driven design project and a conventional project. Instead of optimism turning to concern as the project lingers on, finally turning to disappointment because it doesn't live up to the dream, they will see a period of discussion, maybe some of it heated, and an early realization of the realities of what can be achieved. This will be followed by an implementation that is quicker than before and achieves what it said would be achieved. Over time when they become used to the discipline of context modeling and design, they will become emboldened to ask for more.

IT management will see big differences, too. They may be uncomfortable while the context design is being developed, especially if the project seems to be getting larger, then smaller, then split up, and then larger again. But they can comfort themselves that very little money has been spent. During integration design and other areas where overarching architectural concerns come into play, many IT departments will find the strategic thinking needed to be new and unfamiliar. When the detailed design and implementation start, IT management will feel more at home. When the project is built fast, ideally on time and on budget, and meets the business expectations, they will start to feel good about themselves.

Context-Driven Design Opportunities

As people use context-driven design, they will surely find new improvements to the methods proposed in this book, and especially they will find new analysis techniques. Naturally I would love to see groups building expertise and pushing the boundaries forward. I hope they will talk to each other.

In this section I discuss some of the opportunities for new tools and services and new resources that context-driven design opens up. This section has subsections organized along the lines of the six-box model. These are "Context and Integration Design," "User Interface and Database Design," and "Technical Design." But first, I make some comments on tool development in general because I have had some experience in this area, and, let me say, my experience has been mixed and I should explain why.

New Tools

As I have hinted several times in this book, I have spent a considerable amount of time over the past 15 years writing software to support some of the diagrams and analytic ideas in this book. The basic idea was to capture the design in a database (call it a repository if you like) and to develop software that generated the diagrams. I achieved all of this, but I have learned enough to know that the direction I was taking doesn't work. Since I am discussing the future here and new software development tools are surely part of this future, I thought it would be appropriate to explain what I have learned.

- **If you try to express the richness of the world in diagrams, the number of different symbols becomes large and hard to understand.** This can easily be illustrated by looking at the BPMN diagram notation for drawing business processes [41, 42]. The basic symbols—activities, decision points, and flows—used to draw a business process are simple and easily understood, but when you try to capture all those instances where the basic symbols don't quite express what you want, you end up with a large collection of different symbols. No one deliberately made it complex; it is how it inevitably turns out when you want the diagrams to be comprehensive.

  I don't know a way around this problem. The real world is messy. I have skirted the issue in this book by saying the diagrams are illustrative only and if you want to change them, please go ahead and do so. Perhaps the solution is to teach people the vast array of symbols. But perhaps it is possible to invent a diagramming convention that has a simple core and a way of defining ad hoc extensions. If you are generating diagrams, the difficulty with the simple core approach is that the database schema does not understand the ad hoc extensions, because the diagram generation is driven by the data structures in the database. Therefore, the complexity isn't just in the diagram drawing conventions; it is in the database schema as well, which leads us to the next point.

- **A database schema for design artifacts is complex.** To see how complex the database schema for a repository can become you just need to look at the OMG standards [43]. If you want to generate the diagrams from the database, it is a lot easier to generate simple diagrams from data in a simple database schema.

- **Diagrams of the real world are very cluttered**. A drawing of an application of only medium size will be chock full of boxes and lines. You can write algorithms that neatly draw the lines and try to avoid overlaps where possible, but I sometimes find that neat diagrams are more difficult to understand than untidy ones.

One of the big advantages of generating diagrams, though, is that you can select a single object and draw the diagram centered on it (for instance, seeing everything connected to a single task). Also, you can pan around the diagram and view it at different scales.

- **Editing the design database is clunky.** It is much easier to write notes using a word processor than it is to put the same information into a database using, say, Web forms. In my software I decided to draw all the relationships and tried to make browsing and editing a database as easy as editing a document. It didn't work. It is hard to implement in a database browser something as simple and as powerful as cut and paste. I know because I tried it.

  These last two points make me wonder whether the design repository idea should be abandoned. The answer is no, because without a design repository you can't do any automatic analysis. However, there may be better ways of entering data, in particular, reading documents like the detailed task description and loading them directly. There is a reason why programming languages are languages—no one has found a better way of specifying complex systems.

- **Any tool is going to have to work over the Web.** I wrote my tool for a PC, but the Web is much more capable now (HTML5 incorporates SVG which can be used for drawing diagrams), and I don't think you will be able to persuade people to load a PC application over the Web.

- **You need to convert your design into standard office formats like Power-Point presentations or PDF files.** This is because that is what business managers expect. They do not want any additional software on their workstations, and they are not going to be bothered to learn how to run any additional software.

Finally, I suspect you are going to have to make your tool free. The business model for tool vendors these days seems to be to make the development free and charge for the runtime. That rather kills the market for independent tool vendors.

If you are embarking on developing software like this, your main competitor is not another product; it is office software—word processors, presentation software, and spreadsheets. Remember, too, that you have two user groups: designers who put information in and reviewers who take the information out. While you can demand some level of expertise in your product from designers, you can't expect any from the reviewers.

While I have been a tad negative on tools, I think someone will crack this problem sooner or later. I see designers visiting stakeholders and making notes on a tablet computer and then downloading the notes to a server, which then provides drawings over the Web. And I see the server analyzing the notes and, on request, creating presentations, analyzing the design, and maybe even creating suggestions for the next level of design. Finally, I expect to see the tool generate large amounts of the end user documentation.

Context and Integration Design

The development tool I tried to create, described in the preceding section, was for context design. As I say, someone will crack the problem of tools in this area at some stage, and I hope my advice is useful. The other approach to tools is simply to capture the designs as a number of separate text files (of any format) and record only the dependencies.

Another opportunity in the context design is to provide example context designs, line-of-business context designs if you will. One of the reasons why organizations buy application software is to learn to use the latest methods. Example context designs could help them on the way but still allow infinite tailoring and creativity for each organization to do things its own way.

Generating context models from existing code automatically would be an interesting challenge. I think it is possible at least in part, though ironically I suspect that understanding the code would be one of the lesser problems. The greater problem, I suspect, is knowing what source and schema files are relevant and how they fit together to make up the total system.

The main help that could be given to integration design would be a repository that stored information about not only programs and databases but also context designs. Repositories and their precursors' data dictionaries have been around a long time but have in general never taken off. One reason is the lack of an accepted standard for context designs. The rationale for a repository is primarily to document dependencies, but without the context design the most important dependency of all—from application to business—is not recordable. The other reason repositories have not taken off is the lack of integration between repositories and software version control management systems. This is made worse in some organizations by the fact that application development uses one version control tool while IT operations uses another. I have no solution to this problem except for the platitude that vendors should work together.

User Interface and Database Design

An obvious tool for user interface design would be one that would convert a user interface design directly into code, at least in part. The part that would be difficult would be the code behind the actions. The disadvantage of tackling action logic is that you would have to replace the loose language of the action description with a precise formal language. I'm not convinced that is desirable since such languages tend to be just as wordy and as esoteric as programming source code. But the layout of the screen could be generated automatically up to a point. While it might be cool, I don't think it would make a huge difference in productivity since turning user interface into screen layout is not hard or lengthy.

A more interesting use of the user interface design would be to generate tests and end user documentation. Again, this would be only partial, but help here would be greatly appreciated. The use of a test generator, I think, would help analyze the user interface since it would force you to answer the question, "If I put input into these fields and press a button, what screen should be returned?"

The major assistance for database design would be repositories, discussed in the previous subsection. An organization would like to answer the question, "What data is used where?"

Technical Design

In the future I can see vendors supplying technical designs and associated software. To some extent they do today, but they could go much further. For instance, they could provide the software to drive the tests as well as the software for the framework. Today's frameworks are also very weak on security monitoring and traces for debugging. For example, products do provide low-level traces, but for debugging production systems the first question you need to answer is, "What was the user doing?" Ideally you want simply a record of all the inputs and outputs leading up to the fault and if not the outputs, at least the inputs. I would like to see the framework capture, say, the last five inputs and log them if there was a fault.

Today to build a complex framework you are likely to need to integrate products from several different vendors and maybe add code of your own. It would be nice to have pre-integrated products. Perhaps framework suppliers should be independent of Web server and middleware suppliers. Perhaps I'm dreaming.

Different users have different requirements, of course, so it would be good to see a framework where features can be altered or replaced and the tests rerun. Many organizations would like the ability to start small and grow. At the moment we have server-side scripting products, which are great for small applications, and at the other extreme we have monstrous multitiered homegrown frameworks for large applications. It would be nice if the code that runs in the small could run in the large without change. For instance, code that runs in a single Web server could also run in a configuration that balances the workload across many servers. It would also be nice to be able to incorporate new technology—for instance, biosecurity authentication—and switch off old technology.

This is (even) more difficult than it sounds in spite of the fact that I suspect many sales persons are selling it already! The difficulties can be illustrated by Microsoft security code generated by Visual Studio. What follows goes into some depth, but I know of no easy way to explain the complexity here. It is not meant to be a plug for Microsoft; actually, I am not sure whether Microsoft should be delighted or appalled that I am using their code as an example.

In Visual Studio 2013 Express for Web you can create new Web server projects using the MVC framework, and you will find that by default it generates no fewer than 22 screen definitions (i.e., View files) and enough model and controller code (in C# or VB) to make them work. For an application that doesn't do anything this is a lot of code, so what is happening? Most of the code is about providing authentication security [44] and gives you features such as

- Username and password sign-on

- Sign-on using OAuth and OpenID (which allow you to use Google, Facebook, and other applications to authenticate the user)

- Code for sending e-mails or text messages to people who have lost their passwords

These are useful features, and it is good to have security code that has been developed by people who really understand the issues of security. But what happens if you don't want them all or if a new authentication technology comes along that wasn't supported? And if it does not work the way you want it to work, what happens then?

On the first question you must distinguish between features you definitely don't want and ones you think it is possible you might need in the future. For the features you don't want ever, you can delete the code. For the others you might need it is probably best to disable the code, for instance, by taking out any Web page links to the screens.

Whether you disable or delete the code, you will have to understand all the provided code and retest your modified version of it. In fact, you will almost certainly need to know the code well in any case because you may want to change the database holding the user data, and you may need to put in code to tailor the output according to the privileges of the user. There is an irony here; the richer the feature set of the code being provided for you, the more difficult it is to understand and therefore modify.

On the second question of new security technology coming along, you are on your own. The code is provided only when you first create the application. There are no facilities provided to keep the code current with the latest thinking; it is provided as is when you generate the first version of your program. If, for instance, you want to replace the 2013 version of the code with the 2015 or 2017 version of the code, you will have to generate a new app and move your code over to it. Ideally all of the security code should be in a single module, but the old-fashioned notion of module breaks down in this case because it is implemented in the MVC framework and there are security models, security views (the 22 screens), and security controllers. This is illustrated in Figure 13.1.

I will call this notion of one piece of functionality being implemented by several discrete pieces of code *crosscutting modules*. What I am asking for is the ability to take a crosscutting module out and replace it with something else. Perhaps this is something for the programming theorists and development environment designers to think about.

Back to the example. If the security features don't work in a way you want them to work, you are lost. This was the case with Microsoft MVC security when I last tried to use it. I wanted admin users to have additional buttons on the screen that would not be visible to other users. With the Microsoft approach the buttons would be visible to everyone, but when you click on one and don't have admin privileges, you are presented with a logon screen to log on again. I didn't want this, so I'm sorry to say I gave up on using any of their code.

Thus not only do I want to be able to replace crosscutting modules, what I would like to see in the future is the ability to add features and modify behavior in a module without having to understand large amounts of somebody else's code. This is a really hard problem.

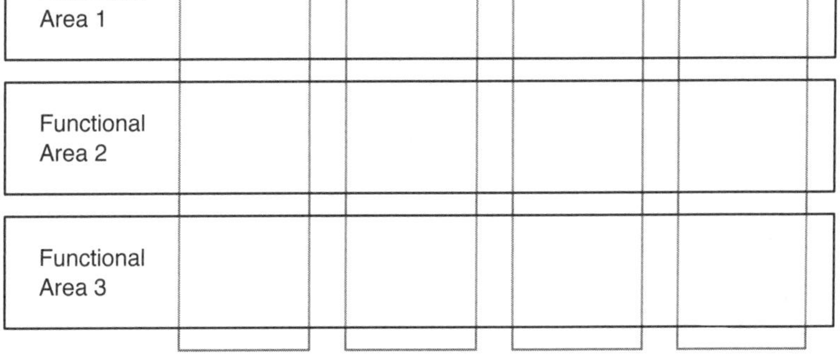

Figure 13.1 *Modern Modules*

Again, this is a supercompetitive area where a lot of very clever people work, so I am hopeful we will see good solutions. Perhaps when you are reading this you will laugh at the primitive tools I have had to struggle with.

The Application Development Challenges

I think all of the challenges described in the previous section can be overcome. It won't be easy, but it's possible. In this section I want to look at more nebulous challenges—challenges for which I think there can and will be movement toward achieving something better than we have today but for which there is no technical solution in sight. The topics I discuss are very much a personal list; they are flexibility, operations, correctness, quality, and professionalism.

Flexibility

IT applications are notoriously hard to change. In Chapter 1, "Introduction to Context-Driven Design," in the first section, "Designing Requirements," I described IT applications as being "as flexible as concrete." The question is, Is there anything we can do about this?

There are several ways in which flexibility can be improved:

- **Keep a record of the dependencies.** This means keeping the context design after the application has been finished and creating context models. It also means recording the relationships between tasks in the context design to screens and screen actions in the user interface design. And it means recording the relationship between screen actions and software components in the implementation. Finally it means recording the relationship between context design data tables and data structures in databases. The benefits are that it gives you traceability and it will help people understand the consequences of change.

- **Some data structures can aid flexibility.** For instance, banks frequently create new kinds of accounts with different interest rates, different limits, and different rules. What you can do is to create a data object to hold all the account type information—the rates, the limits, and the rules—and link the account to the account type object. This was discussed in Chapter 3, "Reusing Existing Methods and Practices," in the section "Why Is BDUF Big?"

- **Crosscutting modules.** The section in this chapter on technical design discusses the notion of crosscutting modules. If these could be implemented, it might be possible for external vendors to develop functional crosscutting modules, possibly even libraries of them. The fly in the ointment is database design. Different functionality tends to imply different data structures. Data structures tend to be used by several functions. Hence a group of functions needs to be replaced at one time. You must know how the functions and data structures fit together.

- **Testing.** Changing the code is relatively simple. The problem is being confident that it works properly. If you could be sure, you wouldn't mind putting the code into production. The obvious way to build this confidence is by testing. To improve flexibility you need to not only test well but test fast. Anything that improves testing should improve flexibility. But as was discussed in Chapter 3, testing tends to be focused on doing the same tests over and over again. While this is fine to achieve a base level of confidence, you need more. In particular, there should be tests that try to break the application, which means trying to use the application in ways it has never been used before. At the moment this is a manual exercise. For instance, if you write a test application that tries to emulate a naïve user by throwing junk data at an application, after a few inputs the application will probably give up and thereafter report errors. An analogy is trying to test how a car behaves with a bad driver. If you just have random controls, the car will crash and the test will be very short. It takes a lot of skill to act like someone stupid but not stupid enough to be disastrous. The second area where testing is often inadequate is testing on lifelike data. I once changed an application to require that a certain field not be null. The test worked perfectly because in the test database the field was never null. I put it on the production database, and it failed the first time it read some old data that had null values in it.

- **Faster deployment from development to production.** Operational procedures can delay the deployment of new code. This is especially true of old complex applications that the organization depends on. This is discussed in the next subsection, "Operations."

If all of this could be achieved, applications would be a lot easier to change quickly and accurately. But there is something else lurking in the background. It is simply the problem that understanding other people's code is hard work. Actually I find that understanding my own code that was written a year ago to be not that easy either. I think there are two difficulties. The first is understanding the deep structure and figuring out how the deep structure is implemented across the code files. The second is understanding the dependencies. The most difficult dependencies to grasp are ordering dependencies. For instance, one code statement calls a function, which calls another function, which updates a variable, and the next code statement uses that variable. It is essential that the two statements be in the order they are, but there are no clues in the code to tell you that.

I would like researchers to look at this problem. I don't know if the solution is better programming languages or better programming tools. In the meantime we can make our applications and procedures more flexible, but there is a long way to go.

Operations

While it is easy to say, "Just install new versions quicker," it is not so easy to do so safely.

In Chapter 2, "A Hierarchy of Designs," in the section on technical design I discussed DevOps—the notion that programmers should be IT operators and know how to do IT infrastructure administration. The rationale for DevOps is to break down the barriers between development and operations. The barriers have to do with mismatch of version control tools, the need to reconfigure the application when moving it from systems test to production, and the long, clumsy processes that have been built up over the years and no one dares change.

I suggest that every application and service can be classified along three risk dimensions:

- **Availability level.** If high it means that the cost of the application being not available is very high. At a first approximation the availability risk level is the number of people who can't do their work times the cost of employing those people. Scalability comes into this measure because if the application is slow, that is equivalent to partial unavailability. Applications that score high on this level should be able to switch to backup quickly.

- **Accuracy level.** If high it means that the application must implement its specification in all its finest detail. Accuracy is not only about programming correctness; it is also about the need for accuracy of the input data and the system software. In the section "NoSQL" in Chapter 9, "Database Design," there was a discussion about trading off accuracy for availability. The higher the score on this level, the more substantial the testing must be.

- **Information security level.** If high it means the damage of information disclosure to unauthorized persons is very high.

These dimensions are independent. There are, of course, applications that score high on all three dimensions (e.g., bank credit and debit account service), and there are applications that are low on all three dimensions (e.g., my private spreadsheet program for tracking my shares). There are programs that are high on one dimension and low on another; for instance, an HR program is high on information security but doesn't have to have superhigh availability levels.

For IT infrastructure management these applications and services could be managed differently. At the moment this tends to be very coarse grained; for instance, every application running in a particular data center is treated the same way. Also, if you have a large program and you split it up, it is likely that the different parts score differently along these dimensions. For instance, few reports have superhigh availability requirements.

For applications that call services, the levels for availability and accuracy cannot be higher than the levels for the service.

If these levels were seriously considered and used to drive technical design and IT infrastructure planning, we would see a much greater readiness to change applications and services when the scores are low.

Correctness

But perhaps a better way to make applications flexible would be to build a tool that could prove that the applications are "correct."

In terms of the six-box model, correctness would mean (at least) the following:

- The context design does not have any consistency or completeness flaws.
- The user interface design implements everything in the context design and nothing more.
- The framework reliably implements crosscutting modules.
- There are crosscutting modules for all screens in the user interface design and for all time-triggered tasks.
- The crosscutting modules implement all the functionality called for in the user interface design correctly and nothing more.
- Everything is installed correctly.
- Hardware exists that is capable of supporting the applications such that the nonfunctional requirements can be implemented.

Even if these were all implemented, the hardware could be unreliable, the data center may not provide a stable environment, the data coming from other applications may arrive unreliably or be wrongly structured, and the context design may not correctly have met the business needs. Correctness does not achieve everything, but in my opinion, at least, any progress on any of these points would be greatly appreciated.

I suspect we will see more use of formal languages [9, 10] in the development of frameworks, especially to handle error recovery and switching to backup. I hope so in any case. For business functional code, I suspect that automatic verifiers of context designs will be more useful than trying to express the context design entirely in formal terms, but I would be delighted if someone proved me wrong. The reason I think a formal context design will prove difficult is the same reason as the fact that trying to be thorough about business process diagramming conventions leads to so much complexity (as discussed in the earlier "New Tools" subsection)—the real world is messy. I suspect that if we ever come to have fully automated application development, it will be done more like a question-and-answer dialogue. The tool will have a formal description of the context design, but it will be hidden from sight and the context design as shown to the stakeholders won't be much different from what is described in this book.

Quality

Quality was discussed in Chapter 3. The question I want to discuss here is whether context-driven design can be used to improve quality.

I know some people find the number of designs in context-driven design rather intimidating. The reason is that I want to describe the flow of thought from idea to implementation, which requires looking at the design from many angles. The length of time taken to do the designs is very unequal. However, by having so many designs we can analyze and improve the practices for each kind of design. It gives us a framework to discuss quality.

Quality improvement is vastly aided by the collection of metrics. In an ideal world I would like to see metrics gathered and compared across many organizations. The metrics I would like to see would be

- **Number of tasks, data tables, and user groups.** This would give a basic measure of how big the job is. (It might be good to rate the complexity of the elements or perhaps use the number of connections between the elements as a measure of complexity.)

- **Number of screens in the user interface design.** Over time one would learn whether this was a simple ratio of task to screen or a more complex relationship.

- **Number of database tables.** Likewise, over time one would learn whether this was a simple ratio of context design data tables to database schema table (or class). If the ratio is not simple, it would be interesting to know why.

- **Time taken and effort expended to develop the different designs.** This would help enormously in sizing new projects.

- **Time taken and effort expended in the different parts of technical design.** In particular I would like to see how long it takes to develop the systems test framework.

- **The number of users and the number of tasks processed in the production system.** This would establish the runtime size of the application, which would be interesting to compare to the time taken to develop the technical design and the time taken to implement each task.

- **Time taken and effort expended for implementation.** Likewise this would help in sizing. It would be especially interesting to compare implementation time with the complexity of the context design and the technical design.

- **Number of late changes to all the different designs.** Late changes are going to impact the delivery time. It would be interesting, eventually, to establish the cost of late changes.

- **Number of errors found in systems test.** A low number is not necessarily good; it could just mean your tests are awful. On the one hand it would be interesting to compare the number of errors against the complexity of the tasks, and on the other hand it would be interesting to compare errors found in systems test against the number of errors found in production.

- **Number of errors found in code inspection.** Similar comments apply.

- **Number of errors found in production.** This would be used as a point of comparison.

- **Technology used.** This is not a metric but would be interesting for analysis of the data.

If we had this data, we would be in a much better position to size application development and to compare and contrast different techniques and approaches. Of course, some of the metrics could also be used to compare application development companies, which is why I'm not actually expecting to see such data published. However, IT organizations should think of capturing the data on their own projects even if it isn't published, and governments should capture it across all their projects.

Professionalism

The IT profession has an ambivalent relationship with professionalism. While many promote it, there are areas in the industry that seem to delight in being unprofessional [45]. There also seems to be huge pressure preventing organizations from being open about their success and failure with IT development. I fully agree with Bertrand Meyer's call to have compulsory reporting of disasters as in the aviation industry [46].

I have also mentioned several times the area where I think professionalism is most important: the development of the context design. It is all too easy for IT departments to wash their hands of this and claim it is the responsibility of the rest of the organization's management. The trouble is that the rest of the organization has no idea how to write a specification for an IT application. Why should they? They are rarely called upon to do so, and they need guidance from the IT department. Particular areas where non-IT management especially needs help are in developing the security plan, deciding on reasonable target metrics, and designing for ease of use.

Ultimately there must be trust between the business management and the IT developers, and professionalism is the basis of that trust.

More specifically, by acting professionally I mean the following:

- Do what you say you are going to do.
- Be open and fair in your dealings with the client.
- Be open and fair in your dealings with other team members.
- Don't contract to do something you don't know how to do.
- Act within the law of the land.
- Be sensitive to the customs of the people you are working with.

But also people who call themselves programmers or IT application designers should have some basic level of knowledge and use some basic good practices. For instance, a programmer should always try to

- Write code without obvious security flaws
- Thoroughly test that the program does what it is supposed to do
- Thoroughly test that the program does not break when the user does not understand the application or when the keyboard is attacked by a one-year-old
- Write code that performs reasonably well

When you hire a builder, you expect a certain level of competence; it should be the same for our profession.

A fuller description of professionalism for software developers is available from the ACM [47].

Concluding Remarks

In this chapter I have looked at how context-driven design changes existing practice. I also looked at the opportunities software vendors and others have to exploit context-driven design as well as at some of the wider issues with application development.

At the beginning of this book I wrote that I want to change application design by

- Basing it on the recognition that you don't gather your IT application requirements, you design them

- Making it more like an engineering discipline, in particular, by analyzing designs and looking for flaws before implementation

- Ensuring that the application works with other applications that exist or are in development to create a coherent IT architecture

I suggest that context-driven design goes a long way toward realizing all three of these objectives. Development won't always be faster than it is today, but it will always be more likely to produce an application the organization wants.

I hope you start using context-driven design. I know I haven't presented a complete cookbook along with surefire recipes for success; you will have to work at it and figure out what works in your organization and what doesn't. Perhaps a little context design or context modeling would be a good starting point.

If you would like to use context-driven design but can't because your organization won't allow it, I hope all the analysis questions make you dangerous.

I know that many in the IT industry will not accept the arguments laid out in this book and certainly won't change their day-to-day practices. I just hope that if you disagree with my arguments, you have a better reason than "I know what works" or "It's an old-fashioned approach."

Whatever your situation, I hope that you have found the ideas interesting, and I hope they will make you a better IT application designer.

Appendix A

Context Design Checklist

The appendix is a checklist for context design and modeling with the purpose of helping you remember all the elements.

Description

There are two layers of description: the process layer and the task details layer.

The overall business objectives should be written in one or two sentences only. Important assumptions (e.g., cooperation from other bodies), constraints (e.g., money, time), opportunities, and risks should also be listed.

The process layer shows how the tasks hang together. I have identified four ways tasks might hang together:

- Business processes (e.g., Figure 5.1)

- Business services

- Resource management (e.g., Figure 5.7)

- Reviewing and monitoring

I suggest that when you identify one or more of these in the domain, you document them using a diagram. The process layer description has explanatory power, but everything in it should be covered by one or more elements in the task layer, including all the dependencies.

The task details layer is described by these elements:

- Tasks

- Task fragments

- Common purpose groups

- Data tables

- Messages

- User groups

- Security threat model

All elements are described by a name and a list of headings under which are a series of points. Some headings that can be used for any element are

- Notes

- Review

- Uncertainty

Tasks, services, user groups, and data tables can be represented diagrammatically by a context diagram (e.g., Figure 5.4). The common purpose groups can be represented by a common purpose group diagram (e.g., Figure 5.6).

Tasks can be described in text with the following headings:

- Task fragments included

- The trigger

- Users

- Data displayed

- Outcomes

- Messages received

- Narrative

- Rules

Task fragments are defined exactly like tasks.

Common purpose groups can be described in text with the following headings:

- Users
- Data displayed
- Tasks
- Messages
- Rules

User groups only need to be listed with possibly some additional comment text. **Data tables** can be described with the following headings:

- Attributes
- Data bags
- Rules

Messages can be described with the following headings:

- Sent by
- Received by
- Reply message
- A list of attributes
- A list of data bags in the message
- Integrity: the default is messages have guaranteed delivery and no duplication

The **security threat model** can be described in text with nested headings being

- Who
- Action
- Damage

Nonfunctional requirements should be set for groups of tasks, for the complete application, and for the whole organization. The nonfunctional requirements typically set at the group of tasks level are volume and availability requirements.

Some pointers for writing the text are:

- Be concise; use headings, lists, and indentation. Aim for a presentation style more than a report style.

- Writing a dictionary of business terms may be useful.

Elaboration

The process layer description should identify the operational tasks. The process diagram itself should be examined to ensure that all errors are handled.

As well as tasks defined for operational reasons, there may be a need for tasks for

- Managers monitoring the business

- Analysts looking at long-term trends

- Application administrators assigning user privileges for the application and possibly doing regular jobs like loading data and running reports.

Also, the application may provide information for another application, which may extend the information gathered.

For reporting you should consider at least

- Alerts

- Performance metrics

- Trends and comparisons

- Textual analysis

Analysis

Process layer:

- Completeness:
  - All errors are handled.
  - All process activities have all needed tasks defined.
  - Tasks exist for all resource state transitions.
  - Tasks exist to handle message replies.

- Tasks exist that help data accuracy if tracking the state of an external entity.

- Data table objects are created, used, and deleted or archived.

- Consistency:

  - Process diagrams are well formed.

  - The process diagram and the task outcome diagram must match.

  - Process integrity constraints are enforced.

- Effectiveness versus objectives:

  - Business objectives are met.

  - Work is not needlessly duplicated.

  - Errors are handled automatically where possible.

  - Is the business process optimized?

  - Does the IT application open up new business risk?

  - Do the IT costs and time frame targets look achievable?

  - How is the customer affected by the new application?

Task details:

- Completeness:

  - All referenced data tables exist, all referenced user groups exist, and all referenced messages exist.

  - All outcomes defined in the process layer are implemented.

  - All tasks have the data to do their job.

  - All tasks are started.

- Consistency:

  - The steps implement the outcomes.

  - The steps and the rules do not contradict each other.

  - The steps and the rules do not contradict the data table rules.

- Effectiveness versus objectives:
    - Task step order is not unnecessarily prescriptive.

Data tables:

- Completeness:
    - All data attributes are mentioned in one or more of the task descriptions.
    - Before a data attribute is used, it must be given a value or the tasks must be able to allow for a null attribute.
    - Rules in the data tables must not be replicated in the task details.

- Consistency:
    - Data table rules must not contradict each other.
    - Are the rules sufficient?
    - Data table rules do not contradict task rules or steps.
    - If a data attribute references another data table object, that object must have already been created.

- Effectiveness versus objectives:
    - Could one or more of the data attributes be calculated from other attributes?
    - Is the effort of acquiring the data worth it?

User groups:

- Completeness:
    - Are there user groups for business operations, managers of business operations, data analysts, and application administrators?
    - Do you want a user group for the application design team itself that receives information about the application's usage and takes feedback and questions from the end users?
    - Do two user groups have the same access control needs and therefore should be merged?

- Within one user group does everyone have the same access control needs? If not, the user group should be split.

- Effectiveness versus objectives:

  - Can such people be identified in your organization?

  - What is the impact of the application on the user group's workload?

  - Do the users have the information to do their tasks?

  - Is the user group compatible with the employee's job description?

- Security—for each user group:

  - Is sensitive information being displayed?

  - Are users being allowed to use functions they shouldn't?

- Application administrators:

  - Can their job be automated?

  - Are there bad consequences of them making errors? If so, how can such actions be prevented?

  - Is there a log of their actions? If so, who reads it?

Messages:

- Completeness:

  - Does all message data have a source?

  - Does the message have a valid sender and receiver?

- Consistency:

  - Is message integrity necessary?

- Effectiveness versus objectives:

  - Are the messages unnecessarily large?

  - Would it be better to put the message data into a data object and store it in a database?

General business effectiveness versus objectives:

- How are the business objectives reached?
- What metrics are needed to measure whether the objectives are achieved?
- What has to be done outside of IT to achieve the goals (e.g., hardware rollout, training)?
- What feedback should be sought and how will it be fed into the planning process?

References

The references in this book are articles or Web sites that I have used to support a point. They are not designed to provide a leaping-off point for further research. There is so much material on the Web and, of course, numerous books about IT application development that anyone who wants to read more is disadvantaged more by a surfeit of information than by a lack of it.

I accessed the Web sites on May 6, 2015, unless otherwise stated.

[1] Wikipedia, "View Model," http://en.wikipedia.org/wiki/View_model.

[2] YouTube, "Tacoma Narrows Bridge Collapse," www.youtube.com/watch?v=lXyG68_caV4.

[3] James Lewis and Martin Fowler, "Microservices," March 25, 2014, http://martinfowler.com/articles/microservices.html.

[4] Wikipedia, "Microservices," accessed on May 19, 2015, http://en.wikipedia.org/wiki/Microservices.

[5] Eric Knorr, "What Microservices Architecture Really Means," *InfoWorld*, September 15, 2014, accessed on May 19, 2015, www.infoworld.com/article/2682502/application-development/application-development-what-microservices-architecture-really-means.html.

[6] Wikipedia, "Standing on the Shoulders of Giants," accessed on May 19, 2015, http://en.wikipedia.org/wiki/Standing_on_the_shoulders_of_giants.

[7] Damon Edwards, "What Is This DevOps Thing, Anyway?," accessed on May 19, 2015, http://dev2ops.org/2010/02/what-is-devops/.

[8] Charles Arthur, "How NatWest's IT Meltdown Developed," *The Guardian*, June 25, 2012, accessed on May 19, 2015, www.theguardian.com/technology/2012/jun/25/how-natwest-it-meltdown.

[9] Chris Newcombe et al., "How Amazon Web Services Uses Formal Methods," *Communications of the ACM* 58, no. 4 (April 2015): 66.

[10] Leslie Lamport, "Viewpoint: Who Builds a House without Drawing Blueprints?," *Communications of the ACM* 58, no. 4 (April 2015): 39.

[11] Tony Morgan, *Business Rules and Information Systems: Aligning IT with Business Goals* (Addison-Wesley, 2002).

[12] Seventeen independently minded practitioners, "Manifesto for Agile Software Development," http://agilemanifesto.org.

[13] Chris Sims and Hillary Louise Johnson, "Scrum: A Breathtakingly Brief and Agile Introduction," accessed on May 22, 2015, www.agilelearninglabs.com/resources/scrum-introduction/.

[14] Don Wells, "Extreme Programming: A Gentle Introduction," accessed on May 22, 2015, www.extremeprogramming.org/.

[15] Alistair Cockburn, "Why I Still Use Use Cases,"http://alistair.cockburn.us/Why+I+still+use+use+cases.

[16] Alistair Cockburn, "Use Case Fundamentals," http://alistair.cockburn.us/Use+case+fundamentals.

[17] Capers Jones, "Evaluating Agile and Scrum with Other Software Methodologies," *InfoQ*, March 20, 2013, www.infoq.com/articles/evaluating-agile-software-methodologies.

[18] Capers Jones, "Laws of Software Engineering Circa 2014," http://namcookanalytics.com/laws-software-engineering-circa-2014.

[19] Capers Jones, "Software Estimating Rules of Thumb," www.compaid.com/caiinternet/ezine/capers-rules.pdf.

[20] Barton P. Miller, Lars Fredriksen, and Bryan So, "An Empirical Study in the Reliability of UNIX Utilities," 1989, ftp.cs.wisc.edu/paradyn/technical_papers/fuzz.pdf.

[21] David Peterson, "What Is Kanban?," accessed on May 22, 2015, http://kanbanblog.com/explained/.

[22] Chris Sauer, Andrew Gemino, and Blaize Horner Reich, "The Impact of Size and Volatility on IT Project Performance," *Communications of the ACM 50*, no. 11 (November 2007).

[23] The Standish Group, "The Chaos Manifesto 2013," versionone.com/assets/img/files/ChaosManifesto2013.pdf.

[24] J. L. Eveleens and C. Verhoef, "The Rise and Fall of the Chaos Report Figures," December 17, 2008, citeseerx.ist.psu.edu/viewdoc/download?doi=10.1.1.143.7918&rep=rep1&type=pdf.

[25] Wikipedia, "NHS Connecting for Health," accessed July 31, 2015, en.wikipedia.org/wiki/NHS_Connecting_for_Health.

[26] Neil Davey, "Why Do Salespeople Hate CRM—and How Can We Help Them Love It?," MyCustomer.com, November 20, 2011, accessed on June 3, 2015,

www.mycustomer.com/topic/marketing/why-do-salespeople-hate-crm-and-how-can-we-get-them-using-it/133778.

[27] JCT (Joint Contracts Tribunal) home page, www.jctltd.co.uk.

[28] NEC (New Engineering Contract) home page, www.neccontract.com.

[29] Henry Mintzberg, Bruce Ahlstrand, and Joseph Lampel, *Strategy Safari: Your Complete Guide through the Wilds of Strategic Management* (Pearson Education, 2009).

[30] Wikipedia, "Non-functional Requirement," accessed on June 5, 2015, https://en.wikipedia.org/wiki/Non-functional_requirement.

[31] Tutorialpoints, "Data Warehousing Tutorial," accessed on June 15, 2015, www.tutorialspoint.com/dwh/index.htm.

[32] L. W. C. Nirosh, "Introduction to Object Oriented Programming Concepts (OOP) and More," accessed on June 15, 2015, www.codeproject.com/Articles/22769/Introduction-to-Object-Oriented-Programming-Concep.

[33] C++ Technology Windows Template Library, accessed on June 15, 2015, www.cppfun.com/wtl.

[34] Rebecca Hiscott, "10 Programming Languages You Should Learn Right Now," Mashable.com, January 21, 2014, accessed on June 18, 2015, mashable.com/2014/01/21/learn-programming-languages.

[35] Cade Metz, "The Second Coming of Java: A Relic Returns to Rule the Web," *Wired*, September 26, 2013, accessed on June 18, 2015, www.wired.co.uk/news/archive/2013-09/26/the-second-coming-of-java.

[36] Wikipedia, "HipHop for PHP," accessed on June 18, 2015, en.wikipedia.org/wiki/HipHop_for_PHP.

[37] Wikipedia, "Programming Languages Used in Most Popular Websites," accessed on June 18, 2015, en.wikipedia.org/wiki/Programming_languages_used_in_most_popular_websites.

[38] Mediant, "APT1 Exposing One of China's Cyber Espionage Units," section on "Attack Lifecycle," accessed on June 19, 2015, intelreport.mandiant.com/Mandiant_APT1_Report.pdf.

[39] OpenID home page, accessed on June 19, 2015, openid.net.

[40] OWASP home page, accessed July 28, 2015, www.owasp.org.

[41] BPMN home page, accessed on June 23, 2015, www.bpmn.org.

[42] Camunda, "BPMN Modeling Reference," accessed on June 23, 2015, camunda.org/bpmn/reference.

[43] OMG, "Unified Modeling Language," accessed on June 23, 2015, www.omg.org/spec/UML.

[44] Pranav Rastogi, Rick Anderson, Tom Dykstra, and Jon Galloway, "Introduction to ASP.NET Security," accessed on June 23, 2015, www.asp.net/identity/overview/getting-started/introduction-to-aspnet-identity.

[45] Phillip G. Armour, "The Business of Software: Vendor: Vidi, Vici," *Communications of the ACM* 57, no. 10 (October 2014): 30.

[46] Bertrand Meyer, "The One Sure Way to Advance Software Engineering," accessed on June 24, 2015, http://bertrandmeyer.com/2009/08/21/the-one-sure-way-to-advance-software-engineering/.

[47] ACM, "Software Engineering Code of Ethics and Professional Practice," accessed on June 24, 2015, www.acm.org/about/se-code.

Index

Numbers

4GL products, 289
80:20 syndrome, software development, 56

A

Access control
    context design analysis of user group, 346
    context design specifying requirements of, 307
    designing, 299
    security design for, 302–303
    security programming vulnerability in,
        316–317
    unchecked by application, 304
    user interface design for, 312
Access devices, designing for, 120, 280
Accuracy, data
    completeness analysis for process layer, 152
    in database design, 216, 233
    integration design improving, 40–41, 186
    as operations challenge, 334–335
ACID (atomicity, consistency, isolation, and
        durability) properties
    of tasks, 29–30, 210–211
    of transactions, 209
Actions, screen
    logical user interface design, 192–193
    recording dependencies for flexibility, 332
    user confirmation box for irreversible, 200–201
Active Server Pages (ASP)
    ASP MVC, 277–278, 280
    ASP.NET, 284–285, 288–290
    memory optimization, 248
    Web Forms, 277
Activities, tasks vs. business process, 30
Ad hoc design
    not working well with IT applications, 7
    overview of, 12–14
    summary of, 18
Address lookup, cache performance, 245–246
Administration
    of applications, 149–150
    organizational nonfunctional requirements
        of, 139
    security, 305–306, 314–315

technical design in, 42, 265–268
    user, 299, 303
Agent programs, 262
Agile design
    BDUF (big design up front) vs., 53
    conclusions, 60
    measuring scope, 84
    overcomplexity less likely in, 72
    supplementing with use cases, 59
    use cases vs. See Use cases
    values/principles of, 54–55
    valuing customer collaboration, 58
    valuing individuals/interactions, 55–56
    valuing responding to change, 59
    valuing working software, 56–58
Alerts
    context design checklist for elaboration
        on, 344
    management monitoring, 143
    sending to tasks in context design, 31
Alexander, Christopher, 10
Alternative technical designs,
        need for, 265
Analysis, copying data for, 148–149
Analysis of design
    by application administrators, 150
    business objectives for, 127
    in context design, 34–35, 151–156
    context design checklist for, 344–348
    in database design, 46–47, 223
    in engineered design, 15–18
    in integration design, 40–41
    overview of, 10–12
    of processes, 123
    of task dependencies, 123–127
    in technical design, 267
    in typical IT applications, 19
    in user interface design for ease of
        use, 206–207
Anonymized data
    database design security, 313
    for sensitive data, 145
Application administrators
    context design checklist for, 344, 346–347

Application administrators *(continued)*
  responsibilities of, 149–150
  security design. *See* Security design
Application designers
  in integration design, 179–180, 187
  reviewing completed context design, 140
  security design not role of, 300
  sensitivity to business needs of
    organization, 116
  in user interface design, 212
Application locks, 250
Applications
  access control design, 302–303
  designing security of. *See* Security design
  high resiliency of, 262
  integration design for, 35–41, 161–162, 312
  look and feel of, 199
  managing operations challenges of, 334–335
  moving forward in transaction steps, 209–210
  organizing according to needs of users, 163
  security monitoring of suspicious activity, 306
  technical design for, 41–44
  types of, 159
  user interface design for, 44–45
  Web security design. *See* Security design
Applications, existing
  change process, 186–188
  fashioning services from, 184–186
  generating context models from, 328
  integration with, 41, 178
  knowing what is there, 178–180
  performing functionality of new
    application, 100
  reconstructing context design from, 41, 156
  replacing, 180–184
Application-wide nonfunctional requirements, 139
Architectural patterns, 277
Artistic work, ad hoc design in, 13
Assumptions, requirements design
  clarity, 4–5, 8
  clarity of feedback, 6, 8
  cost estimates/trade-offs, 6, 8–9
  designing business solution, 8–9
  integration with other applications, 6–7, 9
  no disagreements, 8
  no unknown/ignored stakeholders, 5, 8
  understanding integration options, 8, 9
Asynchronous updates, 167–168
Atomicity
  ACID properties of transactions, 208
  of tasks, 29
  use cases lacking formal concept of, 63–64

Attacks
  cyber, 297–298
  defenses against, 298–299
  technical design countermeasures, 314
Attributes
  columns vs., 220
  in database design, 217–219
  defining name/type of objects/database table
    rows, 223–224
  detailing data table, 136
  detailing message, 137
  keys, relationships and, 228–230
  listing in data bags. *See* Data bags
  naming, 218
  null, 219
  in OO technology, 224
  relational databases using normalization for,
    227–228
  schema storing names of, 239
  using as key to another table, 221–222
Authentication design
  defined, 299–300
  multifactor, 321
  overview of, 300–302
  security programming and, 317
  technical design describing, 314
Automation, eliminating administration
  error, 150
Availability
  business strategy for, 119
  detailing requirements for, 138
  elaborating design hypothesis for, 260
  for high resiliency, 260
  nonfunctional requirements
    for, 41–42
  as operational challenge, 334–335
  technical design for, 94, 266

B

Back-door programs, eliminating, 298
Back-end parallelism, and high
    performance, 256–260
Backups
  extending framework with, 291
  large project technical design for, 94
  sites for disaster, 260
Banking
  authentication design in, 300–301
  insecurity of applications in, 320
  user administration in online, 303
BASE, Basically available, soft state, eventual
  consistency, 240

Batch processing
    application administrators starting, 150
    for existing applications, 181
    in integration design, 37, 159
    large project technical design for, 94
BDUF (big design up front)
    agile design conflict with, 53
    difficulty of measuring scope in, 84
    why it is big, 72–74
Behavior, security encouraging good, 299
Benchmarking
    large project technical design and, 96
    technical design principles for, 263–265
Big design up front. *See* BDUF (big design up
    front)
Biometric authentication, 301, 302
Breaks in services, handling, 139–140
Broadcast updates, databases, 168
Browser, implementing session data in, 254–255
Business
    application development strategy, 118–123
    capturing tasks for services, 112–113
    change issues in large projects, 93
    designing IT applications for, 2, 7–9
    formal methods in applications of, 51
    gathering requirements for, 3–7
    integration design and paybacks to, 186–188
    splitting functionality into tasks, 28–30
Business processes
    analysis of, 123–127
    application development strategy, 118–123
    business services vs., 112–113
    context design review of, 157
    defining users operating, 142–143
    illustrating with process diagrams,
        106–107, 111–112
    integration design changing, 187
    managerial oversight of, 143–147
    mapping tasks onto, 107–108
    resource management vs., 113–114
    review/monitoring vs., 115
    spanning functional areas, 178
    summary remarks, 128
    task steps in, 210–212
    turning into context design, 108–112
    understanding, 106
Buttons, user interface design, 202, 204
Bytecode, Java, 282

C
C language
    choosing, 283

as compiled language, 281–282
    limitations of, 285–286
C# language
    choosing, 287
    as interpretive language, 282–283
    popularity of today, 285
C++ language
    choosing, 283
    as compiled language, 281–282
    as interpretive language, 282
    large companies using, 290
    in performance-critical work, 285
Cache, speeding up applications, 245–247
Calculations, engineered design, 16–17
Candidate keys, 228–229
CAP theorem, 240
Case diagrams, 62–63
Change control
    context design review of, 158
    driving large projects, 102–103
    planning for, 122
    reasons for long-winded, tortuous, 42
    rollout/business issues in large projects, 93
Channels, usage vs. marketing, 163
Check-in/checkout, data duplication, 169
Checklists
    context design. *See* Context design
        checklist
    technology evaluation, 264
Choose and Book application, UK National
        Health Service, 91
CICS transaction monitor, 282
CIL (Common Intermediate Language),
        C#, 282–283
Civil engineering contracts, 97–98
Clarity
    designing requirements, 8
    gathering requirements, 4–5
Class library, OO technology, 225, 237
Classes
    designing after deep program structure, 276
    in OO technology, 224–226
Clustering
    multithreading/multiprocessing and, 249
    task vs. data table, 164
    technical design for large projects, 94
Cockburn, Alistair, 59
Code
    encapsulation, 272
    fashioning services, 162–163
    fashioning services from existing
        applications, 184–185

Code *(continued)*
    improving flexibility with, 333–334
    inspection, 78, 319, 337
    segments in program frameworks, 24
    technical design in large project, 95
    technical design opportunities, 329–330
    technical designer reviewing, 292–293
    as technical design/implementation
        output, 266
    user interface design opportunities, 328–329
    writing common, 293–294
Code-behind file, 277–278
Cohesion, measuring, 273
Collaboration, 58, 97–98
Column NoSQL products, 238
Columns, defined, 220
Commands, monitoring security, 306–307
Comments
    allowing customers/employees to read, 146
    context design document, 130
    monitoring ease of use with user, 208
Committees causing overcomplexity, 72
Common Intermediate Language (CIL),
    C#, 282–283
Common purpose groups
    in context design, 110–111
    context design checklist for description of, 343
    defining task details for, 135–136
    task view diagram of, 32–33
Common utilities, in programming, 24
Comparisons
    context design checklist elaboration of, 344
    management reporting on, 145–146
Compensation Event, NEC contract, 98
Compiled languages, development
    environment, 281–282
Complaints, analysis of, 146
Completeness analysis
    context design checklist for, 344–348
    of data table details, 154
    hierarchy of design vs. engineering design, 49
    of message details, 155
    of process layer, 152
    of task details, 153
Complex queries, and NoSQL, 239
Complexity
    application optimization and, 247
    of business process diagrams, 326
    as enemy of security, 306
    of large IT systems, 85–86, 178
    multiple options in user interface design
        increasing, 90
    technical design levels and, 269

Component-level design, engineered design
    overview of, 15–17
    summary of, 18
    traditional drawings of, 48
Computer operations, technical design, 265
Confirmation bias, designing requirements, 6
Confirmation box, for irreversible
    actions, 200–201
Confusion, in use cases, 64–66, 67
Consistency
    ACID properties of transactions, 209
    eventual, 169–170
    quality and, 75
Consistency analysis
    context design checklist for, 345–348
    of data table details, 154
    hierarchy of designs vs. engineering
        design, 49
    of message details, 155
    of process layer, 152
    of task details, 153–154
Constraints
    access control, 304
    allowing users to report, 122
    NoSQL and, 239, 241
    overarching integrity, 126–127
    process integrity, 152, 345
    referential integrity, 229–230
    relational database model, 227
Context design
    context models vs., 41, 179
    converting process view into task view
        for, 107–108
    creating example context designs, 328
    data tables, 30–31
    defined, 26, 28
    documentation in, 58
    engineering design supported by, 48–49
    estimating cost after completing, 69–72
    existing practices in, 78–79
    feedback from technical design to, 43
    feedback from user interface design to, 197
    improving correctness of, 336
    large project requirements, 88–90
    late-changing requirements, 59
    messages between tasks, 31
    not outsourced, 99
    professionalism in, 338
    putting it all together, 32–34
    reconstructing from existing application, 41
    recording dependencies for flexibility, 332
    reviewing, 156–158
    rollout/business change issues in, 93

security elements of, 307–311
six-box model for, 26–28
stable design after completing, 99
task dependencies. *See* Task dependencies
task details for. *See* Task details
tasks, 28–30
turning business processes into, 106–108
use cases vs. *See* Use cases
user categories in. *See* User categories
user groups, 30
user interface design in, 45, 193–194
Context design, analyzing
data table details, 154–155
message details, 155–156
overview of, 34–35
process layer, 151–153
in review process, 156–158
task details, 153–154
user group details, 155
Context design checklist
analysis, 344–348
description, 341–344
elaboration, 344
Context model architect, 180–184
Context models
analyzing application portfolio with, 186
building from existing applications, 41,
179–180, 324, 328
context design vs., 179
recording dependencies for flexibility, 332
Context-driven design, future of
application development
challenges, 332–338
changing application development,
323–325
integration design opportunities, 328
new tools, 326–328
overview of, 325
technical design opportunities, 329–332
user interface/database design
opportunities, 328–329
Context-driven design, introduction
ad hoc design, 12–14, 18
designing requirements, 2–9
engineered design, 14–18
IT architecture and, 20
making IT design an engineering
discipline, 19–20
overview of, 1
planned design, 14, 18
summary remarks, 21
understanding design, 9–12

Contract negotiations
civil engineering, 97–98
in nonagile projects, 58
outsourcing design/implementation, 99–100
third-party large applications and, 96–97
Cookies
in browser session data, 254
encrypting user identity in, 255
European Union and, 256
programming security for, 318
Correctness, in application development, 335–336
Cost
context design reducing, 89
integration design reducing, 187
large projects driven by, 102
objectives analysis of, 127
performance/availability vs., 119
third-party large projects and, 96–97
user interface design options increasing, 90
Cost estimates
context-driven design, 324
contract negotiations for, 58
problem with, 68–72
technical design process, 268
trade-offs, 6, 8–9
Cost-plus contracts, outsourcing design/
implementation, 99
Coupling, measuring, 273
Creativity, meeting business goals, 118
Credit cards, security monitoring of, 306
CRM (Customer relationship management)
applications, 92–93, 121
Crosscutting modules, 331, 332–333
Cross-site request forgery, 318
Cross-site scripting, 317
Crow's feet diagram, databases, 230
Culture
designing for existing, 120–123
gathering requirements and differences in, 5–6
Customer collaboration, in agile, 58
Customer service objectives, 127
Cyber-spying, 297–299

D

Damage, security threat model, 308–309
Dark room operation, technical design, 94
Dashboards, management metrics, 147
Data
access control design for, 302
accuracy. *See* Accuracy, data
analysis, 148–149
analyzing task dependencies, 126

Data (continued)
   in context design, 158, 216–217
   defining task details, 131–134
   determining service/application size, 40
   governance, 312
   high resiliency of, 260
   in logical user interfaces, 191–194
   meanings of, 216
   organizing services with, 163
   programmer vs. database designer view of, 223–226
   in services interface design, 170, 171
   tracking status of external entity, 126
   used by other applications, 147–148
   in user interface design, 200
Data bags
   in database design, 217–218
   detailing for data tables, 136–137
   detailing for messages, 137
   security access rights for, 312
Data center, high resiliency for, 261
Data marts, data duplication, 169
Data objects, database design, 217–218
Data replication
   advantages/disadvantages of, 166
   controlling data duplication, 168–170
   eventual consistency in, 169–170
   multiple database access, 166–167
   using asynchronous updates, 167–168
Data structure
   aiding flexibility, 332–333
   compiler elements of, 273–276
   complexity of diagrams in database, 279
   in database design, 223, 240
   disk cache and, 247
Data tables
   clustering tasks vs., 164
   completeness analysis of, 152, 154–155
   in context design, 30–31, 217–218
   context design analysis of, 34
   context design checklist of, 343, 346
   dependencies of tasks on, 32
   detailing, 136–137
   determining service/application size, 40
   improving quality with metrics for, 336
   messages between tasks using, 31
   recording dependencies for flexibility, 332
   task view diagram of, 33
Data values, distributing databases, 258–259
Data warehouses, 169, 181
Database data disk I/O, 249–250

Database design
   in context-driven design, 324–325, 327
   database access services, 236–237
   in design hierarchy, 24–25
   encryption principles, 305
   engineering design supported by, 48–49
   in IT architecture, 20
   NoSQL vs. traditional databases, 238–242
   overview of, 46, 215–222
   programmers vs. database designers, 233–236
   recording dependencies for flexibility, 332
   security, 312–314
   six-box model for, 26–28
   theory, 222–233
   in typical IT application, 19
   using existing practices in, 79
Database design theory
   checking correctness of relationships, 230–231
   drawing relationships, 230
   OO technology, 223–226
   referential integrity, 229–230
   relational database model, 226–229
Database designer
   conflict between programmer and, 233–236
   context design review by, 140
   input on data tables for user interface, 212
   role of, 25–26
   task descriptions of, 130
Database locks, 250
Database log, 250
Databases, integration design for, 165–170
Data-focused design, 198
Deadlocks, 250
Debugging
   extending framework with, 291
   technical design opportunities, 329
Decision-making, for IT design requirements, 2
Deep structure
   diagram representing, 274–276
   flexibility of applications and, 333–334
   frameworks as skeletal code for, 276–278
   reconstructing from code, 276
Deferrable service interface, 173–174, 253
Denial-of-service attacks, protection from, 305
Dependencies. See Task dependencies
Description, context design checklist for, 341–344
Design
   ad hoc, 12–14
   change process in, 186–188
   definition of, 9
   engineered, 14–18

with existing applications, 178–186
feedback in, 10–11
iterative context, 156
patterns and, 10
planned, 14
structure of, 10
use cases confusing layers of, 64–66
Development methodology, choosing language
supporting, 289–290
DevOps
developing IT learning culture, 80
overview of, 41–42
rationale for, 334
Diagrams
case, 62–63
case vs. context, 63
context design reviewing, 157
context-driven design, 326
database drawing conventions for, 230
of deep program structure, 274
detailed programming, 57–58
process, 106–107, 111–112
purposes of design, 47
task outcome, 124–125
turning business processes into context
design, 108–111
user interface design disadvantages, 44–45
Dimensions of size, large projects, 84–87
Disagreement, business solution design, 8
Disaster recovery
for high resiliency, 261–263
technical design for large project backup, 94
Disk access time, 244
Disk cache, 247
Disk drives, technical design for large
projects, 94
Distributed databases, 257–259
Document NoSQL products, 238
Documentation
large use cases, 67
logical service interfaces, 176
meeting business goals, 117
purposes of design, 47
task dependencies, 34
technical design elaboration using, 267
user interface design, 194, 329
working software in agile vs.
programming, 56–58
Domain model, 237
Domain name resolution, 252
Domain name server, 252
Domains, relational database model, 227

Duplication
controlling data, 168–169
database design with subclasses
and, 220–221
of database servers, 257–258
integration design eliminating, 187
Durability, ACID properties of transactions, 209

E

Early Warning notice, NEC contract, 98
Ease of use
design steps for, 205–208
in logical user interface design, 45
placing tasks into applications, 162
user interface design. *See* User interface design,
ease of use
Editing design database, 327
Education, preventing cyber-attacks, 298
Effectiveness analysis, context design
checklist, 345–348
Efficiency objective, analyzing, 127
Eiffel programming language, 285
Elaboration
context design checklist for, 344
in ease-of-use design, 206
overview of, 10–12
in technical design process, 267
Elements, context design checklist of, 342
E-mail, preventing cyber-attacks on, 297–298
Encapsulation, 272, 273
Encryption
preventing cyber-attacks, 298
security protection with, 304–305
technical design security elements, 315
user identity, 255–256
End users
defining services for functionality
requirements, 163
large project failure due to resistance of, 91
logic of placing tasks into applications, 162
monitoring use of application, 122
not all security threats coming
from, 311
project study on impact of new application
on, 91–93
relationship with. *See* Task details
security monitoring of, 306
technical design describing vulnerabilities
of, 314
user interface design for, 190
vertical dimension of size in large projects
and, 84–85

Engineered design
   hierarchical series of designs
       supporting, 48–51
   IT design as, 19
   overview of, 14–18
   six-box model of design supporting, 48–51
   summary of, 18
   uses cases poor at supporting, 67
Enterprise JavaBeans servers, memory
       optimization, 248
Entity-relationship diagram, databases, 230
Errors
   completeness analysis for process layer, 152
   context design reducing, 89
   process diagrams analyzing, 111–112, 123
   quality improvement with metrics on, 337
   testing to cause, 77
   testing to find, 50–51
European Union, and cookies, 256
Eventual consistency, 169, 240–241
Example context designs, 328
Existing applications. See Applications, existing
Existing methods/practices. See Reusing existing
       methods/practices
Experimental business programs, managing, 120
Experimental prototypes, technical design, 43–44
"Extend," use case terminology, 67
External channels, analyzing task
       dependencies, 126
External entity
   analyzing task dependencies, 126
   completeness analysis for process layer, 152
   messages sent/received by, 137
External tracking data, 216
Extreme Programming, late-changing
       requirements in, 59

F
Facebook, user administration in, 303
Failures, planning for high resiliency, 260–263
FAQs, user interface design for Help, 203
Fat finger trade, 201
Features, organizing to reduce complexity, 72
Feedback
   designing requirements, 8
   gathering requirements, 6
   and implementation, 47
   improving CRM applications, 93
   monitoring ease of use with user
       comments, 208
   providing mechanisms for, 122

redesign loop, 16–17
   between steps in design process, 10–12
   from technical design to context design, 43
   from user interface design to context
       design, 197
File transfer, 304
Fixed-price contracts, implementation
       design, 99–100
Flexibility
   improving correctness of applications, 335
   improving in application
       development, 332–334
Following plans, in nonagile projects, 59
Foreign keys
   ensuring referential integrity, 229–230
   relational database model, 227
   relationships and, 228–229
Formal methods, in application
       development, 51
Frameworks
   in context-driven design vs. conventional
       projects, 324–325
   extending, 290–293
   most programs built on, 24–25
   program structure explaining, 272–276
   programming language for, 286–290
   running with only one language, 285
   technical design implementation for, 43–44
   technical design opportunities, 329
   understanding, 276–280
Fraud, as application security threat, 310–311
Front-end parallelism, high performance
       of, 252–256
Function
   ease of use and, 199
   placing code into framework, 276
   subdividing applications/databases into areas
       of, 178–179
   user interface design for, 200–201
Function points, project cost estimates, 68–70
Functional access control, 302
Functionality
   implemented by crosscutting
       modules, 331
   implementing common, 293–294
   improving end user response by cutting
       back, 92
   in logical user interface, 45
   in programming, 24
   replacing old applications for new, 181
   testing with skeletal application, 264

Future of application development
    context-driven design changing
        design, 323–325
    context-driven design opportunities, 325–332
    correctness challenges, 335–336
    flexibility challenges, 332–334
    operations challenges, 334–335
    overview of, 323
    professionalism challenges, 337–338
    quality challenges, 336–337
    summary remarks, 339

G

Gaps in requirements, business goals and, 116–117
Gigahertz (GHz), high performance on a single
    machine, 244
Glossary
    of business terms, in context design, 133
    designing user interface for Help, 203
Google Maps, linking data to, 146
Gothic cathedrals, as planned design, 14
Granularity, cache performance, 246
Graph databases, 238
Graphic designer, user interface, 190
Groups
    choosing language for, 287–288
    common purpose. *See* Common purpose groups
    of data objects as data table, 31
    user. *See* User groups

H

Hanssen, Robert, 303
Hardware, high resiliency for, 261
Haskell programming language, 285
Headings, context design checklist for, 342–344
Heartbeat, detecting failure with, 262
Help
    designing user interface for, 203
    ease of use and, 200
    supporting learning organization, 122
Hidden field, browser session data, 254
Hierarchy of designs
    context design. *See* Context design
    database design, 46
    in engineered design, 15
    implementation (programming), 47–48
    integration design, 35–41
    justifying, 23–28
    overview of, 23
    in planned design, 14
    summary remarks, 51–52

supporting engineering design, 48–51
    technical design, 41–44
    user interface design, 44–46
High availability, 94
High resiliency, 260–263
High-level designs, 47, 48
HipHop for PHP, 287
Historical buildings, planned design of, 14
Horizontal dimension of size, large projects,
    84–87
Horizontal scaling (scale-out), 252
HTML, cross-site scripting exploiting, 317
Hypothesis, design
    of deep program structure, 275–276
    for ease-of-use design, 205–206
    for high performance on many servers, 260
    integration design of services, 165
    overview of, 10–12
    scientific theory and, 11–12
    starting programming with, 23
    in technical design, 266

I

Implementation
    in context-driven design vs. conventional
        project, 325
    improving quality with metrics for, 337
    services interface design, 177
Implementation design
    as engineering, 47–48
    existing practices for, 78–79
    fixed price for, 99
    justifying hierarchy of designs, 23–28
Improvement, quality, 75
"Include," use case terminology, 67
Inconsistency, eventual, 169, 240–241
Indexes
    application optimization and, 247
    data and, 216–217
Individuals, agile design values, 55–56
Industry-wide benchmarks, disbelieving, 263
Information
    designing user interface for, 201
    ease of use and, 199
    program structure describing flow
        of, 273–274
    security challenges, 334–335
Infrastructure security
    in context design, 309–310
    in technical design, 315
Inheritance, multiple, 225

Injection attacks, 317
Input parameter, browser session data, 254
Inquiries, task descriptions for, 134
Insecure direct object references, as
    vulnerability, 318
Inspection, and testing, 76–78
Integration design
    applications in, 161–162
    choosing programming language for, 287
    context-driven design opportunities, 328
    context-driven design vs. conventional
        projects, 324
    databases in, 165–170
    defined, 159
    in design hierarchy, 24–25
    designing requirements, 9
    designing reusable services, 177
    documenting, 58
    gathering requirements, 6–7
    in IT architecture, 20
    looking back at design process, 186–188
    making cost estimates, 71–72
    overview of, 35–41, 159–161
    security elements of, 311–312
    services in, 162–165
    services interface design in, 170–178
    six-box model of design in, 26–28
    summary remarks, 188
    testing with skeletal application, 264
    using existing applications in, 178–186
    using existing practices in, 79
Integration designer, 138, 163, 312
Integration model, 179
Integrity
    checking database, 236
    databases supporting referential, 229–230
    designing message, 137–138
    difficulty of implementing in NoSQL, 239
    enforcing constraints for process, 152
    logical user interface design for, 193
    overarching constraints for, 126–127
    transaction and task, 208–212
Interactions, agile design values, 55–56
Interface design
    services. See Services interface design
    user groups. See User groups
Interfaces, definition of, 272
Internal entity data, 216
Internal IT data, 216, 217
Internal presentations, documenting, 58
Internal tracking data, 216

Interpretive languages, 282
Intuitive/likable applications, 203–205
Investment decisions, in business strategy, 118
IP addresses, security monitoring of, 307
IP application designers, 300, 309–310
Is a relationships, 225–226
Isolation, ACID properties of transactions, 209
IT architecture, 20
IT departments, learning culture in, 80
Iterations, 73–74
Iterative context design processes, 156

J
Java
    choosing as language, 287
    as interpretive language, 282–283
    most large companies using, 290
    popularity of today, 285
JavaScript, Web applications, 279
Joint Contracts Tribunal (JCT) contracts, 97–98
"Jones's Law of Programming Language
    Creation" (Jones), 285
JSON format, Document NoSQL, 238

K
Keys, relationships and, 228–229
Keystroke logging programs, 298, 300–301

L
Large applications
    avoiding, 100–103
    changing cost estimates in, 70
    dimensions of size in, 84–87
    disadvantages of, 161
    implementing services for splitting, 40
    lacking end user support, 91–93
    procurement and outsourcing
        problems, 96–100
    requirements problems, 88–91
    summary remarks, 103–104
    technical design problems, 93–96
    underperformance in, 83
    use case documents in, 67
Late-changing requirements
    in agile vs. context design, 59
    changing cost estimate due to, 70
    improving quality with metrics for, 337
    reasons for, 90–91
Learning organization, supporting, 122
Likable applications, 203–205
Links, user interface design, 202–203

Load, testing to break program under, 77
Locks, high performance issues, 249, 250
Log on
    authentication design issues, 300
    holding identity data in browser in, 255
Logical service interface, 173–176
Logical user interface
    design diagram for, 44–45
    overview of, 190
    understanding, 191–194
Login failures, security monitoring of, 306
Logs, monitoring, 307
London Olympics, changing cost estimates, 70–71
London to Channel Tunnel railway line, changing
        cost estimates in, 70
Look and feel, application user interface, 199

M

Maintenance
    analyzing error paths for integrity, 152
    detailing requirements for, 138
    problems with large projects, 97
    proliferation of new programming languages
        and, 285
    restricting access to, 305
Management
    capturing tasks for resource, 113–114
    context design review of, 158
    context-driven design vs. conventional
        project, 325
    designing requirements and, 9
    detailing requirements, 139
    fears of, 55–56
    gathering requirements and, 4–5
    getting perspective of senior, 117
    large project failure/resistance of end users
        and, 92–93
    of large teams, 85
    NEC contracts and, 97–98
    of processes or services, 143–147
    of quality, 75–76
    security vulnerability of operations/
        infrastructure, 311–312
Many-to-many relationships, relational data
        model, 231
Measurement. *See* Metrics
Memory
    multithreading/multiprocessing and, 248–249
    overcoming enormous wait times with
        cache, 245–247
Menus, user interface design, 202

Message queuing, 174, 257–258
Messages
    adding detail to, 137–138
    application optimization and, 247
    completeness analysis for, 152, 155–156
    context design checklist of, 343, 347–348
    defining task details, 131
    encrypting identity data in browser, 255–256
    security protection design, 304
    between tasks in context design, 31
Methodology, language support for
        development, 289–290
Metrics
    establishing target, 5
    improving quality using, 75–76, 336–337
    IT industry deficient in good, 83–84
    management monitoring
        performance, 143–145
Microservices, 38–39
Middleware
    extending framework with, 292
    integration difficulties of, 287
Minimum viable product (MVP), 72
Miranda programming language, 285
Model-View-Controller (MVC) pattern
    ASP, 277–278
    frameworks supporting, 24
    historic, 278–279
    at large-scale/structural level, 277
    overview of, 278
    technical design opportunities, 330–331
Modules
    crosscutting, 331, 332–333
    definition of, 272
    measuring cohesion/coupling of, 273
    modern, 331
    OO classes superseding, 273
Monitoring
    capturing tasks for, 115
    designing for existing culture, 121
    ease of use, 208
    how users use application, 122
    processes or services by management, 143–147
    security, 291–292, 299–300, 306–307
    technical design for, 42
Multifactor authentication, 321
Multiple database access, 166–167
Multiple inheritance, 225, 226
Multiprocessing, speeding up
        applications, 248–252
Multitasking, 248

Multithreading
  detecting application failure, 262
  overcoming enormous wait times, 245
  speeding up applications, 248–252
MVC. *See* Model-View-Controller (MVC) pattern
MVP (minimum viable product), 72

N

Naming attributes, 218
Narrative
  defining task details, 131–134
  logical user interface design, 193
  services interface design, 170
  for task fragments, 135
NatWest Bank fiasco (2012), 42
Navigation
  ease of use and, 199
  user interface design for, 202
Networks
  high performance issues on single
    machine, 250
  high resiliency for failure, 262
  security protection for, 305
New Engineering Contract (NEC), 97–98
NHS National Programmer for IT (in UK), 86, 91
Non-business applications, strategy/planning
    for, 122–123
Nonfunctional requirements
  context design checklist description of, 343
  defining task details for, 138–140
  technical design for, 41–43
Normalization
  design issues/consequences of, 231–232
  relational database model, 227–228
NoSQL products
  eventual consistency in, 240–241
  handling enormous databases with, 240–241
  limitations of not having schema, 239–240
  overview of, 238
Notes
  defining task details for, 131–133
  logical user interface design, 193
  services interface design, 171
Null attributes, in database design, 219

O

Object database models, semantic models
    vs., 225–226
Object identity, 229
Object library, database access services, 236–237
Objectives, programmer vs. database designer, 233

Objectives analysis
  analyzing tasks, 127
  context design checklist for, 345–348
  context design review of, 158
  of data table details, 154–155
  of message details, 156
  of process layer, 153
  of task details, 154
  of user group details, 155
Object-oriented (OO) programming
  classes, 273
  database access services and, 236–237
  database design theory vs., 223–226
  implementing database access
    services, 236–237
  irrelevant questions in, 225
  popularity of patterns in, 277
Objects, in OO technology, 224–226
Offload data, handling existing applications, 183
One-shot service interface, 174–175, 253
Online applications, integration design,
    37, 159–160
Open Web Application Security Project (OWASP)
    vulnerabilities, 316–319
OpenID, single sign-on, 301
Open-tender procurement rules, public-sector
    project failure, 87
Operational procedures
  high resiliency for, 262
  improving flexibility, 333
  technical design for, 42–43
Operations, challenges of, 334–335
Operations plan, 266
Optimization, online database applications, 247
Order processing flow, services interface
    design, 172–173
Organizational nonfunctional
    requirements, 139
Organizational skill set, programming language
    fitting, 287
Outcomes, task flow diagram, 124–125
Outputs, technical design/implementation, 266
Outsourcing
  design and implementation, 99–100
  learning from civil engineering
    contracts, 97–98
  third-party large applications, 96–97
Overarching integrity constraints, task
    dependencies, 126–127
Overengineering security, 315–316
Overhead, from remote database access, 256

OWASP (Open Web Application Security Project)
vulnerabilities, 316–319

P

Packages, failed implementations of, 86
Paper testing, user interface design, 207
Parallelism
back-end, 256–260
front-end, 252–256
Pascal programming language, 285
Pass-through, data duplication, 168–169
Passwords
authentication design issues, 300
identifying users via, 302
keystroke-logging programs reading, 298
not keeping on personal devices, 305
stealing or guessing, 304
vulnerability of recovered, 301
vulnerability of user administration, 303
Patterns
architectural, 277
not useful for large programs, 277
overview of, 10
using frameworks vs., 277
Performance
aging large IT applications and, 86
business strategy for cost/availability vs., 119
choosing programming language and, 287
context design checklist elaboration reports
for, 344
implementing services for, 40
large projects prone to failure, 83–87
monitoring by management, 143–147
nonfunctional requirements for, 41–42
technical design across many servers for
high, 252–260
technical design on single server for high,
244–252
testing with skeletal application, 264
Personal Software Process (PSP), and quality,
75–76
Perspectives, context design review, 157–158
Phase releases, organizing features into, 72
Planned design
dangers of redesign, 17
engineered design vs., 14–15
overview of, 14
summary of, 18
Postmortem, disaster recovery, 262
Precision, in IT applications, 2
Primary keys, 227–229

Principles
agile development, 54–55
database design encryption, 305
of high performance on many servers, 252–260
of high performance on single
machine, 244–252
technical design. See Technical design
principles
Problem solving
complexity dimension of large projects, 85
NEC contracts, 98
Process diagrams
analysis of, 123
completeness analysis of process layer, 152
illustrating business processes, 106–107
incompleteness of, 111–112
task outcome diagrams vs., 125
Process layer
completeness analysis for, 152
context design checklist analysis of, 344–345
context design checklist, description of, 341
context design checklist, elaboration, 344
Processes
agile design values vs., 55–56
analysis of context design, 34
business. See Business processes
as dependencies between tasks, 32
Processors, performance issues on single
machine, 244
Procurement, large project failure and, 96–100
Product decisions, business strategy
guiding, 118
Production, quality improvement with metrics
for, 337
Professionalism, challenges of, 337–338
Program pattern. See Hypothesis, design
Program structure, 19, 272–276
Programmatic interface, 159–160, 238
Programmers
conflict between database designers
and, 233–236
database designer's view of data vs., 223–225
technical design helping, 41, 43–44
in technical design/implementation
process, 266
Programming. See Implementation design
Programming language
choosing framework and, 286–290
choosing in technical design, 93–94
multiple inheritance and, 225
unit testing of, 284

Programming languages
    compiled, 281–283
    interpretive, 282–283
    JavaScript, 285
    OO, 285
    proliferation of, 285–286
    server-side scripting, 284
Project managers
    context-driven design and, 323–324
    meetings with all designers, 212
    resolving conflicts, 233
    technical design involvement of, 163, 268
    user interface design and, 65
    view of business managers vs., 84, 115
Projection, 36–37
Projection, in data copy, 316–319
Projects
    ad hoc design for large, 14
    ad hoc design for small, 12
    choosing software for managing, 288
    defined, 36–37
    documenting management plans, 58
Protection, designing security, 299–300, 304–306
Provably correct, 17
Proxy metrics, monitoring, 144–145
PSP (Personal Software Process), and
        quality, 75–76
Public-sector project failure, 86

Q

Quality
    avoid cutting cost by reducing, 73–74
    context-driven design improving, 336–337
    methods/practices for, 75–76
    testing/inspection for, 76–78
Questions, user interface design for Help, 203

R

RAM access time, 244, 245
Rapid application development (RAD), 289
Read commands, high performance on many
        servers, 257
Reading backup data, security protection
        design, 304
Reading data files, security protection design, 304
Records, creating new, 201
Recovered passwords, 301
Recovery, disaster, 261–264
Redesign, dangers of, 17–18
Redundancy, defining task details, 133
Referential integrity, in NoSQL, 239

Relational database models
    correctness of relationships in, 231–232
    keys and relationships, 228–229
    normalization in, 226–227
    overview of, 226
Relationships
    business. See Business processes
    checking correctness of, 230–231
    drawing conventions showing, 230
    finding design issues/consequences of, 231–232
    implementing tasks in large projects, 85
    keys and database, 228–229
    in OO design, 225–226
    to other IT projects. See Integration design
    with users. See Task details
Releases
    ad hoc design for large projects via, 14
    phased, 72
    staged, 147
Reliability
    detailing requirements for, 138
    of likable applications, 205
Remote database access, and overhead, 256
Remote Procedure Calls, 175
Replacing existing applications, 180–184
Reply messages, task details for, 137
Reports
    of application administrators, 150
    context design checklist elaboration of, 344
    data analysis, 149
    horizontal slicing diagram for delivery of, 49
    managing excessive requirements for, 146–147
    progress, 55
    simplifying, 73
    surveying users, 122
    task view diagram for delivery of, 33
    technical design for error, 42, 95
    in upside-down design, 60–62
Repositories
    context design and, 328
    database design and, 329
Representational State Transfer (REST)
        protocol, 175
Requirements
    business goals vs. formal, 115–118
    ease-of-use design, 205
    fundamental business, 118–123
    handling late-change, 59
    large project problems, 88
    nonfunctional. See Nonfunctional
        requirements

technical design, 266
technical design for nonfunctional, 41–44
trimming, 72
upside-down design, 60–62
Requirements gathering
cultural differences, 5–6
designing business solution vs., 7–9
example of, 3–4
false assumptions in, 4–7
in iterative context design, 156
overview of, 2, 4
of typical IT application design, 19
use cases designed for, 68
in waterfall design, 56
Resiliency, technical design for
high, 260–263
Resistance of end users, large project
failure, 91–93
Resonance, calculating for structure, 17
Resource allocation, as dependencies between
tasks, 32
Resource management
capturing tasks for, 113–114
completeness analysis for process layer, 152
context design review of, 158
high resiliency for, 262
Responding to change, agile design, 59
REST (Representational State Transfer)
protocol, 175
Reusable code
functions, 294
implementation team using, 294
in OO technology, 224–225
services, 39–40, 176–178
Reusing existing methods/practices
agile. See Agile design
big design up front and, 72–74
in context-driven design, 78–79
IT department as learning
organization, 80
iterations, 74–75
overview of, 53–54
problem with estimating cost, 68–72
quality, 75–76
summary remarks, 80–81
testing and inspection, 76–78
Review
capturing tasks for, 115
context design, 156–158
cost estimate, 71–72
defining task details for, 131, 133

Rewrites
packages for large projects vs., 86
public-sector project failure and, 87
Risk
analyzing, 127
developing security plan, 301
Rollback, 208
Rollout, 93
Round-robin algorithm, 252
Routers, 252
Rules
defining task details, 131–134
listing data table, 136
logical user interface design, 193
services interface design, 171

S
Scalability, requirements for, 138
Scale-out (horizontal scaling), 252
Schema, database
choosing language for work in groups, 288
context-driven design opportunities, 326
not having in NoSQL, 238–240
roles of, 239
subclasses and duplication of, 220–221
Scientific theory, hypotheses in design and, 11–12
Scope, IT industry deficient in, 84
Screen design
for existing culture, 120
improving quality and number of screens, 336
logical user interface for, 190–194
Screen traversal, session data used in, 253
Scrum
late-changing requirements in, 59
quality programs in, 75
Searches
designing user interface for, 201
refining with session data, 253
Security
application administrators viewing logs
for, 150
business strategy for, 120
context design review of, 158
designing for existing culture, 121
detailing requirements, 140
elaborating design hypothesis for, 260
extending framework with monitoring for, 291
holding identity data in browser and, 255–256
implementing services for, 40
information, 334–335
loading data into spreadsheets and, 145–146

Security *(continued)*
    session data used in, 253
    technical design for large projects, 94
    technical design of Web applications, 279
    technical design opportunities, 329–331
    technical design process, 266, 268
    testing with skeletal application, 264
Security design
    access control, 302–303
    authentication, 300–302
    context design, 307–311
    database design, 312–314
    integration design, 311–312
    overview of, 297–299
    principles, overview, 299–300
    programming, 316–319
    security monitoring, 306–307
    security protection, 304–306
    summary remarks, 319–321
    technical design, 314–316
    user administration, 303
    user interface design, 312
Security monitoring
    defined, 299–300
    design, 306–307
    extending framework for, 291–292
    technical design describing, 314–315
Select, in data copy, 36–37
Semantic database models, 225–226
Sensitive data
    preventing cyber-attacks, 298
    security programming and, 316–317
Server(s)
    principles of high performance on many,
        252–260
    principles of high performance on one,
        244–252
    restricting access to, 305
    security protection for, 304, 305
    technical design describing security
        of, 315
Server-side scripting languages
    application performance goals, 287
    choosing language for organization's skill set,
        287
    exaggerated productivity advantages of, 289
    for lightweight applications, 287, 290
    overview of, 284
    popularity of today, 285
Service Oriented Architecture. *See* SOA (Service
    Oriented Architecture)

Services
    common purpose groups for, 135–136
    context design improving, 89
    context design review of, 157
    creating from existing applications,
        184–186
    database access, 236–237
    determining size of, 40
    implementation using, 39–40
    integration design for, 37, 159–160,
        162–165, 312
    managerial oversight of, 143–147
    managing operations challenges, 334–335
    reusable, 176–178
    SOA vs. microservices, 38–39
    splitting, 40
    task dependencies, analyzing, 126
    tasks, capturing for business, 112–113
    tasks, detailing breaks in, 139–140
    technical design for, 266
    user interface design for, 45–46
Services interface design
    overview of, 170–172
    for reusable services, 176–178
    service interface definition, 172–176
    storing session data, 253
Session data
    access control design for, 302–303
    elaborating design hypothesis for, 260
    implementing browser, 254–255
    security programming and, 317
    security protection design for, 304–305
    stored in service interfaces, 253
    uses of, 253
Session identifier vulnerabilities, 318
Sharing data, security issues, 312
Shopping carts, 200
Single sign-on, authentication, 301
Six-box model of design
    improving correctness of applications, 335
    overview of, 26–28
    security, 307
    traditional engineering design vs., 48–51
Size
    determining service/application, 40
    large projects and dimensions of, 84–87
    in technical design/implementation, 266
Skeletal code
    in program frameworks, 24, 277
    testing with, 264–265
Snowden, Edward, 303

SOA (Service Oriented Architecture)
  creating large project by moving to, 100–102
  integration design and, 38
  reducing complexity, 72
Social Security number, in database
      identification, 228
Software
  high resiliency and, 261–262
  technical design for large projects, 93–94
  testing product early in large projects, 95–96
  vendor frameworks for, 24, 277
  version control/project management, 288
"Software Estimating Rules of Thumb," 69
Source code
  in interpretive languages, 282
  splitting functionality into programmable,
      287–288
  as technical documentation, 47
Spear phishing attacks, 297–298, 305
Speed
  detailing requirements for, 138
  implementing for development, 119
  of likable applications, 205
Splitting
  databases, 165–166
  large project into smaller projects, 100–103
  protecting highly sensitive data via, 311
Spy programs, 298
SQL
  database access services and, 236–237
  and normalization, 232
SQL-to-LINQ mapping, 236
Stakeholders
  in ad hoc design, 13
  causing late-changing requirements, 90–91
  designing requirements, 8
  gathering requirements, 4–5
  logical user interface design review
      with, 193, 194
  systems test application shown to, 47–48
  in upside-down design, 61–62
Standish Chaos report, 83–84
Static analyzers, quality, 78
Step-by-step move, existing applications, 183
Strategic use cases, 67
Strategy, business, 118–123
Subclasses
  in database design, 219–222
  finding design issues/consequences of, 231–232
  in OO technology, 224–226
  using null attributes for members of, 219

Submenu items, user interface design, 202
Subsets, OO technology, 224
Summary data, 216, 217
Surround existing applications, 181, 183
Symbols, in context-driven design diagrams, 326
System software failures, high resiliency for, 261
Systems management, 291
Systems testing, 47–48, 74

T
Table NoSQL products, 238
Tables, subclasses in database
      design, 220–221
Tacoma Narrows Bridge collapse (1940), 16–17
Task dependencies
  adding details. *See* Task details
  analysis of, 123–127
  disadvantages of small applications, 161
  documenting, 33–34
  flexibility of applications and, 333–334
  improving flexibility by recording, 332
  objectives analysis of, 127
  overview of, 31–32
  task view diagrams of, 33, 107–111
  testing, 77
  well-formed process diagram analysis of, 123
Task details
  completeness analysis of, 153–154
  context design checklist analysis of, 345–346
  defining task fragments, 135
  describing messages, 137–138
  listing data tables, 136–137
  nonfunctional requirements, 138–140
  overview of, 129–130, 131–134
  users of context design, 140
  using common purpose groups, 135–136
Task flow analysis, 124–125
Task fragments
  context design checklist description of, 342
  defining details of, 135
  services interface design, 170–171
Task layer, context design checklist, 342
Task outcome diagram, 124–125, 152
Tasks
  atomicity problem in use cases and, 63–64
  capturing business services, 112–113
  capturing resource management, 113–114
  capturing review and monitoring, 115
  common purpose groups for, 135–136
  completeness analysis for process layer, 152
  in context design, 28–30, 34, 108–112

Tasks *(continued)*
    context design checklist, description
        of, 341–344
    context design checklist, elaboration, 344
    converting to user interface from, 194–198
    data table clustering vs., 164
    defined, 107
    dependencies between. *See* Task dependencies
    existing applications and, 179–180
    finding saved information for incompleted,
        200–201
    grouping, 32–33
    horizontal dimension of size in large projects
        and, 84–86
    improving quality with metrics for, 336–337
    in integration design, 36–41
    integrity of, 208–212
    logical user interface design, 193
    mapping onto processes, 107–108
    messages between, 31
    moving to data-focused design from, 198
    nonfunctional requirements, 139
    placing into applications, 162
    splitting business application functionality
        into, 26
    technical design process, 266
    use cases confusing design for, 64–66
Team Software Process (TSP), and quality, 75
Teams, implementing tasks in, 85
Technical design
    choosing programming language, 288
    context-driven design vs. conventional
        project, 324
    in design hierarchy, 25
    large project failure due to, 93–96
    making cost estimates and, 69, 71–72
    measuring time/effort in, 337
    outsourcing, 99–100
    overview of, 41–44
    process of, 265–268
    security elements of, 314–316
    six-box model for, 26–28
    supporting engineering design, 48–49
    using existing practices, 79
Technical design principles
    of high performance on many
        servers, 252–260
    of high performance on single machine,
        244–252
    of high resiliency, 260–263
    overview of, 243–244

    in technical design process, 265–268
    testing and benchmarking, 263–265
Technical design structure
    choosing programming language/framework,
        286–290
    extending framework, 290–293
    implementing common functionality, 293–294
    overview of, 271
    program structure, 272–276
    summary remarks, 295
    understanding framework, 276–280
    variety of programming languages, 281–286
Technical designer
    context design review by, 140
    extending framework, 292–293
    in integration design, 163
    role of, 25–26
    in service interface design, 212
    working with programmers, 292
Technology
    design in IT architecture, 20
    improving quality by analysis, 337
    replacing existing application due to old,
        180–181
    technical design opportunities, 329–331
Ternary relationships, relational data
        model, 231
Testing
    in context-driven design vs. conventional
        project, 324–325
    early and thoroughly, 265
    in engineered design, 16–17
    extending framework with, 291
    hierarchical series of designs, 49–51
    improving flexibility, 333
    improving quality with error metrics, 337
    ineffectiveness of, 76–77
    inspection and, 76–78
    large application disadvantages, 161
    for security vulnerabilities, 319
    speeding up development by cutting back, 119
    technical design, 43–44, 265, 266, 292
    technical design in large projects, 95–96, 99
    technical design principles for, 263–265
    typical IT application design, 19
    unit, 284
    user interface, 206–207, 329
Text
    consistent in likable applications, 204
    context design checklist for, 344
    designing user interface, 192–193, 202, 203

ease of use and, 200
    services interface design, 173
Textual analysis of information, 146
"The Manifesto for Agile Software
    Development," 54
Theory, database design, 222–233
Third-party applications
    integration design for, 41, 161–170
    outsourcing design/implementation, 99–100
    procurement of, 96–99
Threat model, for security, 307–310, 343
Tiering, technical design of Web application, 279
Time
    improving quality with metrics for, 336–337
Tools
    agile design values vs., 55–56
    context-driven design opportunities, 326–328
    context/integration designs, 328
    technical design, 329
    user interface/database designs, 328–329
Top-level design, engineered design, 15–17
Traceability, engineered design, 49–50
Training
    on CRM applications, 92–93
    on cyber-attack prevention, 298
    in NEC contracts, 98
Transactions
    eventual consistency in NoSQL, 240–242
    integrity of, 208–212
    tasks vs., 29–30
Transparency, 117
Transport Layer Security (TLS), encrypting
    identity data, 255–256
Trends
    context design checklist reports on, 344
    management reports on, 145–146
Triage, for large/small applications, 161
Trimming, reducing complexity, 72
Trust
    business management/IT developer, 338
    security design and, 321
TSP (Team Software Process), and
    quality, 75

U

UML diagrams, 173, 230
Uncertainty
    defining task details on, 131
    handling design, 61–62
Understanding step, design process, 10
Uniqueness constraint, and NoSQL, 239

Unit of release property, application
    development, 38
Unit testing, 284
Updates
    asynchronous database, 166–167
    to banking applications, 183
    cache performance and data, 246
    database transaction, 257–258
    session data ensuring object, 253
Upside-down design, 60–62
URIs
    encrypting user identity, 255
    implementing browser session data, 254
    insecure direct object reference in, 318
Usability lab, testing user interface design, 207
Usability objective, analysis, 127
Use cases
    confusion of design layers in, 64–67
    context design vs., 62–63
    difficulty of understanding large, 67
    lacking formal concept of atomicity, 63–64
    not supporting engineered design, 67–68
    tasks vs., 30
User administration design
    defined, 299–300
    overview of, 303
    technical design describing, 314
User categories
    application administrator, 149–150
    data analysis, 148–149
    data used by other applications, 147–148
    monitoring by management, 143–147
    overview of, 141–142
    process operations, 142–143
User groups
    common purpose. *See* Common purpose
        groups
    completeness analysis for, 155
    in context design, 30
    context design checklist for, 343, 346–347
    context design review of, 157
    context design security issues, 307, 310–311
    database design security design, 313–314
    defining task details, 131–132
    determining service/application size, 40
    existing applications and, 179
    integration design security issues, 311–312
    placing tasks into applications, 162
    quality improvement using metrics for,
        336–337
    task view diagram of, 33

User groups *(continued)*
    technical design process and, 266
    user interface design security, 312
User interface design
    context-driven vs. conventional, 324–325
    database design independent from, 46
    in design hierarchy, 24–25
    documenting, 58
    engineering design supported by, 48–49
    improving quality using metrics, 336
    overview of, 44–46
    screen design, 90, 120
    security elements of, 312
    services. *See* Services interface design
    six-box model for, 26–28
    task description converted into, 134
    task design in use cases vs., 65–66
    uncertainty score based on, 62
    using existing practices for, 79
User interface design, ease of use
    ease-of-use design steps, 205–208
    function, 200–201
    information, 201
    intuitive and likable applications, 203–205
    logical user interfaces, 191–194
    navigation, 202
    other detailed designs, 212
    overview of, 199–200
    studying impact of new, 91–93
    summary remarks, 212–213
    from tasks to clicks, 194–199
    text, 202–203
    transaction/task integrity and, 208–212
User interface designer
    context design review by, 140
    defining contents of data bags, 148
    maximizing flexibility of, 134, 154
    role of, 25–26
    rules giving freedom to, 133
    task descriptions for, 130
    user groups and, 30
    using context design, 134
    working with database/technical
        designers, 212
User iterations, 74
Usernames
    identifying users via, 302
    security monitoring of, 306
    vulnerabilities of user administration, 303

Users. *See* End users
Uses identifiers interface, 174–175, 254
Uses session service interface,
        173–174, 253–254

V
Validation, ease of use via, 200
Value, and null attribute, 219
Value statements, agile design, 54–59
Vendors. *See also* Third-party applications
    frameworks supplied by, 277–281
    technical design opportunities for, 329
    testing software early in large
        projects, 95–96
Version control
    choosing software for, 288
    context-driven design vs. conventional,
        324–325
    technical design for, 42–43
Vertical dimension of size, large projects, 84–85
View, diagram of task, 33
Virtual machines (VMs), 282–283, 285
Visual Studio 2013 Express for Web, Microsoft,
        330–331
Vulnerabilities, OWASP list of, 316–317

W
Wait times, 244, 245
Waterfall design limitations, 56
Web applications
    context-driven design opportunities
        for, 327
    security of. *See* Security design
What, in security threat model, 308–309
Who, in security threat model, 308–309
Working set, cache performance, 245
Working software, agile design, 56–58
Write commands, servers, 257
Write through, data updates/cache performance,
        246
Writing data files, security protection, 304

X
XML format
    designing reusable services, 176
    Document NoSQL, 238